New methods in comparative and historical research in political economy have not been recognized either within an integrated framework or as a major field of comparative research methodology. The most recent works have stressed historical or qualitative approaches, but not the wide range of quantitative work. Existing comparative methodology texts were written before most new methods were in widespread use; Thomas Janoski and Alexander Hicks fill the gap in comparative political economy by focusing on these new comparative/historical methods – time-series, pooled time and cross-sectional, event history, and Boolean analyses. In the introduction, they provide a sweeping overview of the comparative research process and the methods that have been used in the past decade. In subsequent chapters, distinguished scholars in the field introduce specific methods and then demonstrate each one by applying it to social and economic policy in advanced industrialized states. In the conclusion, Janoski and Hicks clarify the slippery topic of "political economy" and identify the four directions they expect the comparative political economy of the welfare state to take over the next few decades.

THE COMPARATIVE POLITICAL ECONOMY OF THE WELFARE STATE

CAMBRIDGE STUDIES IN COMPARATIVE POLITICS

This series publishes comparative research that seeks to explain important, cross-national domestic political phenomena. Based on a broad conception of comparative politics, it hopes to promote critical dialogue among different approaches. While encouraging contributions from diverse theoretical perspectives, the series will particularly emphasize work on domestic institutions and work that examines the relative roles of historical structures and constraints, of individual or organizational choice, and of strategic interaction in explaining political actions and outcomes. This focus includes an interest in the mechanisms through which historical factors impinge on contemporary political choices and outcomes.

Works on all parts of the world are welcomed, and priority will be given to studies that cross traditional area boundaries and that treat the United States in comparative perspective. Many of the books in the series are expected to be comparative, drawing on material from more than one national case, but studies devoted to single countries will also be considered, especially those that pose their problem and analysis in such a way that they make a direct contribution to comparative analysis and theory.

OTHER BOOKS IN THE SERIES

Allan Kornberg and Harold D. Clarke *Citizens and Community: Political Support in a Representative Democracy*

David D. Laitin *Language Repertoires and State Construction in Africa*

Ellen Immergut *Health Politics: Interests and Institutions in Western Europe*

Sven Steinmo, Kathleen Thelen, and Frank Longstreth, eds., *Structuring Politics: Historical Institutionalism in Comparative Analysis*

THE COMPARATIVE POLITICAL ECONOMY OF THE WELFARE STATE

THOMAS JANOSKI
Duke University

ALEXANDER M. HICKS
Emory University

Published by the Press Syndicate of the University of Cambridge
The Pitt Building, Trumpington Street, Cambridge CB2 1RP
40 West 20th Street, New York, NY 10011–4211, USA
10 Stamford Road, Oakleigh, Melbourne 3166, Australia

First published 1994

Printed in the United States of America

Library of Congress Cataloging-in-Publication Data
Janoski, Thomas.
The comparative political economy of the welfare state / Thomas Janoski, Alexander M. Hicks.
p. cm. – (Cambridge studies in comparative politics)
Includes index.
ISBN 0–521–43473–4 (hard). – ISBN 0–521–43602–8 (pbk.)
1. Welfare economics. 2. Welfare state. 3. Comparative economics. I. Hicks, Alexander M. II. Title. III. Series.
HB846. J36 1994
330.12′6 – dc20

93–17335
CIP

A catalog record for this book is available from the British Library.

ISBN 0–521–43473–4 hardback
ISBN 0–521–43602–8 paperback

To our political economy and methodology teachers
at Berkeley and Wisconsin
as well as
Nancy, Ryan, and Nat

Contents

PART II
POOLED TIME-SERIES AND CROSS-SECTIONAL ANALYSIS

PART III
EVENT HISTORY ANALYSIS

PART IV
BOOLEAN ANALYSIS

Contributors

James E. Alt
Harvard University

Susan M. Carlson
University of North Carolina, Charlotte

John R. Freeman
University of Minnesota

Alexander M. Hicks
Emory University

Larry W. Isaac
Florida State University

Thomas Janoski
Duke University

Olli Kangas
University of Turku, Finland

Philip J. O'Connell
University of North Carolina, Chapel Hill
Economics and Social Research Institute, Dublin

Mary P. Mathis
Emory University

Charles C. Ragin
Northwestern University

David Strang
Cornell University

Chikako Usui
University of Missouri, St. Louis

Tables and figures

TABLES

FIGURES

Preface

This book is intended to be an analog of sorts to Theda Skocpol's edited volume *Vision and Method in Historical Sociology*. The format is entirely different in that we organize it around method rather than author, focus it as much on specific policy theories as on general visions, and target it as much on methodological techniques as on designs. Yet the intent is the same – to introduce a broad range of methodological approaches to the comparative social sciences. In keeping with Charles Ragin's concept of *synthetic analysis*, we see this volume joining together an ample range of comparative, quantitative, and, indeed, historical methods. A mesh of methods enriches a field. We hope that our net is tight and broad enough to gather a rich new catch of insights about the welfare state.

This book began in the planning of a Southern Sociological Society session and then reached fruition in the "New Compass of the Comparativist" conference held at Duke University in 1991. Three sources in Durham, New York, and Washington, D.C., provided approximately equal funding to finance the conference on which this book is largely based. First, we would like to thank Edward Tiryakian, Director of the Center for International Studies at Duke University, for providing the seed funding that started the ball rolling on this project. Without his help, this project would probably not have gotten off the ground. Second, we would also like to thank Dr. Ioannis Sinanoglou and the Council for European Studies for their Western European Studies Workshop Grant. And third, we thank William V. D'Antonio for funding from the joint American Sociological Association/National Science Foundation Fund for the Advancement of the Discipline. All three sources contributed equally in making the conference a success and this book a reality.

We would like to thank those who contributed to and participated in the "New Compass of the Comparativist" conference: Peter Bearman of the University of North Carolina-Chapel Hill, Gary Gereffi of Duke

University, Larry Griffin of Vanderbilt University, Larry Isaac of Florida State University, Miguel Korzeniewicz of the University of New Mexico, Peter Lange of Duke University, Philip O'Connell of the University of North Carolina-Chapel Hill, Charles Ragin of Northwestern University, Richard Rubinson of Emory University, David Smith of the University of California-Irvine, David Strang of Cornell University, George Tsebellis of the University of California-Los Angeles, Chikako Usui of the University of Missouri-St. Louis, and Michael Wallerstein of the University of California-Los Angeles. We would especially like to thank Charles Ragin for his roles as discussant and presenter and in helping us obtain two key participants. Graduate students from the Duke University sociology and political science departments played an important role in the conference. They met with paper presenters concerning the methodology and substance of each paper presented. We would like to thank these discussants also: Michael Alvarez, Phillip Atkison, Jihee Choi, Adele Cummings, Stephanie Fonda, Fabrice Laboucq, Patrice LeClerc, Bryan Lyond, P. A. McManus, Stephen Russell, and Vince Salazar. Finally, we thank Judith Dillon for her conference planning and Adele Cummings, Rhonda Dollas, and Brigitte Neary for their logistical support.

At Cambridge University Press, we have a debt of gratitude toward Peter Lange, the series editor, and Emily Loose, social sciences editor. Peter and Emily provided timely editorial input, and Peter also served as a discussant at the conference. Emily Loose gave accurate and optimistic input even when an early review was less than enthusiastic.

We would also like to thank our four anonymous reviewers at Cambridge University Press for their instructive and critical feedback and the seven reviewers connected to funding this project for their views. Finally, Amby Rice and Judith Dillion at the Duke University Sociology Department entered and often reconstructed our tables and figures from a diverse array of styles and programs.

This book is in part dedicated to our political economy and methodology teachers at Berkeley and Madison. Although many teachers made important contributions, the Berkeley author would like to thank Harold Wilensky, who has been a driving force in welfare state analysis and has always warned against methodological dogmatism. The Madison author additionally would like to thank the originators and participants in the weekly "social organization" and "methodology" seminars of the 1970s Sociology Department, exemplary intellectual pluralists all.

1

Methodological innovations in comparative political economy: an introduction

THOMAS JANOSKI AND ALEXANDER M. HICKS

New methods in comparative/historical research have changed the face of analysis in macrosociology. Adam Przeworski has recently stated that

> the number of recent methodological developments are profoundly affecting the practice of cross-national research and provide us with a repertoire of instruments approaching a standard operating procedure. Methodological habits and the knowledge of particular techniques are quite widely diffused among younger scholars. (1987, p. 42)

Yet he states that "all the methodological perspectives" found in the standard research volumes on comparative methods "had been articulated by 1970 and often long before" (p. 34). The problem is that the new methodological developments have not been incorporated into the pedagogic literature of readers and texts, much less integrated with some encompassing and coordinating framework. This volume fills this gap by concentrating on the broadly mathematical contingent of the new comparative/historical methods and doing so with a further focus on their application to the political economy of the nation and the welfare state.

The new methods stress sensitivity to time as well as place. Quantitative approaches to comparative research consist of cross-national, time-series, pooled time and cross-sectional, and event history techniques of analyses. *Cross-sectional* analysis has been done for over 20 years, and its methodological issues remain critical to valid analyses; however, we will not cover them in this volume. *Time-series* analysis has made its mark on single-nation studies in the past few years, but time-series analysis has only begun to be seriously used in comparative research, and it has many problems concerning comparability. *Pooled time-series and cross-sectional* analysis is opening up new vistas, despite controversy about the limits of statistical accuracy and generalizations across time and space. *Event history methods*, elaborated for the analysis of models of pooled data that predict qualitative outcomes, are the most recent new methods now being applied to comparative analysis.[1] The more qualitative methods addressed here, although also mathematical, stand apart because of their approach to conjunctural causation that may be applied to a small numbers of cases (e.g., 5 to 10). The best example is Charles Ragin's *Boolean* approach to comparative/historical methods, which is beginning to be applied in systematic ways to welfare states and revolutions.

We, at this point, should be more precise about what we mean by "methodological innovations." None of the methods arrayed in this volume are entirely new to empirical research. Time-series analysis has been widely used in economics, event history in biomedical and labor market research, pooled methods in macroeconomics, and so on. The chapters in this volume do not radically revise, much less originate, the methods in question. Instead, our innovations consist of applications of these methods outside the contexts in which they have been familiar. In particular, they consist of applications of new methodologies to the political economics and economic politics of (largely industrialized and democratic) nation-states. Many of these methods have previously been applied to individual-level data and not to problems that mainly involve comparing societies or nations. Taking these methods into cross-national terrain is somewhat like transporting a television and VCR into the bush – there are neither electrical sockets nor cable jacks!

The difficulties with using these methods are well exemplified by some differences between persons and nations. To begin with, comparative social research inevitably has a small number of cases. Tied to this is the fact that considerable interaction, and thus interdependence, is not only possible but probable among nations. Survey research can rely on the sampling of a large number of independent cases. Inferences can then be made to populations of indefinitely large scale (e.g., 260 million people in the United States). Most comparative research cannot isolate nations, nor can it sample from millions, or even hundreds, of cases.

A further difficulty is that nations have complex histories and unique structures. Although individual histories may be extremely interesting, they are rarely recorded by the survey researcher. The law of large numbers and sampling methods presumably reduce the distortions introduced into survey samples by the presence of a Mother Theresa, a Charles Manson, a Howard Hughes, or a Henry Kissinger. However, divergent national histories cannot be ignored in a small sample: the law of large numbers no longer operates a priori, especially when extensive histories exist on each country. As a result, comparative research must engage particular histories. For instance, the specificity of Nazi Germany may well transcend all attempts at statistical randomization (see Hicks, Swank, and Ambuhl 1989; Janoski 1990).

Thus, systematic inferences are not made to populations of nations, and researchers must live with or test diffusion effects. And other problems include the nonindependence of temporal observations within nation-states – one year's pension expenditures are much like last years' (e.g., autocorrelation, which will be discussed extensively in the time-series introduction).

A related problem is that of reconciling knowledge of often diverse pathways to common ends with homogenizing tendencies of the general linear model. The Boolean approach of Charles Ragin is an application of methodology that allows for more specific causal pathways and theoretical outcomes. Boolean results may support distinct theories with very few cases. Indeed, the same outcomes in a number of countries may be explained by different theories. Charles Ragin calls this "multiple conjunctural causation."

For the most part, the emphasis here is on the application of various methods in a rather new context, that of comparative political economy. We stress this emphasis on comparative political economy because these new methodologies are not easily accessible to social researchers and graduate students apart from substantively integrated settings and because comparative political economy is one such setting in which our innovations can make, indeed are now making, indispensable contributions. As most of the methods were developed in other areas of the social sciences, their application involves very different problems in comparative/historical research. There is a great need to present systematically the full range of these new methodologies in an integrated context so that they may reach comparative researchers and their graduate students, whatever their interests.

Prior methodology texts date back to the 1960s and 1970s, when a flurry of integrative and pedagogic activity took place among comparativists (Marsh 1967; Przeworski and Teune 1970; Vallier 1971; and Smelser 1976). The appearance of these works fully preceded the application and in some cases the discovery of the new methodologies broached here.

More recent works on comparative/historical methods have been qualitative, where they have focused more on method than substance (Smith 1991, pp. 4–6). Among the more qualitatively oriented works, Theda Skocpol's *Vision and Method in Historical Sociology* (1984) examines traditional historical and documentary approaches to comparative sociology. Charles Ragin's *Comparative Methods* (1987), with its logical, if not mathematical, formalizations, overlaps with the new quantitative methods. Ragin uses variable-based and case-based methods to define the broad range of methods used in this area. However, his book does not extend far into each new quantitative method because he concentrates mainly on his own Boolean approach. In *Issues and Alternatives in Comparative Social Research* (1991), Ragin also examines a number of methods, but he focuses more on "case-based" methods and on synthesizing quantitative and qualitative methodologies. Melvin Kohn's *Cross-National Research in Sociology* (1989) does not discuss time-series, event history, pooled time and cross-sectional, or Boolean research. Despite some focus on Weber's comparative methods, qualitative analyses, and nations as the unit of analysis, Kohn's authors focus mostly on single-nation research outside the United States. Only one article in the book actually addresses quantitative comparisons between countries, and its comparisons are strictly cross-sectional. Another recent book on comparative research – Else Øyen's *Comparative Methodology* (1990) – focuses more on quantitative methods and does include a chapter by Rudolf Andorka on time series. However, with the first half of the book focusing on theory and sociological strategy and the second half covering methods such as content analysis, oral history, sampling, and data archives, overall the book stresses the individual as the unit of analysis.[2]

Thus, our focus on the new methodologies in the comparative investigation of nations fills a critical gap in the research literature. The diversity of new approaches to the comparative analysis of states will be integrated in this volume. Formal integration in methodological introductions will be complemented by substantive integration by including two chapters using each new method such that the formal and the substantive approaches will gain force from each other.

WHAT IS THE UNIT OF ANALYSIS IN COMPARATIVE METHODOLOGY?

The answer to this question can be elusive. From one perspective, comparative sociology is the study of nations, societies, or cultures as wholes.[3] For instance, Reinhard Bendix compared France, Britain, and Russia along with Japan and India. Max Weber studied the rise of the West. This project compared Western civilizations with East Asian and South Asian societies in order to answer the question, Why capitalism in the West and not elsewhere? He also ended up doing a major comparative study of the world's religions: Buddhism, Christianity, Islam, and Confucianism. Tocqueville studied France, Britain, and the United States on democracy. Barrington Moore also studied the course of democracy in the West (United States, Britain, and France) and the East (China,

India, and Japan). Thus, all of these scholars studied large and complex units of analysis from nations to civilizations.

Of course, comparative sociologists and political scientists may study problems that focus on the person or household (Hayashi, Suzuki, and Sasaki 1992). The most frequent unit of analysis may be the individual. Stratification researchers and election analysts are producing a great deal of work that compares individual and other microlevel patterns across countries. This may be comparative political economy, even though traditionalists would say that comparative work has mainly been done through documentary research and by sifting heavily aggregated, national materials. In any case, individual data that formerly could not be compared are now becoming increasingly available. We believe, however, that individual-based research now fits squarely into comparative political economy. In particular, it can be regarded as a variant of "internal" analyses, one facet of a Janus-faced, internal–external image of comparative analysis that we will go into a little later in this introduction. Nonetheless, the focus of this book will be on institutions, states, or societies as the unit of analysis. Despite the comparative uses and legitimacy of micropolitical economics, we stress macropolitical economy for four reasons.

First, political economy generally involves the conflict of class, status, and organizational grouping (workers, Catholics, parties, etc.) in the creation of actions, which can only be measured at the societal level. Second, comparative survey researchers, although they encounter special cross-national challenges, use methods of analysis that do not differ much from those used by single-nation survey researchers. Techniques for improving the statistical comparability of variables and strategies for prudent cross-cultural interpretation of findings are folded into their standard repertoire of techniques.[4] Comparative political economy, however, often employs very small samples from which inferences to populations are often weak or proscribed.

Third, macrocomparative research most often is embroiled in an intense theoretical dialogue with history, whereas comparative survey research often tends much more toward dialogue with social psychology. Comparative political economy more clearly focuses on groups, organizations, and institutions within nations than on individuals and their cultural context. This focus certainly is a distinctive, if not a relatively dominant or unique, mode in political economy. Fourth, using the nation as a unit of analysis pushes the research toward productive analytical complexities. For instance, Rokkan (1966, pp. 19–20) and Przeworski and Teune (1970, pp. 50–1) point to the multiple levels involved in comparative work. And in this complexity some individuals – Otto von Bismarck the prime minister or William Beveridge the planner – are more important than others – Joseph Schmitz the worker or Elizabeth Smith the widowed mother. Sampling may be useful with the second group but not with the first. To be effectively comparative, the analyst must move from the system level to examine at least two subsystems. For these four reasons, this book will focus on the problems associated with nations and/or groups as the unit of analysis.

WHY DO COMPARATIVE POLITICAL ECONOMY?

But after stressing the connections of comparative social science to history, we must also differentiate it from comparative history because social science must be causally analytic as well as interpretive, generalizable as well as historically concrete (Ragin 1987, p. 34). This means that the researcher must not only be able to account for significant historical outcomes in a sensible chronological sequence, but also come up with some covering law and/or set of general causal mechanisms. Genetic, idiosyncratic, and even postmodern causes are discounted, if not eschewed. The social scientist must resolve the tension between nomothetic and idiographic explanations by finding generalizations, and where these two explanatory modes conflict, historians and social scientists will often part company (Semlser 1976; Ragin 1987, p. 35).

Before going into a systematic model of the comparative method, let us look at some reasons why we do comparative sociology (as discussed in Dogan and Pelassy 1990, pp. 3–44).

1. Researchers compare nations in order to find sociological rules or generalizations about societies. Social scientists typically cannot directly experiment on societies, so they are left with the comparative method (or quasi-experimentation) to sort out what has happened over time in different countries. Researchers seek to find systematic differences in class structure, deviance, politics, fertility, and so on. Social scientists, especially in the post–World War II United States, have studied their own society in detail and claim to have found universal sociological regularities. However, whether or not sociological laws exist needs to be verified. Researchers typically find that such regularities are far from being universal laws, even after revisions and replications. Yet sometimes, regularities governing societies, or at least types of societies, emerge.

2. Social scientists compare to escape cultural hegemony (or ethnocentrism), because we all wear blinders of some sort. Certainly, we wear cultural blinders especially connected to language and the society in which we were socialized. Americans readily look at other cultures and assume that their rules apply to those cultures. They are surprised when to find out that Indians from the subcontinent often do not like strawberries or that many Chinese avoid cheese. On a more political level, we

find that our class, cultural, racial, and other biases make it difficult to view the world. But this is only the first stage of the problem. We try to escape our culture's hegemony in order to understand other cultures, but we also try to escape our cultural hegemony in order to understand our own culture. When we see other ways of doing things, we then approach our own culture with new eyes, and new questions emerge: "What prevents us from having another nation's problems" or "Why can't we do it their (better) way." After time and considered analysis, the answers emerge at the level of "social facts" rather than social psychology.

THE STAGES OF THE COMPARATIVE/ HISTORICAL APPROACH TO RESEARCH

Comparative social research can be interpreted in terms of a process model that captures the overall features of this approach to research (Janoski 1991). This model describes the field of comparative research as a whole, not as particular studies; because intensive case studies of 20 or more countries by single researchers are simply not possible. However, it is done at a level that cumulates the work of case-based and variable-based researchers (Ragin 1987). This model of the field of comparative research consists of eight steps in which the middle steps tend to reflect internal analysis and case-based research, while the third and sixth steps tend to describe external analysis and variable-based research (Figure 1.1).

1. *Selection of the problem and theory.* All research starts out with "abduction," a term used by Charles Peirce to indicate the mental baggage or interests that we bring to a study (Collins 1985, p. 188). In comparative research, abduction is especially a problem because researchers are trying to overcome cultural hegemony and ethnocentrism. Thus, social scientists must be alert to their assumptions and biases. This can often be tricky, and it requires a unique degree of reflexivity for the comparativist.[5] Additional aspects of abduction include researcher career values, class position in society, and sources of funding (the National Science Foundation, political foundations, host governments, and so on). Thus, researchers face the general problem of the "sociology of knowledge." Is all knowledge relative to class position as Marxists argue, to gender position as feminists assert, or to cultural position as ethnographers contest, and so on? Comparative researchers must continually guard against such biasing factors by sizing themselves up on abduction – what are our biases, interests, and positions, and how do they might affect our work?[6] Yet elements of abduction may be essential to the posing of questions.

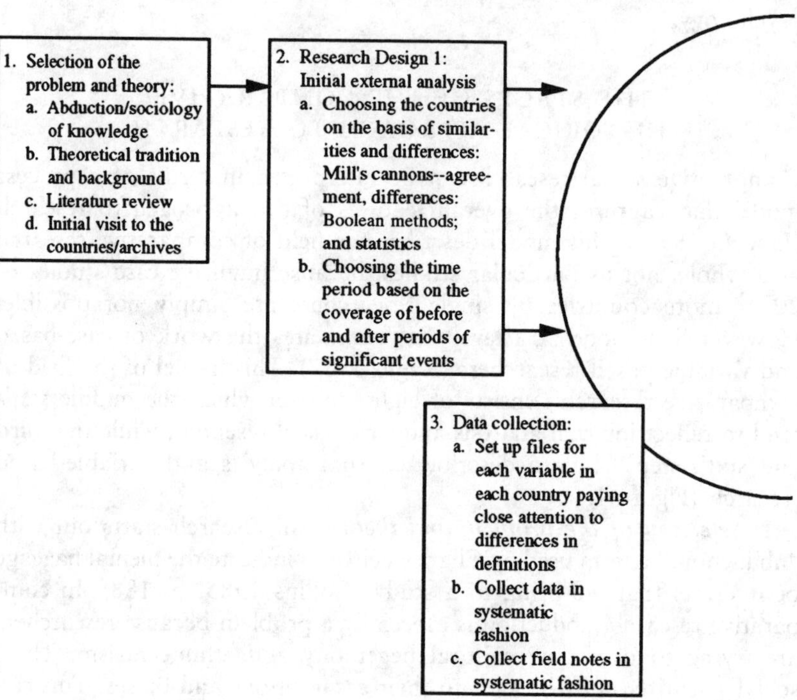

Figure 1.1. A model of the comparative research process.

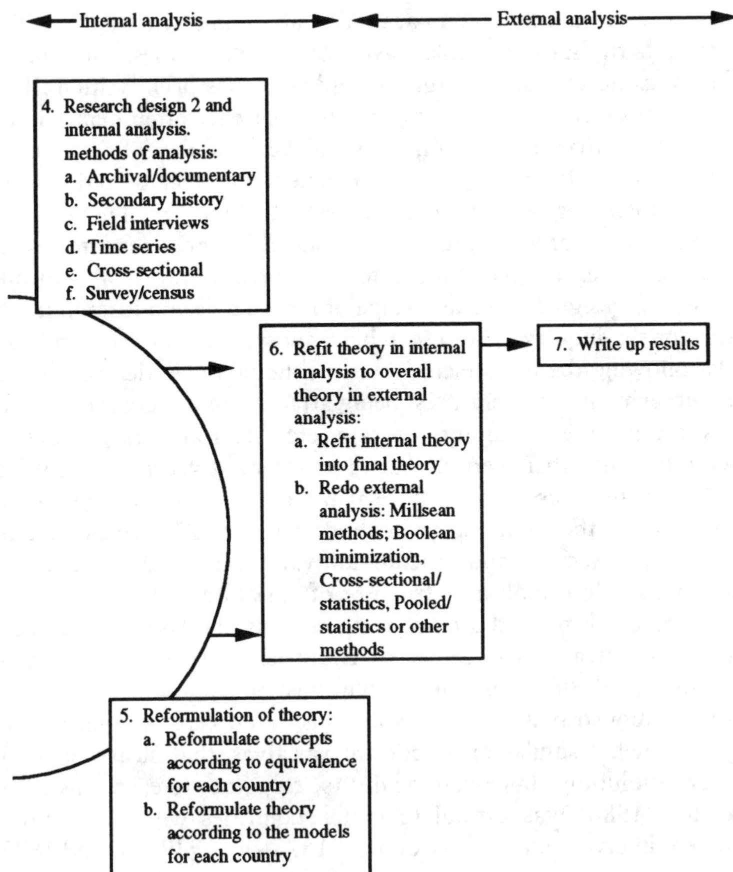
Internal analysis
External analysis
4. Research design 2 and internal analysis. methods of analysis:
a. Archival/documentary
b. Secondary history
c. Field interviews
d. Time series
e. Cross-sectional
f. Survey/census
6. Refit theory in internal analysis to overall theory in external analysis:
a. Refit internal theory into final theory
b. Redo external analysis: Millsean methods; Boolean minimization, Cross-sectional/ statistics, Pooled/ statistics or other methods
7. Write up results
5. Reformulation of theory:
a. Reformulate concepts according to equivalence for each country
b. Reformulate theory according to the models for each country

Like other researchers, comparativists are immersed in theoretical and research traditions. People have done prior studies, and the researcher must access the literature to find what has been written. If the research is case-oriented, the comparative researcher often makes initial visits to the countries in question to assess the feasibility of the research problem. If variable-oriented, the researcher may visit or write to research institutes engaged in such analysis (e.g., the OECD, EEC, and some national research institutes). The social scientist inventories the relevant literatures as deep cultural texts or precise statistical portraits.

2. *Research design 1.* This first stage of research design formulates the structure of the inquiry. The researcher chooses the countries and time periods following the investments made in the first step (learning a language, surveying many literatures, being attached to a theoretical framework, surveying the availability of data, etc.). Researchers pull neither their countries nor their periods out of a statistical urn or magical hat. They choose their cases and historical periods on the basis of experimental design or the comparative method, which applies Mill's methods of difference, agreement, and concomitant variation (1930, pp. 253–66). Mill's canons help establish a structure of variables and constants that direct the research toward a convincing conclusion. Thus, comparative researchers constrain their choice of countries so that some variables can be controlled. In researching revolutions, Skocpol looked for countries that demonstrated "social revolutions," and certain countries, although somewhat similar on important variables, that clearly failed to have such revolutions. In explaining diverse responses to economic crises, Gourevitch (1986) was careful to match countries with and without government interventions in three cycles – 1873–96, 1929–49, and 1973–85. Variable-oriented studies may make an analogous selection of cases or rely on statistical control (Ragin 1987, pp. 61–7). Countries are selected on the basis of similar processes operating within each one. Studies of political economy that rest on principles of social demand – that is, when interest groups push a democratic government toward some end – must select democratic governments in which social demands have some effect. This considerably restricts the sample.

At this point, social scientists are conducting **external analysis**, that is, they compare characteristics between countries or types of countries (e.g., neocorporatist and pluralist types). This is very different from **internal analysis**, which is the analysis of variations within a country. Let us move to the internal analysis stage with its three steps, which tend to emphasize case-oriented more than variable-oriented approaches.

3. *Data collection and field notes.* The researcher has chosen variables and countries. The next step is to examine each country internally. Social scientists set up a file for each country concerning the relevant

data using systematic techniques, which may range from field notes to chronological data. At this stage, researchers also investigate context to see if there are any variables that are not included. Although the ultimate explanatory factors are not definitely known, likely suspects emerge from theory, past findings, and the more general literature review.

4. *Research design 2.* In the internal analysis, social scientists formulate a different sort of analysis design. The first research design concerns how countries can be compared. The second research design concerns how data may be compared (typically over time) within particular countries.[7] This means that the researcher has to come up with a method for extracting knowledge within countries. The candidates are many: historical analysis using secondary materials, primary historical analysis using documents, census or survey research analysis of individual-level data with statistics, participant observation, key informant or elite interviews, time-series studies of particular countries, cross-sectional analysis of subunits within the particular country (e.g., voting districts), and the history of ideas. Each approach requires its own rules of analysis, but it is always constrained by the first research design and the selection of countries. Survey questions require identical or highly similar meanings in each country. Census or government statistical concepts have to have the same meaning and most often have to be collected in the same way. Concepts have to be functionally equivalent, that is, they may take different forms but must supply the same need within each country or refer to the same root concept.

This description applies most directly to case-oriented research, but it affects variable-oriented studies also. In studies of 18 to 100 countries, the researcher cannot know the details of each country's history. Nonetheless, researchers form implicit models of larger multinational domains (e.g., the neocorporatist or the liberal countries). Relying on secondary sources, they form models – for instance, Sweden and Germany have relatively large welfare state expenditures because of trade unions, receptive middle-class groups, and Left-party power. When researchers receive data showing that the Germans spend little, they know from their model and readings of the German literature that the semipublic pension funds may well have been excluded. Researchers may not be able to implement full-fledged multivariate analysis within each nation. However, if variable-oriented researchers do not have a sense of internal analysis and its attendant models, they can produce ridiculous results. Of course, internal analysis will be the strength of the case-based researchers, while external analysis (to come) will be the strength of the variable-based researchers.

5. *Adapting the theory to the specific countries.* Each country is then scrutinized according to a second research design, and the comparative

researcher specifies his or her own theoretical model. At times, this may be an iterative process, that is, it takes place repeatedly with small adjustments. Although we term this stage of analysis "internal," the researcher continues to be cognizant of the internal analyses done in the other countries. As a result, subtle controls are at work (which is quite different from actual operations of external analysis).

In variable-based research, this internal analysis is again somewhat abbreviated since it may rely on secondary materials or small numbers of intranational cases. In some cases internal and external analyses may proceed to some extent concurrently, as in the "within-" and "between-" nation components of "pooled" analyses. Although full-fledged models of each nation may be developed and analyzed in some inquiries, mere scrutinization and refinement of concepts and propositions may comprise other internal analyses. Nonetheless, it is, for the most part, in the next stage that the major portion of variable-based research takes over, and case-based research fades in its contributions.

6. *Specification of theory for all countries.* From the internal analysis of countries, the comparative researcher, especially if he or she is studying a small number of countries, emerges into the external analysis of differences between countries. If an explanation has been located within countries, a different sort of theory may now be used, and a different method may also be used: usually the comparative logic reemerges, or cross-sectional comparisons now come to the fore. An overall interpretation, which was targeted in the research design 1 stage, must now be completed with the data supplied from the internal analysis.

In variable-based research with a wealth and preponderance of cross-sectionally differentiated cases, however, the actual analysis really begins since the internal analysis has been somewhat secondary. Millsean controls are little used because statistical control provides a substitute for such controls in cross-sectional, pooled, or event history analyses. Even the Boolean method can be interpreted as variable-based analysis, although one may choose to stress qualitative variables delineated via a process of intensive historical and/or cultural analysis.[8]

7. *Exit the field or log off the computer to write up the results.* Finally, the comparative researcher exits the field or logs off from the computer and writes up his or her results.

This model describes the cumulative research process rather than any one research project. Clearly, case-based research methods will emphasize internal analysis, and variable-based research will exhibit more strength with external analysis. But the point is that the differentiation of internal and external analyses makes methodological issues more clearly focused, as well as reveals the sometimes obscured but nonetheless complementary relationships between case-based and variable-based methodologies. Although cross-sectional and some pooled analyses contain little explicit internal analysis, their research project rests in many ways on other researchers' internal research. For example, time-series studies of U.S. policy processes enlightened Hicks et al.'s (1989) pooled analysis of changes in welfare spending of 16 nations over 26 years. And with little external analysis, comparative studies of only a few countries may rely on important comparative research projects that do examine many nations. For example, one must ask how much demographic variables would be considered in case studies if not for Wilensky's (1975) work with over 60 nations.

The distinction between internal and external analyses may seem small, but it is not. Most references to comparative research really focus on external analysis alone: Mill's canons of logic apply explicitly to it. However, in most cases, the researcher obtains his or her data either directly or indirectly from a process of internal analysis. For example, economic data used in cross-sectional analyses come from surveys of firms and consumers in individual countries, and characterizations of social structure in case-oriented comparisons of nations are drawn from intensive historical interpretations of nations. Thus, investigations move from internal to external analysis. Similarly, a survey researcher doing an "internal analysis" of three countries uses the individual as the unit of analysis (perhaps over 2,000 individuals in each country). However, as soon as this researcher starts comparing countries, the unit of analysis becomes the country.

Not only should researchers differentiate internal from external analysis in each research project; they can (at least analytically) use this distinction to differentiate the many methods used in this book. And of course, we need to recognize that in comparative research no one method, whether external or internal, exists without the other. The next section will lay out the basic methods covered in this book, classify their use in terms of external and internal analysis, and then relate them to the substantive chapters to follow.

BASIC TYPES OF COMPARATIVE SOCIAL ANALYSES

To illustrate this process model and show the connections of Millsean methods to our new approaches, we will first list the different kinds of comparative societal research and then connect them to the new methods. Mill presents us with two basic approaches to comparative sociology (see Table 1.1),[9] and we will integrate them with five additional methodological approaches.[10]

1. The method of agreement is a repeated juxtaposition of case studies in order to find similar preconditions for all cases with similar outcomes.

Table 1.1. ***Mill's methods of inductive reasoning***

1. Method of agreement: V_1, V_2, and V_3 are all present when V_4 occurs, therefore V_1, V_2, and V_3 cause V_4.

		Country 1	Country 2
Independent variables	V_1	Yes	Yes
	V_2	Yes	Yes
	V_3	Yes	Yes
Dependent variable	V_4	Yes	Yes

2. Method of difference: V_1 and V_2 are present when V_4 occurs and when it does not, therefore V_1 and V_2 cannot explain V_4. Since V_3 is present when V_4 occurs, and not present when V_4 does not occur, V_3 causes V_4.

		Country 1	Country 2
Independent variables	V_1	Yes	Yes
	V_2	Yes	Yes
	V_3	Yes	No
Dependent variable	V_4	Yes	No

3. Indirect method of agreement: V_1 is present in all cases, so it cannot explain V_4. V_2 and V_3 are all present when V_4 occurs and not present when V_4 does not occur, therefore, V_2 and V_3 cause V_4.

		Country 1	Country 2	Country 3	Country 4
Independent variables	V_1	Yes	Yes	Yes	Yes
	V_2	Yes	Yes	No	No
	V_3	Yes	Yes	No	No
Dependent variable	V_4	Yes	Yes	No	No

Skocpol and Somers refer to it as the parallel demonstration of theory because similar processes occur in each country (especially if there are few exceptions and subtypes). Przeworski and Teune (1970) more or less call it the method of most different cases.

The more subtypes designated from the "similar processes," the more the author has disguised positive cases as negative cases and exceptions, and hence, the weaker the argument. Skocpol and Somers (1980, p. 191) claim that the historical analyses themselves cannot validate the theory, but we do not agree. In our terminology, the internal analysis within each case can validate the theory (Bradshaw and Wallace 1991). It can validate a theory that can interpret the data within each country, and this provides the basis for comparison. External analysis can also validate a theory by establishing the commonalities between cases.

A danger with this method is that the author becomes overly enamored with theory and begins to ignore variance between the cases. He or she then simply selects the evidence that is convenient, while ignoring contrary evidence and theories, hence yielding poor comparative results.

This method is congenial to functionalist analysis and the search for cultural universals. As an example, S. N. Eisenstadt's *The Political Systems of Empires* (1963) uses empires as political systems for his unit of analysis. His 13 major cases range from the Pharoahs of Egypt to the Aztecs and even to China, and the cases are selected because they fit the definition of "empire". Theory dominates in this approach, with each case being presented to support an overarching and deductive argument. In the clear use of the method of agreement, Eisenstadt develops the theory in pieces with each case, but clearly the strength of the theory (i.e., the agreements) dominates the uniqueness (i.e., the differences) of each case.[11] Eisenstadt's work demonstrates primary reliance on external analysis with arguments being promoted by the similarity of each case to the theory. Internal analysis is primarily historical or functional in demonstrating the system of each empire or society. This method provides little logical or statistical support for theory beyond that afforded by the several internal analyses it serves to frame.

2. The method of difference (or indirect method of difference) is the selection of countries that have similar features on some variables but are different on other critical variables. One may then attribute causal force to the variables that do not have shared values. This is a combination of positive cases exhibiting agreement and negative cases that do not. This approach combines Mill's methods of agreement and difference.[12]

Theda Skocpol's *States and Social Revolutions* (1978) is the most explicit demonstration of the method of difference available. Skocpol's unit of analysis is the country, and she looks at France, Russia, and China as positive cases. They fit her definition of "social revolution." She then looks at Germany, England, and Japan as negative cases, those in which social revolutions did not occur. Where Moore was somewhat ambivalent on theory, Skocpol is more explicit, and it appears that she develops a structural theory, but she backs off of a completely nomothetic approach in saying that "comparative-historical causal arguments cannot be readily generalized beyond the cases actually discussed" (Skocpol and Somers 1980, p. 195). The clearly structural theory is established by the method of agreement with the countries that experienced a revolution, but then the theory is doubly supported by showing why revolutions did not occur in three countries.[13] This approach to the method of difference stresses external analysis, and its proof lies in the comparison of variables on the positive and negative cases. Internal analysis is not so explicit, yet it is critical to establishing the values for each case. It mainly consists of historical analysis within each country to establish yes or no for the variables in the method of difference. This method can provide no more than the degree of strictly logical or statistical support for theory afforded by a cross-tabulation with every case, yet the cross-tabulation in question is one whose categories have been coded on the basis of careful and richly informed internal analysis. Despite few cases, results may provide powerful support when hypothesized patterns are neatly confirmed as in Stephens (1989) (see also Rueschemeyer, Stephens, and Stephens (1992)).

Beyond these two mainstay methods of comparative research, there are now a number of newer approaches, each unique. Some accentuate external over internal analysis, some focus on cases more than comparisons, and others look to theory. We start with the Boolean method and then go through cross-sectional, time-series, pooled, and event history approaches.

3. The Boolean approach is essentially an extension of the Millsean methods of agreement and difference. It constitutes, however, a heavy formalization and extension of Millsean methods. The innovations that this method develops are (1) techniques for handling a larger number of cases, (2) algorithms for easy data reduction, (3) the inversion of matrices to analyze nonevents (i.e., counterfactual analysis), (4) the ability to produce multiple-conjunctural models based on as few as two cases (an important bridge to qualitative methods), and (5) the extension beyond the sample logics of two-dimensional cross-tabulations. There are parallels between Boolean methods and log-linear analysis, but the Boolean approach substitutes a stress on combinatorial conjunctural effects for the log-linear priority on lower-order effects relative to higher-order interactions. Moreover, it eschews the statistical privileging of more frequent cases. Although the roots of this method are certainly in Mill, the specific formalized method is based on switching circuits, and its computer programs are very new (indeed, they are not yet publically available on the market).

The Boolean approach is preponderantly external analysis, although its qualitative characterizations of cases draw on internal analysis. We can see from Charles Ragin's chapter on welfare state development in Europe that the primary focus is on external comparisons rather than the internal generation of models (see Chapter 13, this volume). However, Ragin does state that before using the method, the researcher must do a careful and exacting history, which of course would entail internal analysis. Thus, Boolean analysis is presumably done the same way as Mill's – relegating internal analysis to a preliminary or background status. However, according to our previous model, internal analysis can be done in any number of ways – even a Boolean approach to subnational units! The external analysis is open to the statistical objection that Boolean algorithms are insensitive to the relative frequencies of cases, blind to the possibilities of random components, and disposed to prematurely disregard simple additive models for arcane multiplicative (or conjunctural) ones.

From the Millsean base in the method of agreement and difference, we now move to correlational methods, which are actually based in Mill's "method of concomitant variation."[14] These correlational methods consist of cross-sectional, time-series, and pooled cross-sectional and time-series analyses.

4. Cross-sectional analysis is well described in Harold Wilensky's *The Welfare State and Equality* (1975). The units of analysis consist of nations at particular points in time. Wilensky selects cases based on having the dependent variable or explanadum that is in the presence of some measurable social security system, no matter how small. The 60 cases, however, are not carefully selected according to Millsean criteria; they are selected simply for being members of a broad category for which data is available (64 "countries," 22 "industrialized countries," and then 14 "industrialized-democratic countries"). The tests of the functionalist theory of industrial development creating social needs is operationalized by GNP per capita and age 65+ as an intervening variable. The method consists of regression equations and path analysis.

This method has all the advantages and disadvantages of the indirect method of difference, and like that method, it is mainly external analysis. To its credit, the methods carry the Millsean method to the point of systematic statistical analysis. To its detriment, it deals in too many cases for the even implicit application of "internal analysis" (e.g., the choice of variables and measures) to be usefully applied. Cross-sectional research can constitute internal analysis (see Tilly's 1964 analysis of French subnational units in the Vendée and Steinmetz's 1990 analysis of German cities), but when it does, it often drops its external analysis (international comparisons).

5. Time-series analysis is demonstrated by Janoski (Chapter 3, this volume) in cross-national research on Sweden, Germany, and the United

States. His cases are constrained by the indirect method of difference. On the dependent variable of active labor market policy expenditures, the analysis searches for the most effective independent variables in politics, demographics, and economics. Thus, the year within one country is the unit of analysis. Janoski uses longitudinal regression within each nation, complete with requisite diagnoses and analysis corrections for autocorrelated error (see the methodological introduction to time series in Chapter 2, this volume). Of particular importance in this analysis are the lagged and distributed effects of the independent variables.

Time-series analysis is clearly internal analysis, and in some sense it can be seen as the quantitative analogue to history. External analysis is really not specified by the method, and the Millsean, Boolean, or cross-sectional methods can be used to compare time-series analyses of a number of countries (Alt and Chrystal 1983; Andorka 1990; and Janoski 1990). This suggests one deficiency of the method: properties of nations (like other temporally invariant factors) do not figure in the calculation of effects. Moreover, data on particular nations may lack sufficient cases to support statistically powerful inferences. Also, stress on nation-specific internal analysis may direct energies away from the identification of cross-nationally general explanations. That is, this method may magnify small differences in national processes by an accumulation of decisions slightly favoring nation-specific variables.

In Chapter 4, this volume, by Larry Isaac, Susan Carlson, and Mary Mathis, the authors examine quality and quantity in the historical analysis of the unemployment and wage relationship in the United States and Sweden. One country fights hard against unemployment while the other does not. In each case internal analysis is important, especially in the sense of finding the country-specific timing of relationships between variables. Larry Isaac has written on this topic in detail in previous articles (e.g., Isaac and Griffin 1989).

John Freeman and James Alt's chapter, "The Politics of Public and Private Investment in Britain," illustrates time series without any explicit comparisons but those across time periods. As such, it provides a purely internal analysis, but one that adds a new dimension in terms of vector autoregression. (In addition to Chapter 5, this volume, see the latter part of the methodological introduction on time series in Chapter 2.)

6. Pooled analysis combines attention to variability across both time and space. Alex Hicks's article, which analyzes "country-years" (i.e., particular nations in particular years) as units of analysis, provides a good exmple of this analytical approach. He uses pooled regression equations with correction for autocorrelation of error across both time and nations (see Chapter 7, this volume). The O'Connell chapter is

another good example. Similar to Hicks's analyses in many respects, O'Connell extends them by employing more distinct foci on separate time-series and cross-sectional analyses. He does so by contrasting the determination of growth in real wage compensation across four contexts defined by combinations of historical/macroeconomic epochs (pre- and post-OPEC), as well as national institutions (corporatist and noncorporatist). O'Connell provides an interesting example of "external" analysis contrasting sets of nations and periods of national history, as well as "internal" analyses within several nation-epochs (see Chapter 8, this volume).

Pooled methods have two weaknesses. First, with so many countries in the study, the researcher cannot know the intimate details of each case. Sometimes this is called the "historical competence problem." This is less troublesome in time series where the number of countries may be limited to two to five. Second, pooled studies tend, in contrast with time-series studies, to reduce the explanation to a single cross-nationally homogenous set of variables and parameters. "Multiple conjunctural causation" allows for multiple causal models; pooled models, contrary to time series, allow for cyclical and structural models. Of course, pooled researchers can come up with different models by elaborating interactions or reducing their sample sizes. However, when interactions proliferate, when models become conceptually and statistically unwieldy, and when sample sizes become too small, the model loses its statistical power to reject null (and articulate other) hypotheses.

Pooled analysis combines internal and external analysis in one whole by using time–space as the unit of analysis. However, internal analyses of separate nations are collapsed across nations, while cross-sectional analyses of nations are collapsed over time. In simpler additive models like those in Hicks and Swank (1992), internal analyses dominate to the extent that longitudinal variation does. In external analyses such as Pampel and Williamson (1988), external analysis dominates to the extent that cross-sectional variation is greater than time variation. Statistical techniques should vary with the extent of cross-sectional, as opposed to temporal, variation. Internal and external analyses may be differentiated by means of distinctive temporal and cross-sectional variances or by means of variables with relatively "fixed-effect" controls for all cross-sectional (or all temporal) variance, through the use of dummy variables for place (or time) (Griffin et al. 1986; Hage, Hanneman, and Gargan, 1989; Hicks et al. 1989).

7. Event history analysis is the newest method to be used in comparative/historical research (Meyer and Hannan 1979; Meyer 1980; Strang 1991). It shifts the analysis from levels of participation or expenditure to actual occurrences or epochal societal events (i.e., the passage

Table 1.2. ***Comparisons using internal and external analysis***

Methodologies	Internal Analysis	External Analysis
The method of agreement	—	Dominant
The method of difference	—	Dominant
Cross-sectional analysis	—	Dominant
Time-series analysis	Dominant	—
Pooled analysis	Considerable	Considerable
Event history analysis	Considerable	Considerable
Boolean analysis	—	Dominant

of a law in a legislature). Chikako Usui follows the legislation of sickness, pension, unemployment, and family allowance programs in the welfare states of 60 nations in Europe and Asia. She pays particular attention to the diffusion effects of international organizations on the developments within nations. This provides a combination of internal and external analysis (see Chapter 10, this volume). David Strang provides a similar analysis focusing on the decolonization of states subject to the United Kingdom (and Commonwealth) and France. His analysis works on both sides of the developed and nondeveloped worlds to show how decolonization works and eventually produces forces for increasing citizenship within the formerly imperial nation. His analysis combines time and space like pooled analysis, but the dependent variable is an event rather than the level of expenditures or participation (see Chapter 11, this volume).[15]

In summing up, the various methods seem to fit the following categories: (1) external analysis is dominant in the Millsean methods, Boolean approaches, and cross-sectional analysis; (2) internal analysis is dominant with time series; and (3) internal and external analysis are combined in pooled analysis and event history (see Table 1.2). Consequently, these methods give us a balanced range of approaches for solving political-economic problems concerning the welfare state.

QUO VADIS POLITICAL ECONOMY

But given these tools, what will the effect be in the comparative political economy of the welfare state? We present four scenarios here. In the conclusion, we take up the prospects for the realization of these scenarios, including components of the methods and theories discussed here.

1. *Quantitative analysis will utilize larger numbers of pooled cases to solve small-n problems and be applied to new approaches to political*

economy. The use of pooled methods and event history by combining internal and external analysis will provide increasing evidence for generalizations that were not previously validated in quantitative analysis.

2. *Quantitative analyses will settle a number of issues with increasing sensitivity to national diversity and time, but still maintain a nomothetic approach to political economy.* The Boolean approach outline by Charles Ragin and the increasing sensitivity of time-series analysis put forward by Larry Isaac, Larry Griffin, and others point in this direction. Primary analyses of single or small numbers of countries will continue to be relied on, but time variability and multiple conjunctural causation will be increasingly used. Sensitivity to flexible time makes quantitative analyses less rigid and recognizes that countries develop at different rates and time. Multiple conjunctural causation allows countries to portray theories when only a very few cases are available. The implications are that questions of power resources, convergence, and world systems, as well as other theories will be confronted with new and powerful evidence that is increasingly sensitive to traditional historical analyses.

3. *Quantitative analysis will tend increasingly toward nation- and period-specific time-series and historical analyses.* Under the pressures of increasing concern for internal analysis, more and more attention will be given to subnational analyses, narratives, and theoretical priors with statistical analysis being cued by and subordinate to qualitative analyses and idiographic explanations.

4. *The political economy of the welfare state will gravitate toward deductive and rational choice models* (Lewin 1988; Kiser and Hechter 1991; and Przeworski 1991). The partially inductive models with somewhat distant connections to social and political theory will give way to more directly deductive models. This will lead to political economy models that will depend much more on decision-making processes. While not necessarily social psychological, this approach will take the theoretical motives of groups into account and then test them.

In our final estimation of *quo vadis* political economy, we will base our conclusions on trends evident in empirical research and disciplinary critiques of research methods.

NOTES

1. Sociologists and political scientists have also begun to use *economic* models such as Cobb–Douglas functions and formal rational choice theory to study economic growth, trade union solidarity, and many other issues (Przeworski 1987, Lewin 1988; and Kiser and Hechter 1991). These more economic approaches are very new to comparative methods outside of the discipline of economics. However, we will not focus on these methods in this book

because they point to theoretical advances rather than methodological innovations.

2. Other works on comparative social science are available, but in most cases they either are much more substantively focused or focus more toward case-based methods. Dierkes et al. (1987) and Manfred and Peschar (1984) examine comparative social policy. J. Michael Armer and Robert Marsh's *Comparative Sociological Research in the 1960s and 1970s* (1982) concentrates on the comprehensive reviews of substantive areas of comparative research. See also Feagin, Orum, and Sjoberg (1991) and Becker and Ragin (1992) on case studies.
3. We use "culture" in a rather broad sense. Swanson's *Birth of the Gods* (1960) dealt with religions rather than nations, but these different religions came close to distinguishing separate societies (1971). Comparative research should distinguish itself from within-country comparisons – for instance, in the comparison of Methodist and Baptist churches in North Carolina, the comparison of two or more bureaucracies in the United States (Graham and Roberts 1972), or the comparison of cities in New England (Schwirian 1974).
4. Of course, the measurement of variables in different countries is a major problem for survey research studies.
5. Consider researchers who study a country very different from their own, say, Americans studying Japan. First, they go through a stage in which they find Japanese ways of doing things rather strange, inefficient, or unfathomable. There is a strong tendency to interpret Japanese behavior and institutions in terms of U.S. society. People who criticize the culture are mired at stage one. Second, they often fall in love with the other country. Everything the Japanese do is embraced unquestionably. The things first thought to be strange become socially useful. Third, researchers reach a more mature point of view where they can see both good points and bad. Some institutions can be copied in another country, but others cannot.
6. According to *Webster's New Universal Unabridged Dictionary*, "abduction" in a logical sense means a kind of argumentation in which "the major is evident but the minor is so obscure as to require further proof." In less technical language, an assumption is being buried.
7. For variable-based research, the internal research design is often rather transparent; however, an internal analysis still underlies this mode of analysis. This will be discussed in the coming paragraphs.
8. However, Ragin chooses to give the Boolean method a qualitative tilt for two reasons. One is the method's stress on qualitative variables, quantitatively coded or not. The other is the method's "case-centered" character. For Ragin, this seems to take the method decisively into the terrain of qualitative history by stressing the researcher's qualitative comprehension of individual cases in all their holistic complexity and integrity as a crucial ground for both model specification and evaluation (see Chapters 12 and 13 and Ragin 1987). Nevertheless, the Boolean method's algorithmic processing of 0–1 variables and formal criteria for adequate Boolean solutions makes the "variable-centered" interpretation a plausible reading as well.
9. Mill (1930, pp. 259–66) also mentions the "method of concomitant variation," which approximates the correlational approach, and the "method of residues," which cannot be used in nonexperimental research.

10. Skocpol and Somers (1980) describe three categories that fit Mill's methods well. First, "parallel comparative history" basically describes the method of agreement. Second, "macro-analytic comparative history" fits the method of difference. Their third category – "contrast oriented comparative history" – is highly idiographic, but it is basically similar to macroanalytic comparative history in its application. It denies that strong generalizations can be made and replaces "theory" with "themes." A good example is Reinhard Bendix's *Nation Building and Citizenship* (1964), in which the cases are the United Kingdom, France, Germany, Russia, India, and Japan. In our view, this method is basically the method of difference, but it is less strictly constructed. The variables in one group do not apply so well to the other group. For instance, Bendix uses the theory of citizenship in Western Europe and then drops it in India and Japan. The "hiatus" between India's modernizing elite and communally tied citizens is apparently too great (p. 4).

    Skocpol and Somers also refer to "paradigm bridgers." For instance, Perry Anderson's *Lineages of the Absolutist State* (1974) is between parallel demonstration of theory and contrast-oriented history. Other examples are Barrington Moore's *Dictatorship and Democracy* (1966), which bridges macrocomparative and contrast-oriented history, and the Tillys' bridging of macrocomparative and parallel demonstration of theory in *The Rebellious Century* (1975). Although these distinctions are interesting mixes of methods, we drop them because they do not present an entirely different method.
11. Another excellent example is Arthur Stinchcombe's *Economic Sociology* (1993) because he looks at three "most different" societies: the United States in the 1970s, France in the 1700s, and the Karimajong herding tribe of Uganda circa 1950. The attempt is to compare these entirely different societies to demonstrate his theory of the mode of production. Stinchcombe uses the method of agreement to show how the mode of production can be used in vastly different societies. In this way, the method of agreement often selects the most different cases.
12. Two criticisms of these studies would come from Bendix (1964) and Wallerstein (1989). First, Bendix would state that the more countries or cases that you enter into the study, the more you affix each country to a Procrustean bed of variables. These variables may have to be stretched to fit each country. Reinhard Bendix might say that researchers should keep their Procrustean beds in their heads as "ideal types" and then deal with the actual variables that are most effective in explaining what happens in each country. Second, world systems theorists would criticize any method based on Mill's principles of experimentation as in error. Countries and cases are connected in vital ways. In their theory of the world system, you cannot treat each country as being determined by its own internal analysis, and external analysis is a network of interrelationships. Hence, the Russian revolution has critical links to the Chinese revolution. Any attempt to treat them as independent will distort reality. Nonetheless, a case-based study can use Millsean methods as a structure, while providing much contextual detail from the world system, and a variable-based study can implement external influences (e.g., the terms of trade with other nations).
13. Technically, the method of difference applies only to differences, and the indirect method of difference applies to the use of agreement and disagree-

ment. Since the indirect method of difference is most commonly used and the method of difference not, we simply refer to them in a combined category (Mill 1930).

14. Correlational methods could be seen as multiplying the "indirect method of difference" (done with continuous as well as categorical variables) into statistical significance, which explains Skocpol and Somer's puzzling remark that Barrington Moore demonstrates a "kind of multivariate analysis" with "too many variables and not enough cases" (1982, p. 182).
15. The rational choice approach has made a considerable impact in political science and has recently begun to penetrate sociological thinking. It operates with deductive theory and formal mathematical modeling (Wallerstein 1987; Hage, Garnier, and Fuller 1988; Tsebelis 1990; and Kiser and Hechter 1991). We have not included it in this book because it is a theoretical approach to political-economic problems rather than a methodological approach to analyzing data. Nonetheless, rational choice provides an important contribution in this area. Karl Ove Moene and Michael Wallerstein presented a paper at the conference that brings rational choice theory to bear with the solidaristic bargaining of skilled workers who would appear to have more to gain by going it alone. By deductively showing that workers pursue the equality of wages and at the same time raise the productivity level of industry, worker solidarity is shown to be a rather "counterintuitive" rational choice. This presents a very fruitful avenue of approaching theory.

REFERENCES

Alt, James E., and K. Alec Chrystal. 1983. *Political Economics*. Berkeley: University of California Press.

Anderson, Perry. 1974. *Lineages of the Absolutist State*. London: Verso.

Andorka, Rudolf. 1990. "The Use of Time Series in International Comparison." In Else Øyen (ed.) *Comparative Methodology*, pp. 203–23. London: Sage.

Armer, J., Michael Armer, and Robert Marsh. 1982. *Comparative Sociological Research in the 1960s and 1970s*. Leiden: E. J. Brill.

Becker, Howard, and Charles Ragin. 1992. *What Is a Case? Exploring the Foundations of Social Inquiry*. Cambridge University Press.

Bendix, Reinhard. 1964. *Nation Building and Citizenship*. New York: Doubleday.

Bradshaw, York, and Michael Wallace. 1991. "Informing Generality and Explaining Uniqueness: The Place of Case Studies in Comparative Research." In Charles Ragin (ed.), *Issues and Alternatives in Comparative Social Research*, pp. 154–71. Leiden: E. J. Brill.

Collins, Randall. 1985. *Three Sociological Traditions*. Oxford: Oxford University Press.

Dierkes, Meinolf, Hans Weiler, and Ariane Antal. 1987. *Comparative Policy Research*. New York: St. Martins.

Dogan, Mattei, and Dominique Pelassy. 1990. *How to Compare Nations: Strategies in Comparative Politics*, 2d ed. Chatham, N.J.: Chatham House.

Eisenstadt, S. N. 1963. *The Political Systems of Empires*. Glencoe, Ill.: Free Press.

Feagin, Joe, Anthony Orum, and Gideon Sjoberg. 1991. *A Case for the Case Study*. Chapel Hill: University of North Carolina Press.

Gourevitch, Peter. 1986. *Politics in Hard Times: Comparative Responses to International Economic Crises*. Ithaca: Cornell University Press.

Graham, William, and Karlene H. Roberts. 1972. *Comparative Studies in Organizational Behavior*. New York: Holt, Rinehart & Winston.

Griffin, Larry, Pamela Barnhouse Walters, Philip O'Connell, and Edward Moor. 1986. "Methodological Innovations in the Analysis of Welfare State Development." In Norman Furniss (ed.), *Futures of the Welfare State*, pp. 101–38. Bloomington: Indiana University Press.

Griffin, Larry, Christopher Botsko, Ana-Maria Wahl, and Larry Isaac. 1991. "Theoretical Generality, Case Particularity: Qualitative Comparative Analysis of Trade Union Growth and Decline." In Charles Ragin (ed.), *Issues and Alternatives in Comparative Social Research*, pp. 110–36. Leiden: E. J. Brill.

Hage, Jerald, Maurice Garnier, and Bruce Fuller. 1988. "The Active State, Investment in Human Capital, and Economic Growth." *American Sociological Review* 53:824–37

Hage, Jerald, Robert Hanneman, and Edward Gargan. 1989. *State Responsiveness and State Activism*. London: Unwin Hyman.

Hayashi, C., T. Suzuki, and M. Sasaki. 1992. *Data Analysis for Comparative Social Research: International Perspectives*. Amsterdam: North Holland.

Hicks, Alexander, and Duane Swank. 1992. "Politics, Institutions, and Welfare Spending in Industrialized Democracies, 1960–1982." *American Political Science Review* 86:658–74.

Hicks, Alexander, Duane Swank, and Martin Ambuhl. 1989. "Welfare Expansion Revisited." *European Journal of Political Research* 17:401–30.

Isaac, Larry, and Larry Griffin. 1989. "Ahistoricism in Time-Series Analyses of Historical Process: Critique, Redirection, and Illustrations from U.S. Labor History." *American Sociological Review* 54:873–90.

Janoski, Thomas. 1990. *The Political Economy of Unemployment: Active Labor Market Policy in West Germany and the United States*. Berkeley: University of California Press.

1991. "Synthetic Strategies in Comparative Sociological Research: Methods and Problems of Internal and External Analysis." In Charles Ragin (ed.), *Issues and Alternatives in Comparative Social Research*, pp. 59–81. Leiden: E. J. Brill.

Kiser, Edgar, and Michael Hechter. 1991. "The Role of General Theory in Comparative-Historical Sociology." *American Journal of Sociology* 97(1):1–30.

Kohn, Melvin. 1989. *Cross-National Research in Sociology*. Newbury Park, Calif. Sage.

Lewin, Lief. 1988. *Ideology and Strategy*. Cambridge University Press.

Marsh, Robert. 1967. *Comparative Sociology: A Codification of Cross-Societal Analysis*. New York: Harcourt, Brace & World.

Meyer, John. 1980. "The World Polity and the Authority of the Nation-State." In A. Bergeson (ed.), *Studies of the Modern World-System*, pp. 109–38. New York: Academic Press.

Meyer, John, and Michael Hannan. 1979. *National Development and the World System: Educational, Economic, and Political Change 1950 to 1970*. Chicago: University of Chicago Press.

Mill, John Stuart. 1930. *A System of Logic: Ratiocinative and Inductive*. London: Longmans, Green.

Moore, Barrington. 1966. *Social Origins of Dictatorship and Democracy*. Boston: Beacon.

Neißen, Manfred, and Jules Peschar. 1984. *International Comparative Research*. Oxford: Pergamon Press.

Øyen, Else. 1990. *Comparative Methodology: Theory and Practice in International Social Research*. London: Sage.

Przeworski, Adam. 1987. "Methods of Cross-National Research, 1970–83: An Overview." In Meinolf Dierkes, Hans Weiler, and Ariane Antal (eds.), *Comparative Policy Research*, pp. 31–49. New York: St. Martins.

1991. *Democracy and the Market*. Cambridge University Press.

Przeworski, Adam, and Henry Teune. 1970. *The Logic of Comparative Social Inquiry*. New York: Wiley.

Ragin, Charles. 1987. *The Comparative Method*. Berkeley: University of California Press.

1991. *Issues and Alternatives in Comparative Social Research*. Leiden: E. J. Brill.

Rokkan, Stein. 1966. "Comparative Cross-national Research: The Context of Current Efforts." In Richard Merritt and Stein Rokkan (eds.), *Comparing Nations*, pp. 3–26. New Haven, Conn.: Yale University Press.

Rueschemeyer, Dietrich, Evelyne Huber Stephens, and John D. Stephens. 1992. *Capitalist Development and Democracy*. Chicago: University of Chicago Press.

Schwirian, Kent. 1974. *Comparative Urban Structure: Studies in the Ecology of Cities*. Lexington, Mass.: Heath.

Skocpol, Theda. 1984. *Vision and Method in Historical Sociology*. Cambridge University Press.

1978. *States and Social Revolutions*. Cambridge University Press.

Skocpol, Theda, and Margaret Somers. 1980. "The Uses of Comparative History in Macrosocial Inquiry." *Comparative Studies of Society and History* 22:174–97.

Smelser, Neil. 1976. *Comparative Methods in the Social Sciences*. Englewood Cliffs, N.J.: Prentice-Hall.

Smith, Joel. 1991. "A Methodology for Twenty-first Century Sociology." *Social Forces* 70(1):1–18.

Steinmetz, George. 1990. "The Local Welfare State: Social Domination in Urban Imperial Germany." *American Sociological Review* 55(6):891–911.

Stephens, John D. 1989. "Democratic Transition and Breakdown in Western Europe, 1870–1939: A Test of the Moore Thesis." *American Journal of Sociology* 94(5):1019–77.

Stinchcombe, Arthur. 1983. *Economic Sociology*. New York: Academic Press.

Strang, David. 1991. "From Dependency to Sovereignty: An Event History Analysis of Decolonization, 1870–1987." *American Sociological Review* 55(6):846–60.

Swanson, Guy. 1960. *The Birth of the Gods*. Ann Arbor: University of Michigan Press.

Swanson, Guy. 1971. "Frameworks for Comparative Research: Structural Anthropology and the Theory of Action." In Ivan Vallier (ed.), *Comparative Methods in Sociology*, pp. 141–202. Berkeley: University of California Press.

Tilly, Charles. 1964. *The Vendée*. Cambridge, Mass.: Harvard University Press.

1984. *Big Structures, Large Processes and Huge Comparisons*. New York: Russell Sage, Foundation.

Tilly, Charles, Louise Tilly, and Richard Tilly. 1975. *The Rebellious Century, 1830–1930*. Cambridge, Mass.: Harvard University Press.

Tsebelis, George. 1990. *Nested Games*. Berkeley: University of California Press.
Vallier, Ivan. 1971. *Comparative Methods in Sociology*. Berkeley: University of California Press.
Wallerstein, Immanuel. 1989. *The Modern World-System*. Vol. 3. San Diego: Acadamic Press.
Wallerstein, Michael. 1987. "Unemployment, Collective Bargaining, and the Demand for Protection." *American Journal of Political Science* 31:729–52.
1989. "Union Organization in Advanced Industrial Democracies." *American Political Science Review* 83:481–501.
Wilensky, Harold. 1975. *The Welfare State and Equality*. Berkeley: University of California Press.

PART I

Time-series analysis

2

Introduction to time-series analysis

THOMAS JANOSKI AND LARRY W. ISAAC

Beginning with time series is perhaps the best point of entrée for the new methods of comparative research because its chronologically ordered data come closest to familiar notions of history. Yet rather than simply describing "one damn year after another," time-series analysis tests for the relationships between variables. When time-series analysis is done in a sensitive, theory-driven, historically grounded manner, it can ring true with conventional historical analysis by enriching and being enriched by historical inquiry.[1]

THE SCOPE AND LOGIC OF TIME-SERIES ANALYSIS

Time series, as currently used, most often cover variables in comparative political economy in nations or states from 20 to 100 years. Most studies of the welfare state focus on state expenditures, but participation in programs or demographic outputs have also been used (Hage and Hanneman 1980; Griffin, Devine, and Wallace 1983; Hicks 1984; Korpi 1989; Hage, Hanneman, and Gargan 1990). Political scientists have pursued the election cycle and macroeconomic policies (Hibbs 1977; Monroe 1979, 1984; Hibbs and Vasilatos 1981; Beck 1982; and Hibbs, Rivers, and Vasilatos 1982). And sociological and economic researchers have also focused on strikes (Shorter and Tilly 1974; Snyder

This introduction has the limited intent of introducing the reader to the procedures, strengths, weaknesses, and promises of time-series analysis. It then provides leads to important sources that treat each topic in much more detail. Consequently, much of this introduction treats very complicated materials in a quick and simple way. We implore our readers' indulgence with our generalizations and direct them to the more complex treatments of each issue in the texts that we reference.

We would like to thank Alexander Hicks for his careful readings and suggestions, as well as John Freeman and James Alt for supplying the short explanation of vector autoregression on which we have heavily relied. Any errors, of course, are our own.

1975; Edwards 1981; and Isaac and Griffin 1989). Time-series methods, however, can be applied to any social or political variable that can be regularly measured over a given time frame (i.e., over standard calendar units of years, quarters, months, etc.).

The basic logic of time-series regression analysis is simply that of ordinary regression, but with a few twists concerning the independence of observations over time and the time lags of variables. Put most simply with two variables (X and Y), time-series regression analysis draws and then expresses a straight line (in an equation) through the observed points (X_i, Y_i) on a graph that will minimize the summed distances from the observed points to the proposed line.

This method involves several common limitations. First, a researcher needs consistent measurements of variables over a relatively long period of time. While the absolute minimum for producing a line is two cases, this is insufficient for computing covariance-based estimates. The lowest number of years we have seen in the political economy regression literature is 8 years (Tufte 1978), with a more common lower limit between 20 and 30 years. Consistent measurements over long lengths of time, however, are not always available. Second, a nation's historical "constants" (e.g., political structure for the United States or Sweden since World War II) are not well expressed in many time-series analyses but the very longest. As a result, certain theoretical arguments (e.g., many state-centric theories) that include structural variables that do not vary much over time cannot be adequately tested. The regression constant can be used as a residual for all such theoretical constants, but the α is too indefinite to provide a case for state-centric theories.[2] And third, multicollinearity – too many variables being too closely related in the analysis – may distort regression estimates and is a common problem in time-series analysis because of the trending of aggregate variables. Multicollinearity can leave some analyses indeterminate. (See pp. 36–7, this chapter for some possible solutions.) But given relatively uncorrelated explanatory variables in a regression model defined over a reasonable period of time, time-series analysis can be a very effective method of testing social and political theories.

TIME-SERIES DATA

Time-series data need to be collected consistently over a number of years (quarters, months, etc.). In the comparative political economy of the welfare state, Peter Flora (1986 and 1987) has published a large inventory of time-series data for 11–12 nations over 30 years. The OECD, UN, ILO, and other supragovernmental organizations collect data, but it is most often for economic purposes. Individual nations are now publishing large amounts of data going back to the turn of the century. However, as yet an institution equivalent to the Inter-University Consortium for Political and Social Research (ICPSR) has not been established for comparative welfare state research.[3] Unfortunately, most analysts must collect and code their own data, and that is a complicated, labor-intensive, and time-consuming task.

THE BASICS OF TIME-SERIES REGRESSION METHODOLOGY

The inherent chronological ordering of variable observations is the major strength of time series because certain features of time and temporality in social process can be explicitly modeled, yielding a much stronger case for causal inference than in a cross-sectional research design. Time ordering of observations in time-series regression analysis is the source of certain strengths as well as the source of some of the more thorny technical problems. Autocorrelation, lag structures, causal order, and multicollinearity are among the more commonly encountered difficulties. We give a brief review of each.

Autocorrelation

Because time-series data for any one year are often closely related to the previous year's values, ordinary least squares (OLS) regression procedures need to be modified in certain ways. The relationship between last year's value and the present year's figure is called autocorrelation, and it violates the OLS regression assumption of the independence of cases (i.e., years). Error terms are correlated and may not be normally distributed with a mean of zero, nor have constant variance. The existence of autocorrelated error causes the coefficients to be inefficient, estimated standard errors to contract, and significance levels to inflate. Consequently, the results of an insignificant equation may appear to be significant. There are three standard ways of dealing with this problem: (1) ordinary least squares regression with a lagged endogenous variable, (2) differencing variables in the equation, and (3) using a generalized least squares (GLS) procedure (e.g., the Cochrane-Orcutt method generalized into a two-step full-transform method).[4]

When a lagged dependent variable appears on the right-hand side of the equation (i.e., as an independent variable) and errors are serially correlated, OLS estimates of regression coefficients will be less biased and inconsistent. Moreover, the conventional Durbin-Watson "*d*-test" that is often used to diagnose autocorrelation is biased in such situations, and the bias is typically toward the null hypothesis. Therefore, it is customary to rely on Durbin's "*h*-test" when estimating such models 1970).[5] However, if autocorrelation is still present, the researcher might entertain moving to OLS or differencing procedures. Differencing as a solution to autocorrelated error can also be quite effective. One may look at rates or first differences such as $X_t - X_{t-1}$ (e.g., one value might be $X_{1970} - X_{1969}$), which intrinsically are less dependent on earlier years. The researcher, however, often creates a new variable with differences and must be prepared to alter his or her theory to match the new meaning. If the theory is already expressed in rates or differences, there is no theoretical problem.[6]

Although Cook and Campbell (1979) and others recommend that time-series data always be detrended (i.e., made into rates of change) before analyzing data, there are a number of reasons for not differencing variables. First, using rates of change may be appropriate when analyzing "quasi-experimental research based on stimulus–response models," but most work in the political economy of the welfare state is more complex and hardly as responsive as "stimulus–response" relationships (Jennings 1983, p. 1232). Jennings even states that differencing "could undermine any attempt to detect relationships between levels of system components (p. 1232). He also points out that this simple differencing correction for autocorrelation can consume variance in the dependent variable that other independent variables would have explained. Whether level variables or change variables are employed must ultimately depend on the theoretical purposes of the analysis.[7]

Using GLS procedures to correct for autocorrelation may help avoid this disqualification of variables. In this procedure, OLS are used to implement a regression model. The residuals from the OLS equation are used to estimate serial correlation (autocorrelation). The estimated simple forms of serial correlation are then used in a generalized differencing transformation that purges regressand and regressors of serial linear dependence. An estimation equation then yields revised parameter estimates for the original OLS equation. The new regression residuals are then used to reestimate serial correlation, and generalized differencing may continue iteratively until the researcher is satisfied that new estimates of serial correlation no longer differ from the previous estimates (and are as good as this procedure allows). Final estimates are then used to correct inflated significance statistics.[8]

Thus, there are at least three solutions to autocorrelation. However, it is important for the analyst to remember that each approach alters the model's structure in certain ways.

Lag Structure

Lag structures, which allow for the delayed effects of economic and social processes, often receive little attention in political science and sociology. Lags are most often short – one to two years – probably because (1) they reduce the time-series length and most social policy data sets are rather short to begin with, and (2) economics, where time-series analysis has been most popular, assumes stimulus–response reactions between money-based variables with relatively short lags.

However, political-economic variables may not respond so fast or in a discrete one-to-one fashion, and lags that are distributed over a number of years might be a more accurate portrayal. For example, the political process acts as a filter through which state expenditures and program participation must pass, thus lengthening and diversifying time lags in four ways: (1) *budgetary lags* – the preliminary budget is made and approved about a year in advance of actual presentation of a budget to the legislature; (2) *legislative lags* – new legislation may take one to three additional years depending on support or opposition; (3) *regime change lags* – it may take up to four years to replace a president or even longer to replace a chancellor; and (4) *implementation lags* – the bureaucracy needs time to spend money and, more generally, to put plans and people into action. It may not be uncommon for political lags to run from a minimum of one year to as much as five years. For instance, one could compute a four-year lag based on the U.S. recession in 1958 causing the passage of the Manpower Development and Training Act in 1962. An arbitrary lag of one year, then, might not be appropriate.

A variable with a distributed lag influences expenditures in a number of subsequent years – a sort of ripple effect – rather than only in one year. The weighting of distributed lags specifies the years that should have the greatest impact (see in Johnston 1984, chap. 9, for Almon and Koyck lags). For example, the following lag goes back one and two years, and the weights (W_1, W_2) might be equally divided (e.g., would equal .50):

$$X_{\mathrm{DL1-2}} = W_1(X_{t-1}) + W_2(X_{t-2}).$$

Some political variables may have a distributed lag of four years with the weights creating an inverted U-curve. The theory behind such a lag configuration is that political effects build up and then decline, with their peak influence coming in the second and third years. Although such lags can be formally tested (e.g., Almon lags), a researcher could construct such a lag for an independent variable as follows:

$$X_{\mathrm{DL1-4}} = W_1(X_{t-1}) + W_2(X_{t-2}) + W_3(X_{t-3}) + W_4(X_{t-4}).$$

Here the inverted U-pattern weights might be as follows: $W_1 = .10$, $W_2 = .40$, $W_3 = .30$, and $W_4 = .10$. Demographic variables may follow a similar pattern but peak a year later. Economic variables often have peak influence in the first year and then decline, for example, geometrically, because economic information is quickly disseminated throughout society. This geometric decay of weights in the Koyck distributed lag model might have the following weights: $W_1 = .70$, $W_2 = .50$, and $W_2 = .20$.

$$X_{DL1-3} = W_1(X_{t-1}) + W_2(X_{t-2}) + W_3(X_{t-3}).$$

Despite highly multicollinear Xs, formal polynomial or Almon lags can be constructed for the inverted U-curve and tested for significance; a geometrically declining pattern of lags can be estimated via the Koyck procedure (Johnston 1984, chap. 9). In any event, the time-series analyst should provide a theoretical or substantive rationale for such lags, since they form an important portion of model specification.

Causal order and Granger causality tests are topics related to the issue of lags structures. For instance, in testing the causal order between the size of the bureaucracy (X) and social policy expenditures (Y), one might regress the lagged bureaucracy variable on unlagged social policy expenditures and then regress the lagged social policy expenditures on the unlagged size of the bureaucracy. That is, we may stipulate that

$$Y_t = f(X_{t-1}), \text{ and}$$
$$X_t = f(Y_{t-1}).$$

If the lagged bureaucracy variable explains variance that the lagged social policy variable does not, we can say that this is evidence that causality moves from the size of the bureaucracy to social policy spending (Granger 1969; Freeman 1983). But again, reciprocal causation is possible, and this technique is no substitute for causal theory.[9]

Multicollinearity

It is not uncommon for aggregate variables gauging the level of economic, social, or political activity of a nation to display substantial time trend.[10] When several trending variables are placed in a multivariate regression model, it is not unusual to find nontrivial levels of multicollinearity. Serious multicollinearity in an equation can be identified by a number of diagnostics: β's have large changes when a variable is added or deleted, when important variables appear in certain equations to have no effect, when the signs of β's change in ways contrary to theoretical expectations and prior equations, and when confidence intervals are extremely wide (Neter, Wasserman, and Kutner 1985,

p. 390). Regression coefficient instability in a number of equations can be detected by sign reversals, large significance-level fluctuations, and drastic changes in the values of the α's. If the parameter estimates exhibit stability, then they can be more readily accepted – "no harm, no foul" (Wonnacott and Wonnacott 1979; Achen 1982; and Pindyck and Rubinfeld 1990).

Without choosing to change the basic variables through differencing, more formal methods are available for dealing with multicollinearity. Variance inflation factors (VIF) measure the degree to which "the variances of the estimated regression coefficients are inflated as compared to when the independent variables are not linearly related," and ridge regression modifies the method of least squares to "allow biased estimators of the regression coefficients" (Neter et al. 1985, pp. 391–400). However, VIFs elaborate the problem without providing an easy way out, while ridge regression trades off instability in a sometimes questionable exchange for bias (Belsey et al. 1980; Smith and Campbell 1980; Neter et al. 1985, pp. 394–400; and SAS 1986, 1992).[11] Perhaps the easiest solutions to multicollinearity problems occur when we feel substantively warranted to index collinear variables into simple measures or to allow one of a set of collinear variables to explicitly stand in for the rest.

Results and Comparisons

The results of time-series regression analyses are equations of the form

$$Y = \alpha + \beta_1 X_1 + \beta_2 X_2 + \ldots + \beta_n X_n + e.$$

The equation results come with a regression coefficient (R^2) and standard errors for the estimates. The researcher's object often is simply to obtain significant coefficients (significance levels and standard errors of α's and β's) showing that regressors are significantly related to regressands and that R^2 values are high, "explaining" a large percentage of the variance in dependent variables.[12] The researcher often has to decide which equations perform best in relation to his or her theory. In comparing countries, choosing the best equations can be a problem because what works in one country may not work in another. One's capacity for generalized theorizing and historical insight may present challenging trade-offs; indeed, the general and specific may seem pitted against each other.

Although there are tests in regression analysis for the significance of individual β's and R^2 values, these tests are inherently involved with internal rather than external analysis (see the distinction made in Chapter 2, this volume). Comparisons between equations from different nations are somewhat difficult. However, once reasonable equations have been estimated for both countries, the most important test is the *F*-test to assess the approximate equivalence of equations for two or more countries. This test, which is analogous to the Chow test for structural equivalence across time, is not typically generated by computer programs and must be done by obtaining the error sum of squares for two different equations from two different time-series data sets. This *F*-test compares the error sum of squares for "two country specific models" with the error sum of squares for both countries (pooled) (Cohen 1983, p. 90; Pindyck and Rubinfeld 1990, pp. 115–116).[13]

$$F_{k,\,N+M-2k} = \frac{[ESS_{\text{pooled}} - (ESS_{\text{country A}} + ESS_{\text{country B}})]/k}{(ESS_{\text{country A}} + ESS_{\text{country B}})/(N + M - 2k)}.$$

Or, for ease of computation the following equation can be used:

$$F_{k,\,N+M-2k} = \frac{N+M+2k}{k} \cdot \frac{ESS_{\text{pooled}} - (ESS_{\text{country A}} + ESS_{\text{country B}})}{(ESS_{\text{country A}} + ESS_{\text{country B}})}.$$

In each equation, *k* stands for the degrees of freedom (number of parameters estimated including both α's and β's), *N* is the sample size of the first country data set, *M* is the sample size of the second country data set. ESS_{country} is the error sum of squares for one (or the other) country, and ESS_{pooled} is the error sum of squares for both countries combined into one data set. The computed *F*-results are then compared to the *F*-statistics reported at various levels of significance. If the computed *F*-value is higher than the table value, one can reject the null hypothesis that the two equations are equivalent. Thus, a computed *F*-value greater than the table means that the equations for countries *A* and *B* are significantly different, while a computed *F*-value less than the critical value means that the equations for the two countries are quite similar. However, if the variables in each country's equation are different, the comparison becomes intrinsically qualitative, although R^2 values can still be roughly compared for overall explanations of variance within each country (Chow 1960; Cohen 1983; Neter et al. 1985, pp. 343–51; and Conerly and Mansfield 1989).

NEW APPROACHES

Two papers in this volume demonstrate sophisticated "twists" to time-series analysis. First, Larry Isaac and coauthors demonstrate the *time-varying parameter models*, or TVP approach to time series, which is designed to be more sensitive to *historical* process. In contrast to conventional time-series regression with temporally fixed coefficients, TVP models are designed to allow parameters (or covariance structures) linking independent to dependent variables to change through time.[14] While the emphasis in this literature is on the time-varying "parameter (coefficient) structure" of the model, certain types of TVP models can be manipulated to allow "process structure" to change through time as well.[15] Based on this logic, the more inclusive terminology might be "time-varying parameter/process" (TVP/P) models.

There are two basic motives to apply TVP models. One reason is that such approaches can be used to check the stability of a more general model. In this approach, the stability of a fixed-coefficient time-series regression model is questioned. As represented by Newbold and Bos (1985, pp. 11–12):

> The multiple linear regression model with fixed coefficients . . . is frequently fitted to data by social scientists. As we have just suggested, one should be skeptical about the assumption, implicit in such analyses, about the constancy through time of model parameters.

The point is that the stability of coefficients should be checked just as autocorrelation or heteroscedasticity is questioned. If it cannot be verified as a whole, one avenue that might be open to the researcher is to break the regression model into a number of different time periods (Quandt 1958; McGee and Carlton 1970).

The other reason to use TVP models is that temporal invariance is expected in a parameter or suspicion of a sociohistorical process that changes the relations between variables (e.g., policy shift, legislative change, revolutionary event). This involves searching for an interrupted time-series process without assuming when the interruption actually occurs. The basic idea is to take the empirically generated results of the TVP estimation as "new data" about some sociohistorical process.[16] The permitted heterogeneity in parameter and/or process structure allows for a deeper historical narrativity than previously imagined. Consequently, TVP models can play an important role in comparative/historical research in synthesizing the strengths of social science causality and historical contingency (Isaac and Leicht 1992).

Estimation strategies for TVP regression models fall into two types: (1) "moving" or "recursive" regressions, and (2) Kalman filtering estimators.[17] The first approach using moving regressions is more straightforward. It estimates the time-series model for a time-specific subsegment of the entire series ($t_{t}, \ldots, t_T$); estimation continues in an iterative manner as the time-specific subsegment is "moved" along the overall series, so that the next regression differs from the previous by only one year.[18] Within the class of "moving regression" (or covariance) models, there are three strategies. (1) In *forward movement*, all estimations are anchored on the first year in the series; an initial subperiod is estimated and then estimation continues moving forward by adding another year to the period on which the estimation is done; this continues seriatim until the entire series is exhausted. (2) *Backward movement* follows the same principle as "1" but reverses the chronological movement by anchoring all estimations on the last year in the series and moving incrementally one year at a time in a backward manner until the entire series is exhausted. (3) In *diagonal movement*, the subperiod segment length is defined (e.g., 15 years) and is then "moved" through the entire series by changing the beginning and ending anchors on each estimation. For the first two strategies, the "window" of estimation actually expands in size, either forward or backward in time; for the diagonal strategy the window of estimation remains fixed in length but moves through the series.[19]

The other approach to estimation – Kalman filtering – is computationally more complex,[20] and a detailed presentation is beyond the scope of this introduction. In brief, the Kalman filter approaches to stochastic parameter regressions rely on maximum likelihood estimators employing all available information from the time series to derive (under specified assumptions) coefficients (β_t/T) for each year (t) of the entire series (T). The vector of time-varying coefficients is then tested against the assumption of fixed or temporally constant coefficient models.[21]

TVP models allow for consideration of sites of possible change (Hernes 1976) within time-series models that may be linked to important temporal concepts (Aminzade 1992). Table 2.1 presents a cross-classification with descriptions in each cell. For instance, we often think in terms of temporality and change in terms of single time-series variables. This can be seen in the first column – "output structure." Notions of trend (trajectory), fluctuation, and cycles are familiar descriptions, but "turning points" are also used to describe peaks and troughs in a series (e.g., Kendall 1973 and Chatfield 1989). Typically applied to time series prior to being modeled, such temporal richness becomes relatively worthless because the conventional time-series modeling process tends to lose or repress these temporal contours by rendering parameter or process structures fixed or time-invariant.

Unlike conventional time-series analysis, TVP models seek to preserve temporal nuance. The use of TVP models generates the possibility of exploring and theorizing potentially rich sources of temporality in parameter and process structure (see the second and third columns in Table 2.1). In the case of parameter structure, TVP models generate a vector of historically contingent coefficients rather than the single-parameter estimate in conventional time-series models. Such coefficients

Table 2.1. *Types of temporal concepts and locations of possible change in time-series models of historical process*

	Locus of possible change in time-series models		
Temporal concept	Output structure	Parameter structure	Process structure
Trend (trajectory)	Trend in actual series (e.g., trend in inflation)	Trend in parameter structure (e.g., temporal drift in relation between unemployment and inflation)	—[a]
Fluctuation	Short-term fluctuation in series (e.g., fluctuation in unemployment)	Short-term changes in parameter structure (e.g., temporal fluctuation in relation between unemployment and wages)	—[a]
Cycle	Regular periodic swing in a series (e.g., business cycle movement in unemployment)	Regular periodic swing in the parameter structure (e.g., business cycle movement in Phillips curve)	—[a]
Turning point	Inflection point, peak, or trough in series (e.g., trough in unemployment during a recession)	Inflection point in parameter structure or abrupt parameter "shift" (e.g., an abrupt shift in the Phillips curve)	Inflection point at which the model's functional form shifts (e.g., from linear to nonlinear)

[a] In most time-series model applications, the temporal concepts of trend, fluctuation, and cycle in characteristics of the model's process structure would be extremely difficult to monitor because it would call for continuous examination of multiple characteristics that are usually considered fixed (or constant) in time.

could display (1) relative homogeneity or time invariance, (2) incremental or decremental change in coefficients ("parameter drift" in Beck 1983), (3) short-run fluctuations in coefficients, (4) cyclical behavior in coefficients showing a regular periodic swing, perhaps in conjunction with economic or electoral cycles or long waves, and (5) rapid or abrupt coefficient "shift" or change indicating major turning points.

Although much less common and likely more challenging, one may examine historically contingent temporality and change in a time-series process structure. For example, the changing institutional, legal, or political conditions in the post–World War II decades may have altered the lag lengths governing the relationship between strikes and wage changes. Or a model may shift from a linear to a nonlinear form. Further, shifts in the error structure of time-series models may indicate that the omission of a variable is a problem in one historical period but not another. Analyzing the temporal variability in parameter and process structures is likely to lead to richer and more historically grounded models. An additional benefit results from taking seriously the rich and diverse forms of that much maligned "mundane variable" – time (e.g., Stock and Watson 1987, 1988; Isaac and Griffin 1989; and Griffin and Isaac 1992).

Second, John Freeman and James Alt use *vector autoregression* (VAR) analysis as an alternative to more familiar structural equation approaches to theory testing. VAR modeling focuses on a reduced form of a political economic system in which each variable is regressed on its own past history and on the past histories of the other variables in the system. It thus seeks to reveal the major contours and basic causal character and dynamics of what is essentially an unknown underlying structural equation model and, by implication, what theories are and are not supported by the data (Sims 1980a). As a reduced form, the VAR model subsumes multiple theoretical perspectives in that intervening mechanisms are not explicitly represented. This analysis allows the researcher to narrow the class of competing structural equation models – and hence competing theories – to a subset that is consistent with the data.[22]

Three complementary types of tests are performed by VAR analysts. First, they determine whether the coefficients in an estimated VAR model have the properties associated with the causal claims associated with competing theories. An *F*-test is often used for the joint statistical significance of sets of coefficients, as in standard regression practice (Freeman 1983). The validity of hypotheses is also assessed through innovation accounting, essentially a simulation exercise that gives insight into the magnitude and direction of effects that one variable has on others. The coefficients of a recursive moving-average representation of the model are calculated from the estimated coefficients of the autoregressive model.[23] This recursive moving-average representation of the system is then used to study how the system responds to (1) the shock in each individual variable alone, which yields insights into the *qualitative* effect of specific kinds of political and economic innovations or "surprises," and (2) a set of shocks in all the variables in the system, which reveals the *relative* impact that these same shocks have on the forecast error variance for each of the variables.

Innovations or shocks in the variables are defined as follows. Suppose that $\hat{y}_t$ is the best linear forecast of y_t based on y_s where $s < t$. Then the *innovation* in y_t is $y_t - \hat{y}_t$ (Sims 1981, p. 284). For example, say part of the policy-making process is based on planning and that this part gives rise to a best linear forecast of the policy variable. Then the forecast error in the policy variable represents the "policy innovation," or the new policy choice that results from some previously unanticipated event or consideration.

The innovation accounting is "historically grounded" in the sense that (1) the hypothetical shocks are set equal to the observed standard deviation of the residuals obtained from estimating the model for a particular time period, and (2) the recursive moving-average representation of the model is composed of parameters derived from the estimated parameters of the VAR model for the same period.

A recursive form of the moving-average representation is used because the residuals from different equations in the estimated, nonrecursive VAR model are serially uncorrelated but probably contemporaneously cross-correlated. Hence, it usually is difficult to discern the effect that a shock or set of shocks in a variable(s) has on the other variables in the model. This problem is circumvented if a recursive form of the moving-average representation – obtained by orthogonalizing the error vector for the model – is used. Orthogonalization preserves the connection between the disturbances in the respective variables in the model in the sense that each (transformed) error is the normalized error in forecasting the respective variable from past values of all the other variables and current values of certain other variables in the model. The deeper presumption for orthogonalization is that behaviorally distinct sources of stochastic variation in social systems should be independent of one another (Sims 1986).

Orthogonalization assumes a specific causal chain of contemporaneous effects. For instance, if the variables in the model are X, Y, and Z (in that order), then shocks in X are assumed to have immediate effects on X, Y, and Z; shocks in Y have immediate effects only on Y and Z; and shocks in Z have immediate effects only on Z. This triangulation of contemporaneous effects makes possible an assessment of the moving-average response to a shock in an individual variable and to shocks in all the variables in the system.

Innovation accounting yields important information about the character of political-economic systems. For example, when the recursive moving-average representation of a system is subjected to an orthogonalized set of shocks in the variables, a large part of the forecast error variance in a variable, say *Y*, is attributable to the shock in another variable, say *X*. This is evidence that *X* is causally prior to *Y*. On the other hand, there is good reason to believe that *Y* may be econometrically exogenous in the system if shocks in *X* account for little of the forecast error variance in *Y*; instead, the forecasted error variance in *Y* is attributed mostly to shocks in that same variable.[24]

The VAR method has been and can be used in a number of settings. Hansen and Sargent (1980) use a VAR model for the decisions of a single firm choosing wage and capital rental rates in a competitive market, which follows the theoretical underpinnings of microeconomic theory. Sargent conceives of VAR models as the realization of a dynamic game between economic agents and the government where the actors use rational expectations (aggregate effects of rationality being represented in the reduced-form equations), while unanticipated changes in model variables are also taken into account (represented in the error terms). Political scientists have recently begun to evaluate and employ VAR (Freeman, Williams, and Lin 1989), and Williams (1990) uses shocks in vote intention as measures of electoral uncertainty in determining monetary policy.[25]

THE PROMISE OF TIME SERIES

Time-series analysis is the form of quantitative analysis most complementary to historical narrative. Not only can it test the relationship between two variables, but it can do so utilizing real historical covariations between temporally lagged "causes" and subsequent effects on controlling for the effects of other variables. Narrative history can be usefully brought into time-series analysis by employing dummy variables for events and eras (e.g., wartime), using time-varying parameter/process models, and using VAR models in combination with detailed historical narrative on social, political, and economic processes. For instance, the relatively intractable state-centric hypotheses can be tested with time-series data on the organizational structure and resources of bureaucracies from 1850 to the present. In this way, a constant in the short term (e.g., bureaucratic structure) is made into a variable in the long term. The promise of time series is in sophisticated statistical analysis that is coupled with ever more relevant social and political data. The real challenge in many ways lies in theoretically conceptualizing and then collecting this extremely difficult to obtain data.[26] With new data and increasing sensitivity of structural changes, time series will bring increased methodological rigor and theoretical insight to comparative political economy.

ANNOTATED BIBLIOGRAPHY

In this final section, we discuss entrée articles that give a good feel for time-series analysis, methodological texts going into detail on more technical issues, and the most prevalent computer packages in use. The more accessible materials are generally listed before the more complex treatments.

Entrée point books and articles

Ostrom, Charles. 1990. *Time Series Analysis: Regression Techniques. 2d ed.* Newbury Park, Calif.: Sage.
This work provides a short introduction to time-series analysis.

Hibbs, Douglas A. 1974. "Problems of Statistical Estimation and Causal Inference in Time-Series Regression Models." In Herbert L. Costner (ed.), *Sociological Methodology 1973–74*, pp. 252–308. San Francisco: Jossey-Bass.
Good basic treatment of some major technical issues with empirical examples.

Isaac, Larry, and William Kelly. 1981. "Racial Insurgency, the State and Welfare Expansion." *American Journal of Sociology* 86:1348–96.
The Isaac and Kelly article provides a contextualized approach to time-series analysis of the riot–relief relation, making its use clear to the reader.

Mintz, Alex, and Alexander Hicks. 1984. "Military Expenditures in the U.S., 1949 to 1976: Disaggregating Military Expenditures and Their Determination." *American Journal of Sociology* 90:411–7.
Mintz and Hicks provide a concise example of the time-series regression models of Department of Defense military spending divided into function-specific areas.

Methodology and statistical texts

Most materials on time series come from econometric applications. Few have been directly written for political science and sociology. The references are listed from most to least accessible.

Pindick, Robert, and Daniel Rubinfeld. 1990. *Econometric Models and Economic Forecasts*. New York: McGraw-Hill.

This is one of the more accessible texts. See chap. 6 for autocorrelation and chap. 9 for distributed lags. Pt. 3 is devoted to time-series models, but most of the discussion involves ARIMA and forecasting, which is not that useful in political science and sociological work.

Belsey, D. A., E. Kuh, and R. E. Welsch. 1980. *Regression Diagnostics*. New York: Wiley.

This is an excellent source for regression diagnostics to help in the practical analysis of regression problems.

Neter, John, William Wasserman, and Michael Kutner. 1985. *Applied Linear Statistical Models*. Homewood, Ill.: Irwin.

This is a comprehensive textbook on statistical modeling. Chap. 13 contains an excellent discussion of autocorrelation in time series, and chap. 11 handles multicollinearity.

Johnston, J. 1984. *Econometric Methods*. New York: Wiley.

Chap. 8 discusses GLS with applications to autocorrelation. The approach is generally accessible with matrix notation, but some partial differentiation is involved. Chap. 9 contains an excellent discussion of lagged variables with details on Koyck or geometric and Almon or polynomial distributed lags.

Judge, G. G., W. E. Griffith, R. C. Hill, and T. C. Lee. 1985. *The Theory and Practice of Econometrics*. New York: Wiley.

This text covers the most complete range of issues – autocorrelation, multicollinearity, lagged variables, and more. However, the presentation is more difficult than some of the other texts listed here.

Other useful texts are listed in the references: Chatfield (1989), Dhrymes (1974), Granger (1989), Gujarati (1978), Intriligator (1978), Harvey (1981a, b), Kendall (1973), Kmenta (1971), Maddala (1976), Theil (1971), and Wonnacott and Wonnacott (1979). For ARIMA methods, see McCleary and Hay (1980) and SAS (1986).[27]

Computer programs

The SAS ETS (Econometrics and Time-Series Analysis), SHAZAM, and SPSS Trends packages provide programs for dealing with autocorrelation, lags, and ARIMA programs. Each program package provides a short introduction to the statistical procedures. Many other time-series programs also exist (TSP, LIMDEP, RATS, and PC-GIVE), but the three already mentioned represent of the most frequently used packages.[28]

SAS. 1986. *SAS System for Forecasting Time Series.* Cary, N.C.: SAS Institute.
This SAS manual focuses heavily on ARIMA, but chap. 1 provides a good overview of time series and chap. 2 has a good discussion of autoregression.

1988. *SAS/ETS User's Guide, Version 6*: 1st ed. Cary, N.C.: SAS Institute.
Although the examples are overwhelmingly for economics and business (e.g., Grunfield's investment model has been used in the last four manuals), the introductions provide useful summary descriptions of most procedures. See the AUTOREG program for the generalized Cochrane-Orcutt procedure.

1991. *SAS/ETS Software: Applications Guide 1: Time Series Modeling and Forecasting, Financial Reporting, and Loan Analysis.* Version 6, 1st ed. Cary, N. C.: SAS Institute.
Although oriented toward business applications, this SAS applications manual may also be useful.

Shazam. 1988. *Shazam Econometrics Computer Program: User's Reference Manual, Version 6.1.* New York: McGraw-Hill.
This stand-alone program provides excellent time-series regression programs.

SPSS. 1988. *SPSS-X Trends.* Chicago: SPSS Inc.
This is a complete time-series package with autoregression models including the Cochrane-Orcutt, Prais-Winsten, and exact maximum likelihood procedures.

1990. *SPSS Reference Guide.* Chicago: SPSS Inc.
The SPSS manual does not devote much space to time series. However, the regression program can be used with the Durbin-Watson statistic.

NOTES

1. For many purposes, however, "ringing true" with theoretical histories will require important reforms in time-series technology and interpretation.
2. Residual variance can be approached in more creative (though not necessarily more valid) ways than in the past. In the economic study of productivity in advanced industrialized nations, Dennison (1979) has used residual variance as a measure of "contributions to knowledge." Researchers in the sociological area of discrimination have decomposed residuals and attributed much to discrimination effects (Iams and Thornton 1975; Jones and Kelley 1984). In a similar way, comparative researchers would have a case to attribute residual variance to cultural (inherently national) differences. These procedures are, however, subject to extensive criticisms.
3. Peter Flora has recently started a research center at the University of Mannheim that will be directed toward data dissemination and collection.

4. AUTOREG in the SAS time-series package can be used to control for *n*th-order auto-correlation (SAS 1982; Pindyck and Rubinfeld 1990).
5. The Durbin *h*-statistic is designed to signal first-order autoregressive (AR) error processes. More general tests exist. For example, Godfrey (1978) has developed a test against *n*th-order autoregressive (AR) and moving average (MA) processes in models with lagged dependent variables.
6. ARIMA (autoregressive, integrated, MA) models also incorporate differences, but as yet their more sophisticated approaches have been used mostly with univariate models, and they make greater demands for a larger number of cases to estimate effectively most models (McCleary and Hay 1980, p. 20).
7. If major ambiguities are present, it is often prudent to analyze both level and change representations of a model.
8. This discussion closely follows the work of Pindyck and Rubinfeld, but we have left out the equations. The process is obviously more complicated than presented here. The reader can follow the statistical presentation of these statistics in Pindyck and Rubinfeld (1990, pp. 138–43), Neter et al. (1985, pp. 455–6), and Johnston (1984, pp. 321–41).
9. The Granger procedure involves fastidious consideration of autocorrelated errors (Granger 1969; Freeman 1983).
10. The issue of "trend" is one of those seemingly simple ideas that have the property of becoming more and more complex as one ponders them. What we perceive as trend is largely a consequence of a priori theoretical sensitization to expected contour in a variable (e.g., one analyst's "trend" is another analyst's "cycle") and the temporal window produced through left- and right-hand censoring of chronological time. It is also possible to think in terms of multiple and variable-shaped trends in single series (see Stock and Watson 1988).
11. With these methods there is often a trade-off between efficiency and bias. For the Haitovsky test of multicollinearity, see Rockwell (1975).
12. In time-series analysis with trending data, R^2 values tend to be higher than in cross-sectional research. For instance, a cross-sectional researcher may be satisfied with an R^2 of .40, but a time-series researcher may be unhappy with an R^2 of .80. Indeed, R^2 values .90 are fairly common with time series, especially those for "trends" as opposed to "change" data. However, because time-series data are typically aggregated and permit distributed lag structures, they tend to generate high coefficients of determination for valid as well as nonfactual reasons.
13. The *F*-tests using the OLS results may come to the same conclusion as results from autocorrelated programs; however, one should use the corrected error sum of squares (ESS) from the Cochrane–Orcutt results (Yule–Walker estimates).
14. The technical details and varieties of time-varying parameters or stochastic parameter models are laid out in Beck (1983) and Newbold and Bos (1985). A useful annotated bibliography is contained in Johnson (1977).
15. Hernes's (1976) typology of the major structural components in models of social change is useful: (1) output structure – the distribution of a given dependent variable series; (2) parameter structure – definite magnitudes governing the process of relations between variables (e.g., the coefficients, to be estimated, linking "independent" and "dependent" variables); and (3) process structure – the logical form of the variables and process posited as

generating the output structure results (e.g., functional form, lag structure, error structure).

16. See the section entitled Parameter Historicity and Explanation in Isaac et al. in this volume (Chapter 4) for further elaboration.
17. On "moving" or "recursive" regressions see Quandt (1958), Brown, Durbin, and Evans (1975), Isaac and Griffin (1989), and Griffin and Isaac (1992). For the Kalman filtering estimators, see Beck (1983), Johnson (1977), Newbold and Bos (1985), Engle and Watson (1987), and Harvey (1987).
18. For convenience, we refer to "year" as the time period used to organize the series. The unit of analysis could just as easily be quarters, months, or other regular time periods.
19. For further discussion of these moving strategies and their implications for historical analysis, see Isaac and Griffin (1989), and Griffin and Isaac (1992). For additional empirical examples, see Isaac et al., Chapter 4, this volume, and Isaac and Leicht (1992).
20. In analyzing the temporal variability of process structure, the "moving-regression" approach would have an advantage over the Kalman filter class of estimators since the latter are designed exclusively to estimate time-varying parameters.
21. For a simple model relating inflation and Treasury Bill rates for U.S. quarterly data from 1953 to 1980 under various estimation assumptions, see Newbold and Bos (1985).
22. The VAR method was developed by the Minnesota School of Economics to test the theory of rational expectations (Hansen and Sargent 1980; Sims 1980a, b; and Sargent 1984).
23. Any autoregressive process may be approximated as a moving-average process of some order. In the latter representation, the variables in the system are expressed in terms of the accumulated past error or shocks that the system has experienced.
24. In reference to structural stability, Sims (1980a, pp. 17–18) explains why conventional tests are likely to be biased when dummy variables are used to check for structural instability. He proposed a correction to the log-likelihood ratio statistic, which takes into account the number of variables in each unrestricted equation. The modified test takes into account the degrees of freedom in the asymptotic chi-square distribution for the likelihood ratio statistic, which is approximately the same magnitude as the degrees of freedom left in the data after the vector autoregressive model is estimated. The usual test statistic is $T(\log|D_R| - \log|D_U|)$, where D_R and D_U are the matrices of the cross-products of residuals for the restricted and unrestricted models, respectively. This is modified to be $(T - k)(\log|D_R| - \log|D_U|)$, where k is the total number of regression coefficients minus the number of equations in the model.
25. The VAR method is also used for policy analysis and forecasting by several Federal Reserve Banks (Litterman 1984).
26. Another challenge to sociologists and political scientists doing time series will come from the problems of co-integration and unit roots. This will become more apparent as data sets become larger with increasing years. For a review of this problem, see Fromby and Rhodes (1990).
27. For good reviews of a large number of econometrics texts and regression books, see Jain (1982) and Balach (1982).

28. For computer manuals for RATS, see Doan (1989), and for PC-Give, which has a moving-TVP regression procedure, see Hendry (1986).

REFERENCES

Achen, Christopher. 1982. *Interpreting and Using Regression.* Beverly Hills, Calif.: Sage.

Aminzade, R. 1992. "Historical Sociology and Time." *Sociological Methods and Research* 20:456–80.

Balach, George. 1982. "A Comparative Review of Econometrics Books." *Journal of Marketing Research* 19(Feb.):156–63.

Beck, Nathaniel. 1982. "Parties, Administration and American Macroeconomic Outcomes." *American Political Science Review* 76:83–93.

1983. "Time-Varying Parameter Regression Models." *American Journal of Political Science* 27(3):556–600.

Belsey, D. A., E. Kuh, and R. E. Welsch. 1980. *Regression Diagnostics.* New York: Wiley.

Brown, R., J. Durbin, and J. Evans. 1975. "Techniques for Testing the Constancy of Regression Relations over Time." *Journal of the Royal Statistical Society*, series B(37):149–92.

Chatfield, C. 1989. *The Analysis of Time Series: Theory and Practice* (4th ed.) London: Chapman Hall.

Chow, C. G. 1960. "Tests for the Equality Between Sets of Coefficients in Two Linear Regressions." *Econometrica* 28:591–605.

Cohen, Ayala. 1983. "Comparing Regression Coefficients Across Subsamples." *Sociological Methods* 12:77–94.

Conerly, Michael, and Edward Mansfield. 1989. "An Approximate Test for Comparing Independent Regression Models with Unequal Error Variances." *Journal of Econometrics* 40:235–55.

Cook, Thomas, and Donald Campbell. 1979. *Quasi-Experimentation: Design and Analysis Issues for Field Settings.* Chicago: Rand McNally.

Dennison, Edward. 1979. *Accounting for Slower Economic Growth.* Washington, D.C.: Brookings Institute.

Dhrymes, P. J. 1974. *Econometrics: Statistical Foundations and Applications.* New York: Springer.

Doan, Thomas A. 1989. *RATS: Regression Analysis of Time Series.* Evanston, Ill.: VAR Econometrics.

Durbin, J. 1970. "Testing for Serial Correlation in Least-Squares Regression When Some of the Regressors Are Lagged Dependent Variables." *Econometrica* 38:410–21.

Edwards, P. K. 1981. *Strikes in the United States, 1881–1974.* New York: St. Martins.

Engle, R. F., and M. W. Watson. 1987. "The Kalman Filter: Applications to Forecasting and Rational-Expectations Models." In Truman Brewley (ed.), *Advances in Econometrics*, pp. 245–83. Cambridge University Press.

Flora, Peter. 1986. *State, Society and Economy in Western Europe.* Vol. 1. Frankfurt: Campus.

1987. *Growth to Limits: The Western European Welfare States Since World War II, Volume 4, Appendix.* Berlin: De Gruyter.

Freeman, John. 1983. "Granger Causality and the Times Series Analysis of Political Relationships." *American Journal of Political Science* 27:327–58.

Freeman, John, J. T. Williams, and Tse-min Lin. 1989. "Vector Autoregression and the Study of Politics." *American Journal of Political Science* 33(4):842–77.

Fromby, Thomas, and George Rhodes, Jr. 1990. *Advances in Econometrics: Co-Integration, Spurious Regressions and Unit Roots.* Greenwich, Conn.: JAI.

Godfrey, L. G. 1978. "Testing Against General Autoregressive and Moving Average Error Models When the Regressors Include Lagged Dependent Variables." *Econometrica* 46:1293–1301.

Granger, C. W. 1969. "Investigating Causal Relations by Econometric Models and Cross-Spectral Methods." *Econometrica* 37:424–38.

1989. *Forecasting in Business and Economics.* 2d ed. New York: Academic Press.

Griffin, Larry, Joel Devine, and Michael Wallace. 1983. "On the Economic and Political Determinants of Welfare Spending in the Post–WWII Era." *Politics and Society* 12:331–72.

Griffin, Larry J., and Larry W. Isaac. (1992). "Recursive Regression and the Historical Use of 'Time' in Time-Series Analyses of Historical Process." *Historical Methods* Volume 25:166–79.

Gujarati, Damodar. 1978. *Basic Econometrics.* New York: McGraw-Hill.

Hage, Jerald, and Robert Hanneman. 1980. "The Growth of the Welfare State in Britain, France, Germany and Italy." *Comparative Social Research* 3:45–70.

Hage, Jerald, Robert Hanneman, and Edward Gargan. 1990. *State Responsiveness and State Activism.* London: Unwin Hyman.

Hansen, L. P., and T. Sargent. 1980. "Formulating and Estimating Dynamic Linear Rational Expectations Models." *Journal of Economic Dynamics and Control* 2:7–46.

Harvey, A. C. 1981a. *The Econometric Analysis of Time Series.* Oxford: Philip Allan.

1981b. *Time Series Models.* Oxford: Philip Allan.

1987. "Applications of the Kalman Filter in Econometrics." In Truman Brewley (ed.), *Advances in Econometrics*, pp. 285–313. Cambridge University Press.

Hendry, David. 1986. "Using PC-Give in Econometrics Teaching." *Oxford Bulletin of Econometrics and Statistics.* 48(1):87–98.

Hernes, G. 1976. "Structural Change in Social Processes." *American Journal of Sociology* 82:513–87.

Hibbs, Douglas. 1974. "Problems of Statistical Estimation and Causal Inference in Time-Series Regression Models." In Herbert L. Costner (ed.), *Sociological Methodology, 1973–74*, pp. 252–308. San Francisco: Jossey-Bass.

1977. "Political Parties and Macroeconomic Policy." *American Political Science Review.* 71:1467–87.

Hibbs, Douglas, R. Douglas Rivers, and Nicholas Vasilatos. 1982. "On the Demand for Economic Outcomes." *Journal of Politics* 44:426–62.

Hibbs, Douglas, and Nicholas Vasilatos. 1981. "Macroeconomic Performance and Mass Political Support in the United States and Great Britain." In D. Hibbs and H. Fassbender (eds.); *Contemporary Political Economy*, pp. 31–48. Amsterdam: North Holland.

Hicks, Alexander. 1984. "Elections, Keynes, Bureaucracy and Class." *American Sociological Review* 49:145–82.

Iams, Howard, and Arland Thornton. 1975. "Decomposition of Differences: A Cautionary Note." *Sociological Methods and Research* 3:341–52.

Intriligator, M. D. 1978. *Econometric Models, Techniques and Applications* Englewood Cliffs, N.J.: Prentice-Hall.

Isaac, Larry W., and Larry J. Griffin. 1989. "Ahistoricism in Time-Series Analyses of Historical Process: Critique, Redirection, and Illustrations from U.S. Labor History." *American Sociological Review* 54:873–90.

Isaac, Larry W., and William Kelly. 1981. "Racial Insurgency, the State and Welfare Expansion." *American Journal of Sociology* 86:1348–96.

Isaac, Larry W., and Kevin Leicht. 1992. "Regimes of Power and the Power of Analytic Regimes: Historical Contingency and Continuity in Policy Regimes of the U.S. 'Welfare-Warfare State.'" Paper presented at the American Sociological Association Convention, Pittsburgh.

Jain, Arun. 1982. "Recent Books on Regression Analysis: A Comparative Review." *Journal of Marketing Research* 19(Aug.):392–401.

Jennings, Edward. 1983. "Racial Insurgency, the State and Welfare Expansion." *American Journal of Sociology* 88:1220–36.

Johnston, J. 1984. *Econometric Methods.* New York: Wiley.

Johnson, L. W. 1977. "Stochastic Parameter Regression: An Annotated Bibliography." *International Statistical Review* 45:257–72.

Jones, F. L., and Jonathan Kelley. 1984. "Decomposing Differences Between Groups: A Cautionary Note on Measuring Discrimination." *Sociological Methods and Research* 12:323–43.

Judge, G. G., W. E. Griffiths, R. C. Hill, and T. C. Lee. 1985. *The Theory and Practice of Econometrics.* New York: Wiley.

Kendall, M. G. 1973. *Time Series.* New York: Macmillan.

Korpi, Walter. 1989. "Power, Politics, and State Autonomy in the Development of Social Citizenship." *American Sociological Review* 54(3):309–28.

Kmenta, J. 1971. *Econometrics.* New York: McGraw-Hill.

Litterman, R. B. 1984. "Forecasting and Policy Analysis with Bayesian Vector Autoregressive Models." *Federal Reserve Bank of Minneapolis Quarterly Review* 8:30–41.

Madalla, G. S. 1976. *Econometrics.* New York: McGraw-Hill.

McCleary, Richard and Richard Hay. 1980. *Applied Time-Series Analysis for the Social Sciences.* Newbury Park, Calif.: Sage.

McGee, V., and W. Carleton. 1970. "Piecewise Regression." *Journal of the American Statistical Association* 63(331):1109–24.

Mintz, Alex, and Alexander Hicks. 1984. "Military Expenditures in the U.S., 1949 to 1976." *American Journal of Sociology* 90:411–7.

Monroe, Kirsten. 1979. "Economic Analysis of Electoral Behavior." *Political Behavior* 1:137–73.

1984. *Presidential Popularity and the Economy.* New York: Praeger.

Neter, John, William Wasserman, and Michael Kutner. 1985. *Applied Linear Statistical Models.* Homewood, Ill: Irwin.

Newbold, P., and T. Bos. 1985. *Stochastic Parameter Regression Models.* Newbury Park, Calif.: Sage.

Ostrom, Charles. 1990. *Time Series Analysis.* Newbury Park, Calif.: Sage.

Pindyck, Robert, and Daniel Rubinfeld. 1990. *Econometric Models and Economic Forecasts.* 3d ed. New York: McGraw-Hill.

Quandt, R. 1958. "The Estimation of the Parameters of a Linear Regression System Obeying Two Separate Regimes." *Journal of the American Statistical Association* 53:873–80.

Rockwell, R. L. 1975. "Assessment of Multicollinearity: The Haitovsky Test of the Determinant." *Sociological Methods and Research* 3(Feb.):308–20.

Sargent, T. 1984. "Autoregressions, Expectations, and Advice." *American Economic Review* 74:408–15.

SAS. 1986a. *SAS System for Forecasting Time Series.* Cary, N.C.: SAS Institute.

1986b. *SUGI Supplemental Library User's Guide. Version 5.* Cary, N.C.: SAS Institute.

1988. *SAS/ETS Users Guide. Version 6, 1st ed.* Cary, N.C.: SAS Institute.

1991. *SAS/ETS Software: Applications Guide 1. Version 6, 1st ed.* Cary, N.C.: SAS Institute.

1992. *SAS Technical Report P-229: SAS/STAT Software: Changes and Enhancements*, Cary, N.C.: SAS Institute.

Shorter, Edward, and Charles Tilly. 1974. *Strikes in France, 1830–1968.* Cambridge University Press.

Sims, C. 1980a. "Macroeconomics and Reality." *Econometrica* 48(1):1–48.

1980b. "Comparison of Interwar and Postwar Business Cycles: Monetarism Reconsidered." *American Economic Review* 70(2):250–7.

1981. "An Autoregressive Index Model for the U.S., 1948–1975." In J. Kmenta and J. B. Ramsey (eds.), *Large Scale Macroeconomic Models: Theory and Practice*, pp. 283–329. New York: North-Holland.

1986. "Are Forecasting Models Usable for Policy Analysis?" *Federal Reserve Bank of Minneapolis Quarterly Review* 10(1):2–16.

Smith, Gary, and Frank Campbell. 1980. "A Critique of Some Ridge Regression Methods." *Journal of the American Statistical Association* 75(369):74–81.

Snyder, David. 1975. "Institutional Setting and Industrial Conflict: A Comparative Analysis of France, Italy, and the United States." *American Sociological Review* 40:259–78.

SPSS. 1988. *SPSS-X Trends.* Chicago: SPSS.

1990. *SPSS Reference Guide.* Chicago: SPSS.

Stock, James, and Mark W. Watson. 1987. "Measuring Business Cycle Time." *Journal of Political Economy* 95:1240–61.

1988. "Variable Trends in Economic Time Series." *Journal of Economic Perspectives* 2:147–74.

Theil, H. 1971. *Principles of Econometrics.* New York: Wiley.

Tufte, Edward. 1978. *The Political Control of the Economy.* Princeton, N.J.: Princeton University Press.

Williams, J. 1990. "The Political Manipulation of Macroeconomic Policy." *American Politial Science Review* 84(3):767–96.

Wonnacott, R. J., and T. H. Wonnacott. 1979. *Econometrics.* 2d ed. New York: Wiley.

3

Direct state intervention in the labor market: the explanation of active labor market policy from 1950 to 1988 in social democratic, conservative, and liberal regimes

THOMAS JANOSKI

Prior studies of the political economy of the welfare state have focused on programs that automatically respond to demographic or economic pressures: students cause educational expenditures, unemployment causes unemployment compensation, poverty causes public assistance, and persons over 65 cause old-age pensions.[1] At the very least, such demographic pressures largely determine short-run fluctuations in such spending. However, active labor market policy (ALMP) – direct government intervention into labor markets to decrease unemployment through job-placement, job-training, and job-creation programs – is preponderantly discretionary and not dominated by demographic fluctuations. Thus, ALMP can be either a major recipient of fiscal resources – Sweden spent 2.10 percent of GNP in 1984 – or relatively ignored by politicians and budget makers – the United States spent only 0.17 percent of GNP in the same year (see Table 3.1 for additional years and countries). As testimony to the discretionary character of ALMP, countries as similar as West Germany and Austria have ALMP/GNP figures that differ by factors of 4 to 10.

Sweden, West Germany, and the United States effectively represent

I wish to thank Harold L. Wilensky and Alexander Hicks for detailed comments on this paper. Critical assistance was provided by Dr. Günther Schmid of the Wissenschaftszentrum, Berlin, Jürgen Kühl of IAB in the Bundesanstalt für Arbeit, and Jan Johannsesson of EFA in the Swedish Ministry of Labor. Thanks also go to Betty Lou Bradshaw, Basil Browne, Steven Gold, Charles Ragin, Kenneth Spenner, Davida Weinberg, and Robert Yamashita. Support on Swedish policies was provided by the Swedish Information Service through their Bicentennial Swedish–American Exchange Fund.

Table 3.1. ***Government expenditures on active labor market policy divided by GNP (countries ranked according to 1987 figures)***

Country	1960	1970	1975	1980	1984	1987
Sweden	0.80%	1.10%	1.16%	2.06%	2.10%	1.83%
Ireland	—	—	—	0.17	—	1.88
Belgium	—	—	0.70	—	—	1.31
Netherlands	—	—	0.22	0.42	—	1.24
Denmark	—	—	0.20	1.51	—	1.19
Finland	—	1.36	0.56	0.71	—	1.01
United Kingdom	—	—	0.43	0.72	—	1.01
West Germany	0.26	0.30	0.54	0.58	0.62	0.95
France	—	—	0.17	0.28	—	0.85
Italy	—	—	—	—	—	0.83
Spain	—	—	—	—	—	0.82
Norway	—	—	0.90	0.63	0.63	0.79
New Zealand	—	—	—	—	—	0.78
Canada	—	—	1.10	0.51	0.58	0.66
Portugal	—	—	—	—	—	0.46
Australia	—	—	0.30	0.34	—	0.41
Turkey	—	—	—	—	—	0.20
Japan	—	—	0.43	0.72	—	0.18
United States	0.03	0.10	0.18	0.28	0.17	0.16
Switzerland	—	—	—	—	—	0.13
Iceland	—	—	—	—	—	0.01
Greece	—	—	—	—	—	0.01
Austria	—	—	0.05	0.15	—	—

Sources: The United States, West Germany, and Sweden were calculated from national sources, which are described in the Appendix. All other 1987 figures were calculated according to my own definition from OECD 1990. Austrian figures come from Soldwedel (1984, p. 93). Irish figures were calculated from Dineen (1984, p. 269).
Belgian figures are from OECD (1974, p. 53). Finnish figures were calculated from Finland (1966-82). The remaining figures come from OECD (1978, 1982).

this range of ALMP efforts with high, moderate, and low ALMP expenditures, respectively. Moreover, they are also good examples of Esping-Andersen's social democratic, conservative, and liberal regime types (1990, pp. 69–78). "Regimes" represent basic characteristics of the welfare state system – institutional arrangements, program rules, expenditure developments, and problem definitions – and to Esping-

Andersen, they also represent basic aspects of political economy (p. 80). In cross-sectional correlations of 18 countries in 1987, the social democratic ($r = .50$) and liberal regime types ($r = -.68$) are significantly correlated with ALMP/GNP spending.[2] Thus, the countries selected in this chapter represent the distinctiveness of each of three regimes: (1) as a social democratic regime, Sweden demonstrates, on average, strong universalism, high benefit equality, and high ALMP expenditures; (2) as a conservative regime, West Germany has diverse occupationally based pension schemes, a privileged civil service, and moderate ALMP spending; and (3) as a liberal regime, the United States exhibits widespread means-tested poor relief, high levels of private welfare spending, and low ALMP expenditures.[3]

Although Esping-Andersen bases his regime approach to citizenship on decommodification (1990, pp. 35–54), ALMP, especially in Sweden, focuses on preparing workers for entering the labor force (Furåker and Johansson 1990). In this active approach to labor markets, employers find more appropriate and highly skilled workers through ALMP, but workers are also reequipped to cope effectively with market forces. Consequently, Esping-Andersen's emphasis on passive (decommodification) policies seems somewhat out of place in discussing ALMP. In his analysis of ALMP/GDP expenditures in 1975, Esping-Andersen found that Left coalition power ($r = .70$) is strongly connected to ALMP/GDP spending, but he does not present a multivariate analysis of ALMP expenditures (pp. 132, 162–90).

This chapter will explain the determinants of ALMP for each country in accord with its regime type. Commodification will be a variable characteristic of each explanation, not an assumption. The next few sentences preview my argument. In the parsimonious Swedish model, employment needs cause ALMP/GNP spending, but Left-party power does not because it is hegemonic after World War II (i.e., a constant rather than a variable). In the West German political economy model, Left-party power and unemployment cause ALMP, while the declining manufacturing sector and the first oil shock impede it. In the fragmented U.S. model, the demographic pressures on the labor market cause ALMP/GNP expenditures with a small assistance from Left-party power and a foreign oil shock. These differences illustrate the Swedish and West German "work models" that respond to working-class problems and demands, as well as the U.S. "socialization model" that creates a large and somewhat underpaid service sector with its own problems and pressures. These differing models clearly show the discretionary nature of ALMP, with Left politics and the unemployed having a great effect on policy in one country but not in another.

Direct state intervention in the labor market

THE THEORY OF ACTIVE LABOR MARKET POLICY EXPENDITURES

Three major approaches attempt to explain the growth of public expenditures: needs–constraints, social demands, and bureaucratic models.[4]

Needs versus constraints

Needs and constraints can come in many different forms. Some refer to these models as functionalist, but more fundamentally, they point to forces largely outside the conflict arenas that drive social policies. Three variants of need models are particularly important: the business cycle, industrial structure, and labor market pressure models.

Pro-cyclical and counter-cyclical models. Such models consider the effect of the business cycle on politics and social welfare programs. How have the year-to-year fluctuations of unemployment (and also inflation and economic growth) affected ALMP/GNP spending? Because ALMP has explicitly been formulated as a counter-cyclical or Keynesian theory, the state should intentionally increase spending during economic crisis to reduce unemployment. However, a pro-cyclical hypothesis indicates that slow economic growth, meager profits, and overall economic misery constrain government expenditures. High economic growth allows more spending on ALMP during good times; but during recessions, low growth sharply constrains ALMP. The pro-cyclical hypothesis also coincides with the belt-tightening policies of Right-political parties (Nolan and Sabel 1982; Gourevitch 1986; and Hall 1986). Unemployment, inflation, and economic misery are economic problems, and when the state responds to these needs with increasing ALMP spending, it confirms the counter-cyclical hypothesis. Consequently, unemployment and inflation variables should have a positive correlation with ALMP to verify the counter-cyclical hypothesis. Growth is an economic resource to the state and should be negatively correlated with ALMP to support the counter-cyclical hypothesis. Opposite results support the pro-cyclical or constraint theory (Gourevitch 1986; Hall 1986).

Structural change models. In each of two model variants, societal changes dilute predictable state responses. In the service society "pull" model, citizens with higher disposable income demand more state and private services. Women enter competitive employment and expand the service sector through the growth of female-dominated semiprofessions – teaching, nursing, social work – and the demand for services for working mothers – child care, cleaning services, and food services. The education system produces large numbers of white-collar workers creating a surplus of workers that must be absorbed by the state. As the state and local governments reach their fiscal limits in taking up labor market slack, they turn to the federal government. The federal government subsidizes state and local government expansion through public service employment; consequently, most ALMP job creation comes in the form of government services. Thus, the service sector "pulls" ALMP into its financially needy arms by providing both the supply (employing college graduates) and demand (increasing government service jobs) pressures for ALMP.

In the industrial society "push" model, the decline in manufacturing employment as a percentage of the total labor force pushes workers into unemployment or blocks younger workers' entry into manufacturing jobs (Lindbeck 1988). The reality or specter of decline promotes ALMP expenditures. Although automation and robotics may not take jobs away from workers, manufacturing ceases to create new jobs while production continues to rise. For example, the oil crises accelerated the decline of manufacturing employment by pushing productivity growth through labor-saving capital investment and relocation of plants in Third World countries. States react to the needs of manufacturing workers and others with ALMP. (Political reaction by unions will be discussed in the upcoming power resources section.) Thus, the size of the manufacturing sector should be negatively related to ALMP/GNP spending and positively related to unemployment.

Labor market pressure models. These models focus on three factors that strain labor markets: working women, large cohorts of young adults, and immigrants. In the United States and Sweden, the entrance of married women and the baby boom generation into the labor force has increased job competition,[5] while immigration has also been a small factor.[6] In West Germany, women have not entered the labor market as in the United States and Sweden, and the baby boom was much smaller and came in the 1980s. But guest workers have crowded West German labor markets.

The effects of the labor market pressure model are direct and indirect. Labor market pressure *indirectly* influences policy when it increases the unemployment rate, which is a hypothesized cause of ALMP. Labor market pressure *directly* influences policy through worker insecurity on the job. Workers experiencing labor market pressure through organizational crowding react through political attitudes and demands for increasing employment regardless of the unemployment rate. Thus, labor market pressure directly influences ALMP through the insecurity of the employed, and this can be seen when we control for unemployment.

Direct state intervention in the labor market

First, female labor force participation rates should be strongly connected to ALMP in two ways. As women work they become more conscious of labor market issues and demand equal employment opportunity; their demands should include ALMP. Increases in female participation rates may also indirectly threaten men through tighter labor market conditions. The political effects may initially come from more concern for unemployed men, while concern for women takes the form of civil rights protections. ALMP expenditures should increase because employed men want insurance against competition in the labor market, and women want fairness at work and access to jobs.

Second, an influx of young persons creates crowding in the labor market. In the mid-1970s, U.S. baby boomers entered the labor market, caused higher unemployment, and demanded ALMP. By the 1980s, the peak of the baby boom had passed with most of the youth cohort reaching stable employment, while succeeding cohorts were smaller and less politically demanding. Thus, the size of the cohorts aged 16–19 and/or 20–24 as a percentage of the total population should exert a positive influence on ALMP/GNP spending.

Third, immigration should also cause ALMP. In West Germany, the steady growth of guest workers exerted pressure on labor markets. With the threat of guest workers gaining skills in the 1960s, the West German government recognized the potential problem of guest workers taking jobs from West German natives and used ALMP to promote the native labor force over guest workers. Similar governmental tendencies concerning immigrants and illegal aliens in the United States may be apparent although no explicit policy for promoting natives existed.[7]

The power resources approach

This approach regards governmental processes as an independent causal force, rather than as a superstructural reaction to societal cleavages or economic fluctuations. Political party power directly determines public expenditures in two ways: a step function increase of expenditures through new legislation and the incremental increase in expenditures through yearly budgetary decisions. Interest groups have a powerful but more indirect effect on legislation through consultation, lobbying, and campaign finance. Trade unions in particular should have an interest in labor market activities (Wilson 1979). Although some claim that socioeconomic conditions are more powerful than political variables in cross-sectional and time-series analysis, political power variables should have a strong and positive effect that is greater than socioeconomic variables because ALMP is a discretionary rather than an automatic policy.[8]

Social movements focus more on informal and less unorganized activities as causing higher public expenditures. Although the labor movement was the main social movement of the pre–World War II period, civil rights, women, youth, and antiwar groups were prevalent since the 1950s. These social movements have pressured the state into providing increased social expenditures. For instance, jobs for blacks was considered a major riot issue in the United States, and violent protest measured by yearly riots should test this hypothesis with ALMP. The lag structure is critical. Hicks (1984, p. 178) claims that immediately after riots state managers reduced social spending and stepped up infrastructural and police spending in order to restore business confidence. Then a few years later, with business confidence reestablished, steps were taken to address the underlying problems of riots. ALMP may have been one of these steps.

Even though protest demonstrations represent diverse actions – black civil and economic rights, welfare rights, and protests against the Vietnam War – they all can be connected to social policy of which ALMP is a part. Civil rights protests had a direct connection to employment rights. The high number of Vietnam War protest demonstrations in the 1960s threatened defense expenditures and thus provided an indirect demand for greater social spending. In West Germany, protests were directed against refugee unemployment in the 1950s, emergency powers and imperialism in the 1960s, and environmental destruction and youth unemployment in the 1970s and 1980s (Mushaben 1985, pp. 27–35).[9] Protests against rearmament and nuclear weapons were also evident throughout the post–World War II period. Protests present alternatives to government military expenditures, and full employment is often a major "opportunity" option. Thus, protests, despite their indirect connection, should be positively correlated with ALMP/GNP spending.

High strike rates, measured by total yearly days lost due to strikes, represent a similar need for the government to respond to conflict with higher social expenditures (Shorter and Tilly 1974). According to this hypothesis, the government should spend more when strike rates are high. However, in the neocorporatist approach to labor–capital conflict, social partners trade increases in social policy expenditures for moderation in wage bargaining. Although countries that are successful in these policies have low strike rates, worker demands that are controlled for long periods of time by elite bargaining may erupt to produce a renewed emphasis on ALMP. As a result, strikes in corporatist countries should demonstrate these latent social demands and should be positively connected to ALMP/GNP expenditures.

Proponents of this theory also indicate that elites recognize the potential political power of these movements and will attempt to co-opt them under their coalitions (Piven and Cloward 1971; Isaac and Kelly 1981; and Hicks and Swank 1984). In the United States, the post–World War II Democratic coalition especially cultivated the black vote when southern Democrats proved increasingly intractable on welfare issues, and farmers and small businesses dwindled to a minuscule voting bloc. This may have produced co-optation. In West Germany during the early 1970s, a similar phenomenon occurred with the SPD (Social Democratic Party of Germany) trying to assimilate the Left, the middle-class, university students, and graduates. This led to the rise of the JUSOs (Young Socialists), who clearly opposed the old labor bureaucrats in the SPD who saw ALMP as a central policy issue.[10]

Bureaucratic models

Although bureaucracies have an interest in the growth and stability of their budgets, bureaucratic interests vary according to elite and common civil service systems. Elite bureaucratic systems keep the size of the bureaucracy lean since power depends on maintaining scarcity and the wealth of their treasury. In that way, increasing budgets will inordinately benefit civil servants (Esping-Andersen 1990, pp. 69–73). Restrictions on enrollments – the "numerus clausus" in West Germany – help control the supply of university graduates for elite bureaucratic jobs. Thus, elite systems exert upward pressure on bureaucratic budgets but not on employment size. A different process takes place in nonelite bureaucratic systems because mere bureaucratic employment does not entail special privilege. Only expanding the number of employees will yield additional specialties and further promotions through greater hierarchy. The path to increased size lies in accumulating duties, responsibilities, and programs. But in either system, organizational growth must also be balanced with stability. Thus, there is a trade-off between the size of the bureaucracy and the richness of the bureaucrats, which can be seen most effectively in cross-sectional analysis.[11]

The effect of the bureaucracy on ALMP expenditures can be estimated by the ratio of employment service employees to the civilian labor force. A two-year distributed lag represents both immediate bureaucratic spending and delays in the hiring of a full staff, that is, a new law often takes a year before all the necessary employees can be hired, and even then the employees themselves may not press for expansion or promotion until they have assessed their organization's potential. However, state and local bureaucracies in the United States rather than the United States Employment Service (USES) are more precisely connected to ALMP because they implemented the Comprehensive Employment and Training

Act (CETA) and actually hired workers through ALMP job-creation policies (Alt 1985; Skocpol and Orloff 1986). However, the size of the bureaucracy should not affect ALMP in Germany or Sweden.

THE DATA

ALMP consists of direct government intervention into labor markets for the primary purpose of reducing unemployment. It presumes that participants are ready and willing to work and are adults, not students. Macroeconomic policies to increase economic growth are excluded because they are indirect and often have uncertain effects on labor markets. Thus, ALMP is job placement (matching the appropriate people to the appropriate jobs), job training (teaching new skills to people for jobs left unfilled because of skill shortages), and job creation (direct government efforts to create jobs). Despite two decades of use, ALMP is still a new term. Most national governments and international statistical agencies have not compiled systematic ALMP data, and few analyses exist on this policy.[12] As a result, painstaking efforts were made to measure the dependent variable and make it comparable between the three countries used. For comparative purposes, the main dependent variable was computed so that U.S., West German, and Swedish figures clearly match (see the data appendix for sources).

Job-training expenditures

In both Sweden and Germany, job-training expenditures consist of basic training, advanced training, retraining, support payments, institutional promotion of education, and the promotion of in-the-firm or apprenticeship training. In the United States, these expenditures tended to fall into the areas of retraining and basic training. They specifically include the Manpower Development and Training Act (MDTA), CETA Titles IIB and IIC job-training programs, the Job Corps, Job Opportunities in the Business Sector, and Job Training and Partnership Act (JTPA) expenditures.

Job-placement expenditures

Such expenditures include money spent for the employment service, the administration of the employment service, other expenses and publicity, and special labor market placement programs. In Germany, this includes some special placement programs for Berlin, and in the United States this included the Concentrated Employment Program and CETA Title III program support for community-based organizations.

Direct state intervention in the labor market

Job-Creation program expenditures

Such policies produce public- and private-sector jobs for many different groups of people. In Sweden, job-creation programs focus on older worker programs and have included work-creation programs in forestry and road building. In Germany, job-creation programs include Work Creation Measures (ABM) and redundant worker programs. In the United States, job-creation programs include measures for older citizens, CETA-IID structural unemployment, public service jobs programs for structural unemployment, and CETA-VI counter-cyclical unemployment programs.

Exclusions

Exclusions were generally made when programs applied to students rather than adults, to subsidy or regional policy programs, and to all passive programs ranging from unemployment insurance to public assistance. In Sweden, inventory stockpiling support, regional development programs, and refugee supports were excluded. In Germany, ALMP expenditures exclude some job-creation programs – short-time work, bad weather payments, and winter payments – because they support workers already in jobs and the construction industry as a whole. Speech and skill training for foreign students who will leave West Germany after training were both excluded. In the United States, ALMP expenditures exclude Department of Health, Education, and Welfare (HEW) vocational rehabilitation, Veteran's Administration (VA) education and training benefits, and youth stay-in-school programs such as the Neighborhood Youth Corps. And for all three countries, passive labor market policy programs – unemployment compensation and unemployment help – were excluded because they do little or nothing to connect a person to a job.[13]

ALMP expenditures are standardized by GNP. Rates of change in expenditure variables were not used because social pressures do not monotonically or mechanistically stimulate spending. The policy process is not a stimulus–response relationship. Economic variables may react immediately (i.e., within a year) and consistently to some events, but the pressures from political and social variables are often exerted through large time cushions and percolator effects. The data for political, economic, and demographic variables for all three countries are rather straightforward and come from standard government statistical sources (see the Appendix for sources).

Two issues may be controversial. First, the Left party in the United States excludes southern Democrats because of their conservative politics

(Shelley 1983). This does not make the concept of the U.S. Left party totally equivalent to social democratic parties in Sweden and Germany, but it does bring it much closer. Second, unemployment is endogenous in Sweden because its ALMP has a much larger impact on unemployment than in other countries. As a result, vacancies as a percentage of the labor force will be used as an equivalent measure of social demands in Sweden.[14]

In order to reduce the complexity of the data and multicollinearity, two indices were constructed. The "labor market pressure index" is the percentage of women in the labor force, plus the percentage of young adults in the labor force, plus immigrants as a percentage of the population. "Left-party power" indices of executive and legislative party power were constructed for Sweden and West Germany. In the United States, the Left president was ignored and an index constructed of House and Senate power.[15] None of these indices are standardized because they are all composed of relatively equivalent percentages of what is being measured.

THE TIME-SERIES METHODOLOGY

Due to autocorrelation, I used a generalized version of the Cochrane–Orcutt method in a "two-step full-transform" method to control for error and bias. This method was chosen over simple regression with a lagged dependent variable because it is simpler to explain and allows for the inclusion of variables that might be highly correlated with the lagged dependent variable.[16] It was chosen over ARIMA models, which need at least 50 cases, and may be statistically so conservative that it suppresses notable effects (McCleary and Hay 1980, p. 20; SAS 1982; see also Jennings 1983).[17]

Lag structures "allow a reasonable period of adjustment by state managers" (Isaac and Kelly 1981, p. 1365). I avoid short lags of one year in favor of distributed lags because the political process lengthens and diversifies time lags in four ways. First, the budget is executively formulated at least a year in advance of its legislative revision and certification. Second, new legislation may take an additional one to three years depending on the alignments and dynamics of conflicting legislative parties, factions, and alliances. Third, it may take up to four years or more to replace a president or chancellor and enact bottled-up opposition proposals. And finally, the bureaucracy needs time to implement legislation.[18] Since budgetary decisions are dependent on the previous year, the autocorrelation function covers the incremental effects of the one-year lag. A two-year lag would take into account congressional elections. The legislative process clearly produces larger increases in expenditures than do budgetary politics, but its effects can take one to three years. The four-year lag covers bureaucratic implementation, regime changes due to elections, and infrequent and unpredictable political events like impeachments and foreign policy crises. However, strong emphasis of four-year lags might be misguided since elections occur much more frequently than such a long lag implies. Here, two- and three-year distributed lags will be used for political variables. A two-year lag indicates a responsive enactment of policies, while a three-year lag involves a difficult legislative process with voters replacing at least some unresponsive representatives.

Two other sets of independent variables had different lags. First, unemployment, inflation, and other cyclical economic variables are widely publicized in the media, and government bureaucracies may quickly increase expenditures for existing programs. Although measures of unemployment and inflation have longer lags when affecting the political process, their length here is relatively short with distributed lags of one and two years. Second, structural, labor market, and other demographic variables are clearly indirect because they do not signal an immediate problem that would require political action. They come into the spotlight when causing overcrowded schools or unemployment. Consequently, these variables have a distributed lag of three to four years.

A variable with a distributed lag influences expenditures in a number of years rather than only in one year. The weighting of distributed lags specifies the years that should have the most effect. For political and demographic variables, the distributed lags follow a four-year inverted U-curve. Political variables have a build up and decline with their peak influence coming in the second and third years; demographic variables follow the same pattern but peak a year later. I first weighted these lags at 10, 30, 40, and 10 percent, but then shortened them by eliminating the first and second years, which had little or no effect on results. Economic variables, however, have a peak influence in the first year and then decline because economic information is quickly disseminated throughout society. I put most emphasis (70 percent) on a one-year lag for budgets and bureaucratic discretion and less emphasis (30 percent) on a two-year lag in affecting legislation.[19] These lags were largely supported by statistical tests with polynomial and geometrical lags.[20]

MULTIVARIATE TIME-SERIES ANALYSIS OF ALMP/GNP EXPENDITURES

The multivariate analysis shows that each country is somewhat unique. In explaining ALMP/GNP spending, the Swedish model concentrates on vacancy rates – a more accurate measure of employment need than of unemployment – while Left-party power varies inversely with ALMP/GNP expenditure in time. The West German model highlights Left-political power, the industrial push version of the structural economic theory, and cyclical economic variables, especially unemployment. The U.S. model, despite minor Left-legislative power effects, is essentially a social structural/labor market model – a service-sector pull model strongly supplemented by labor market pressure variables.

Time-series data are especially prone to multicollinearity, especially for trend-dominated variables. Thus, many of the correlations with ALMP/GNP expenditures in Table 3.2 are large. Neither dependent variable is trend-dominated: ALMP/GNP spending in Sweden and even more so in West Germany forms a U-curve. In the United States, it approximates a late-peaking, inverted U-curve. However, many of the independent variables are trend-dominated – showing an almost constant increase or decrease over time – and as a result they are susceptible to multicollinearity. The presence of multicollinearity considerably restricts the analysis and the number of variables that can be put into one equation. Thus, the analysis can best proceed by restraining the number of variables in each equation, rather than by crowding all contentious variables representing each theory into one equation.[21]

The determinants of Swedish ALMP expenditures

The Swedish model is not straightforward because two variables that should work – Left-party power and unemployment – do not. Left-party power has most certainly led to high ALMP expenditures in Sweden but has been above a threshold, making it a virtual constant that is not very helpful when entered into equations for the 1950 to 1988 time period (Petterson 1976; Jorgensen and Lind 1987; and Brown and King 1988). In regression equations (Equations 1 and 2 in Table 3.3), the effects of Left-party powers are actually negative with ALMP/GNP spending. Unemployment is not at all significant when coupled with Left-party power (Equation 1 in Table 3.3). Thus, the most obvious political economy model does not explain longitudinal fluctuations. To explain this, one must either extend the time period or go beyond fluctuations to cross-national comparisons of a larger number of countries. Left politics and unemployment do form the heart of the Swedish model but in a slightly different way (Therborn 1986). Employment need, as measured by the vacancy rate, and Left bargaining power, as measured by strike frequency, are the two strongest predictors of ALMP/GNP expenditures.[22] Together they explain 91 percent of the variance in

ALMP/GNP spending, with both coefficients being significant (Equation 3 in Table 3.3). The model is clearly counter-cyclical in its reaction to employment need – as vacancies increase ALMP goes down, and vice versa. Thus, the Swedish model is not quite so different as it initially appears.

The oil shock period also has a complex relationship to ALMP/GNP policy expenditures in Sweden because the bourgeois coalition took power in 1976. The first oil shock is negative, but it most often does poorly in regression equations. Early in the first oil shock, the Social Democratic (SAP) government spent little on ALMP (as indicated by the residuals of strikes and vacancy rates), because the shock did not have the typical contractionary effect in Sweden until quite late in 1976 (Martin 1985; Heclo and Madsen 1987, pp. 57–79). Consequently, the first oil shock is negative ($\beta = -.0006$ in Equation 4). The second oil shock hit hard. Much more money was spent on job maintenance policies and other ALMP by the bourgeois government. One could even interpret this as overspending, and the coefficient for the second oil shock is positive. However, neither oil shock variable is significant, and both add only about 1 percent to the variance explained. In the end, employment need (the vacancy rate) and Left bargaining power (strike rates) provide the most powerful and parsimonious explanation (Equation 3 in Table 3.3).

Membership in the Swedish Federation of Trade Unions, the (LO) is highly correlated with ALMP/GNP expenditures ($r = .81$). LO power as measured by membership figures has not faced a major decline. This trade union strength combined with strikes brings much more pressure for ALMP expenditures. However, the LO, which mainly represents blue-collar workers, has also had help from the white-collar employees union, the TCO (Tjänstemännens, Centralorganisation), which of course wants to maintain high government employment.

Sweden has the most parsimonious political economy model where simple need – the vacancy rate – along with strikes and the second oil shock explains over 96 percent of the variance in ALMP/GNP expenditures. The approximate levels of ALMP are not a political issue; the system responds to threats to unemployment. Left political forces and even bourgeois parties respond directly to threats of unemployment and slight declines in manufacturing employment with increases in social policy. The polity and economy are integrated in the world's strongest counter-cyclical model that appears ready to search and destroy threats to unemployment. Gearing up political forces that require massive external threats is not necessary. Of course, this is not to say that considerable political effort from unions and the SAP is not required to keep the Swedish policies intact.

Table 3.2. *The determinants of active labor market policy expenditures, 1950-87: hypotheses with correlation coefficients*

Hypotheses[a]	Sweden	West Germany	United States
I. Needs versus constraints models			
A. Cyclical hypotheses:			
Unemployment rate	-.11	.51	.41
Inflation rate	.93	.72	.56
Real growth rate	.56	-.25	.36
Economic misery index	.22	.81	.57
B. Structural change hypotheses:			
Percentage of service-sector employees in the civilian labor force	—	.73	.75
Percentage of manufacturing employees in the civilian labor force	—	-.52	-.76
C. Labor market pressure hypotheses:			
Female labor market participation rate	.79	.31	.68
Young workers as a percentage of the labor force	.29	.02	.79
Immigrant/guest worker percentage of labor force[b]	.36	.82	.50
Labor market pressure index	.73	.74	.84
II. Power resourses model			
A. Formal political hypotheses:			
Left-party power index	-.48	.83	.69
Left executive power	-.63	.77	.06
Union membership ratio	.81	.86	-.84
B. Social movement hypotheses:			
Riot frequency	-.18	.23	.08
Protest frequency	.41	.16	.34
Strike frequency	.71	.17	-.23
III. State-centric models			
A. State managerialism hypotheses:			
Executive election cycle	.03	.14	.01
Legislative election cycle	.03	.14	-.13
B. Bureaucratic expansion hypotheses:			
Employment service employees in labor force	—	.76	.34
State and local employees in labor force	—	.72	.79

Table 3.2. *(cont.)*

Hypotheses[a]	Sweden	West Germany	United States
C. Bureaucratic capacity hypothesis:			
Bureaucratic confusion	—	.13	.04
IV. External variables			
1st oil shock dummy variable	.26	.29	.66
2d oil shock dummy variable	.47	.51	.46

[a] All variables but those for election cycle and oil shocks have distributed lags as indicated in the text.
[b] The U.S. variable uses ages 16-24; West Germany uses 15-20.

The determinants of West German ALMP expenditures

Left political power, both legislative and executive, is the strongest determinant of ALMP expenditures, closely followed by unemployment and the declining manufacturing sector. Each of these variables works well in two-variable regression equations. Left control of the chancellorship and unemployment in regression equations are strong ($\beta = .0037$, $p = .0001$; $\beta = .0348$, $p = .0001$, respectively) and explain 87 percent of the variance in ALMP expenditures (see Equation 1 in Table 3.4). An index of Left-party legislative power and the Left chancellor does less well with unemployment, but it still explains 69 percent of the variance, and Right-party power is in between and negative. Clearly, Left power has led to higher ALMP expenditures, while Right power has reduced expenditures. Unemployment, closely connected to the decline in manufacturing, is a strong positive predictor of ALMP, and this relationship is consistently counter-cyclical, that is, the government responds to unemployment with greater ALMP. The equation with unemployment and the Left chancellor is the strongest of all two-variable equations.

The variables for Left chancellor ($\beta = +.0039$, $p = .0001$) and the declining manufacturing sector ($\beta = -.0750$, $p = .0001$) are also strong. They explain 83 percent of the variance – also a high percentage for only two variables. The manufacturing sector is negatively related to ALMP as expected, meaning that the declining manufacturing sector produces more ALMP. When ALMP spending was high in the 1950s, the manufacturing sector was small and struggling to get on its feet again after World War II. When ALMP spending was low during the

Table 3.3. *Sweden: the determinants of active labor market policy expenditures over GNP, 1950-88: regression results controlling for autocorrelation*

	Unstandardized ß's predicting ALMP over GNP				
Variables[a]	(1)	(2)	(3)	(4)	(5)
Vacancy rate	—	-.1894 (.0001) [.0137]	-.1741 (.0001) [.0112]	-.1711 (.0001) [.0103]	-.1706 (.0001) [.0103]
Unemployment rate	.0013 (.3873) [.0015]	—	—	—	—
Left-party power	-.0143 (.07) [.0076]	-.0120 (.0007) [.0032]	—	—	—
Strike frequency	—	—	.00007 (.0001) [.0000]	.00005 (.0001) [.0000]	.00005 (.0001) [.0000]
1st oil shock dummy variable	—	—	—	-.0006 (.4744) [.0008]	—
2nd oil shock dummy variable	—	—	—	—	.0007 (.4252) [.0008]
R^2	.12	.91	.95	.96	.96
n	38	38	38	38	38

Note: Significance levels in parentheses; standard errors in brackets.
[a] All variables have distributed lags as indicated in the text, except the oil shock variables, which are not lagged.

economic miracle, the manufacturing sector reached a world high, and when the oil crisis hit in the mid-1970s the manufacturing sector recorded a small decline. The decline in manufacturing employees in the labor force produces unemployment, and these two variables are highly correlated ($r = -.87$). Actually, the manufacturing sector changed little

Table 3.4. ***West Germany: the determinants of active labor market policy expenditures over GNP, 1952-88: regression results controlling for autocorrelation***

	Unstandardized ß's predicting ALMP over GNP				
Variables:	(1)	(2)	(3)	(4)	(5)
Left chancellor[a]	.0037 (.0001) [.0003]	.0039 (.0001) [.0004]	.0040 (.0001) [.0003]	.0034 (.0001) [.0004]	.0035 (.0001) [.0003]
Unemployment rate	.0348 (.0001) [.0044]	—	.0348 (.0001) [.0038]	.0334 (.0001) [.0046]	.0336 (.0001) [.0042]
Manufacturing/ sector employment	—	-.0750 (.0001) [.0116]	—	—	—
1st oil shock dummy variable[b]	—	—	.0004 (.3210) [.0004]	—	.00002 (.9705) [.0004]
2d oil shock dummy variable[c]	—	—	—	.0006 (.1571) [.0004]	.0005 .2453 [.0004]
R^2	.87	.83	.91	.85	.88
n	36	36	36	36	36

Note: Significance levels in parentheses; standard errors in brackets.
[a]All variables have distributed lags as indicated in the text except the oil shock variables, which are not lagged.
[b]The 1st oil shock represents 1974-7.
[c]The 2d oil shock represents 1979-82.

during this period, unlike the steady decline in the United States. Also unlike the United States, the West German service sector is not a mirror image of the manufacturing sector since these two sectors are only weakly correlated ($r = -.24$). Agricultural employment fueled the growth of manufacturing and services at the same time, and the women did not swell the service sector. Due to causal priorities and multicollinearity problems, however, I will put the manufacturing sector later in time order as a cause of unemployment and use unemployment as the main, direct cause of ALMP/GNP spending.

One could argue that the Left chancellor variable is simply a proxy for the oil shock period. The total oil shock and the Left chancellorship variables are too highly correlated to include in the same regression equation to settle the question. If we put Left-party power, which is a standardized index of Left Bundestag power and the Left chancellor, and the oil shock variables together, the multicollinearity can be greatly reduced. In an equation that explains 88 percent of the variance in ALMP/GNP expenditures, the direct effects of the oil shock are woefully insignificant, while the Left power and unemployment variables are both significant. Thus, in West Germany the oil shock simply does not match the important effect of Left-party power on ALMP.

But the oil shock period has a complex relationship to ALMP/GNP expenditures in West Germany. The oil shock most often does poorly in regression equations with unemployment. If we look closer at the residuals of the two best two-variable equations (i.e., the Left chancellor with unemployment and then with the manufacturing sector), we find that during the first oil shock, the government spent much more in 1975 than predicted, but serious shortfalls below predicted expenditures appear in 1976, 1977, and 1978. But in 1979, 1980, and 1981, the second oil shock produced mildly higher than expected expenditures. The West German government expected a short recession, so they increased ALMP in 1975. When they found out how long the recession would last, they severely cut expenditures in the next three years. When the second oil shock appeared, they had some experience with the problem, and expenditures were a little higher than expected. If the oil shock period is divided into two variables of three years each and the overly optimistic first year is eliminated, the oil shock variables produce significant results. The first oil shock is negative as expected with the Left chancellorship and unemployment variables in explaining 91 percent of the variance in ALMP/GNP expenditures (Equation 3 in Table 3.4). The second oil shock is positively correlated in a similar equation and more significant than the first oil shock (Equations 4 and 5 in Table 3.4).

Membership in the dominant trade union federation, the DGB, is highly correlated with ALMP. Unlike the United States, where trade unions have seriously declined, DGB power as measured by membership figures has faced only a mild decline. This trade union strength helps to motivate the SPD to respond to unemployment and manufacturing declines with more ALMP expenditures. However, despite a strong zero-order correlation, DGB power does not work well with unemployment and other variables in explaining ALMP expenditures. The coefficients are significant, but the variance explained is low. The SPD has to be in power for the DGB to exert its direct influence; otherwise, the more moderate Catholic trade unions have the upper hand in policy. Thus, the effect of trade unions is more indirect.

Numerous other variables fail to explain much variance in ALMP. The labor market pressure index is weak, and even alterations in the index to stress guest workers fare poorly against Left politics and unemployment variables. Strife, strikes, riots, and protests did nothing to explain the residuals of Left power and unemployment variables. The bureaucratic expansionism hypotheses failed because the causal order tests indicate that ALMP causes the bureaucracy to grow and not the other way around.

West Germany has a parsimonious political economy model in which three variables – the left chancellor, unemployment, and the first oil shock – explain over 91 percent of the variance in ALMP. One can refer to this as a "work model" of political economy because it is so closely connected to trade unions, their problems, and their party. ALMP is controlled by an internal set of Left political forces – Left-party and trade union power – responding directly to changes in unemployment, the manufacturing sector, and the different effects of the two oil shocks. The polity and economy are integrated in a counter-cyclical model that responds in a regular fashion to workers' needs.

Explaining U.S. ALMP expenditures

If the strongest two variables from West Germany – executive power and the unemployment rate – are used in U.S. equations, a striking difference appears. The Left chancellor and unemployment variables explained 87 percent of the variance in West Germany, while the variables for Left president and the unemployment rate explain only 15 percent of the variance in the United States. Substituting a measure of presidential ideology does no better. Replacing the variable for Left president with one for Left-party power increases the variance explained to 21 percent, but this still pales in comparison to the 87 percent variance explained in West Germany. Clearly, the United States diverges from the West German model.

U.S. unemployment does not produce a consistent reaction in ALMP. On the contrary, when unemployment is perceived to be internally induced (1950–73, 1982–present), unemployment generates a procyclical response with ALMP (i.e., higher unemployment means less ALMP), and when unemployment is perceived to be externally induced

(1974–81), it generates a counter-cyclical response (i.e., higher unemployment means more ALMP). Indeed, instead of an integration of polity and economy, the United States only responds with extensive ALMP when threatened by foreign powers during the oil shock. An internal system of political economy does not exist with a consistent relationship between U.S. ALMP and unemployment.

Instead, labor market and political variables explain the most variance in U.S. ALMP/GNP expenditures.[23] Unlike West Germany, where demographic factors have little impact, the U.S. labor market pressure index explains a large amount of variance. This index and one for Left-party legislative power explain 43 percent of the variance in ALMP/GNP spending. If we decrease the political lags from two and three years to one and two years on the Left-party power measure and the demographic lags from three and four years to two and three years on the labor market pressure index, the amount of variance explained increases to 67 percent. With these changes, the regression coefficient for the labor market pressure index is strong and significant ($\beta = .03$, $p = .0001$) and Left-party power measure is somewhat close to significance ($\beta = .0003$, $p = .25$; see Table 3.5). When one controls for unemployment, labor market pressure is still strong. Thus, labor market pressure causes ALMP/GNP expenditures through labor market crowding and political demands, rather than through indirect effects by creating unemployment.

The influx of young adults due to the baby boom, working women, and a moderate amount of immigrants hit the labor market in the 1970s to produce severe job competition, labor market insecurities, and some unemployment. The liberals in the Senate and House pushed hard for ALMP. The strength of the Left legislative index and weakness of the Left presidency measure show the preeminence of the legislature in predicting ALMP/GNP expenditures (Orfield 1975). In the United States, consequently, measures of Left legislative power – weaker than in West Germany and excluding the executive – and labor market pressure explain ALMP/GNP spending.[24]

The Left power and labor market variables explained a smaller share of variance than in the other two countries. Clearly, the U.S. model is not parsimonious, and two additional variables were used to approach the power of the other models. First, a total oil shock variable explains an additional 10 percent of the variance with the political and labor market variables ($R^2 = .77$), but the oil shock is only significant at $p = .068$. Using a dummy variable for the first oil shock, the positive effect of the oil crisis can be more precisely singled out (see Equation 2 in Table 3.5). The first oil shock is strong ($\beta = .0013$), highly significant ($p = .0004$), and adds 37 percent to the variance explained ($R^2 = .80$).

Table 3.5. *United States: the determinants of active labor market policy expenditures over GNP, 1950-88: regression results controlling for autocorrelation*

	Unstandardized ß's predicting ALMP over GNP				
Variables[a]	(1)	(2)	(3)	(4)	(5)
Labor market pressure index	.0300	.0195	.0337	.0230	.0336
	(.0001)	(.0038)	(.0041)	(.0068)	(.0004)
	[.0001]	[.0061]	[.0107]	[.0078]	[.0082]
Left-party power index	.0003	.0004	.0004	.0004	.0003
	(.2452)	(.0281)	(.1590)	(.0407)	(.0953)
	[.0003]	[.0002]	[.0003]	[.0002]	[.0002]
1st oil shock dummy variable[b]	—	.0013	—	.0012	-.0006
		(.0013)		(.0053)	(.1455)
		[.0004]		[.0004]	[.0004]
2d oil shock dummy variable[c]	—	—	-.0009	-.0004	—
			(.1207)	(.4648)	
			[.0006]	[.0005]	
Reagan administration dummy variable	—	—	—	—	-.0012
					(.0293)
					[.0004]
R^2	.43	.80	.46	.77	.84
n	38	38	38	38	38

Note: Significance levels in parentheses; standard errors in brackets.
[a]All variables have distributed lags as indicated in the text except the oil shock variables, which are not lagged.
[b]The 1st oil shock represents 1974-7.
[c]The 2d oil shock represents 1979-82.

Further, labor market pressure and Left-party power are strong and significant. Testing for the second oil shock provides no such improvement (Equation 3 in Table 3.5). Thus, only the first oil shock creates the massive consensus to pass job-creation programs and foster a countercyclical reaction to unemployment. And the fact that the signs of the first and second oil shocks in both Sweden and West Germany are exactly opposite their counterparts in the United States, shows entirely different methods for dealing with the domestic turmoil that external shocks produce.

In addition, a Reagan administration dummy variable can explain the precipitous decline in ALMP that takes place from 1981 to 1984 in the face of record high unemployment. The Reagan presidency explains 2 percent more variance ($R^2 = .82$) than Equation 2. Including the labor market pressure index and measures of Left-party power and the first oil shock along with the Reagan administration variable produces the best equation (Equation 5 in Table 3.5), in which 84 percent of the variance in ALMP/GNP expenditure is explained with only the first oil shock moving out of significance.

In contrast to those of Sweden and West Germany, U.S. demographic variables are strong as well as significant, and contribute to a high amount of variance explained. Female labor force participation rates and the influx of workers due to the baby boom swelled ALMP in the 1970s, and now that the influx is over and demographic pressures are stabilizing, ALMP has gone down. But the actual decreases in ALMP during the 1980s are much greater than predicted by the labor market pressure index and Left-party power measure because Reagan decimated ALMP. Without Reagan, ALMP/GNP expenditures most likely would have slowly rather than precipitously declined because labor market pressures due to the baby boom were subsiding.

Two variables that have some success in Sweden and Germany have none in the United States. First, unemployment has had unstable and even contradictory effects on ALMP expenditures. Unemployment has an inconsistent relationship with ALMP/GNP spending, and only during the external threat of the first oil crisis did unemployment bring the fragmented political system together to generate extensive job-creation policies. U.S. policymakers typically point to low unemployment as an indicator of general economic well-being. It is logical but perhaps naive to think that high unemployment would represent a strong cue to government that ALMP intervention is necessary. But unemployment as a variable has little systematic effect. At some points after World War II, job loss and higher prices were accompanied by aggressive moves to manipulate U.S. labor markets; at other points, these economic downturns signaled a stability or decline in ALMP.[25] In short, U.S.

responses to unemployment and inflation are sufficiently inconsistent that cyclical economic fluctuations fail to predict policy interventions or expenditures.

Second, U.S. trade union power is even further removed from the "work model" demonstrated in Germany because U.S. trade unions could be grouped with the Republican Party as a factor operating against ALMP (Janoski 1990, pp. 243–44). While this is preposterous given the hard work of the AFL-CIO and UAW for ALMP, these results suggest that trade union power simply cannot be a systematic determinant of ALMP.

Instead of a tightly grouped system of political economy variables, as in Sweden and West Germany, the United States fits a "socialization model" that emphasizes demographic changes and the service sector. Politics are fragmented with the Left president measure having no effect, while the Left legislative measure has only a moderate impact. In concluding about the United States, politics – fragmented into multifarious centers with veto powers – produced ALMP on a bipartisan level only when threatened by a hostile oil shock from abroad, aided by a service sector expanding with a massive influx of women and baby boomers into the labor market. Thus, the U.S. "socialization model," with the traditional emphasis on the service sector and government employment in reaction to labor market pressure and Left-party power, gives a smaller boost to ALMP, which needed a major input from the oil shock. In the West German work model, the emphasis on manufacturing and trade union power increases Left power in the face of unemployment to provide ALMP/GNP spending. In the "pro-active" Swedish work model, the emphasis on declining vacancy rates and trade union power quickly increases ALMP/GNP spending.

Direct comparisons between models are somewhat difficult; however, an attempt is made in Table 3.6. In the work model, Sweden and Germany do well, but the unemployment rate in the United States is not at all significant. In the socialization model, the United States does the best and Germany does poorly. However, Sweden also does well in this model, but the signs for Left power and labor market pressure measures totally contradict the theory and make the model implausible. To some extent because of the large increase in government employment and female labor force participation, Sweden is closer to the U.S. model than Germany, but another essay would be needed to go into the odd symmetry involved. These comparisons do not pit the best equations from each country against each other because the best equations are simply too different. Comparisons with the same models are most often quite suboptimal. Nonetheless, the comparable models do demonstrate basic differences and some similarities between these three countries.

Table 3.6. *Comparisons of regression equations for Sweden, West Germany, and the United States*

	Unstandardized ß's predicting ALMP over GNP					
	Work model			Socialization model		
Variables[a]	Sweden	West Germany	United States	Sweden	West Germany	United States
Unemployment/ vacancy rate[b]	-.1887	.0334	.0578	—	—	—
	(.0001)	(.0001)	(.1893)			
	[.0138]	[.0046]	[.0420]			
Left-party power[c]	-.014	.0034	.0002	-.015	.0007	.0195
	(.0015)	(.0001)	(.0006)	(.0161)	(.0201)	(.0038)
	[.0041]	[.0004]	[.0002]	[.0050]	[.0003]	[.0061]
Labor market pressure index	—	—	—	-.0006	.0085	.0004
				(.0004)	(.3610)	(.0281)
				[.0001]	[.0092]	[.0002]
1st oil shock dummy variable	—	—	.0014	—	—	.0013
			(.0021)			(.0013)
			[.0004]			[.0004]
2d oil shock dummy variable	.0012	.0006	—	-.0025	.0004	—
	(.3567)	(.1571)		(.1844)	(.3911)	
	[.0013]	[.0004]		[.0019]	[.0005]	
R^2	.91	.85	.61	.77	.48	.80
n	38	37	38	38	37	38

Note: Significance levels in parentheses; standard errors in brackets.

[a] All variables have distributed lags as indicated in the text, except for the oil shock dummy variables.

[b] The vacancy rate is used in Sweden instead of the unemployment rate because the Swedish unemployment rate is so heavily influenced by ALMP. See the text for further discussion.

[c] The left-party power indices include the chancellor and Riksdag for Sweden, only the chancellor for West Germany, and the two legislaures in the United States.

Table 3.7. *Summary of results*

Variables	Sweden	Germany	United States
Employment need			
Unemployment	n/a	+++	0
Vacancies	+++	n/a	n/a
Labor market pressure	-	+	+++
Social demands			
Left policies	0	+++	+
Right policies	0	- - -	- - -
Strikes	+++	0	0
State bureaucracy			
Government size	0		
Employment service	0	0	++
		0	- -
Crises			
1st oil shock	-	-	+
2d oil shock	+	+	-

Note: +++ is a stronger positive factor; ++ is moderate; + is a weakly positive factor. - - - is a stronger negative factor; - - is moderate; - is a weakly negative factor. 0 is a non-factor. n/a means the relationship was not tested.

CONCLUSION AND SUMMARY

The determinants of ALMP/GNP expenditures in these three countries are strikingly different (see Table 3.7), and they are indeed "three worlds of welfare capitalism" (Esping-Andersen 1990). The Swedes invented the active approach to the labor market (Meidner 1948; Rehn 1948). Its emphasis on retraining and jobs through social policy is strongly driven by employment needs. Left politics (Left-party and trade union power) help explain this system, but Left hegemony results in a post-World War II constant rather than a variable. As such, it does not explain variation in ALMP. Strikes have supplied the variable motive force in pushing Left-party power and ALMP. In the end, the Swedish government, even when in the hands of bourgeois parties, clearly generates ALMP funds in a counter-cyclical manner. Service-sector variables along with demographic pressures from women and the baby boom play a smaller but still important role in Sweden. The oil shock

– not necessary as a consensus maker – plays a less important role in Sweden than in either Germany or the United States. In fact, the first oil shock had a slight negative impact on ALMP as policymakers reassessed the effects of high ALMP spending. Thus, the determinants of ALMP/GNP expenditures can be stated simply in Sweden: the government responds to the need for enhanced employment before the situation degenerates into unemployment. This approach fits strongly with the social-democratic regime type, which had the strongest cross-national correlation of the three regimes tested with ALMP.

West German ALMP, with its work approach to social policy, has a model strongly driven by Left politics (Left-party and trade union power), cyclical unemployment, and an economic structure heavily weighted in favor of manufacturing. The government clearly generates ALMP funds in a counter-cyclical manner, but Left power is contested rather than hegemonic as in Sweden. Service-sector variables along with demographic pressures from women and the baby boom do not play an important role in West Germany. The oil shock – the big consensus maker in the United States from 1974 to 1978 – plays a positive role only from 1979 to 1981 because West Germany's counter-cyclical approach immediately pumped money into ALMP. In fact, the first oil shock had a negative impact on ALMP as policymakers reassessed the effects of high ALMP spending. These variables form a tightly knit political economy model focused on traditional working-class institutions and issues. The determinants of ALMP/GNP spending in Germany are more complicated than those in Sweden, but they can still be parsimoniously listed as follows: Left power, unemployment, a declining manufacturing sector, and the negative impact of the first oil shock.

West Germany fits the conservative welfare regime type of Esping-Andersen. These regimes can go a number of directions, and indeed Austria and West Germany diverge completely on ALMP. The weak correlation with ALMP/GNP expenditures of the conservative regime type belies this split and shows that these countries may indeed have the most discretion in pursuing labor market and industrial policies.

The U.S. model is fragmented and otherwise completely different from Swedish and West German models. Early U.S. ALMP policies operated in a pro-cyclical fashion. Only the first oil shock pushed ALMP into a counter-cyclical mode. The U.S. socialization model is based on the service sector – private and state – putting pressure on the labor market to absorb women, baby boomers, and immigrants. Demographic pressures on the number and types of jobs available to workers proved to be powerful pressures to increase ALMP intervention by creating insecurity about the availability and stability of jobs. This insecurity is felt by people who hold jobs, as well as those who are looking for jobs, and is reinforced by weak unions, large secondary labor markets, and a stigmatizing welfare state.

The U.S. response is an expected result from a liberal regime type. The liberal regime variable is almost an anathema to ALMP – why reskill or find jobs for workers when labor discipline can be effectively enforced to keep wages low and unemployment high? The underfunded U.S. ALMP programs are explained by more marginal factors that come about during good times, when the government has more money to spend, or during the initial stages of a foreign threat.

Thus, the political economy of unemployment clearly fits with the welfare regime types outlined by Esping-Andersen. Social democratic regimes are strongly correlated with ALMP/GNP spending in cross-sectional analysis, and the Swedish model demonstrates the effects of employment need and Left bargaining strength. Conservative regimes are weakly correlated with ALMP/GNP spending, indicating that this regime type may go either way. West Germany tends toward the work model of Sweden, and unemployment and Left-party power are strong causes of ALMP/GNP expenditures. Liberal regimes are strongly but negatively correlated with ALMP/GNP levels, and their model shows how unemployment and Left power are not factors in explaining those levels. Consequently, where direct intervention into capitalist labor markets is concerned, regime types rather than demographic forces make the most difference in providing the causal factors of political economy.

APPENDIX

Data sources

Sweden. AMS-V: AMS, *Arbetsmarknaden: Verksamhetsberättelse*, for 1947–88; AMS-P: AMS, *Arbetsmarknadsstatistik: Platsstatistiken 1902–1982*; AMS-HT: AMS, *Arbetsmarknadsstatistik: Historiska tabeller*, for 1989; LO: LO, for 1948–90; *Annual Reports*; SAS: Statistiska Centralbryån, *Statistisk Arsbok för Sverige.*

Federal Republic of Germany. BAA-AN and BAVAV-AN: Bundesanstalt für Arbeit, *Amtliche Nachrichtung der Bundesanstalt für Arbeit*, for 1952–84; BAA-GB and BAVAV-GB: Bundesanstalt für Arbeit Geschaftsbericht; BAA-AA: Bundesanstalt für Arbeit, *Auslandische Arbeitsnehmer*; BMA-HAS: Bundesministerium für Arbeit, *Hauptergebnisse der Arbeits- und Sozialstatistik*, for 1954–84; SJ-BRD: Bundesrepublik Deutschland, *Statistisches Jahrbuch für die Bundesrepublik Deutschland*, for 1950–84; JG: Sachverständigenrat

Jahresgutachten, for 1970–1, 1984–5; SB: Bundesrepublik Deutschland, Statistisches Bundesamt, *Bevölkerung und Kultur – Reihe 2*, for 1975.

United States. AFL-CIO/BCR: AFL-CIO, *Biannual Convention Reports*; BUSG: *Budget of the U.S. Government*; ETRP: U.S. President, *The Employment and Training Report of the President*, for 1962 –80; ECRP: U.S. President, *The Economic Report of the President*, for 1984–5; DOL-EHE: U.S. Department of Labor *Employment, Hours and Earnings: U.S. 1909–1984 Volume II*; DOL-HLS: U.S. Department of Labor *U.S. Handbook of Labor Statistics*; DOL-MLR: U.S. Department of Labor, *Monthly Labor Review*; INS: U.S. Immigration and Naturalization Service, *1981 Annual Report*; UAW-AAR: UAW, *Annual Audit Reports*.

General sources. OECD-NAS: OECD, *National Accounts Statistics, Main Aggregates*, for 1960–85; OECD-LFS: OECD, *Labour Force Statistics*; OECD-LMP: OECD, *Labour Market Policies for the 1990s*.

Variable construction

Active labor market policy expenditures. ALMP expenditures are the sum of job-placement, job-retraining, and job-creation programs, and they were constructed from national sources in all three countries.

Sweden. Figures were taken from Johannesson (1989), Johannesson and Persson-Tanimura (1978), and Ohman (1970) but were supplemented from the annual AMS-V reports for all years.

Federal Republic of Germany. BAVAV-AN and BAA-AN for most years, BMA-HAS for 1965–67, and Wittich (1966) to clarify the early 1950s.

United States. ALMP expenditures are scattered: ETRP for most data after 1962, an "internal DOL budget office report" for the 1970s, and BUSG for USES, HEW, Office of Economic Opportunity, and other expenditures. All U.S. expenditures were converted to calendar years.

18 OECD Countries.

ALMP data for 1987 were taken from OECD (1990).

Government Employment. The government employment figures were divided by the total civilian labor force.

Sweden. Total of AMS permanent employees comes from AMS-V. Other government employees were taken from Flora (1983) and supplemented by SAS.

Federal Republic of Germany. Total BAA permanent employees: BAA-

GB and BAVAV-GB. Other government employees were taken from Flora (1983) and supplemented by the SJ-BRD.

United States. USES federal and state national staff years (i.e., full-time employee equivalents) were obtained from an "internal DOL budget department memorandum." Total federal, as well as state and local government, employment were taken from the DOL-EHE.

Political variables. The Left legislative variable is a percentage derived from party seats divided by total members, and the Left executive measures consist of dummy variables. The figures for Sweden and Germany with midyear election dates and representatives who crossed over to other parties are adjusted to calendar years (Burkett 1975, Conradt 1978).

Sweden. Left-party power in the chancellorship was coded 1 when the SAP was in power and 0 otherwise. Party power in the Riksdag was taken from Rose and Mackie (1990).

Federal Republic of Germany. Left party power in the chancellorship was coded 1 when the SPD was in power and 0 otherwise. Party power in the Bundestag was taken from the SJ-BRD and Smith (1979).

United States. Left presidential party power was coded 1 for a Democratic president and 0 for a Republican. Left-party power in the legislature is measured separately for each branch. Three parties are delineated: Mainstream Democrats, Republicans, and southern Democrats – Ala., Fla., Ga., Ky., La., Miss., N.C., Okla., S.C., Tenn., Tex., and Va. (Shelley 1986). An index of Left-party legislative power was constructed from House and Senate party power by standardizing each variable.

Trade unions. Trade union power consists of union membership figures divided by the civilian labor force.

Sweden. Trade union power is LO and TCO membership, which is taken from SAS.

Federal Republic of Germany. Trade union power is DGB membership, which is taken from the SJ-BRD.

United States. Trade union political power consists of AFL-CIO membership, which is taken from the AFL-CIO/BCR. Union expenditure figures were also taken from UAW-AAR and AFL-CIO/BCR.

Social movement variables. Protest demonstrations and riots for all three countries were taken from Taylor and Hudson (1975) and Taylor and Jodice (1983). Each variable constitutes frequency and not seriousness or participation.

Sweden: Days lost in strikes and lockouts are from SAS.

Federal Republic of Germany. Days lost in strikes and lockouts are from SJ-BRD.

United States. Strikes as days idle as a percentage of estimated working time are from the DOL-MLR.

Industrial structure. The distribution of the labor force in manufacturing and other sectors is divided by the civilian labor force.

Sweden. The source is SAS.

Federal Republic of Germany. The sources are the BAA-GB and BAVAV-GB.

United States. The source is ETRP.

Economic variables. GNP at factor cost, computed from from the OECD-NAS, was deflated and divided by the population for GNP per capita. Economic growth is the yearly rate of change in GNP at factor cost.

Sweden: Figures for unemployment and inflation rates with 1970 as the base year are from SAS. Vacancy rates were taken from AMS-PS.

Federal Republic of Germany. Figures for unemployment and inflation rates with 1970 as the base year are from JG.

United States. Unemployment and inflation rates are from ECRP.

Demographic variables

Sweden. Figures for total population, labor force participation rates, guest workers, and civilian labor force are from SAS. The percentages of the population in various age groups and for immigrants come from SAS.

Federal Republic of Germany. The total West German population and civilian labor force is from the BMA-HAS. The labor force participation rates are from JG. The female labor force rate was calculated from BMA-HAS and, for 1950–1 and 1983, from SJ-BRD. The age groups of the population were calculated from SJ-BRD and SB. Guest worker figures in the labor force come from BAA-AA and SJ-BRD, with those for 1950–3 estimated from immigration figures for those countries that provided guest workers later.

United States. Population and labor force participation rates – total, female, and male – come from ECRP. The civilian labor force figures by age and totals come from DOL-HLS. Total immigration divided by population was taken from the INS.

NOTES

1. These points are widely supported, and one can look to Wilensky (1975, 1976), O'Connor and Brym (1988), and Pampel and Williamson (1988) for explanations.

2. The conservative regime type was not significant ($r = .17$), but that in itself shows that these countries are different from the other two. This regime type includes the vastly different ALMP programs of Germany and Austria.
3. The regime variable was calculated from the scores provided by Esping-Andersen on his corporatism, etatism, means-test, private pension, private health, average universalism, and average benefit equality variables (1990, p. 71). However, I found his scoring to be somewhat arbitrary (pp. 74, 77–78), so I standardized each variable and added the scores. As a result, my scores tend to range from −1.0 to +1.0, while his range from 0 to 8 or 0 to 12. The resulting differences between the correlations, however, are minor. See Charles Ragin (chapter 13, this volume) for a further discussion of Esping-Andersen's regime types.
4. On each one of these theories, see Esping-Andersen and van Kersbergen (1992), Pampel and Williamson (1988), Devine (1985), Mintz and Hicks (1984), Griffin, Devine, and Wallace (1983), Hage and Hanneman (1980), Peters and Klingman (1978), Cameron (1978), and Tarschys (1975).
5. The tremendous rise in female labor force participation rates has come from married women because single women have always had a high labor force participation rate. Further, most of the rise in the married women rates comes from the middle and upper classes, since lower-class (especially black) married women have also had relatively high labor force participation rates.
6. Labor market crowding may be isolated in specific segments. For instance, the West German baby boom swelled enrollments in higher education and by the late 1970 caused severe crowding in public bureaucracy and other professional labor markets. The increased number of college-educated workers diverted attention from ALMP, which is usually aimed at secondary labor markets and blue-collar rather than white-collar occupations.
7. This hypothesis applies even though most illegal immigrants and guest workers do not take jobs from native workers. Employers reorient future investment and reallocate tasks in the face of immigration and the possibilities of cheap labor. This often pressures native men and women in the secondary sector to seek better work or else be subject to downward wage pressures. The fact is that native Germans were on the automobile assembly lines in the 1950s, and now many guest workers are in those jobs, but few if any guest workers took jobs away from unionized German workers. Though similar examples are not as dramatic in the U.S. automobile industry, displacement does occur in the secondary labor market. However, the pressure index represents pressure, not displacement. "Pressure" refers to the allocation of work and investment decisions. "Displacement" refers to taking jobs directly from natives, a rather small phenomenon that I am not addressing.
8. On the socioeconomic versus political variable debate, see Lewis-Beck (1977), Dye (1981), Hibbs (1977), Hibbs, River, and Vasilatos (1982), Hibbs and Vasilatos (1981), and Beck (1982).
9. Protests against unemployment in West Germany were more evident in strikes like the 35-hour strike in 1982. Ethnic conflict and discrimination involving guest workers was most often protested through wildcat strikes (Kirchlechner 1978). This analysis, however, does not include extensive protests against unemployment subsequent to German reunification.
10. The old labor representatives favoring tripartite bargaining conflicted with

the more social-movement-oriented JUSOs, who were less favorable to unemployment initiatives. However, JUSOs played a subordinate role here to the churches. On the whole the JUSOs could be said to put ALMP much lower on their list of political objectives in comparison with the trade union representatives.

11. From my own correlations, etatism (the expenditures on pensions for public employees in 1980) and the size of the bureaucracy (bureaucratic employees divided by the total labor force in 1977) are negatively correlated (Lindblom 1980; Jackson 1982, pp. 13, 121–72; Gruber 1987, pp. 85–120; and Esping-Andersen 1990). This provides some evidence for elite and common bureaucratic systems. Etatism also provides part of the definition of conservative welfare regimes.
12. ALMP data on Sweden have been collected by Furåker and Johansson (1990) from 1970 to 1987, but they do not perform a causal analysis. Johannesson (1989), and Johannesson and Persson-Tanimura (1978) collect data on ALMP, but they are more interested in evaluation research than expenditure analysis. As yet, no quantitative causal analysis has appeared on Sweden. A number of scholars have collected ALMP data on West Germany: Wittich (1966) for 1950–61, Hardes (1983) for 1970–80, Soldwedel (1984) for 1972–80, and Schmid, Reissert, and Brache (1992) for 1973–88. However, none of these data sets cover more than 15 years. In the United States, Gottschalk (1983) looks at data for 1964–83 but does not do correlations. Devine (1985, p. 151) collects "social consumption expenditures" for 1947–77 but includes health, housing, and urban renewal expenditures in with ALMP.
13. A number of mixed programs existed in the United States: CETA-III nationally administered migrant and Native Indian programs, the Work Incentive Program, the Private Sector Initiative Program, CETA-III nationally administered special job training, and private sector hiring programs. These combined programs were divided into job-placement, job-training, and job creation programs.
14. Vacancies are not entirely exogenous; however, they are much more exogenous than is unemployment. Obviously, the more job placement and training the state engages in, the more likely vacancies are going to be filled. However, the Swedish government has been accused of swelling the job-training rolls with the unemployed. This effectively reduces unemployment, but it would have little or no impact on vacancies registered by employers. In essence, the state can more easily tamper with unemployment as a supply factor than with vacancies as a demand factor. For this reason, vacancies make a much less endogenous variable than does unemployment.
15. As a Republican president, Richard Nixon spent large amounts of money on social welfare programs by introducing automatic "cost-of-living adjustments." A Democratic Congress pressed for large amounts of ALMP at the same time over Nixon's opposition. Earlier Democratic presidents such as Truman and Kennedy spent little on ALMP, and even Lyndon Johnson's War on Poverty program had only small amounts of labor market policy (Janoski 1990).
16. I used AUTOREG in the SAS time-series package to control *n*-order autocorrelation. See Chapter 2 for more details on autocorrelation and methods to correct for it.

17. See Chapter 2 for a discussion of using a lagged dependent variable in order to control for autocorrelation.
18. This last point is not trivial. Bureaucracies must create programs, write regulations, hire new employees, and then finally start the actual program. This takes time.
19. Some differences in the length of lags are due to the nature of the dependent variables. For instance, wage–capital ratios are rather immediate phenomena, i.e., they are paid during the same year in which they occur; they do not have two- to four-year gestation periods. Even public assistance expenditures are much more responsive to needs than is ALMP because they are the last line of defense. However, ALMP is a more discretionary policy and is more likely to have longer lags.
20. Formal polynomial or Almon lags were constructed for the political variables, and geometrically declining or Koyck lags were attempted for economic variables. Although these lags support my lag theory, they were not statistically significant.
21. In order to detect disqualifying multicollinearity, the following rules of thumb were used: (1) the correlation between independent variables should not be more than the correlation of each independent variable with the dependent variable, except when intercorrelations between independent variables fall below .70; (2) when intercorrelations are below .70 but are higher than the direct correlation with the dependent variable, these independent variables may be included if the results indicate that β's are stable. Instability will be detected by sign reversals, large significance-level fluctuations, and drastic changes in the values of β's. If these independent variables exhibit β stability, they will be guardedly accepted (Achen 1982, Pindyck and Rubinfeld 1981).
22. The vacancy rate is a demand measure, while the unemployment rate is a supply measure. The more vacancies a country has, the less unemployment it should suffer. Consequently, both variables represent employment needs, but that need is represented by a negative correlation between vacancy rates and ALMP/GNP spending and a positive correlation between unemployment rates and ALMP/GNP spending.
23. In the United States, two bureaucratic variables were also strong with ALMP, but they come in time order before politics and the labor market. Further, they are both multicollinear with the labor market pressure index and with each other. State and local government employment as a percentage of civilian employment and private service-sector employment as a percentage of civilian employment were impossible to include in the same equation. The differences in variance explained between using these variables in place of the labor market pressure index were not large, but they still performed less well. These variables are not a factor in Germany because of misplaced causal order. In a causal order test with U.S. variables, ALMP/GNP expenditures lagged for two years explain only 15 percent of the variance in local and city government employment, while local and city government employment lagged for two years explains 45 percent of the variance in ALMP/GNP spending. Thus, the bureaucracy can be considered a cause of ALMP in the United States. However, in Germany ALMP/GNP expenditures lagged for two years explains 48 percent of the variance in bureaucracy, while the bureaucracy measure lagged for two years explains

only 19 percent of the variance in ALMP/GNP spending. Consequently, the U.S. bureaucracy causes ALMP to grow, but the reverse is true in Germany (Granger 1969; Freeman 1983).

24. Another Left-party power variable combining a measure of Senate and House legislative power with the proportion of Democrats controlling the House Rules Committee – a strategic committee for social legislation – could not be used because it is too highly correlated with labor market pressure index. Nevertheless, this revised Left variable would have more strongly demonstrated the fragmentation of the U.S. political process in scattering political power within the legislature.
25. Setting unemployment in alternate years to zero, we obtain contradictory correlations. Externally induced unemployment (1974–81) is positively correlated with ALMP/GNP spending (r = .80), while internally induced unemployment (1950–73 and 1982–4) is negatively correlated (r = –.87).

REFERENCES

Achen, Christopher. 1982. *Interpreting and Using Regression.* Newbury Park, Calif.: Sage.

Albritton, Robert. 1979. "Social Amelioration Through Mass Insurgency." *American Political Science Review* 73:1003–12.

Alt, James. 1985. "Political Parties, World Demand, and Unemployment." *American Political Science Review* 79:1016–40.

Arbetsmarknadsverket (AMS). 1949–89. *Arbetsmarknaden, 1948(–89): Verksamhetsberättelse.* Solna: AMS.

1983. *Arbetsmarknadsstatistik: Platsstatistiken, 1902–1982.* Argång 31. Solna: AMS.

AFL-CIO. 1950–84. *Biannual Convention Report.* Washington, D.C.: AFL-CIO.

Beck, Nathaniel. 1982. "Parties, Administration, and American Macroeconomic Outcomes." *American Political Science Review* 76:83–93.

Brown, Alice, and Desmond King. 1988. "Economic Change and Labour Market Policy: Corporatist and Dualist Tendencies in Britain and Sweden." *West European Politics* 11(3):75–91.

Bruche, Gert, and Bernd Reissert. 1985. *Die Finanzierung der Arbeitspolitik – System, Effectivität, Reformansatze.* Frankfurt: Campus.

Bundesanstalt für Arbeit (BAA). 1969–84. *Amtliche Nachrichten der Bundesanstalt für Arbeit – Jahreszahlen.* Nuremberg: BAA.

1969–84. *Geschaftsbericht.* Nuremberg: BAA.

1981. *Auslandische Arbeitnehmer.* Nuremberg: BAA.

Bundesanstalt für Arbeitsvermittlung und Arbeitslosenversicherung (BAVAV). 1954–68. *Amtliche Nachrichten der Bundesanstalt für Arbeitsvermittlung und Arbeitslosenversicherung.* Nuremberg: BAVAV.

1954–68. *Geschaftsbericht.* Nuremberg: BAVAV.

Bundesministerium für Arbeit. 1954–84. *Hauptergebnisse der Arbeits- und Sozialstatistik.* Bonn: Bundesminister für Arbeit und Sozialordnung.

Bunderepublik Deutschland. 1950–85. *Statistisches Jahrbuch für die Bundesrepublik Deutschland.* Stuttgart: Kohlhammer.

1975. *Bevölkerung und Kultur – Reihe 2.* Mannheim: Statistisches Bundesamt.

Burkett, Tony. 1975. *Parties and Elections in West Germany.* London: C. Hurst.

Cameron, David. 1978. "The Expansion of Public Economy." *American Political Science Review* 72:1243–61.

Conradt, David. 1978. *The German Polity*. New York: Longman.

Cook, Thomas, and Donald Campbell. 1979. *Quasi-Experimentation: Design and Analysis Issues for Field Settings*. Chicago: Rand McNally.

Devine, Joel. 1985. "State and State Expenditures." *American Sociological Review* 50:150–65.

Dineen, Donal. 1984. "Anti-Unemployment Policies in Ireland Since 1970." In Jeremy Richardson and Roger Henning (eds.), *Unemployment: Policy Responses of Western Democracies*, pp. 238–76. Newbury Park, Calif.: Sage.

Dye, Thomas. 1981. *Understanding Public Policy*. New York: Prentice-Hall.

Esping-Andersen, Gøsta. 1990. *The Three Worlds of Welfare Capitalism* Princeton, N.J.: Princeton University Press.

Esping-Andersen, Gøsta, and Kees van Kersbergen. 1992. "Contemporary Research on Social Democracy." *Annual Review of Sociology* 18:187–208.

Finland. 1966–82. *Finnish Statistical Yearbook*. Helsinki: Central Statistical Office.

Flora, Peter. 1983. *State, Economy and Society*. Chicago: St. James.

Freeman, John. 1983. "Granger Causality and the Times Series Analysis of Political Relationships." *American Journal of Political Science* 27:327–58.

Furåker, Bengt, and Lief Johansson. 1990. "Unemployment and Labour Market Policies in the Scandinavian Countries." *Acta Sociologica* 33(2):141–64.

Gottschalk, Peter. 1983. "U.S. Labor Market Policies Since the 1960s." Madison, University of Wisconsin Institute for Research on Poverty Discussion Paper 730–83.

Gourevitch, Peter. 1986. *Politics in Hard Times* Ithaca, N.Y.: Cornell University Press.

Granger, C. W. 1969. "Investigating Causal Relations by Econometric Models and Cross-Spectral Methods." *Econometrica* 37:424–38.

Griffin, Larry, Joel Devine, and Michael Wallace. 1983. "On the Economic and Political Determinants of Welfare Spending in the Post-WWII Era." *Politics and Society* 12:331–72.

Gruber, Judy. 1987. *Controlling Bureaucracies: Dilemmas in Democratic Governance*. Berkeley: University of California Press.

Hage, Jerald, and Robert Hanneman. 1980. "The Growth of the Welfare State in Britain, France, Germany and Italy." *Comparative Social Research* 3:45–70.

Hall, Peter. 1986. *Governing the Economy*. New York: Oxford University Press.

Hardes, Heinz-Dieter. 1983. "Ausgaben für operative Leistungen der Arbeitsmarktpolitik." *Schriften des Vereins für Sozialpolitik* 133(I):45–87.

Heclo, Hugh, and Henrik Madsen. 1987. *Policy and Politics in Sweden: Principled Pragmatism*. Philadelphia, Pa.: Temple University Press.

Hibbs, Douglas. 1977. "Political Parties and Macroeconomic Policy." *American Political Science Review* 71:1467–87.

Hibbs, Douglas, R. Douglas Rivers, and Nicholas Vasilatos. 1982. "On the Demand for Economic Outcomes." *Journal of Politics* 44:426–62.

Hibbs, Douglas, and Nicholas Vasilatos. 1981. "Macroeconomic Performance and Mass Political Support in the United States and Great Britain." In D. Hibbs and H. Fassbender (eds.), *Contemporary Political Economy*, pp. 31–48. Amsterdam: North Holland.

Hicks, Alexander. 1984. "Elections, Keynes, Bureaucracy and Class." *American Sociological Review* 49:145–82.

Hicks, Alexander, and Duane Swank. 1984. "On the Political Economy of Welfare Expansion." *Comparative Political Studies* 17:81–119.

Isaac, Larry, and William Kelly. 1981. "Racial Insurgency, the State and Welfare Expansion." *American Journal of Sociology* 86:1348–96.

Jackson, P. M. 1982. *The Political Economy of Bureaucracy*. Oxford: Philip Alan.

Janoski, Thomas. 1990. *The Political Economy of Unemployment: Active Labor Market Policy in the United States and West Germany*. Berkeley: University of California Press.

Jennings, Edward. 1983. "Racial Insurgency, the State and Welfare Expansion." *American Journal of Sociology* 88:1220–36.

Johannesson, Jan. 1989. "On the Composition and Outcome of Swedish Labour Market Policy, 1970–1989." EFA-Delegation for Labour Market Policy Research. Stockholm: Swedish Government Printing Office.

Johannesson, Jan, and Inga Persson-Tanimura. 1978. "Labour Market Policy in Transition: Studies About the Effects of Labour Market Policy." EFA-Delegation for Labour Market Policy Research. Stockholm: Regeringskansliets Offsetcentral.

Jorgensen, Henning, and Jens Lind. 1987. "Decentralized Welfare Capitalism: The Case of Employment and Industrial Policies" *Acta Sociologica* 30(3–4):313–37.

Kirchlechner, Berndt. 1978. "New Demands or the Demands of New Groups?" In C. Crouch and A. Pizzorno, *The Resurgence of Class Conflict*, pp. 161–76. London: Macmillan Press.

Lewis-Beck, Michael. 1977. "The Relative Importance of Socioeconomic and Political Variables for Public Policy." *American Political Science Review* 71:559–66.

Lindbeck, Assar. 1988. *The Insider–Outsider Theory of Employment and Unemployment*. Cambridge, Mass.: MIT Press.

Lindblom, Charles. 1980. *The Policy Making Process*, 2d ed. Englewood Cliffs, N.J.: Prentice-Hall.

LO. 1948–90. *Annual Reports*. Stockholm: LO.

Martin, Andrew. 1985. "Wages, Profits and Investment in Sweden." In Leon Lindberg and Charles Maier (eds.), *The Politics of Inflation and Economic Stagnation*, pp. 403–66. Washington, D.C.: Brookings Institution.

McCleary, Richard, and Richard Hay. 1980. *Applied Time-Series Analysis for the Social Sciences*. Newbury Park, Calif.: Sage.

Meidner, Rudolph. 1948. "Lönepolitikens dilemma vid full sysselsättning." *Tiden* 9:464–70.

Mintz, Alex, and Alexander Hicks. 1984. "Military Expenditures in the U.S., 1949 to 1976." *American Journal of Sociology* 90:411–17.

Mushaben, Joyce. 1985. "Cycles of Peace Protest in West Germany: Experiences from Three Decades." *West European Politics* 8:24–40.

Nolan, Mary, and Charles Sabel. 1982. "Class Conflict and the Social Democratic Reform Cycle in Germany." *Political Power and Social Theory* 3:145–73.

O'Connor, Julia, and Robert Brym. 1988. "Public Welfare Expenditure in OECD Countries: Towards a Reconciliation of Inconsistent Findings." *British Journal of Sociology* 39:47–68.

Ohman, Berndt. 1970. "Arbetsmarknadspolitikens utveckling, 1948–1969". *Meddelanden från Utredningsbryån OECD* (17):1–44. (Stockholm: AMS.)
1960–89. *Labor Force Statistics*. Paris: OECD.
1960–89. *National Accounts Statistics, Main Aggregates*. Paris: OECD.
1990. *Labour Market Policies for the 1990s*. Paris: OECD.
Orfield, Gary. 1975. *Congressional Power*. New York: Harcourt Brace Jovanovich.
Pampel, Fred, and John Williamson. 1988. "Welfare Spending in Advanced Industrialized Democracies, 1950–1980." *American Journal of Sociology* 93:1424–56.
Peters, Guy, and David Klingman. 1978. "Patterns of Expenditure Development in Sweden, Norway, and Denmark." *British Journal of Political Science* 7:387–412.
Pettersen, Per Arnt. 1976. "Parliamentary Attitudes Towards Labor Market Policies." *European Journal of Political Research* 4:399–420.
Pindyck, Robert, and Daniel Rubinfeld. 1981. *Econometric Models and Economic Forecasts*, 2d ed. New York: McGraw-Hill.
Piven, Frances Fox, and Richard Cloward. 1971. *Regulating the Poor*. New York: Pantheon.
Rehn, Gosta. 1948. "Ekonomisk politik vid full sysselsättning." *Tiden* 3:135–42.
Rose, Richard, and Thomas Mackie. 1990. *International Almanac or Electoral History*. 3d ed. London: Macmillan.
Sachverständigenrat. 1970–1. *Jahresgutachten: Konjunktur im Umbruch – Risken und Chancen*. Stuttgart: Kohlhammer.
1984–5. *Jahresgutachten: Chancen für einen langen Aufschwung*. Stuttgart: Kohlhammer.
Schmid, Günther, Bernd Reissert, and Gert Brache. 1992. *Unemployment Insurance and Active Labor Market Policy*. Detroit: Wayne State University Press.
SAS. 1982. *SAS/ETS Users Guide: Econometric and Time-Series Library*. Cary, N.C.: SAS.
Shelley, Mack. 1983. *The Permanent Majority*. University: University of Alabama Press.
Shorter, Edward, and Charles Tilly. 1974. *Strikes in France, 1830–1968*. Cambridge University Press.
Skocpol, Theda, and Ann Orloff. 1986. "Explaining the Origins of Welfare States." *In* S. Lindenberg, J. Coleman, and S. Nowak (eds.), *Approaches to Social Theory*, pp. 229–54. New York: Russell Sage Foundation.
Smith, Gordon. 1979. *Democracy in Western Germany*. New York: Holmes Meier.
Soldwedel, Rüdiger. 1984. *Mehr Markt am Arbeitsmarkt*. Munich: Philosophia Verlag.
Statistiska Centralbryån. 1950–90. *Statisktisk Arsbok för Sverige*. Stockholm: Statistiska Centralbryån.
Tarschys, Daniel. 1975. "The Growth of Public Expenditures." *Scandinavian Political Studies* 2:9–31.
Taylor, Charles, and Michael Hudson. 1975. *Political and Social Indicators*. New Haven, Conn.: Yale University Press.
Taylor, Charles, and David Jodice. 1983. *Political and Social Indicators*. New Haven, Conn.: Yale University Press.

Therborn, Goran. 1986. *Why Some Peoples Are More Unemployed than Others*. London: Verso.
United Autoworkers (UAW). 1948–88. *Annual Audit Reports*. Detroit: UAW.
U.S. Department of Labor. 1970–85. *Monthly Labor Review*. Washington, D.C.: GPO.
1980. *U.S. Handbook of Labor Statistics*. Washington, D.C.: GPO.
1985. *Employment, Hours and Earnings: U.S. 1909–1984*. Bulletin 1312–12, Washington, D.C.: GPO.
U.S. Government. 1950–82. *Budget of the United States Government*. Washington, D.C.: GPO.
U.S. Immigration and Naturalization Service. 1982. *1981 Annual Report*. Washington, D.C.: GPO.
U.S. President. 1962–82. *The Employment and Training Report of the President* (ETRP). Washington, D.C.: GPO.
1984–85. *The Economic Report of the President*. Washington, D.C.: GPO.
Wildavsky, Aaron. 1979. *The Politics of the Budgetary Process*, 3d ed. Boston: Little, Brown.
Wilensky, Harold. 1975. *The Welfare State and Equality*. Berkeley: University of California Press.
1976. *The New Corporatism: Centralization and the Welfare State*. Newbury Park, Calif.: Sage.
Wilson, Graham. 1979. *Unions in American National Politics*. New York: St. Martin's.
Wittich, Günther. 1966. "The German Road to Full Employment." Ph.D. diss. University of California, Berkeley.

4

Quality of quantity in comparative/historical analysis: temporally changing wage labor regimes in the United States and Sweden

LARRY W. ISAAC, SUSAN M. CARLSON,
AND MARY P. MATHIS

Comparative/historical social inquiry is enjoying a renaissance (Sztompka 1986; McDonald in press) signified in the reevaluation and reform of metatheoretical, strategic, and methodological practices. Although not always explicit, there is a growing awareness that comparative/historical inquiry could be improved by creative attempts to bridge the gulf between intensive-qualitative, case-centered research and extensive-quantitative, variable-based analysis. Ragin (1987), a pioneer of one particularly creative bridging strategy, has argued that "new directions in comparative research over the next several decades will involve greater attention to the gulf between intensive and extensive research and more creative effort to bridge the gulf" (Ragin 1989, p. 61). Following Ragin's forecast while recognizing limitations of his bridging strategy for the kind of research question addressed here (Griffin et al. 1991), we propose an alternative – an "intensive comparative/historical time-series" approach. We argue that this strategy (1) is capable of spanning the intensive–extensive gulf, (2) allows for changing qualitative features of quantitative relations, (3) increases the prospects for constructing historically contingent causality (Abbott 1990, 1991), and (4) can accommodate both internal and external comparison (Janoski 1991). Following

Earlier versions of this paper were presented in April 1991 at "The New Compass of the Comparativist" conference at Duke University and in November 1991 at the annual meeting of the Social Science History Association, New Orleans. For useful comments on these earlier drafts, we thank Larry Griffin, Alex Hicks, Tom Janoski, Jill Quadagno, Charles Ragin, and Rick Rubinson. This research was supported, in part, by a grant to the senior author from the American Sociological Association/National Science Foundation "Advancement of the Discipline Fund."

brief discussion of the gulf and the foundations of our bridging strategy, we illustrate this approach in a comparative/historical analysis of U.S. and Swedish wage labor regimes.

THE GULF: INTENSIVE-QUALITATIVE VERSUS EXTENSIVE-QUANTITATIVE STRATEGIES

Comparative/historical inquiry currently follows two primary paths (cf. Rubinson 1977; Bach 1977; Treiman 1977; Burawoy 1977). More than just alternatives, these two are often characterized as alien to one another, separated by a substantial philosophical and practical gulf. This is evident in the basic composition of the intensive and extensive strategies of comparative/historical analysis, which include the following bifurcated elements (see e.g., Abrams 1982; Sayer 1984; Ragin 1987; Abbott 1988; Isaac and Leicht 1992): (1) *empirical organization*: case-centered versus variable-centered; (2) *research style*: qualitative-historical (e.g., narrative focused) versus quantitative-ahistorical (e.g., cross-sectional, conventional time series, pooled cross-sectional/time-series); (3) *mapping goal*: holistic configurations across case time versus variables over time within or between cases; (4) *mapping emphasis*: internal process or event-sequence of substantial relations versus external quantitative relations reduced to a summary-singular point estimate; (5) *kind of outcome*: changing qualitative outcome (magnitudes typically deemphasized) versus changing quantitative outcome (qualitative change typically ignored); (6) *type of causality*: complex conjunctural determination versus linear, additive "effects" of a single variable or sum of variables; (7) *features of causality*: temporally heterogeneous, path/sequence-dependent with the possibility of multiple paths to a single outcome versus temporally homogeneous with event sequence and path conditions typically ignored; (8) *treatment of "deviant" cases*: centrally theorized versus eliminated or stabilized for purposes of generality, tractability, and "fit" of a homogeneous model; (9) *dominant rhetoric*: "close presentational" narrative versus narrative of "perspective."

Focusing exclusively on comparative-historical designs – that is, those containing both explicit time–space dimensions – we identify three major strategies spanning the extensive–intensive continuum. First, there is a *temporally and spatially extensive* approach perhaps best represented in the conventional pooled cross-sectional/ time-series design (see Hannan and Young 1977; Stimson 1985). This strategy accomplishes a generalization of the conventional extensive time-series and cross-sectional analyses: a general set of parameter estimates linking independent to dependent variables are typically assumed to be constant or homogeneous through extensive time–space dimensions (see e.g., Pampel and

Williamson 1988; Korpi 1989). Consequently, time is reduced to space (cf. Lukacs 1923/1971), and relational magnitudes between variables are emphasized rather than the historical processes that gave rise to those quantitative relationships. For many purposes in sociohistorical inquiry, such ("pooled") generalization lacks sufficient concern with historicity in theory and/or model building (see Hannan and Young 1977, pp. 58–9). In a sense, "regressions in time and space" (Stimson 1985) end up repressing the content of time and space.

Second and at the other end of the continuum, we can locate a *temporally and spatially intensive* approach found in some multiple case study designs. The typical analytic emphasis is on cross-time, cross-space qualitative conjunctural change in historical processes, rather than on magnitudes of covarying relations between variables (e.g., Burawoy 1983; Stephens 1989). This intensive, qualitative, case-centered strategy has the virtue of highlighting specificity and event process. Often such strategies are more successful than others in theoretically appropriating history instead of presupposing a division (as theory–fact separation) leading to an adjudicative confrontation between theory as explanation and history as data. More so than extensive designs, this intensive approach centers human agency in a narrative representation of historical processes and qualitative change in social relations. The primary weakness of this strategy is its neglect of relations between quantitative variables in comparative (time–space) perspective.

Finally, there is a third approach that might be termed a *temporally extensive/cross-space comparative* strategy, which can be located between the aforementioned extensive and intensive strategies. A typical study in this genre employs conventional extensive time-series analysis procedure to compare models across several separate spatial units (e.g., countries). This design yields temporally constant ahistorical parameter estimates that may be compared across space (e.g., Snyder 1975; Hibbs 1987, chap. 3). However, the ability to allow cross-space specificity in parameters and theorization gives this comparative approach a definite advantage over the temporally and spatially extensive or "pooled" design.

The intensive–extensive distinction involves scope – that is, depth and breadth – as well as differential attention to historical process versus formal quantitative relations between variables. But there is more. On one side, all the elements emphasize *historical contingency*,[1] complexity, and diversity in social relations and processes of change – that is, why we should expect it; why we need to attend to it in sociohistorical theoretical inquiry; and how we might examine it. On the other side, the simplicity, generality, and ahistorical homogeneity of external form of relations among (macro) conditions and circumstances are emphasized without the internal and often hidden historical processes that produced the quantitative traces. These quantitative traces of (macro) circumstances – as outcomes (e.g., unemployment, inflation, wage rates, etc.) – are presented as static objects in most research. Attention, then, is fixed on the relations among "things" of circumstance, rather than on relations between people that gave rise to these "circumstances." Historicity of event sequence, human agency, and movement are silenced, abstracted, or emptied out. Consequently, we are left with a picture of precision accompanied by the still life that precision requires.

Focusing on the differential bases of extensive versus intensive strategies alerts us to the uneven emphases contained within the metatheory of research method and strategy – that is, the various emphases on quantity versus quality, generality versus particularity, variables versus cases, external formal relations versus internal substantial relations, structure versus agency, and outcome versus process. Moreover, recognizing these compositional bases for the two sides of the gulf is the first step toward producing a bridging strategy – an approach that will allow the integration of various strengths situated on opposite sides of the divide – that can simultaneously sustain a "rhetoric of perspective" and a "rhetoric of close presentation" (Abrams 1982).

BRIDGING THE GULF: TOWARD THE QUALITY OF QUANTITY IN COMPARATIVE/HISTORICAL INQUIRY

As one way to bridge the gulf, we propose to focus on changes in the quality of social relations as they shape and are shaped by the quantity of activity internal to them. This involves an attempt to "intensify" the treatment of historical process in the analysis of quantitative time series – the "historicization of method" in Isaac and Griffin (1989).

Time and time-series analysis

Theoretical history, relationally structured human agency, and the quality of quantity are all crucial to any bridging strategy seeking to span the extensive–intensive dualism. But the accomplishment of such a synthesis requires a greater sensitivity to time than has typically been the case in the social sciences (Abrams 1982; Adam 1990). The central thematics of intensive historical sociology demand a recognition of *sociohistorical time* (as content) internal to the logic of *ahistorical* clock time (as form). The internality of historical time leads directly to a concern with historical contingency. Theorizing historical contingency points away from exclusive concerns with the smooth continuity of history (represented in homogeneous, monolithic time-series model parameters) toward the possibility of discontinuity and turning points. The continuity that exists in history is an uneven, rugged, nonlinear continuity that resembles global geographic topography more than the smooth linear space of a billiard table. Human actors face differing historical conditions, and their action is therefore contingent and uneven in time (and space) leaving behind lumpy products or outcomes, rather than a smooth linear surface. Theoretical-historical concern with discontinuities and turning points, in turn, raises important questions about the practice of time and temporality *internal* to time-series analyses and how these might be modified operationally to avoid an exclusive reliance on ahistorical Newtonian time.[2]

The model estimation element of our proposed strategy is a variation of time-varying parameter (TVP) models discussed by Janoski and Isaac in Chapter 2, this volume. In particular, portions of the analyses that follow employ an analysis of time-varying covariance structures to examine the historicity, turning points, and trends in relations (Isaac and Griffin 1989) between unemployment, consumer price inflation, and wages. We are especially interested in how these macrosocioeconomic magnitudes move singularly and in relation to each other across time within and between policy regimes of a nation (Isaac and Leicht 1992), and in comparison to policy regimes cross-nationally. Because we are focusing on developmental sequence in changing relations and the chronological reconfiguration of regimes, we employ the "forward-moving" strategy to TV covariance analysis (Griffin and Isaac 1992).

TVP models, capable of detecting nonlinear movements or "shifts" in coefficients, highlight "unusual," "deviant," or "outlier" cases (time points – years in the present examples). Such temporal points are crucial in the historical intensification of time-ordered data analytic procedures. Serious theoretical treatment can simultaneously inform generality while yielding unique explanation (Bradshaw and Wallace 1991). Importantly, TVP models have the virtue, among others, of retaining the power of time-series techniques in examination of quantitative formal relations without necessarily purchasing a notion of "general linear reality" (Abbott 1988) in process or parameter structure (see Isaac and Leicht 1992; Janoski and Isaac, Chapter 2, this volume).

We have argued for the historical intensification of the time-series strategy because it is capable of revealing (rather than repressing) certain features of historical contingency in formal quantitative relations (i.e., the *why* of what we are proposing). We have also indicated that one possible operational basis for accomplishing this task resides in TVP models applied to time-ordered data (i.e., the *how* of what we are proposing). The question of what the resulting product might achieve, as a form of explanation, remains.

Parameter historicity and explanation

There is more involved here than merely making quantitative analysis more historical. The issue of explanation is also called into question. To state the point in boldest terms: *not only do summary-singular coefficients that are taken to be homogeneous or time invariant repress too much complexity or historicity necessary for adequate sociohistorical explanation, they do not constitute meaningful explanation in the first place.*

For purposes of elaboration, consider two cross-time variables, x_t and y_t, linked by "causal" parameter b_{yx}. Assume further that all "third" factors (sources of potential spuriousness) have been eliminated (controlled) or are otherwise nonproblematic. The b_{yx} does not constitute an explanation, but rather a quantitative parameter, which in itself may be interesting data. Even if we "elaborate" the relation by introducing sequentially connected "intervening" variables ad nauseam, we have not really explained anything because the same question can be repeatedly asked: what does this coefficient mean? What processes must occur to produce this set of relations connected by a parameter of such magnitude? (See Abell 1987.) As additional descriptive parameters (b_{yz}, s) linking intervening variables are added, the b_{yx} and/or b_{yz}, s must themselves be explained discursively in a theoretical-historical/biographical manner; that is, the coefficient magnitudes (or mappings) require a theoretical explanatory narrative – a sort of "imaginative re-enactment" to use Beer's (1963) phrase – that puts the substantive process in context and "makes sense" of it. The more we attend to issues of active movement and human agency in the making of history, the more we require a narrativity of "close presentation" (Abrams 1982).

Now further imagine that we have two theoretically interesting variables – x_{nt} and y_{nt} – measured across time (T) within two different spatial units (N). TVP models (e.g., TV covariances for simplicity) are estimated, so we have two space-specific vectors of temporally varying relations between x and y. These resulting products do not amount to explanation in any meaningful sense. Assuming that the coefficients are varying through time and across space, the question for the conventional approach is: Which one of the point estimates constitutes the correct explanation? There is no way of choosing an estimate for purposes of hypothesis testing. The picture is seemingly chaotic. However, if we accept the coefficients as another form of data to be explained, then the picture is no more chaotic than any other problem of empirical explanation. The historically contingent coefficients reveal a certain time–space topography – a potential unevenness, or lumpiness in relational magnitudes across time and space. And it is precisely this variability or lumpy historical topography that requires explanation.

How do we proceed to explain this topographical variability? Although a variety of possibilities might be imagined, we mention two for present purposes. One approach follows a theoretically based historically detailed narrative of imaginative reenactment explaining events and processes that generated the temporal–spatial contour of relations, concentrating especially on major "watershed shifts" in relations. A second possibility takes the spatially specific vector of changing relations between x and y (i.e., covariances of x and y) as dependent variables to be mapped to sets of independent variables in what might be termed a "second-order time-series model." But here, too, the second approach *without* theoretically based historical narrative would amount only to new (albeit potentially interesting) data. Whether a second-order time-series model is employed or not, theoretically/historically grounded narrative must form the substantive "guts" necessary for explanation of the historically varying quantitative relations. And no algorithm, irrespective of "labor-saving" or ingenious qualities, can substitute for this necessary theoretical labor.

In the light of such historical intensification of time-ordered data analysis, ahistorical theoretical questions that ask if variable x affects variable y are supplanted by historically focused questions: *When* (and *where*) does variable x affect variable y? How is the overall historical contour or topography of their relationship shaped or molded across time and space?

Cases versus variables? Regimes as variable-constituted cases

Recall that the intensive–extensive divide also differentiates between a case-centered and a variable-centered focus (Ragin 1991). There has been considerable discussion of the strengths and weaknesses of each (e.g., Abell 1987; Ragin 1987; Bradshaw and Wallace 1991) with several creative strategies for combining and synthesizing the two (e.g., Abell 1987; Ragin 1987). While the problems associated with any particular approach are unlikely to be resolved "once and for all" by any new "method," a specific metatheory may be more or less congenial to a given theoretical question under investigation, and hence provide greater analytic utility than other possibilities. Exactly what constitutes a case, what variables are relevant, and the like should result from theoretical premises and questions. Here we suggest that a potentially fruitful avenue for further research lies in the possibility of combining spatial case units (e.g., countries), temporal case units (e.g., chronological calendar time years), and the intersection of time–space in the notion of qualitative configurations of relations, or *regimes*. Our argument is that within the concept of regime we can merge historicity of relations (in time–space), extensive-intensive strategic characteristics with the substantial (qualitative)-formal (quantitative) relations of interest (Isaac and Leicht 1992). Our concept of regime has a dual character. It is at once a *case* – (i.e., a temporally–spatially specific form/content of relations that has a regulative coherence but is also capable of transformation by way of internal contradiction) and also a *variable* (i.e., magnitude or quantity of relations as in "parameter regime") (Quandt 1958; Isaac and Leicht 1992; or Hernes's (1976) use of "parameter structure"). It is in regime as a qualitative configuration of relations with quantitative magnitudes of relational coupling that we can begin to speak of the "quality of quantity." As quantitative relations change markedly across time and space, it may be indicative of a changing qualitative configuration of relations in event sequence and structure.

An example may be useful. The standard treatment of the unemployment–wage relation by orthodox economics – cast in the language of the "Phillips Curve" (see, e.g., Phillips 1958; Bodkin 1969; Brunner and Meltzer 1976; Neftci 1978; Geary and Kennan 1982; Bils 1985; and Sumner and Silver 1989) – conforms to the ahistorical, extensive, quantitative strategy. One of the core ideas is that an equilibrium adjustment operates – either as a long-term trade-off or a short-term adjustment – independent of or only marginally affected by the historical changes in institutional structures and/or internal contradictions of the wage relation itself over the past two centuries of capitalist development. Given this approach, the corresponding object of econometric studies is to demonstrate a time-invariant general relationship, even if the analytic interpretation might differ across studies (Boyer 1979). This tendency runs counter to theoretical-historical analyses that entertain the possibility of both *continuity* (the continuation of capitalist development, the subsumption of labor in the wage relation) and *discontinuity* (the institutionally specific and historically changing configurations that constitute wage labor regimes). (See, e.g., Aglietta 1979; Edwards 1979; Boyer 1979; Gordon, Edwards, and Reich 1982; Burawoy 1983; Davis 1986; and Esping-Andersen 1990.) Such studies point to historically changing conditions of capitalist development that are likely to produce temporally and spatially contingent rather than universal relations between unemployment and wages. The usefulness of our "intensive comparative/historical time-series" approach is that it examines relations between variables expected to vary through time and space. We take parameter variation as data to be explained via event-sequence history and political regime reconfigurations. This strategy allows for multiple points of historically specific comparison and demands a narrative of "close presentation," while maintaining the virtues of the extensive cross-space, cross-time quantitative approach with its rhetoric of "perspective." Importantly, the "making" and "unmaking" of specific kinds of regimes can be tracked temporally within a spatial unit, compared across spatial units, and examined for cross-time, cross-space synchronic movement – that is, to what extent do central characteristics comprising a regime tend to be moving in a coordinated manner across time and space? Moreover, this strategy is "open" in the sense that it does not require allegiance to a particular regime theorization as point of departure (Isaac and Leicht 1992). In addition to articulating with a variety of current theoretical developments, our bridging strategy empowers a quantitative variable-based analysis spanning extended time–space dimensions, while it preserves the most important basic properties of the intensive analytic approach. In fact, we preserve all five basic properties of the intensive analytic strategy, which Ragin (1989, pp. 69–70) convincingly argues should be preserved in any synthesis of the extensive and intensive strategies.[3]

A COMPARATIVE/HISTORICAL ILLUSTRATION: THE UNEMPLOYMENT–WAGE RELATION IN THE UNITED STATES AND SWEDISH WAGE LABOR REGIMES

To illustrate our bridging strategy, we focus on two advanced capitalist nations – the United States and Sweden – that occupy positions of maximum difference (see, e.g., Hage 1975) on central macrosocio-economic policies (see, e.g., Cameron 1978; Schott 1990). For each country, we demonstrate how unemployment, prices, wages, and their *relations* become quantitatively reconfigured within qualitatively different wage labor regimes. *As we identify changes in the topography of these various macro-socioeconomic products, we characterize the content and internal movement of the historically specific regime within capitalism – that is, the processual substance giving rise to change in quantitative contour.*

Using wage labor regimes as cases, we ask: How do certain quantitative features of these historically specific wage labor regimes configure and reconfigure institutionally as a result of internal political-economic processes? Specifically, how do historical legacies as well as current processes and events shape the level of and relations between unemployment and wages in nation-specific capitalist development? More concretely, how does the quantitative relation between surplus labor power (in the form of "official" unemployment) and real consumption wages (wage rate deflated by price increases in consumer commodities) change into and as a result of qualitative reconfigurations in the institutional complex of wage labor regimes?

United States: two twentieth-century wage labor regimes

Since the turn of the century, unemployment, inflation, and wages have shaped and been shaped by two major wage labor regimes. The first, an unstabilized, competitive-monopoly capitalist wage labor regime, spans the years from the depression of the 1890s to the depression of the 1930s. The 1930s and 1940s represent a transitional period in which U.S. wage labor was reconfigured in significant respects. The resulting institutional configuration, a military-industrial Keynesian-stabilized wage labor regime, characterizes the decades following 1950. In what follows, we present the quantitative cross-regime unemployment–wage topographies between the historical narrative documenting processes that account for special features of these specific regimes.

The unstabilized, competitive-monopoly capitalist wage labor regime. Between the 1890s and the 1930s, the United States was characterized by features of a nineteenth-century laissez-faire liberalism dominated by relatively competitive markets, on the one hand, and the rapid, if uneven, rise of large-scale corporate capitalism with some oligopolistic markets, on the other. The uneven quality in capitalist organization and market began to differentiate the wage relation. Certainly the dominant wage form was still the product of simple *direct* individual sale of labor power in which the monetary terms of exchange were elastic with both nominal and real wages and highly sensitive to the rhythms of capitalist accumulation. During this early period, U.S. labor was caught between the coercion of the market under conditions of high unemployment, on the one hand, and the forceful repression of unions and strike activity (e.g., in Homestead in 1892 and Pullman in 1894), on the other. Moreover, with the exception of the "occasional soup lines" or the "odd local workhouse," this regime provided meager, if any, relief for the unemployed. Not surprisingly, the most dramatic expression of a "labor market organized on pure principles of Sumnerian liberalism" were "the armies of tramps that periodically foraged the land in hard times" (Davis 1986, p. 106).[4]

Even as these conditions continued, other features began to develop within the wage relation. During the "progressive era," the federal government passed legislation to promote "corporate responsibility," regulate rails, reform the monetary system, and lower tariffs, while local state governments "regulated the working conditions of women and children, enacted protective laws for men laboring in dangerous occupations, established systems of workmen's compensation, and initiated programs of housing reform" (Dulles and Dubofsky 1984, p. 176). And though many small- and medium-sized firms "remained obdurately fixed in the liberal, competitive framework," most mass-production industries experimented with "Fordist-style self-organization" (Davis 1986, p. 108). Recognizing the limits of the intensive regime of accumulation created in mass-production industries – in certain ways reminiscent of limits earlier encountered in the extension of the length of the working day (Marx 1867/1967, chap. 10) – some larger firms followed the pioneering lead of Henry Ford and John D. Rockefeller (see Rockefeller 1916) deploying "satellite employee self-government through works councils and company unions" (Davis 1986, p. 109). More broadly, early U.S.-style "welfare capitalism" included experiments with life insurance schemes, health/accident/retirement benefits, stock-purchasing plans, company credit, safety and sanitation programs, along with social "scientific" personnel practices for regulating work and worker in the factory and home.

However important, this nascent (localistic) welfare capitalism was coupled with a direct repressive capitalist offensive against the labor movement that colors fundamentally any simple reform image of the era. Beginning significantly with the "open-shop drive" launched by the National Association of Manufacturers in 1903 through subsequent extension into the American Plan of the 1920s, the capitalist countermovement to labor attempted, according to Griffin, Wallace, and Rubin (1986), the following: (1) *reduce working class unity and strength* by the use of immigrant labor power as a reserve, the mechanized reorganization and serialization of the labor process, and new systems of factory administration; (2) *weaken the organizational and mobilization capacity of organized labor* via boycotting union goods, hiring labor spies and agent provocateurs, bribing union officials, blacklisting union workers, forcing workers to sign binding oaths and "yellow-dog contracts," moving production facilities from high to low union density areas, organizing national lobbies against proposed pro-labor legislation, and promoting and sponsoring trade schools and industrial education programs to increase the supply of nonunion skilled workers; (3) *decrease the efficacy of union collective action to deepen their organizational base* by furnishing employers with strikebreakers, subsidizing and policing firms engaged in open-shop battles, and using local police, state militia, and private agents – Pinkertons and Baldwin Felts – to harass, to suppress free speech, and to generally intimidate and repress with open force; and (4) *limit the structure of political "opportunities" available to the working class through processes of delegitimation and generally raising the costs of organized labor's mobilization* via propaganda disinformation tactics, and by using local, state, and federal legislation to cripple unions. Quite simply, an evaluation of labor's attempt at self-organization must be made not only within the context of "state reforms" and "industrial administration reforms" associated with welfare capitalism, but also within the context of active, open-season repression of the labor movement. And by all accounts, the state and capital successfully repressed the labor movement before the Great Depression. Capitalists enjoyed greater productivity and lower labor costs (Griffin et al. 1986), while the setback suffered by labor may be equalled only by that registered during the decade of the 1980s (cf. Piven and Cloward 1982; Davis 1986; and Goldfield 1989).

If there was an "active labor market policy" (ALMP) in this regime, it was this: the simple direct wage relation, embedded in a highly competitive labor market, where workers were disciplined *directly* by despotic paternalism on a local enterprise basis coupled with powerful capitalist repressive offensives and *indirectly* by the labor-reserve army. Moreover, this configuration of "local action" was underwritten, aided and abetted by a state that was "a very active participant in union-busting in the first third of the 20th century" (Griffin et al. 1986, p. 161). The organizational and strategic forms constituted the regulatory conditions of the wage relation, first in terms of exchange relations of labor power in the market and then as capitalist consumption of labor in the "hidden abode." As Davis put it:

> Nowhere in the world was the sale of labor-power conducted under conditions of such savage "freedom" of the market as in the non-Southern parts of the United States. . . . In this competitive stage of accumulation, where the power of employers was measured by the number of Pinkertons they could hire, wage and price depreciation cyclically produced immiseration [*sic*]. (1986, p. 106)

This direct wage/nascent welfare capitalism both succeeded and failed as a wage labor regime. Success (in the form of expanded capitalist enterprise) and failure (in the transformation to a new regime) resulted because it heightened rather than stabilized the volatility and contradictions inherent in the wage relation. It ultimately led to a transformative crisis because its design and implementation was localistic and highly privatized like the valorization process on which it fed. Regulation of both labor power in circulation and labor in production was carried out on localized micro (company) levels. The containment of labor's militant self-organization followed a direct, repressive, confrontational strategy inherent in the daily terrorism epitomized in factory and community life of company towns, while the open-shop drive and American Plan combined with welfare capitalism schemes of "productivity persuasion." During this period, welfare capitalism was fundamentally a localistic strategy to a basically global (macro) problem of synchronizing effective aggregate demand (mass consumption) with rising productive volume and capacity (mass production). Moreover, individualized enterprise Fordisms were more than offset in the aggregate by the success of the capitalist offensive against organized labor. Ironically, that very success – limiting union expansion and undercutting wage rates – worked at odds with the volume of aggregate purchasing power needed to absorb growing industrial output. This was the acute contradiction of attempts to produce an intensive mass-production wage labor regime "inside a liberal, nineteenth-century state" (Davis 1986, p. 109). These contradictory tendencies contributed in no small way to ushering in the Great Depression of the 1930s. And in many ways it was the "long New Deal" spanning the depression and war years that amounted to the "long turning point" between the first and second major wage labor regimes in the twentieth-century United States.

Next, we present a brief look at the historically contingent character of the unemployment–wage relation associated with both the unstabilized and stabilized wage labor regimes. The historical narrative forming the content of the second regime follows this discussion.

Cross-regime unemployment and wage topographies. The dominant forms assumed by the wage relation, the industrial relations system, and state generated a volatile and highly uneven topography of unemployment, commodity inflation, and wage fluctuations in the years between 1890 and the Great Depression. Before the 1930s, unemployment and prices swung up and down with staccato-like pulsation. From 1890 to the 1930s, the rate of unemployment overshadowed the rate of inflation in all but the World War I years, with deflation punctuating the period in 1894–5, 1908, 1921–2, 1927–8, and then massively in the opening of the Great Depression (see Figure 4.1).[5] Deflation during the 1930s was more than matched by the massive rise in the unemployment rate unequalled before or since.

However, by the immediate post–World War II years, certainly by 1950, the cyclical pulsation of unemployment and general price inflation had calmed. While unemployment remained enormously high (by most Western European standards) throughout the post–World War II era, cyclical frequency and amplitude were greatly reduced relative to the earlier unstable regime.

In the earlier regime, average nominal and real consumption wage rates in manufacturing moved closely together but so slowly that the standard of living for the vast proportion of the industrial working class changed little (data not shown). The annual rate of change in the real, but especially the nominal wage fluctuated widely with the business cycle, but without any pronounced trend throughout the early period

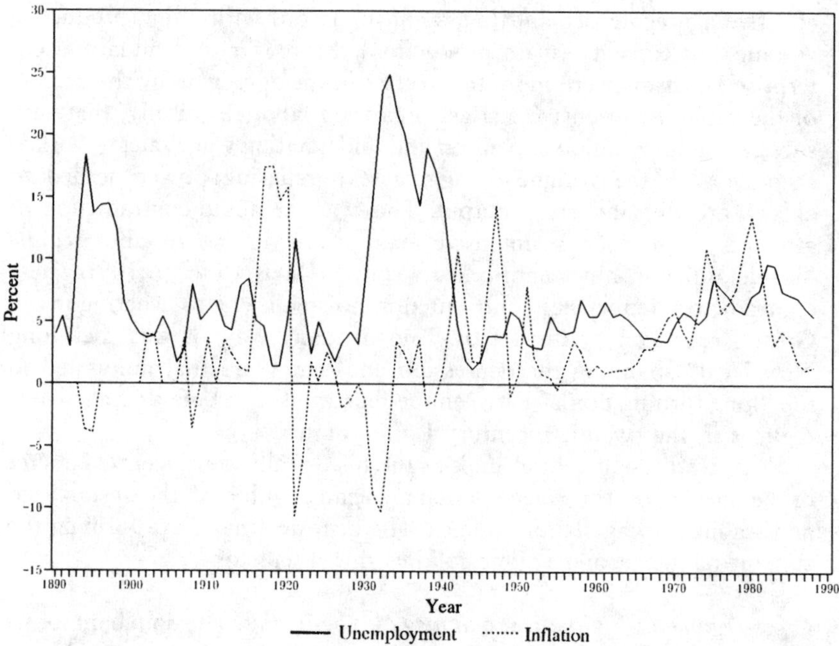

Figure 4.1. Rates of unemployment and inflation: United States, 1890-1988

(see Figure 4.2). During the first several decades of this century, "the material conditions of the great bulk of working people did not keep pace with the enormous growth in national wealth. The real income of workers in fact grew less rapidly than that of professionals, stock- and bondholders, and property owners in general" (Dulles and Dubofsky 1984, p. 176).

Most notable in the movement of manufacturing wage rates is the substantial growth in the nominal wage during the post–World War II years, while the real wage tended to plateau by the late 1960s and early 1970s. Although not pronounced in these data, there is a dip in the real wage in the 1980s corresponding to the attack on labor and the social wage during the Reagan years in particular (Piven and Cloward 1982). In the comparison of the nominal and real wage rates, the gap in the 1970s and 1980s is remarkable. The monetary base for the stabilization of the postwar regime was beginning to have an accumulative negative effect on the reproduction wage of the industrial working class during the past two decades.

Figure 4.3 charts the temporally varying covariance structure for the *relation* between unemployment and the percent change in real wages.[6]

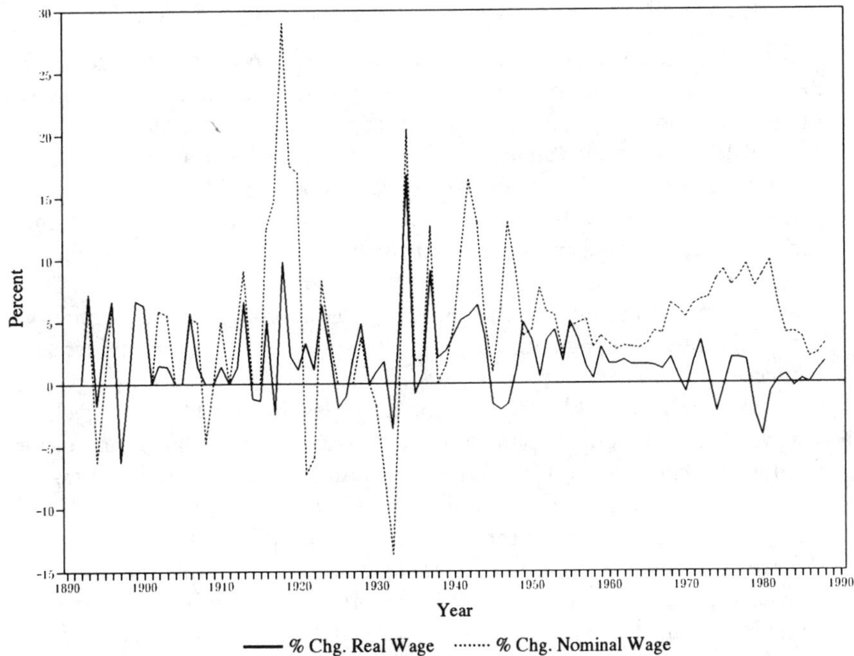

Figure 4.2. Percent change in nominal and real wage rates: United States, 1891-1988

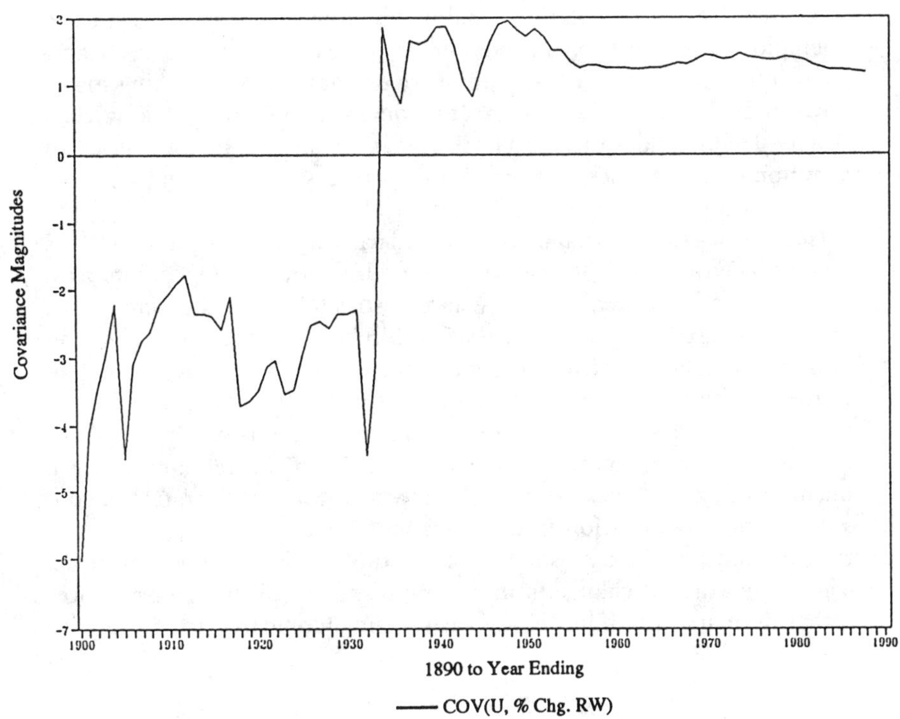

Figure 4.3. Temporally-moving covariances between unemployment and percent change in manufacturing hourly real wage rates: United States, 1890-1900, ..., 1890-1988

Most strikingly, the expansion in surplus labor power translated into declines in real consumption wage rates throughout the entire pre–Great Depression regime (see Figure 4.3). With each decline in the general level of employment, immiserization was the plight of the "industrial reserve army" as well as those who continued to receive a direct wage that consequently procured a lower standard of living. In this early regime, the industrial reserve army played its classic role: disciplining labor and containing the real wage movements of employed workers. The extreme volatility in the annual rate of change in the relation between unemployment and change in real wage rates is evident in Figure 4.3.[7]

In the early unstable regime, the vagaries of the business cycle – always a part of any capitalist regime – were particularly vicious in forging the rhythms and conditions of industrial working-class life: no social relief wage for the unemployed and, as a partial result, reduced real purchasing power for those employed. In addition to the substantial weakening of the labor movement delivered by capitalist counter-offensives, the underdevelopment of institutional complexes capable of containing surplus labor power (e.g., large standing military, long schooling duration for large proportions of the population, extended prison and other institutional confinements, pensions and retirement programs) also contributed to employers' ability to resist even nominal wage increases. With inflation usually quite low and inversely related to unemployment, most expansions in the industrial reserve army translated into reduced real consumption wages. Far from overriding major horizontal divisions and political fractionalization of the working class (Davis 1986), widespread cyclical damage was *one* major source of common class interest in an era that displayed some meaningful homogenization of wage workers (Gordon et al. 1982).

Comparing the covariance parameter structures across the pre-1930s and post–World War II years indicates dramatic turning points as a result of the New Deal-World War II restructuring of the wage labor regime. In particular, while the relationship between unemployment and inflation remains negative throughout the twentieth century, the extent of the inverse relation began to diminish shortly after 1950 and continued to follow an upward trend throughout the postwar period (not shown here). Even more striking is the shift in the relation between unemployment and the real wage. By the mid-1930s, the erratic but consistently negative relation in the unstable regime shifted into a positive relation and remained reasonably stable throughout the postwar years. The annual rate of change in the unemployment–real wage covariances reveal dramatic instability in the early regime compared to the relative "flat line" of the postwar era. What lies inside this transition to relative stabilization?

The military-industrial Keynesian-stabilized wage labor regime. The New Deal-World War II years brought about a fundamental institutional reconfiguration in the U.S. wage labor regime. Although the initial short-term consequences were anything but tranquil and stabilizing, the ultimate aim of the massive reform package of the long New Deal was stabilization of various problematic features of the capitalist social formation, especially the wage relation and its consequences. The initial phases of the New Deal brought forth a flurry of legislation including, among others, the Norris–LaGuardia Act (1932), the National Industrial Recovery Act (1933), the Wagner Act (1935), and the Social Security Act (1935). In combination, these legislative initiatives partially supplanted (at least within leading industries) the instability of the earlier despotic factory regimes (Burawoy 1983), empowered workers' organizational capacity (Davis 1986), policed workers' strike activity (McCammon 1990), and contributed some margin of income security in old age (and other forms of labor power disruption) by means of a deferred (social) wage organized primarily around the insurance principle (Quadagno 1984).

Some of this new stabilization strategy of the early New Deal was Keynesian-inspired. But, Keynesian theory and practice were never interpreted or embraced in a uniform fashion among specific class factions in single countries – including the United States (see, e.g., Collins 1981) – or across capitalist countries (see, e.g., Cameron 1978; Schott 1990). To the extent that Rooseveltian New Deal policy was Keynesian in direction, it was at best a timid variety (Weir and Skocpol 1985). Moreover, while the early New Deal programs set the stage, the institutional reconfigurations and "accords" (Bluestone and Harrison 1982; Bowles, Gordon, and Weisskopf 1983) of the immediate postwar years largely determined the shape of the wage labor regime to come. Emerging victorious and relatively unscathed from World War II, the United States fundamentally reconfigured the institutional bases for the wage relation at home and abroad. Largely between the years of 1946 and 1950, a domestic and international restructuring took place that was geared toward containing three major forms of *destabilizing threat* posed to U.S. capitalism under immediate postwar historical circumstances. In particular, policy was directed toward the *stabilization* of (1) the macroeconomy – to smooth out the wild swings in prices and unemployment, especially to counter deep downturns in the business cycle, (2) the labor movement – to regulate and channel labor organizing into "acceptable" forms of unionization that would minimize the disruptive potential of labor militancy and contribute to economic growth, and (3) the international order, especially those international circuits on which U.S. capital and economic growth seemed to depend – initially this included mostly the Atlantic circuit and the containment of movements that threatened to seal off crucial markets (Block 1980; Van der Pijl 1984).

The domestic restructuring consisted of three major pillars. First, the *capital–labor accord*, a second-phase Fordism, was initiated as large manufacturing capital's response to the labor threat during the 1930s and 1940s. This strategy was also more broadly a response to completing the production–consumption circuit on a mass scale. Conceived in the Roosevelt-Truman Labor/Management Conference of 1945, the Fordist tendency of restructuring was inaugurated concretely in the Wilson Formula in 1949 and the Treaty of Detroit a year later. In the factory regimes of leading mass-production industries (especially autos), such agreements purchased a certain "consent" from unionized labor through the progressive wage that provided an "annual improvement factor" (i.e., productivity share) of 3 percent along with a cost-of-living adjustment tied to the consumer price index, typically supplemented with private pensions and health insurance (Davis 1986, p. 112). In combination with the seniority system and promotion within internal labor markets, the unionized mass-production core of the economy established a wage relation that, for a time, was relatively immune to cyclical downturns and tides of the industrial reserve army (Davis 1986).[8]

Second, the capital–labor accord was complemented by an ongoing *capitalist offensive* ("anti-New Dealism") against labor and all labor-empowering legislation. In response to "the labor threat" of "pro-labor New Deal" legislation, smaller labor-intensive capitalists tied mostly to smaller domestic markets in the nonunionized parts of the economy fought to reshape labor legislation. Spearheaded by conservative Republican and Dixiecrat politicians, their major achievement was the Taft–Hartley Act of 1947, which, in effect, gutted or repealed any labor-empowerment force that Wagner (see note 8) may have had (Tomlins 1985).

The third pillar of domestic restructuring – *the state–citizen accord* (Bowles et al. 1983) – was constituted as a fiscal-monetary policy direction designed to foster economic growth while producing macroeconomic stabilization and expanded social services and programs providing some economic security for the aged, the unemployed, and the poor through direct social spending and "social wage," however meager. Although there was an Employment Act (of 1946), commitment to a full-employment economy was never part of this institutional reconfiguration. Even the AFL and the CIO – both supportive of the goal of full employment – disagreed on the proper strategy for achieving that end. Most telling, the meaning of "full-employment targets" – as maximum acceptable levels of unemployment – shifted upward over the entire post–World War II period (Duboff 1977), along with decade averages in the actual unemployment rate.

The international restructuring geared toward "stabilizing" the political and economic climate of the capitalist world system in the U.S. image was ostensibly rooted in a fear of external attack, containment of international communism in general and the Soviets in particular, and a belief that access to major international markets (especially Europe) would be necessary to prevent any return to depression conditions (Block 1980). In brief, the major institutional developments came in the form of the Bretton Woods Agreement (1944), the United Nations (1945), the development of atomic power and the "national security bureaucracy" (with the Finletter Commission in 1948), economic containment in the Truman Doctrine (1947), and the Marshall Plan (1948–51).

In 1949–50, a conjuncture of forces, including waning political support for the Marshall Plan, a secret planning strategy (NSC–68), and the beginning of the Korean War, provided the needed political purpose that would ostensibly accomplish all the major goals of stabilization while providing a Keynesian-type growth motor for economic expansion (Block 1980). This strategy of large-scale, permanent military spending was not just a "commercial Keynesianism" (Lekachman 1966), nor unilateral state domination of military contractors (Melman 1970), nor a simply fashioned "military Keynesianism" (Baran and Sweezy 1966). Instead, this military-industrial Keynesianism (MIK) wedded state macrolevel fiscal and stabilization policy to the microlevel concerns of many large, leading corporate producers, eventually locking state and corporate sector into a symbiotic web of stabilization/procurement. Under the aegis of "national defense," MIK was used to regulate the level of unemployment within organized labor and the rate of monopoly-sector profits (Griffin, Devine, and Wallace 1982; Mintz and Hicks 1984), while the Pentagon served as the hub for a "de facto industrial policy" (Hooks 1990).[9]

These "accords" formed the foundation for a new wage labor regime forged in the face of macroeconomic, global political, and labor movement instabilities that ripped apart the earlier wage labor regime of the 1930s and 1940s. In general, the institutional practices established in the accords led to a relatively small and divisive, rather than universal, social wage. The industrial relations system was characterized by decentralized enterprise-level bargaining in the organized sectors of the economy, and strong state regulation of labor organization and the right to strike (Burawoy 1983; Davis 1986; and McCammon 1990). Dualistic direct wage policies were complemented by dualistic social wage policies. One major result was a highly segmented and disorganized working class with no program for full employment or wage solidarity.

The MIK strategy, far from securing an increased standard of living for the working class as a whole, stabilized and promoted rapid economic growth from the end of World War II to the end of the 1960s. However, by the early 1970s, virtually all major pillars supporting the MIK regime had greatly weakened or totally collapsed. In the mid-1970s, declining corporate profitability, expanding government deficits, rising inflation and unemployment, declines in union density (Goldfield 1989), anti-social wage backlash to the reform gains of the previous decade, reduced military budgets, and OPEC "oil shocks" were all symptomatic of a weakened MIK wage labor regime. In the current context of renewed destabilization of the past two decades, a new capitalist offensive against labor (organized or not) was launched (Davis 1986; Bowles et al. 1983; and Piven and Cloward 1982). The result has been a new unstabilized despotic wage labor regime (Burawoy 1983) increasingly incapable of reproducing labor power at higher standards of living. As a result, nominal wages have climbed with inflation and unemployment; the cyclical relation between inflation and unemployment has moved rather consistently from a strong negative at the end of World War II to a strong positive ("stagflation") relation in the 1970s and 1980s. However, the cyclical relation between unemployment and changes in the real consumption wage have become increasingly inverse. The growth of surplus labor power in recent decades, far from boosting real wages of those still employed, has cut deeply into the living standards of most wage earners. The hypermobility of capital, deindustrialization, a weakened labor movement, a major capitalist offensive, casualization of labor, and wage concessions are all part of a climate that resurrects and reinforces the industrial reserve army's effect on real wages in the late twentieth century.

The global restructuring of the capitalist world economy is certainly involved in these U.S. processes, but the local–national rhythm and social consequences are filtered or conditioned by particular historical paths that created very different cultural and institutional outcomes. This becomes especially evident when we introduce a cross-national dimension in the form of a third wage labor regime. We now turn to an analysis of the Swedish wage labor regime that also grew from the global crisis during the 1930s and 1940s.

Sweden: a social Keynesian-stabilized wage labor regime

In the midst of global depression, the Social Democratic Labour Party (SAP) came to power in the 1932 election, promising to reduce unemployment and restore economic prosperity in Sweden. Within a year, SAP struck a deal with the Agrarian Party to pass an economic recovery package that included deficit-financed public works that paid workers the going union wage, agricultural loans, protective tariffs, and subsidies to shore up the price of agricultural commodities (Korpi 1978; Martin 1979; and Weir and Skocpol 1985). This move represented a marked shift from the unemployment policy implemented after World War I.[10]

The main effect of the Social Democratic depression-era strategy was not so much immediate economic recovery (Ohlin 1977; Weir and Skocpol 1985; and Heclo and Madsen 1987) as it was the production of domestic conditions necessary for export-led expansion in the short run (Weir and Skocpol 1985) and a stable political-economic base for continuous power (1932–76) in the longer term. The support of the Agrarian Party for the Social Democratic agenda continued until the late 1950s and was absolutely critical in the immediate post–World War II period. More importantly, the SAP's commitment to fiscal policy to secure full employment won the continued support of the LO.[11] Until recently, the SAP and unions affiliated with the LO identified themselves as parts of the unified SSD labor movement (Pontusson 1991).

The LO and SAF[12] signed the historic "Basic Agreement" at Saltsjöbaden in 1938. The Saltsjöbaden accord (1) provided for a thorough regulation of labor market relations; (2) attempted to limit industrial disputes by codifying specific terms of wage contracts, refined legal provisions, and bound labor and management to negotiate before engaging in overt conflict; (3) empowered the labor court to rule on interpretive conflicts over existing agreements while enforcing a strike/lockout ban; and (4) provided for arbitration to settle other disputes (Heclo and Madsen 1987, p. 112). In turn, the Basic Agreement "rested on the unions' tacit acceptance of paragraph 32 of the SAF statutes, which stipulated that any collective bargaining agreement entered into by an SAF affiliate must explicitly recognize managerial prerogative to hire and fire workers and to direct the labour process" (Pontusson 1987, p. 8). Indeed, capital's cooperation with the full-employment agenda of the SAP rested on unfettered exercise of precisely this capitalist "right."

Major modifications to the Basic Agreement occurred in the immediate postwar years. In 1951, economists Gösta Rehn and Rudolf Meidner authored a key document – "Trade Unions and Full Employment" – that served as the blueprint for postwar economic policy. The goal of the postwar strategy was to produce a depression-proof economy characterized by full employment, low inflation, stable growth, and an equitable distribution of the social product. The model contained four critical and interdependent elements: wage solidarity, centralized wage bargaining, ALMP, and counter-cyclical fiscal strategies – specifically, state control over credit, the timing of investment, and indirect taxation.

Wage solidarity served as the cornerstone of this policy matrix. In the 1950s, the LO began to implement solidaristic wage policy in its contract negotiations with SAF – a policy based on the general principle of equal pay for equal work irrespective of an employer's ability to pay or the labor market power of particular groups of workers (Pontusson 1987, p. 9). Under this principle, workers would receive the same wage/piece rate for doing the same job regardless of the relative competitiveness of their employer or their employment sector. Wage solidarity also entailed narrowing income differentials between high- and low-wage workers through use of progressive taxation.

In the Rehn–Meidner plan, wage solidarity would produce stable economic growth and, presumably, higher levels of employment. National wage rates would squeeze the profits of the least efficient producers. In general, the policy of state-backed profit squeeze was designed to heighten pressure for capitalist investment to produce more efficient operations or be driven from the market (Pontusson 1987; Milner 1989). Wage solidarity policy was expected to be the engine of stable, steady economic growth and expansion of employment as more competitive firms grew to absorb, at least in part, workers sloughed off by declining firms and industries. However, smooth implementation of wage solidarity required two additional policy elements: (1) centralized wage negotiations to control inflation produced through interunion rivalry and (2) active labor market policy to buffer the impact of wage-solidarity-induced economic structural dislocation on workers.

Occurring in two- or three-year cycles (Martin 1979), centralized wage negotiations for white- and blue-collar workers were institutionalized in the early 1950s and have operated continuously since 1956 (with branch-level bargaining formally resurfacing in 1983; see Heclo and Madsen 1987; Pontusson 1991). A key goal was to tie wage increases for blue-collar workers to average productivity increases in the export-goods-producing sector so that Swedish goods would remain internationally competitive while keeping domestic inflation under control, consistent with full-employment policy (Heclo and Madsen 1987). In a typical bargaining round, SAF and LO would reach agreement on minimum wage (usually piece) rates (Fulcher 1973). Then branch- and firm-level negotiations would adjust to the national rate for low-wage workers, thereby minimizing "wage drift" – the difference between national and local wage rates. And although not always without conflict, centralized bargaining included white- as well as blue-collar workers.

When an LO/SAF settlement was near, a second tier of pattern bargaining would occur between SAF and the private-sector white-collar federations, typically negotiating similar wage increases for white-collar workers.

Some worker dislocation was expected from wage solidarity – the result of removing less productive firms – and was countered by state-directed labor market policy to maintain full employment. The core of the program was a mixture of supply- and demand-side strategies for "getting people to productive work and productive work to people" (Milner 1989, p. 115). Supply-side strategies included retraining, job relocation, and job-information services, while demand-side programs featured expansion of employment opportunities through selective public investment or incentives, or as a final resort, public works projects. Without these programs the unemployment rate for the years 1976–82 would have been in the vicinity of 6–7 percent instead of below the 3 percent mark (Heclo and Madsen 1987, pp. 74–5).

State policy in support of wage solidarity involved regulation of investment activity through an investment reserve fund program. Companies were allowed to set aside 50 percent of their pre-tax profits, at least half to be deposited in special Bank of Sweden accounts. These corporate profits remained tax exempt if they were invested during recessionary periods or in depressed regions, as dictated by the government (Milner 1989). Noncompliance meant the funds were subject to normal tax rates.

During the 1960s, three socioeconomic conditions promoted the success of the Rehn–Meidner plan to minimize unemployment, inflation, and wage differentials (Heclo and Madsen 1987). First, a stable international economic environment enabled reliable projections of the impact of wage changes. Second, marginal tax rates guaranteed correspondence between pre- and post-tax wage increases. Together, these two factors ensured that wage changes and their effects could be assessed in terms of impact on the competitiveness of Swedish goods in the international market and on purchasing power of workers at home. Finally, the dominant position of the LO among labor union federations limited wage drift and facilitated agreement on centralized wage settlements. The absence of interunion struggle and labor militancy were also crucial to production of the long period of stable relations following World War II.

The results of the successful implementation of the Rehn–Meidner model between the mid-1950s and the late 1960s can be seen in Figures 4.4, 4.5, and 4.6.[13] For example, Figure 4.4 shows minimal fluctuation in the unemployment rate, which hovered around 1.5–2 percent while inflation was in the 3–4 percent range. In the early postwar years, the

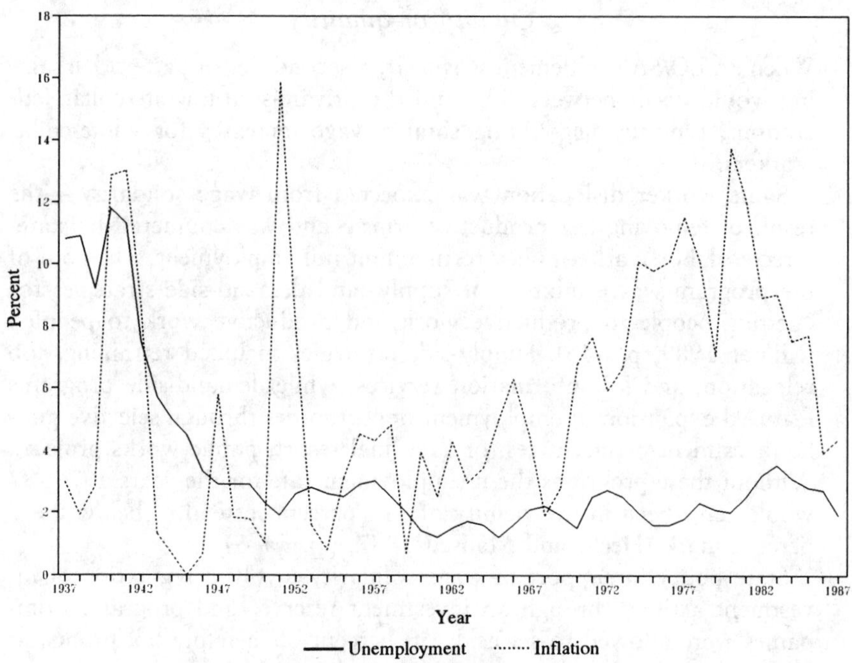

Figure 4.4. Rates of unemployment and inflation: Sweden, 1937-87

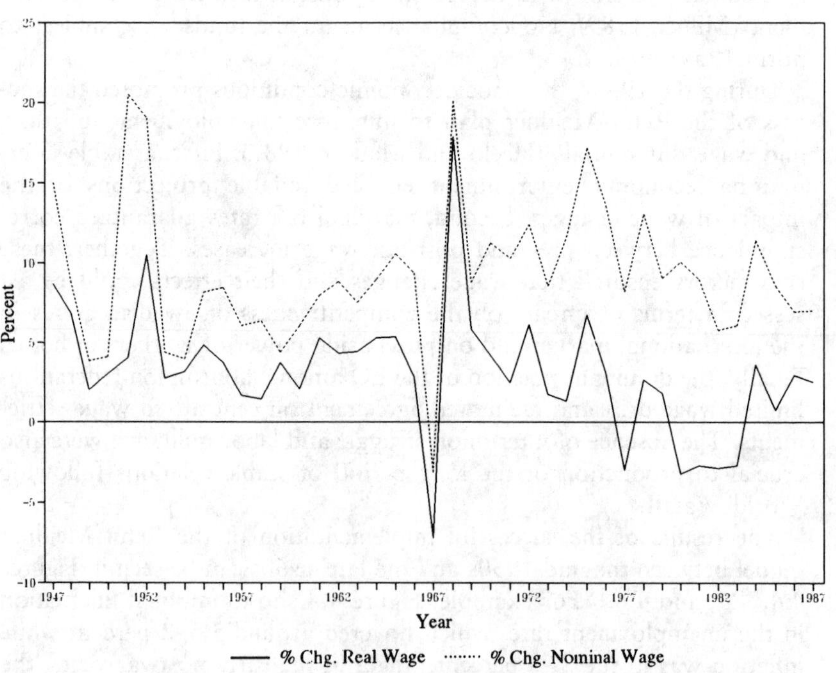

Figure 4.5. Percent change in nominal and real wage rates: Sweden, 1947-87

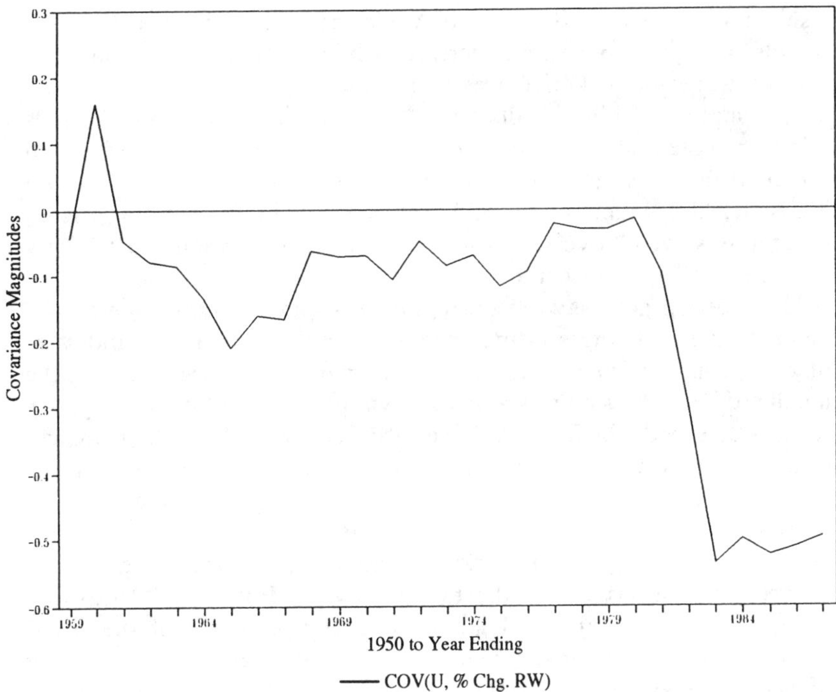

Figure 4.6. Temporally moving covariances between unemployment and percent change in manufacturing hourly real wage rates: Sweden, 1950-59, ..., 1950-87

gap between average nominal and real wages in manufacturing was small but increased over time. The tight coupling between changes in nominal and real consumption wages in manufacturing, shown in Figure 4.5, reflects this as well as the relative stability of the economic environment. Finally, the lack of marked shifts in the pattern of moving covariance coefficients in Figure 4.6 indicates the relatively smooth operation of the Rehn–Meidner inspired policies.

The dramatic shift in the unemployment–inflation relationship in 1951 (Figure 4.6) can be explained by the institutionalization of centralized wage bargaining and the endorsement of wage solidarity by the LO Congress. After World War II, the SAP continued to use wartime controls as well as new strategies to manage the economy. To prevent a repeat of runaway unemployment, as occurred following World War I, the government instituted wage freezes in 1949–50 agreed to by the LO and other producer groups (Martin 1979). However, when prices rose sharply in 1951 as a result of the Korean War, the LO rejected additional stabilization policy to control unemployment and prices if predicated solely on wage restraint. The 1951 branch-level wage negotiations resulted in extreme differences in wage increases. The first of these rounds brought a 6 percent increase, while the last resulted in a 22 percent wage jump. Differences in productivity across branches, and hence employers' ability/willingness to pay, led to wage differentials that were potentially divisive, convincing the LO leadership of the need for centralized bargaining to maintain union solidarity (Heclo and Madsen 1987). Likewise, the SAF was persuaded that centralized wage negotiations were necessary to prevent wage escalation, particularly within an inflationary context.

The growing gap between unemployment and inflation (Figure 4.4), nominal and real wages in manufacturing (not shown here), and rates of change in nominal and real wages (Figure 4.5) beginning in the middle to late 1960s reflects a breakdown of the institutional and policy context that made the Rehn–Meidner plan successful. Important changes included (1) growing instability in the international economy and deterioration of Sweden's position within it, (2) increasing conflict between manual and nonmanual unions over wages, (3) escalation of labor militancy over wages and working conditions, (4) increasing tension between the unions within the LO over wage drift, and (5) growing conflict between capital and labor over relative shares of the social product and capital's investment strategies. Simultaneously, mistiming of demand management strategies by the state and growing deficits contributed to a deteriorating situation (Martin 1979).

As crises deepened between 1967 and 1976, four conditions undermined the legitimacy of wage solidarity policy (Pontusson 1987): (1) an uncertain global economy made it difficult to determine how much wage restraint was necessary to maintain/restore the competitiveness of Swedish goods in the international market; (2) firms that benefited most from wage solidarity policy (e.g., engineering and chemicals) simultaneously increased their direct foreign investment and the capital intensiveness of the labor process in their operations at home; (3) the increased wage militancy of nonmanual unions (most official strikes during the period were by nonmanual unions and the most intense strike/lockout activity was in the public sector between SAV and SACO/SR;[14] see Fulcher 1973) and wage drift among LO unions made it increasingly difficult for the LO and SAF to reach centralized wage agreements; and (4) solidaristic wage policy in the mid-1970s began to revolve around distributing the burden of losses rather than wage increases.[15]

This conjuncture of forces meant that while the Swedish government could continue to underwrite full employment via state expenditures (albeit at increasing cost), it could no longer successfully control externally and internally produced inflation.[16] When the state increased taxes to dampen demand and meet the cost of the social wage bill, "accelerated inflation and steep marginal tax rates . . . severed the connection between nominal wage changes and real disposable take-home pay" (Heclo and Madsen 1987, p. 120). The gap between unemployment and inflation grew, contributing to a steady deterioration of the working-class consumption wage, particularly among blue-collar industrial workers.

Deterioration of the working-class consumption wage, the position of Sweden in the international market, and wage solidarity led to the defeat of the SAP in the 1976 elections. The incoming conservative government followed many of its predecessor's strategies for controlling unemployment when the worldwide recession hit Sweden belatedly in the late 1970s. But as public employment rolls, social welfare expenditures, and subsidies to employers in declining sectors increased, the budget deficit grew because increased expenditures more than offset efforts to cut the public budget. To increase the competitiveness of Swedish goods, the government devalued the crown by 15 percent during the 1976–7 crisis, reduced employer taxes, and enacted tax policies to buffer the impact on real wages. The tax policies reduced state revenues, driving up the deficit even further. As economic crisis continued into 1981, the bourgeois government resorted to a 10 percent devaluation of the crown and implemented mechanisms to protect purchasing power.

The six-year legacy of the conservative government is mixed. While international competitiveness had improved, huge deficits and spiraling inflation continued to exist at home. When the SAP returned to power in 1982, it immediately implemented a market-oriented neoliberal recovery strategy, the major thrust of which was to free resources for public and private investment by restraining aggregate consumption (Heclo and Madsen 1987; Pontusson 1991). A 16 percent currency devaluation increased international demand for Swedish exports while it reduced the real wages of workers (Figure 4.5) and the disposable income of pensioners (Heclo and Madsen 1987). Moreover, increases in indirect consumption taxes eroded purchasing power, while deregulation of financial markets led to a credit boom that exacerbated inflationary tendencies (Pontusson 1991). This "middle way" recovery strategy was successful in eliminating the budget deficit without cutting welfare entitlements. It restored a balance of trade surplus, reduced unemployment, and spurred economic growth (Pontusson 1991). However, the cost of the recovery was borne by the working classes: for the first time in post–World War II history, Swedish citizens suffered a net decline in their standard of living.

Not surprisingly, deterioration of the real wage in Sweden has led to intensified wage struggles between factions of the working class – between manual and nonmanual federations, and among LO unions –

making coordinated bargaining virtually impossible. This has resulted in decentralized wage negotiations since 1983. And divided industrial workers have not recouped wage losses; the average real consumption wage in manufacturing in 1987 stood at its 1978 level.

In the final analysis, counter-cyclical movement in the real wage–unemployment relation during the 1980s (Figure 4.6) resulted from the unequal distribution of the burden of a market-driven economic recovery. The working class was forced to consume less, because of increases in taxes and devaluation of the crown, but also because of state cutbacks in employment expansion and loss of work due to "rationalization" of the labor process within export-oriented firms. This resulted in the highest unemployment rates since World War II. The breakdown of wage solidarity and its necessary supports – centralized wage bargaining and active labor market policy – suggests that, at least in the short term, the counter-cyclical movement of unemployment and change in real wages is likely to be maintained and reproduced.

External comparison of regimes

An "external" (Janoski 1991), cross-regime comparison illustrates several important general points regarding the volume of unemployment, inflation, and wages under different historical conditions of capitalist development. First, the average level and variation in cyclical components of unemployment and inflation vary dramatically within and between wage labor regimes (see Tables 4.1, 4.2). By contrast, the early U.S. regime was indeed remarkably "unstable." Unemployment was generally higher (approximately three times greater than the postwar Swedish average) and far more variable, while average inflation is much lower but nonetheless highly volatile. And these magnitudes exclude the Great Depression decade.

Second, the average annual change in wages shows the reverse (relative to unemployment) ranking across regimes. Both nominal and real wages were lower and more stable in the early U.S. regime than in either the military-industrial Keynesian (MIK) or social Keynesian (SK) counterparts. However, average annual increments in real wages were not radically different.

Third, the behavior of covariance structures across regimes demonstrates how misleading it is to assume that the relation between inflation and unemployment follows some transhistorical or universal "Phillips curve" form. The magnitude of the temporally varying covariances ranges from a maximum of 2.22 (in the postwar U.S. regime) to a minimum of –14.37 (in the early predepression U.S. regime). And while the average for the Swedish SK regime shows a small inverse relation, it is

Table 4.1. *Summary statistics for "output" and "parameter" structures in the United States*

Panel A. Unstabilized competitive-monopoly capitalist wage labor regime: 1890-1930

	Output structures				Parameter structures		
	U^a	I^b	NW^c	RW^d	$Cov\ (U,I)^e$	$Cov\ (U,NW)^f$	$Cov\ (U,RCW)^g$
Mean	6.11	1.73	0.01	0.01	-8.71	-12.15	-2.83
Std. dev.	4.04	5.79	0.02	0.02	3.07	3.40	.85
C. of var.	0.65	3.35	2.00	2.00	-0.35	-0.28	-0.30
Max.	18.40	17.50	0.08	0.08	-4.63	-8.29	-1.51
Min.	1.40	-10.70	-0.04	-0.04	-14.37	-18.18	-6.03

Panel B. Military-industrial Keynesian-stabilized wage labor regime: 1950-88

	Output structures				Parameter structures		
	U^a	I^b	NW^c	RW^d	$Cov\ (U,I)^e$	$Cov\ (U,NW)^f$	$Cov\ (U,RCW)^g$
Mean	5.70	4.12	0.23	0.03	0.20	0.95	-0.63
Std. dev.	1.68	3.45	0.17	0.05	1.27	1.18	0.37
C. of var.	0.29	0.84	0.74	1.67	6.35	1.24	-0.59
Max.	9.70	13.50	0.72	0.11	2.22	3.21	-0.15
Min.	2.90	-0.40	0.04	-0.13	-1.16	-0.07	-1.26

[a] *U* = percent labor force unemployed. [b] *I* = rate of inflation (Consumer Price Index). [c] *NW* = change in average hourly money wage in manufacturing industry. [d] *RW* = change in average hourly real consumption wage in manufacturing industry. [e] *COV(U,I)* = covariance between the rate of unemployment and rate of inflation. [f] *COV(U,NW)* = covariance between the rate of unemployment and change in average hourly money wage in manufacturing industry. [g] *COV(U,RCW)* = covariance between the rate of unemployment and change in average hourly real consumption wage in manufacturing industry.

Table 4.2. *Social Keynesian-stabilized wage labor regime: Sweden, 1950-87*

	Output structures				Parameter structures		
	U^a	I^b	NW^c	RW^d	$Cov\ (U,I)^e$	$Cov\ (U,NW)^f$	$Cov\ (U,RCW)^g$
Mean	2.21	6.18	1.59	0.07	-0.16	-0.35	-0.16
Std. dev.	0.57	3.65	1.54	0.11	0.15	0.12	0.18
C. of var.	0.26	0.59	0.97	1.57	-0.94	-0.34	-1.13
Max.	3.50	15.80	5.53	0.46	0.11	-0.16	0.16
Min.	1.20	0.70	-0.30	-0.20	-0.56	-0.79	-0.54

[a] *U* = percent labor force unemployed.
[b] *I* = rate of inflation (Consumer Price Index).
[c] *NW* = change in average hourly money wage in manufacturing industry.
[d] *RW* = change in average hourly real consumption wage in manufacturing industry.
[e] *COV(U,I)* = covariance between the rate of unemployment and rate of inflation.
[f] *COV(U,NW)* = covariance between the rate of unemployment and change in average hourly money wage in manufacturing industry.
[g] *COV(U,RCW)* = covariance between the rate of unemployment and change in average hourly real consumption wage in manufacturing industry.

remarkably stable by contrast, at least once centralized wage bargaining was established in 1950.

Finally, the pattern of temporally varying covariation between unemployment and real wage change across regimes illustrates that, on average, surplus labor power moves counter-cyclically with real wages across all regime types. The industrial reserve army is, therefore, apparently always something of a wage threat. However, the severity of that threat is substantially mitigated by the institutional quality of the ALMP across regimes. The Swedish SK regime does a better job of protecting workers from the likelihood of joblessness while substantially dampening the wage-suppressing effects of unemployment.

A comparison of temporally changing relations between unemployment, inflation, and wages across the post–World War II U.S. and Swedish regimes yields additional insights not fully captured by regime summary statistics shown in Table 4.1. For instance, Table 4.3 reveals accelerating stagflation from the 1970s into the mid-1980s for the United States. The trend moves in the same direction for Sweden, but is much less pronounced. Likewise, as the post–World War II decades unfolded the wage "cost" of unemployment has increased for both U.S. and Swedish workers, but the short-term downward pressure is greater in the United States.

Both countries have felt the impact of altering national positions within the world economy as global restructuring was set in motion by the destabilization of their respective regimes in the 1970s, and both country patterns have been stamped by the neoconservative macroeconomic policies in the 1980s.[17] However, and perhaps only momentarily, respective *prior* institutional and policy histories have made the difference: the negative impact of global and regime destabilization cum neoconservative policy wave has been muted somewhat by the social democratic legacy in Sweden relative to the United States. Surplus labor is an increasing threat to the reproductive wage rate across capitalist nations. But the depth of the threat is, at least, partially contingent on past history (cf., Therborn 1986; McBride 1987).

CONCLUSIONS AND IMPLICATIONS

Our analysis of unemployment, prices, and wages in Sweden and the United States demonstrates the substantial time–space variability in actual output magnitudes of several crucial macrosocioeconomic conditions as well as substantial historical contingency in *relations* among these products. Within the historical scope of our analysis, patterns of "output" and "parameter" regimes feature nonrandom topographies comprehensible in terms of three differing regime-regulative strategies

Table 4.3. *Time-varying covariances between unemployment, inflation, and wages:[a] subperiod averages for post-World War II United States and Sweden*

Panel A. United States

Subperiod[b]	*Cov (U,I)*	*Cov (U,NW)*	*Cov (U,RW)*
1950s	-1.11	-1.55	-0.39
1960s	-0.97	-1.42	-0.45
1970-4	0.82	-1.00	-0.20
1975-9	0.77	0.30	-0.53
1980-4	1.98	0.91	-1.09
1985-8	1.75	0.55	-1.24

Panel B. Sweden

Subperiod[b]	*Cov (U,I)*	*Cov (U,NW)*	*Cov (U,RW)*
1950	-0.56	-0.79	-0.04
1960s	-0.20	-0.32	-0.09
1970-4	-0.12	-0.22	-0.08
1975-9	-0.25	-0.34	-0.06
1980-4	-0.07	-0.40	-0.29
1985-7	0.07	-0.46	-0.51

[a] All variables as previously defined. The wage data are average annual hourly direct (excluding deferred and indirect) wages in manufacturing industry.

[b] Subperiod averages are computed for vectors of forward-moving covariances estimated on temporal windows: 1950-9, 1950-60, ..., 1950-88 (for United States) ... 1950-87 (Sweden).

governing the wage relation, differing institutional outcomes, and alternative paths of capitalist development. However, this historical variability in unemployment–wage movements, resulting from underlying struggles and institutional reconfigurations, is contained within one general formative relation – the commodity form of social life: the subsumption of human life activity into relations that are *simultaneously* value-in-use and value-in-exchange (Isaac 1990). This subsumption of life activity – labor – occurs within the wage relation in which labor power (value-in-exchange) is sold and converted into actual labor (value-in-use). The expansion of this process *is* the accumulation of capital, itself inherently and internally contradictory and antagonistic; class struggle turns on the sale of labor power and the extraction of actual labor from the "purchased" commodity. An important feature of this antagonism resides in the production of surplus life in the form of unemployed, redundant labor power in reserve. Yet just how that reserve translates into changes in real consumption wages varies by type of capitalist wage labor regime. For instance, the Swedish Social Democratic wage policies were relatively successful in insulating real wage rates from the rhythms of the business cycle, but only within a unique national regime–world economy conjuncture (cf. Fagerberg et al. 1990 on Norway). While evidently always detrimental to working class interests, the fluctuating volume of the industrial reserve army has no single transhistorical or universal quantitative consequence for the real wage. These three historically distinct wage labor regimes with their respective qualitative–quantitative conditions of the surplus labor power/real consumption wage relation indicate the futility of ahistorical, extensive research strategies as well as ahistorical general theories of wage cyclicality on which they are based. Both neoclassical and neo-Keynesian theories of real wage cyclicality are equally ill prepared to explain the historically contingent character of real wage movement. Theories of the wage relation must appropriate, rather than suppress, such historical variability.

We have one major conclusion: *the gulf between intensive and extensive research strategies can and should be avoided.* Our central purpose has been the explication of *one* (but certainly not the only) strategy for bridging the gulf between extensive and intensive designs in comparative/historical research. For many historically grounded research questions involving change and temporality, it is possible and desirable to expand investigation of the scope of time-varying processes. Such an intensive expansion of scope becomes increasingly sensitive to processes of discontinuity and historically significant turning points in configurations of relations rather than remaining confined to quantitative notions of change located exclusively in single-variate distributions governed by ahistorical process and parameter structures. Changing parameter (or process) regimes signify a complex, uneven (rather than a smooth, linear, even) topographic product that should be the expected (as an unexceptional) result of historical determinative agency that is itself dialectical and nonlinear (see, e.g., Sewell 1987; Hazelrigg 1991). When we recognize that, as a result of such agency, historical contingency can manifest itself in diverse forms and in multiple sites within the structure of a time-series model, new opportunities are created for integrating social science causality and the contingencies of historical narrative.

Several implications follow from this conclusion. First, temporally universal ahistorical theories (Kiser and Hechter 1991) are likely to be casualties of the kind of practice we advocate here and elsewhere (see Isaac and Griffin 1989; Griffin and Isaac 1992; and Isaac and Leicht 1992) as they have increasingly been called into question by historical sociologists practicing intensive research strategies (Ragin 1989; Quadagno and Knapp 1992). Especially problematic are the overly structural theorizations in both their conservative structural-functionalist manifestations (see Ragin 1989) and various "radical" structural varieties (see Schmidt 1981). Ahistorical macroeconomic theories of the unemployment–wage relation are burdened with many of the same liabilities.

Second, quantitative coefficients (e.g., a parameter regime of a time-series model) cannot be taken as ends in themselves – that is, in the sense of an "explanation." Because the parameters are likely to vary through time (and across space) – that is, to display a form of historical contingency – they provoke a closer consideration of historically specific theoretical arguments that take human agency seriously and make greater demands on comparative/historical narrative. Multiplicity of parameters in time and space is likely to be received as "chaotic" in some quarters. After all, parameter complexity is avoidable through repression of historicity in extensive designs. Such a "chaos" receptivity is a result of the stance that desires one parameter linking any given set of variables so that deductive theories and hypotheses may be "tested" against the data (history). However, if there are many parameters, hypothesis testing in the conventional sense becomes awkward if not downright impossible. The multiplicity of parameters showing historicity in relations reveals that such parameters cannot serve well as explanations in themselves, but are instead important data to be explained.

Third, the temporally extensive capability of quantitative time-series procedures coupled with the ability to highlight intensive historical concerns through temporally varying "windows" enables one to add a diachronic dimension to the singular synchronic aspect of conjunctural analysis – for instance, as in McMichael's (1990) discussion of "singular form incorporated comparison." In brief, we can examine the quantitative variability of relations over time contained within a particular historical conjuncture. Historical analysis of regimes as cases is one way to theorize general cross-time patterns without losing sight of historical contingency and relational processes of change.

Fourth, our examples highlight the historically specific quality of quantity as regime types that normally would be repressed in conventional time-ordered data analyses done in the classically extensive manner. However, our strategy does not move from the extensive-quantitative design by simply rejecting the quantitative in historical analysis (Skocpol 1987). Instead, the retention of quantitative mappings of variables allows us to examine the extensive contour of (varying) relations that would be impossible to track and to theorize had we exclusively relied on qualitative case study designs.

Fifth, our bridge across the extensive–intensive gulf carries potential for spanning macro–micro divisions. On the macrolevel side, quantitative mappings of relations are especially useful in combination with a "rhetoric of perspective" for comparison of social form. On the microlevel side, an understanding of the underlying processes, labors, struggles, and movements giving rise to the macrolevel conditions demands detailed narrativity focusing on human agency and a "rhetoric of close presentation" to compare a historical movement in the content/substance of the form (see Abrams 1982; White 1987). Bringing the two together can be done in a single study when historical contingency is permitted in the quantitative mappings of variables. For example, in our study we attempt to bridge the gap between a macrolevel-oriented political economy stressing quantitative dimensions with microlevel-oriented, qualitative policy and labor history.

The current renaissance in comparative/historical sociology, on which we opened, is generating a flurry of new theoretical-historical questions, research strategies, and methodological innovations. While we can concur with Ragin's (1989) explanation for this activity, we believe other forces are operative too. The return to the classics in some areas of sociology (and comparative/historical is certainly one) coupled with close critical attention to standard methodological (usually quantitative) techniques (Abbott 1988) is generating *part* of the fertile discontent of the "historic turn in the human sciences" (McDonald in press). With this turn, the disciplinary divisions between the social sciences and history may continue to erode and with them the extreme separations between theory and history, structure and agency, causality and contingency, and quantity and quality.

NOTES

1. By "historical contingency," we mean the embeddedness or nestedness of processual relations internal to broader relational conditions that are changing through time–space as both product and condition of human historical agency (see Isaac and Griffin 1989; Isaac and Leicht 1992). Here we examine historical contingency in the form of differentiation and discontinuity in quantitative marcrosocioeconomic relations. More concretely, we demonstrate how the relations between surplus labor (as unemployment) and wage rates change and are changed by institutional configurations that regulate labor power, money, and capital accumulation.
2. Most discussions of the theory of time-series analysis are remarkably mute on the subject of time. This makes Kendall's (1973, p. 1) opening statement all the more atypical and blunt: "Time is perhaps the most mysterious

thing in a mysterious universe. But its esoteric nature, fortunately, will not concern us in this book. For us, time is what it was to Isaac Newton, a smoothly flowing stream bearing the phenomenal world along at a uniform pace."

3. According to Ragin (1989, pp. 69–70), the particularly valuable features of intensive (small-*N*) research that should be preserved are (1) cases as wholes or configurations of parts, (2) qualitative outcomes, (3) causal conjunctures, (4) causal heterogeneity, and (5) "deviant" cases and concern for invariance.
4. Although there were some notable events – e.g., "Coxey's Army of unemployed marching on Washington – the dearth of protest or insurgent activity directly aimed at unemployment during this early regime was remarkable. By 1930 this relative quiescence of the unemployed began to change (see Kerbo and Shaffer 1992).
5. All U.S. data employed are national annual time-series observations. Unemployment is the percentage of the total nonagricultural labor force unemployed; inflation is the annual percentage rate of change in the Consumer Price Index; nominal wage is the average hourly money wage rate (in dollars) in manufacturing industry; real consumption wage is the nominal hourly wage rates in manufacturing industry deflated by the Consumer Price Index. The real consumption wage rate comes closer to assessing the level of labor power's reproduction (standard of living) than measures that deflate by the Wholesale Price Index or the GNP deflator. (Sources for all variables: U.S. Bureau of the Census 1975; various years.)
6. The time varying covariances shown in Figures 4.3 and 4.6, as well as in Tables 4.1 and 4.2, were estimated using a "forward-moving" strategy most compatible with a narrative of developmental sequence (see Griffin and Isaac 1992). For the United States, this strategy produces a turning point in the sign of the relationship between unemployment and real wages when 1934 is brought into the estimation window. Alternatively, the "backward-moving" strategy (not displayed here) generates a turning point circa 1938–9. For purposes of this analysis, we are primarily indicating that the New Deal-war years constituted a "long turning point" in the employment–wage relationship as part of the changing structure or regime of accumulation.
7. Additionally, the relationship between unemployment and inflation was negative from the 1890s forward, the "trade-off" becoming increasingly pronounced as the nation approached the Great Depression of the 1930s. Unemployment also maps negatively with nominal wage changes. Before the 1930s, the strongest sustained counter-cyclicality in money wage rates occurred during the 1920s, when wage resistance by employers was likely at its peak: the growth of the industrial labor reserve and the accumulated successes of the capitalist offenses against labor (organized or not) translated into downward pressure on money wages, with sharp year-to-year fluctuations around a virtually nonexistent trend.
8. The "new receptivity" to organized labor, at least in some state-Keynesian/mass-productivist quarters, was seen along with "business competition" as one of the twin cylinders of the newly emerging growth motor. As Robert F. Wagner stated in an address to the Institute of Social Order in 1947: "The function of unions, broadly considered, is to maintain purchasing power at a high enough level to absorb the products of business competition.

Business competition and national unions are the indispensable blades of our twin scissors of supply and demand" (quoted in Tomlins 1985, p. 282).

9. Many other dimensions of an ALMP are part of this story. For additional direct discussion on ALMP in the post–World War II United States, see Janoski (1990).
10. In Sweden, the use of public works projects to combat unemployment dates back to the early twentieth century. In 1914, the Swedish government established the Unemployment Commission as an advisory and investigatory board to address the problem of postwar unemployment (Weir and Skocpol 1985, p. 123). Soon thereafter, the commission began to provide relief for the unemployed thrown out of work during the transition from a war- to a peacetime economy. Public works were implemented in the 1910s and 1920s as a form of "humanitarian" relief that paid workers considerably less than the market wage (Korpi 1978, p. 80; Valocchi 1992). The national recovery policy adopted in 1933, in contrast, was based on the Stockholm school's underconsumptionist theory, which saw insufficient aggregate demand as the cause of economic depression, rather than excessively high wages. Accordingly, deficit-financed expansion of consumption was a necessary means for stimulating demand and hence spurring economic recovery. Along these lines, public works that paid workers the going union wage were implemented as a form of humanitarian demand stimulus within an overall strategy for national recovery.
11. The LO (Landsorganisationen i Sverige) is the National Confederation of (blue-collar) Trade Unions. Since its inception in 1898, the LO has had formal ties with the SAP. However, collective affiliation between the LO unions and SAP ended in 1991 as a result of a decision by the SAP.
12. The Swedish Employers' Confederation (SAF; Svenska Arbetsgivareföreningen) was formed in 1902 in response to the national organization of labor. Individual employers belong both to the SAF and one of its 35 sector branch associations. SAF has a collective bargaining relationship with the LO and other federations that organize member unions in the private sector.
13. All Swedish data employed are national annual time-series observations. Unemployment is the percentage of the total nonagricultural labor force unemployed (statistika Central bryån, *Statistisk Arsbok för Sverige,* for 1952–87; U.N., *Monthly Bulletin of Statistics,* for 1937–42 and 1958–61); inflation is the annual percentage rate of change in the Consumer Price Index (*Statistisk Arsbok för Sverige*); nominal wage is the average hourly money wage rate (in Kronors) in manufacturing industry (ILO, *Yearbook of Labour Statistics*); real consumption wage is the nominal hourly wage rate in manufacturing industry deflated by the Consumer Price Index (source: constructed).
14. Other major worker-employer organizations include the following: (1) The Central Organization of Salaried Workers (TCO; Tjänstemännens Centralorganisationen) was founded in 1944 and includes white-collar unions in the private and public sectors; the TCO seeks to organize all salaried employees irrespective of occupation and education (Heclo and Madsen 1987), and in recent years this vertical integration strategy has caused boundary conflicts between the TCO and SACO/SR; (2) The Swedish Association of Professional Associations (SACO; Centralorganisationen Sveriges Akedmikers) was formed in 1947 as a confederation of white-

collar professional associations organized horizontally; until recently, a university degree was required for membership; after public employees were given the right to strike and bargain collectively in 1965, SACO merged with the National Federation of Civil Servants (SR; Centralorganisationentatsjänstemannens Riksfförbundet) in 1974 to form SACO/SR made up of 27 professional associations that repressent white-collar professionals, higher-level civil servants, and military officers; (3) The SAV (Statens Avtalsverk) is the state administrator's association to bargain with nonmanual public-sector workers; it is the SAF counterpart in the public sector (Fulcher 1973; Heclo and Madsen 1987; and Milner 1989).

15. In 1974 the Codetermination Act was passed to offset the harsh consequences of the exercise of managerial prerogative – e.g., speedup, authoritarian managerial regimes, and hazardous working conditions and related labor militancy in the late 1960s and early 1970s. The law makes working conditions and the organization of the labor process subject to collective bargaining. According to the act, public and private employers are to negotiate any changes that might affect the work force (e.g., changes in the organization of work, management and supervision, new technologies, plant location) with workers' union representatives (Heclo and Madsen 1987). If enforced, this law would effectively nullify paragraph 32 of the SAF statutes. In practice, however, the law has been ineffective largely because private-sector employers have refused to play by the new rules (Pontusson 1987).
16. During the three intense profit squeeze–wage drift cycles that occurred from 1964 through the mid-1970s, private-sector expansion was, for the first time, unable to absorb workers who lost their jobs due to plant closings or "rationalization" of the labor process. This was due both to the lack of domestic employment expansion and to increased foreign investment of Swedish firms. As a consequence, the public sector had to pick up the slack in order to meet its full-employment commitment, resulting in a growing budget deficit. In turn, public-sector unions benefited by the influx of new employees (Martin 1979).
17. However, along with the United States, Sweden is quite likely in for more, given recent trends and the SAP defeat in the fall 1991 elections (Olsen 1991; Valocchi 1992). For a discussion of related processes in Norway, see Fagerberg et al. (1990).

REFERENCES

Abbott, A. 1988. "Transcending General Linear Reality." *Sociological Theory* 6(Fall):169–86.

1990. "Conceptions of Time and Events in Social Science Methods." *Historical Methods* 23:140–50.

1991. "History and Sociology: The Lost Synthesis." *Social Science History* 15(Summer):201–38.

Abell, P. 1987. *The Syntax of Social Life*. Oxford: Clarendon.

Abrams, P. 1982. *Historical Sociology*. Ithaca, N.Y.: Cornell University Press.

Adam, B. 1990. *Time & Social Theory*. Cambridge: Polity Press.

Aglietta, M. 1979. *A Theory of Capitalist Regulation*. London: New Left Books.

Bach, R. 1977. "Methods of Analysis in the Study of the World-Economy." *American Sociological Review* 42(Oct.):811–14.
Baran, P., and P. Sweezy. 1966. *Monopoly Capital.* New York: Monthly Review.
Beer, S. 1963. "Causal Explanation and Imaginative Re-Enactment." *History and Theory* 3(1):6–29.
Bils, M. 1985. "Real Wages over the Business Cycle: Evidence from Panel Data." *Journal of Political Economy* 93(Aug.):666–89.
Block, F. 1980. "Economic Instability and Military Strength: The Paradoxes of the 1950 Rearmament Decision." *Politics & Society* 10(1):35–58.
Bluestone, B., and B. Harrison. 1982. *The Deindustrialization of America.* New York: Basic.
Bodkin, R. 1969. "Real Wages and Cyclical Variations in Employment: A Re-Examination of the Evidence." *Canadian Journal of Economics* 2(Aug.):353–74.
Bowles, S., D. Gordon, and T. Weisskopf. 1983. *Beyond the Waste Land.* New York: Doubleday.
Boyer, R. 1979. "Wage Formation in Historical Perspective: The French Experience." *Cambridge Journal of Economics* 3:99–118.
Bradshaw, Y., and M. Wallace. 1991. "Informing Generality and Explaining Uniqueness: The Place of Case Studies in Comparative Research." *International Journal of Comparative Sociology* 32(1–2):154–71.
Brunner, K., and A. Meltzer (eds.). 1976. "The Phillips Curve." In *The Phillips Curve and Labor Markets*, pp. 1–18. New York: North Holland.
Burawoy, M. 1977. "Social Structure, Homogenization, and 'The Process of Status Attainment in the United States and Great Britain.'" *American Journal of Sociology* 82(Mar.):1031–42.
1983. "Between the Labor Process and the State: The Changing Face of Factory Regimes Under Advanced Captialism." *American Sociological Review* 48:587–605.
Cameron, D. 1978. "The Expansion of the Public Economy: A Comparative Analysis." *American Political Science Review* 72(Dec.):1243–61.
Collins, R. 1981. *The Business Response to Keynes, 1929–1964.* New York: Columbia University Press.
Davis, M. 1986. *Prisoners of the American Dream.* London: Verso.
Duboff, R. 1977. "Full Employment: The History of a Receding Target." *Politics & Society* 7:1–25.
Dulles, F., and M. Dubofsky. 1984. *Labor in America.* Arlington Heights, Ill.: Harlan-Davidson.
Edwards, R. 1979. *Contested Terrain.* New York: Basic.
Esping-Andersen, G. 1990. *The Three Worlds of Welfare Capitalism.* Princeton, N.J.: Princeton University Press.
Fagerberg, J., A. Cappelen, L. Mjoset, and R. Skarstein. 1990. "The Decline of Social-Democratic State Capitalism in Norway." *New Left Review* 181(May–June):60–94.
Fulcher, J. 1973. "Class Conflict in Sweden." *Sociology* 7:49–70.
Geary, P., and J. Kennan. 1982. "The Employment–Real Wage Relationship: An International Study." *Journal of Political Economy* 90(Aug.):854–71.
Goldfield, M. 1989. *The Decline of Organized Labor in the United States.* Chicago: University of Chicago Press.

Gordon, D., R. Edwards, and M. Reich. 1982. *Segmented Work, Divided Workers*. Cambridge University Press.

Griffin, L., C. Botsko, A. Wahl, and L. Isaac. 1991. "Theoretical Generality, Case Particularity: Qualitative Comparative Analysis of Trade Union Growth and Decline." *International Journal of Comparative Sociology* 32(1–2):110–36.

Griffin, L., J. Devine, and M. Wallace. 1982. "Monopoly Capital, Organized Labor, and Military Expenditures in the United States, 1949–1976." *American Journal of Sociology* (Suppl.) 88:s113–s153.

Griffin, L., and L. Isaac. 1992. "Recursive Regression and the Historical Use of 'Time' in Time-Series Analyses of Historical Process." *Historical Methods* 25(Fall):166–79.

Griffin, L., M. Wallace, and B. Rubin. 1986. "Capitalist Resistance to the Organization of Labor Before the New Deal: Why? How? Success?" *American Sociological Review* 51(Apr.):147–67.

Hage, J. 1975. "Theoretical Decision Rules for Selecting Research Designs: The Study of Nation-States or Societies." *Sociological Methods & Research* 4(Nov.):131–65.

Hannan, M., and A. Young. 1977. "Estimation in Panel Models: Results on Pooling Cross-Sections and Time-Series." In D. Heise (ed.), *Sociological Methodology*, p. 52–83. San Francisco: Jossey-Bass.

Hazelrigg, L. 1991. "The Problem of Micro–Macro Linkage: Rethinking Questions of the Individual, Social Structure, and Autonomy of Action." *Current Perspectives in Social Theory* 11:229–54.

Heclo, H., and H. Madsen. 1987. *Policy and Politics in Sweden*. Philadelphia, Pa.: Temple University Press.

Hernes, G. 1976. "Structural Change in Social Processes." *American Journal of Sociology* 82:513–47.

Hibbs, D. 1987. *The Political Economy of Industrial Democracies*. Cambridge, Mass.: Harvard University Press.

Hooks, G. 1990. "The Rise of the Pentagon and U.S. State Building: The Defense Program as Industrial Policy." *American Journal of Sociology* 96(Sept.):358–404.

International Labour Organization. Various years. *Yearbook of Labour Statistics*. Geneva: ILO.

Isaac, L. 1990. "The Value of Value in Marx and the Political Economy of Labor: Classical Theory, Contemporary Debates." Paper presented at the annual meeting of the American Sociological Association, Washington, D.C.

Isaac, L., and L. Griffin. 1989. "Ahistoricism in Time-Series Analyses of Historical Process: Critique, Redirection and Illustrations from U.S. Labor History." *American Sociological Review* 54(Dec.):873–90.

Isaac, L., and K. Leicht. 1992. "Regimes of Power and the Power of Analytic Regimes: Historical Contingency and Continuity in Policy Regimes of the U.S. 'Welfare-Warfare State.'" Paper presented at the American Sociological Association Meetings, Pittsburgh.

Janoski, T. 1990. *The Political Economy of Unemployment*. Berkeley: University of California Press.

1991. "Synthetic Strategies in Comparative Sociological Research: Methods and Problems of Internal and External Analysis." *International Journal of Comparative Sociology* 32(1–2):59–81.

Kendall, M. G. 1973. *Time-Series*. New York: Hafner.

Kerbo, H., and R. Shaffer. 1992. "Lower Class Insurgency and the Political Process: The Response of the U.S. Unemployed, 1890–1940." *Social Problems* 39(May):139–54.

Kiser, E., and M. Hechter. 1991. "The Role of General Theory in Comparative-Historical Sociology." *American Journal of Sociology* 97(July):1–30.

Korpi, W. 1978. *The Working Class in Welfare Capitalism: Work, Unions, and Politics in Sweden.* London: Routledge & Kegan Paul.

1989. "Power, Politics, and State Autonomy in the Development of Social Citizenship: Social Rights During Sickness in Eighteen OECD Countries Since 1930." *American Sociological Review* 54:309–28.

Lekachman, R. 1966. *The Age of Keynes.* New York: Random House.

Lukacs, G. 1923/1971. *History and Class Consciousness.* Trans. R. Livingstone. Cambridge, Mass.: MIT Press.

Martin, A. 1979. "The Dynamics of Change in a Keynesian Political Economy: The Swedish Case and Its Implications." In C. Crouch (ed.), *State and Economy in Contemporary Capitalism*, pp. 88–121. New York: St. Martin's.

Marx, K. 1867/1967. *Capital.* Vol. 1. New York: International.

McBride, S. 1987. "The State and Labour Markets: Toward a Comparative Political Economy of Unemployment." *Studies in Political Economy* 23:141–54.

McCammon, H. 1990. "Legal Limits on Labor Militancy: U.S. Labor Law and the Right to Strike Since the New Deal." *Social Problems* 37:607–24.

McDonald, T. (ed.). In press. *The Historic Turn in the Human Sciences.* Ann Arbor: University of Michigan Press.

McMichael, P. 1990. "Incorporating Comparison Within a World-Historical Perspective: An Alternative Comparative Method." *American Sociological Review* 55(June):385–97.

Melman, S. 1970. *Pentagon Capitalism.* New York: McGraw-Hill.

Milner, H. 1989. *Sweden: Social Democracy in Practice.* Oxford University Press.

Mintz, A., and A. Hicks. 1984. "Military Keynesianism in the United States, 1949–1976: Disaggregating Military Expenditures and Their Determination." *American Journal of Sociology* 90:411–17.

Neftci, S. 1978. "A Time-Series Analysis of the Real Wages–Employment Relation." *Journal of Political Economy* 86(Apr.):281–91.

Ohlin, B. 1977. *The Problem of Employment Stabilization.* Westport, Conn: Greenwood.

Olsen, G. 1991. "Labour Mobilization and the Strength of Capital: The Rise and Stall of Economic Democracy in Sweden." *Studies in Political Economy* 34:109–45.

Pampel, F., and J. Williamson. 1988. "Welfare Spending in Advanced Industrial Democracies, 1950–1980." *American Journal of Sociology* 93(May):1424–56.

Phillips, A. 1958. "The Relation Between Unemployment and the Rate of Change of Money Wage Rates in the United Kingdom, 1861–1957." *Economica* 25(Nov.):283–99.

Piven, F., and R. Cloward. 1982. *The New Class War.* New York: Pantheon.

Pontusson, J. 1987. "Radicalization and Retreat in Swedish Social Democracy." *New Left Review* 165:5–33.

1991. "The Crisis of Swedish Social Democracy." Paper presented at the Center for Social Theory and Comparative History, UCLA.

Quadagno, J. 1984. "Welfare Capitalism and the Social Security Act of 1935." *American Sociological Review* 49(Oct.):632–47.

Quadagno, J., and S. Knapp. 1992. "Have Historical Sociologists Forsaken Theory? Thoughts on the History/Theory Relationship." *Sociological Methods & Research* 20(May):481–507.

Quandt, R. 1958. "The Estimation of Parameters of a Linear Regression System Obeying Two Separate Regimes." *Journal of the American Statistical Association* 53:873–80.

Ragin, C. 1987. *The Comparative Method: Moving Beyond Qualitative and Quantitative Strategies.* Berkeley: University of California Press.

1989. "New Directions in Comparative Research." In M. Kohn (ed.), *Cross-National Research in Sociology*, p. 57–76. Newbury Park, Calif.: Sage.

1991. "Introduction: The Problem of Balancing Discourse on Cases and Variables in Comparative Social Science." In C. Ragin (ed.), *Issues and Alternatives in Comparative Social Research*, pp. 1–8. Leiden: E. J. Brill.

Rockefeller, J., Jr. 1916. "Labor and Capital-Partners." *Atlantic Monthly* 117:12–21.

Rubinson, R. 1977. "Reply to Bach and Irwin." *American Sociological Review* 42(Oct.):817–21.

Sayer, A. 1984. *Method in Social Science.* London: Hutchinson.

Schmidt, A. 1981. *History and Structure.* Trans. J. Herf. Cambridge University Press.

Schott, K. 1990. *Policy, Power and Order.* New Haven, Conn.: Yale University Press.

Sewell, W., Jr. 1987. "Theory of Action, Dialectic, and History: Comment on Coleman." *American Journal of Sociology* 93:166–72.

Skocpol, T. 1987. "Social History and Historical Sociology: Contrasts and Complementarities." *Social Science History* 11(Spring):17–30.

Snyder, D. 1975. "Institutional Setting and Industrial Conflict: Comparative Analyses of France, Italy and the United States." *American Sociological Review* 40(June):259–78.

Statistiska Centralbyrån. Various years, 1952–89. *Statistisk Arsbok för Sverige.* Stockholm: Statistiska Centralbyrån.

Stephens, J. 1989. "Democratic Transition and Breakdown in Western Europe, 1870–1939: A Test of the Moore Thesis." *American Journal of Sociology* 94 (Mar.):1019–77.

Stimson, J. 1985. "Regression in Space and Time: A Statistical Essay." *American Journal of Political Science* 29(4):914–47.

Sumner, S., and S. Silver. 1989. "Real Wages, Employment, and the Phillips Curve." *Journal of Political Economy* 97(June):706–20.

Sztompka, P. 1986. "The Renaissance of Historical Orientation in Sociology." *International Sociology* 1:321–37.

Therborn, G. 1986. *Why Some Peoples Are More Unemployed Than Others: The Strange Paradox of Growth and Unemployment.* London: Verso.

Tomlins, C. 1985. *The State and the Unions.* Cambridge University Press.

Treiman, D. 1977. "Toward Methods for a Quantitative Comparative Sociology: A Reply to Burawoy." *American Journal of Sociology* 82(Mar.):1042–56.

United Nations. Various years. *Monthly Bulletin of Statistics.* New York: U.N. Department of International Economic and Social Affairs, Statistical Office.

U.S. Bureau of the Census. 1975. *Historical Statistics of the United States:*

Colonial Times to 1970. Bicentennial edition. Washington, D.C.: U.S. GPO.

Various years. *Economic Report of the President*. Washington, D.C.: U.S. GPO.

Valocchi, S. 1992. "The Origins of the Swedish Welfare State: A Class Analysis of the State and Welfare Politics." *Social Problems* 39(May):189–200.

Van der Pijl, K. 1984. *The Making of an Atlantic Ruling Class*. London: Verso.

Weir, M., and T. Skocpol. 1985. "State Structures and the Possibilities for 'Keynesian' Responses to the Great Depression in Sweden, Britain, and the United States." In P. Evans et al. (eds.), *Bringing the State Back In*, pp. 107–63. Cambridge University Press.

White, H. 1987. *The Content of the Form: Narrative Discourse and Historical Representation*. Baltimore: Johns Hopkins University Press.

5

The politics of public and private investment in Britain

JOHN R. FREEMAN AND JAMES E. ALT

Many writers attribute Britain's comparatively poor economic performance and, by implication, the failings of its welfare state to deficiencies in the country's investment mix. Some argue that public investment (particularly in the nationalized industries as opposed to general government capital spending) has been used inappropriately as a tool of economic adjustment, others that it has been unduly inflated, either by pressure from the particular clienteles of those industries (unions seeking jobs or customers seeking subsidized goods) or by managers oriented to quantitative growth of production in the absence of a competitive fiscal constraint. Behind these specific arguments lie two general themes or beliefs about public ownership and investment, beliefs that mirror the larger debate.

On the one hand, John Moore, MP (1986) exemplifies those who believe that the elections lead politicians to interfere in public investment for distributional reasons. He writes that public managers are "constantly at risk from political and bureaucratic interference. . . . Are the industries businesses or social services?" (p. 83). For those like Moore, political influence in the shadow of electoral competition prevents state managers from undertaking socially preferred investments: inefficiency results from *too much popular control.* On the other hand, Aharoni (1988) speaks for those who believe that public control allows managers to evade market discipline, while elections provide an inadequate means for voter-consumers to gain satisfaction. He writes that "the many oscillations of government's politics had been a major problem." With political parties unable to remain in office for long periods, state managers are able to create a pattern of investment that serves their own selfish interests at the expense of society's collective interests. Inefficiency results from *too little popular* control.

Our chapter resolves some of this controversy. It is divided into two parts. In the first part, we examine the rationale for guardianship or technocratic control over public investment and show it to be manifest in the British case. We then review the argument that elections inhibit guardianship of public investment rights and thus allow too much popular control over public investment decisions, as well as the argument that state managers are unwilling or unable to act as guardians, so that elections produce too little popular control. These two arguments, plus the further possibility that technocratic control has been realized, form three competing perspectives on democracy and investment in Britain.

These competing accounts are tested in the second part of the chapter. Using British data for the period from 1955 to 1984 and a multiequation time-series technique, we show that electoral politics has not necessarily affected public or private investment. The effects of unexpected changes or shocks in citizens' voting intentions on both public and private investment have been short-lived and relatively small in magnitude. This is in spite of the fact that British citizens and their parties have very different views about public ownership and about how the nationalized industries ought to be managed. While all three perspectives find some support, the data go against many claims derived from the view that elections afford too much popular control over public investment. The results also show that public investment has been motivated not by managerial self-interest but by trends in such macroeconomic variables as (aggregate) consumption. However, public investment has not had lasting impacts on consumption or on other variables like unemployment. Therefore it appears that despite the electoral outcomes of the past three decades, technocratic control over public investment has remained intact in Britain. But neither technocracy nor electoral democracy provide citizens with an effective – namely, welfare-enhancing – means of executing public investment rights. The implications of our results for future research on the investment rights question are discussed briefly in the concluding section.

ELECTIONS AND INVESTMENT

The rationale for public guardianship

Technocratic execution of public investment rights, according to theories of the public sector, brings about a welfare-enhancing mix of public and private investment, as in correcting various kinds of "market failures."[1] Government planners presumably are guided by an appreciation for the value that future generations place on the returns from these investment streams. For example, they employ a discount rate that is lower than the market rate of interest because the lower rate better accounts for the gains to future (unborn) citizens. In a larger sense, government planners act as *guardians* of the public interest. They execute public investment rights on behalf of citizens, living and unborn, so as to realize productively efficient, welfare-enhancing investment mixes (Arrow and Kurz 1970, esp. p. 6).

In theory Britain's nationalized industries originally were to be operated by a group of public guardians. The Morrisonian conception of the public corporation – pioneered by Labour Minister Herbert Morrison – entrusted the execution of public ownership rights to benign groups of state managers. It provided for an "arms length" relationship between state managers and government. Public corporations were to be operated by socially conscious managers who did not have to answer to Parliament or even to ministers for their decisions. However, over the years, state managers have been subject to more ministerial and parliamentary supervision (see upcoming sections). Efforts also have been made in various official White Papers to rationalize the operation of the nationalized industries both internally and in relation to patterns of private investment. These include attempts to stipulate minimum rates of return (1961), to employ long-term marginal cost pricing in the nationalized industries, to apply "test discount rates" to their public investments (1967), and more recently, to reconcile the external financing limits of the nationalized industries with governments' general macroeconomic strategies (1978). In this way, the British experience reveals a belief in the possibility of guardianship of the public ownership rights (Garner 1979, 1985; Redwood 1980; and Redwood and Hatch 1982).

Too much popular control

General argument. At the heart of the first perspective, that elections allow too much popular control over public investment decisions, is the claim that changes in the investment mix are a direct outgrowth of electoral competition. This is an example of the general argument that the instability of social choice makes majority rule undercut otherwise stable systems of property rights (see, e.g., Usher 1981). That is, electoral politics prevents state managers from discovering and implementing optimal mixes of investment, investment mixes that serve society's collective interest by inducing political parties instead to use public investment to (re)distribute wealth to their particular supporters. Most simply, if citizens prefer fundamentally different public investments and fiscal policies, volatile electoral outcomes will reflect their disagreement (Heurtebise 1978).

Further, to stay in office, parties must implement fiscal policies and make public investments that serve the interests of their living constituents at the expense of the interests of their living opponents and, perhaps, the interests of future, unborn citizens. For example, Cohen and Noll (1984) show how a system in which electors vote "retrospectively" by observing their benefits from incumbents' policies induces politicians desiring reelection to defer capital projects (which pay off later) in favor of current consumption. It follows that parties which support the principle of public guardianship cannot get (re)elected. Since party leaders know this and are self-interested, they use fiscal policy and public investments to win the support of their particular (living) constituents. If this change in the structure of property rights makes private investors unnecessarily uncertain about rates of return, asset markets are distorted, and the level and pattern of private investment also is adversely affected.[2]

The idea that electoral politics prevents the realization of a collectively preferable investment mix recurs in debates over the British experience. Some contend that in violation of the "arms length" dicta, elected officials have continually intervened in the price, wage, and other policies of public enterprise managers, perhaps more visibly from the mid-1960s onward. Even Thatcher's governments, while somewhat reducing the scope of public investment, are charged with using the nationalized industries to promote the interest of conservative voters in the automotive industry, in rural parts of Britain, and in various other constituencies.[3] Indeed, Brittan (1983) claims that Britain's electoral volatility has made private investors uncertain about long-range rates of return from new investment, as well as about the structure of property rights. In turn, private investors supposedly eschewed the kind of investment that produces lasting gains in productive efficiency, employment, and real growth of incomes and consumption.

Specific implications of the first perspective. As a starting point, the first perspective stresses the role of distributive concerns in electoral politics. Its central implication is that public investment responds more to macroeconomic conditions that have clear distributional and hence partisan consequences, like unemployment and inflation, than to such conditions as aggregate consumption that have more collective, intergenerational welfare consequences.[4] A second implication is that the impact of public investment should be more apparent on those macroeconomic variables with the clearest distributional consequences. Third, trends in public investment should depend directly on trends in support of incumbent political parties. Moreover, trends in support of incumbent political parties should depend at least indirectly on the macroeconomic consequences of public investment if not directly on public investment. That is, when changes in relevant economic conditions (unemployment and inflation) occur such that popular support falls off, public investment will be adjusted so as to restore the welfare of the government's supporters, and if effective, this will bolster popular support. Fourth, the effects of public investment on inflation and unemployment vary depending on the identity of the incumbent political party since each party's supporters prefer a different mix of investment and, by implication, a different blend of welfare outcomes (Hibbs 1977). Fifth, and finally, if elections produce uncertainty that undercuts private investment, then private investment depends on (at least unanticipated) changes in levels of popular support of incumbents. (Because this last claim relates to the effects of unanticipated changes in popular support, it will be tested separately.)[5]

Too little popular control

General argument. The second theoretical perspective stresses the problems posed by the separation of ownership and control. It holds that the managers of firms have incentives to further their own particular interests at the expense of shareholders' interests, private and public, and, in turn, at the expense of society as a whole. Various institutions exist to help private owners control private firms. These institutions, which promote productive efficiency and therefore enhance the welfare of society, include stockholders' meetings, company law, managerial labor markets, and capital markets. The most effective means private owners have to reassert control – to promote efficiency – is share trading. By selling shares in private firms, private owners presumably can punish managers for inefficient behavior. Of course, to the extent that private equity transactions are based on information owners receive from managers, asset markets can be imperfect, ownership will remain separate from control, and socially suboptimal welfare outcomes can occur. Private managers' abilities to control the agendas of stockholders' meetings and/or to manipulate accounting data make this situation worse.

Even so, this problem is much more severe in the case of public ownership. First, performance criteria for public enterprise are difficult to define and apply, allowing more possibilities for managers to misrepresent firms' performance. Second, public ownership rights are compulsory by virtue of residence and cannot be sold. For each member of the public, unlike shareholders in joint stock companies who can sell their shares, the costs of influencing government enterprise policy can considerably outweigh any benefits gained from a change in policy. Then, citizens will not hold public managers accountable for policy. Managers have greater freedom to make mistakes or simply to pursue their own selfish interests; and inefficient patterns of public investment and, in turn, social welfare losses, therefore occur because electoral institutions are no substitute for markets as a source of managerial control (see Millward and Parker 1983; Aharoni 1988).

The second perspective also is common in literature on Britain. Some writers argue that private managers have seized control of British firms and, out of selfishness or a deep cultural aversion to industrialism, have made inefficient decisions (Knight 1983). In the nationalized industries, public managers have neither guarded the public interest nor promoted any social conception of distributional equity. Rather, by lobbying or ignoring Parliament, nationalized industries' managers and public planners in general have preserved their (or their clients') control over the public's property. British citizens, whether out of ignorance or excessively high political transaction costs, have not been willing or able to hold state managers accountable for their (public) investment decisions. Thus, for most of the past 40 years there has been no effective means for public owners to control public managers (Pryke 1981, esp. pp. 249–50).

Specific implications of the second perspective. First, elections have little impact on public investment, which remains unaffected by trends or by unexpected fluctuations in popular support for incumbent political officials. This is either because public managers are able to prevent those officials from holding them accountable to citizen-owners or because citizen-owners do not use these expressions of support to punish or reward state managers. Moreover, citizens' support for incumbent political officials does not depend on public investment, as citizens display little understanding of how their welfare depends on public investment. Hence, it also is the case that electoral outcomes, including changes in the partisan identity of governments, have no effect on public investment or on the welfare consequences of investment generally.

Finally, the view that elections allow too little popular control over public investment implies that trends in private and public investment are best explained by their own past histories. In other words, each kind of investment is self-reinforcing; each is designed to serve the respective managers' (or some narrow clientele's) selfish interests more than to serve the interests of society. The close links with the distributive outcomes implied by the first perspective in particular are absent. Any impacts of private or public investment on consumption, employment, and the like are short-lived.[6]

Technocracy realized: a third perspective

General argument. A third perspective holds that the rationale for guardianship of public investment rights is real and that it enjoys widespread public support (see, e.g., Shonfield 1965). Citizens and their elected officials willingly surrender their public investment rights to state managers and government planners who pursue a meaningful conception of the public interest beyond direct electoral reach. This third perspective is somewhat different from the first and second perspectives. This "technocratic perspective" shares both the first perspective's belief in the *possibility* of technocratic control over public investment and the second perspective's appreciation of the problem of holding state managers and planners accountable through democratic institutions. However, this third view rejects the other perspectives' claims that elections invariably subvert technocratic control on the one hand and that state managers and planners promote their self-interest on the other.

The third perspective is less prevalent in British studies. Some students of the nationalized industries contend that Morrisonian doctrine was adhered to in the 1950s and 1960s because of the consensus that existed among party leaders about the virtues of technocratic control over public investment (Millward 1976; Pryke 1981; and Redwood and Hatch 1982). However, most of the same writers contend that electoral politics eventually undermined Morrisonianism in particular and government investment planning in general. As a consequence, a socially harmful pattern of public investment supposedly was realized in Britain. To our knowledge, none of these analysts have seriously investigated the possibility that public investment decisions continued to be made technocratically throughout the 1970s and into the 1980s.

Specific implications of the third perspective. As with the other two, the technocratic perspective has a set of testable implications. What most clearly differentiates the technocratic perspective from both the others is the argument that a concern for future aggregate welfare outcomes motivates public investment. The socially beneficial effects of technocratic control are reflected in the lasting, positive impacts that public investment has on macroeconomic variables like consumption. If state managers are concerned with enhancing the collective welfare of current and future generations, the technocratic perspective implies (contrary to the view that elections allow too much popular control) that public investment is motivated more by trends like aggregate consumption than by trends in unemployment and inflation.[7] Then, like the second perspective but not the first, the technocratic perspective implies that trends and unexpected changes in citizens' voting intentions have little impact on public investment. While citizens' voting intentions could (but need not) depend directly on public investment or indirectly on the welfare consequences of the investment mix, public investment is not motivated by this or other aspects of electoral competition. Hence, also, changes in the partisan identity of governments have little effect on the causes or welfare consequences of public investment. Finally, contrary to the expectations of the others, the technocratic perspective implies that public investment consistently is designed to complement private investment in a way that reflects state managers' and government planners' conceptions of the public interest.

METHODOLOGY AND DATA

Methodology

In an ideal world, our statistical analysis could be carried out within a structural equation framework. To each perspective would correspond a formal model embodying its arguments about how politicians, planners, investors, and citizens make decisions as well as the process by which these decisions interact to produce the actual investment mix. Each of these three models would imply a testable structural equation model for the relationships in Table 5.1, Panel B. We would specify a *general* structural equation model that subsumes all three, in which each equation would express a row or left-hand-side variable in terms of one or more of the column or right-hand-side variables. If we could identify such a model, estimating it would tell us exactly which sets of coefficients actually are statistically significant and are of particular signs and magnitudes, and thus which perspective best accounts for the British experience in the sample time period. A model general enough to subsume all the perspectives will require all six variables to be endogenous and will allow few zero restrictions to be made for identification purposes. Hence, an identified structural model will require some new, presumably exogenous right-hand-side variables.

However, the literature on public investment contains no such widely accepted models (Freeman 1983a), nor could leading scholars direct us to any (e.g., Robert Millward, personal communication). Indeed, the lack of such a theoretically derived model is why we have described "perspectives" and "claims" rather than "theories" and "hypotheses." Inventing such a model would require us to make some stringent, possibly erroneous assumptions about the exogeneity of certain variables within equations and within the system as a whole for identification purposes. Since the existing literature provides little guidance, any choice we made would be controversial. The most we could do is to suggest some structural model consistent with each perspective, but then we cannot directly test the perspectives against each other, since the same information will not be used in each model.

For our purposes in this chapter then, vector autoregression (VAR)

Table 5.1. *Vector autoregressive (VAR) model and theoretical predictions*

Panel A. VAR model for analyzing the causes and welfare consequences of public and private investment

$$C_t = a_{10} + \sum_i a_{11i}\, C_{t-i} + \sum_i a_{12i}\, U_{t-i} + \sum_i a_{13i}\, P_{t-i} + \sum_i a_{14i}\, PRV_{t-i} + \sum_i a_{15i}\, PUB_{t-i} + \sum_i a_{16i}\, SUP_{t-i}$$

$$U_t = a_{20} + \sum_i a_{21i}\, C_{t-i} + \sum_i a_{22i}\, U_{t-i} + \sum_i a_{23i}\, P_{t-i} + \sum_i a_{24i}\, PRV_{t-i} + \sum_i a_{25i}\, PUB_{t-i} + \sum_i a_{26i}\, SUP_{t-i}$$

$$P_t = a_{30} + \sum_i a_{31i}\, C_{t-i} + \sum_i a_{32i}\, U_{t-i} + \sum_i a_{33i}\, P_{t-i} + \sum_i a_{34i}\, PRV_{t-i} + \sum_i a_{35i}\, PUB_{t-i} + \sum_i a_{36i}\, SUP_{t-i}$$

$$PRV_t = a_{40} + \sum_i a_{41i}\, C_{t-i} + \sum_i a_{42i}\, U_{t-i} + \sum_i a_{43i}\, P_{t-i} + \sum_i a_{44i}\, PRV_{t-i} + \sum_i a_{45i}\, PUB_{t-i} + \sum_i a_{46i}\, SUP_{t-i}$$

$$PUB_t = a_{50} + \sum_i a_{51i}\, C_{t-i} + \sum_i a_{52i}\, U_{t-i} + \sum_i a_{53i}\, P_{t-i} + \sum_i a_{54i}\, PRV_{t-i} + \sum_i a_{55i}\, PUB_{t-i} + \sum_i a_{56i}\, SUP_{t-i}$$

$$SUP_t = a_{60} + \sum_i a_{61i}\, C_{t-i} + \sum_i a_{62i}\, U_{t-i} + \sum_i a_{63i}\, P_{t-i} + \sum_i a_{64i}\, PRV_{t-i} + \sum_i a_{65i}\, PUB_{t-i} + \sum_i a_{66i}\, SUP_{t-i}$$

Panel B. Specific predictions of theoretical perspectives with respect to parameters in VAR model in Panel A.

Too much popular control	Too little popular control	Technocratic control
$a_{52i} \neq 0;\ a_{62i} \neq 0$	$a_{51i} = 0;\ a_{15i} = 0$	$a_{51i} \neq 0;\ a_{15i} \neq 0$
$a_{53i} \neq 0;\ a_{63i} \neq 0$	$a_{52i} = 0;\ a_{25i} = 0$	$a_{54i} \neq 0;\ a_{45i} \neq 0$
$a_{56i} \neq 0;\ a_{66i} \neq 0$	$a_{53i} = 0;\ a_{35i} = 0$	$a_{55i} \neq 0;\ a_{65i} = 0$
$a_{25i} \neq 0;\ a_{35i} \neq 0$	$a_{55i} \neq 0;\ a_{65i} = 0$	$a_{56i} = 0$
	$a_{56i} = 0$	

Note: C_t, U_t, P_t, PRV_t, PUB_t, and SUP_t denote levels of consumption, unemployment, prices, private investment, public investment and government support, respectively. (See text for specific definitions.)

has some advantages over structural equation methods (cf. Janoski and Isaac, Chapter 2 this volume; the principal citation in political science is Freeman, Williams, and Lin 1989). VAR does not force us to make stringent assumptions for identification, and its results are less likely to be affected in what they reveal about causal relationships by the possible omission of truly relevant lags of variables. In this way, VAR allows comparison of the competing perspectives and indeed lets us gain information valuable in constructing a structural model, while avoiding many of the inferential problems associated with the structural equation approach. Of course, it too has certain shortcomings. The method still forces us to impose some (weaker) restrictions on our equation systems, restrictions that could be inappropriate. In its unrestricted form, the method's usefulness is limited to the analysis of small- and medium-scale systems like the one we are studying here. As the number of variables in the model increases, a rapidly growing number of coefficients must be estimated. Degrees of freedom quickly diminish, and statistical inference becomes more problematic. Confidence intervals in the innovation accounting can become large (see Sims 1987). Nevertheless, for an application like our effort in using British data to test such theories, where the existing competing theoretical arguments are so poorly developed, the virtues of VAR clearly outweigh its drawbacks.

Model restrictions and data

The general form of our VAR model is contained in Table 5.1, Panel A. Each of the six variables – three welfare consequences, the two investment variables, and government support – are functions of their own past histories and the histories of the remaining variables. From a substantive standpoint, the inclusion of past histories in this full reduced form model allows current consumption to vary with past consumption (the essence of the life cycle-permanent income hypothesis; Hall 1978), "bureaucratic inertia" to exist in public investment behavior (Frey and Schneider 1978), current and past levels of private investment to be related in accordance with the tenets of prevailing economic theories (Bean 1981a, b) and noneconomic, autonomous sources in support for governments to exist (Hudson 1985). The other variables on the right-hand sides of the equations capture various other sources of change in the left-hand-side variables, for instance, the impact of "wealth effects" on permanent income calculations in the consumption equation (Hall 1978), the effects of financial considerations and changes in factor demands in the private investment equation (Bean 1981a, b), and the impacts of consumption, unemployment, prices (Hibbs 1982), and past support (Hudson 1985) in the government support equation.

VAR models for Britain were constructed in the following way. Quarterly data on the six variables in Table 5.1, Panel A, were assembled for the time period from 1955-I through 1984-II. Variables include (gross) consumer spending, private investment (an aggregate of gross domestic fixed capital formation by industrial and commercial companies and by financial institutions), and public investment (gross fixed capital formation by British public corporations and local and central governments combined). (We later note the results – essentially the same – from estimating models with capital formation by public corporations alone.) These series were all seasonally unadjusted and in current prices. "Unemployment" was defined as the seasonally unadjusted number of people without jobs, including school leavers. The index of retail prices was used for the price variable. All these series were taken from the 1985 Annual Supplement of *Economic Trends*.[8]

What measures how citizens execute their public ownership rights? Ideally, we would like to have an indicator that taps citizens' evaluations of governments' investment activities. Unfortunately, continuous quarterly time series of this kind are not available. In this chapter, we substitute a measure that is a quarterly indicator, the proportion of the public intending to vote for the incumbent party in the next election (VOTE). While this taps a much broader political orientation than the question of public investment, empirical work has demonstrated the electorate's close cognitive link between the British political parties and the parties' positions on public ownership (Alt, Sarlvik, and Crewe 1976), and public investment has been linked to voting outcomes, at least anecdotally (Hart 1986). For consistency with the literature (see Frey and Schneider 1978), models with two other indicators also were analyzed: the proportion of citizens approving of government's (overall) performance (*APP*) and the percentage lead that the incumbent party enjoys over its main opposition in terms of expressed voting intentions (*LEAD*).

These measures allow us to test the central tenets of the competing perspectives pertaining to the impact that electoral politics has on investment activity. For instance, if the too much control perspective is correct and electoral politics undermines technocratic control over public investment decisions, we might observe significant changes in the behavior of public investment corresponding to changes of party control of government. Alternatively, at least vote intention should be causally prior to public investment. If changes in vote intention represent direct threats to the authority of political officials, incumbent parties have a clear incentive to alter public investment in response to these changes. According to this view, unexpected changes or shocks in vote intention ought to produce concomitant fluctuations in private investment.

Of course, changes of party control, vote intention, and other measures of government support may be imperfect reflections of citizens' evaluations of (efforts to change) public investment. In fact, the other two theoretical perspectives stress precisely this fact. Especially the second (too little popular control) emphasizes the imperfect means that citizens, as public owners, have to execute their investment rights. However, these two perspectives make different claims about the welfare consequences of this aspect of political-economic reality.

The theoretical debate is represented in the following way. The competing claims amount to different *sets* of predictions about the coefficients in the general VAR model in Table 5.1, Panel A. Specifically, each theoretical perspective makes the predictions summarized in Table 5.1, Panel B. Additionally, the first perspective implies that the coefficients that embody these relationships change with shifts in partisan control of government. Each perspective also makes predictions about the ways the British system responds to shocks or innovations in the variables. For example, the too much control perspective predicts that a positive surge in vote intention will produce lasting decreases in public investment, while the too little control and technocratic perspectives predict that these same shocks will have no lasting impact on public investment. Similarly, the too much control perspective predicts that most of the forecast error variance in public investment will be due to shocks in vote intention relative to shocks in other variables. The other two perspectives predict that the forecast error variance in public investment will be accounted for mostly by shocks in public investment itself (too little control) or by shocks in consumption (technocracy). The overall accuracy of the perspectives can be assessed by examining the number of theoretical predictions with which the data are consistent.

We concentrate on a specific six-variable system composed of the welfare consequences consumption (*C*), unemployment (*U*), and the index of retail prices (*P*); private investment (*PRV*); public investment (*PUBGOVT*); and the government support variable (*VOTE*). VAR models with these and other variables were estimated with both six and eight lags and with and without trend terms included in each equation. We focus on the specification with six lags of the right-hand-side variables and with equations containing constants but not trend terms. With the exception of government support, all variables were transformed into logarithms prior to estimation. This is a standard way to stabilize the variance in the time series and does not affect the results of the causality tests (Pierce and Haugh 1977). In order to determine how robust the results are, a collection of simpler three-, four-, and five-equation systems containing some alternative indicators were also estimated. Details of measurements and results are available from the authors.[9]

For the innovation accounting, we chose the ordering *C, PRV, PUBGOVT, U, P, VOTE*. This ordering embodies an essentially Keynesian view of the economy in which shocks in consumption and private investment have immediate effects on all the other variables in the model. Shocks in both private and public investment have immediate impacts on unemployment, prices, and voting intentions, and shocks in voting intentions do not have immediate impacts on other variables. Shocks in all variables have *lagged* effects on all other variables. We call this ordering, in which economic shocks have contemporaneous effects on vote intention but political shocks affect economic variables only with a lag, the "economics of politics" ordering.[10]

EMPIRICAL EVALUATION OF THE COMPETING PERSPECTIVES

In presenting our results, first we consider the evidence about the *existence* of causal relationships as predicted by each perspective. Then we establish the *stability* of these relationships across partisan eras. Finally, we examine the *direction* and *magnitude* of certain causal relationships as indicated by the response of our system of equations to simulated shocks.

Hypothesis-testing: the existence of predicted causal relationships

Table 5.2 contains the *F*-statistics for the tests of the bivariate relationships. Notice first that the results are consistent with much of the conventional wisdom about the structure of the British political economy. For example, the current level of private investment depends on past consumption (a surrogate for expected output), on past unemployment (an indicator of "factor demand"), and on past private investment (Bean 1981a). Unemployment appears to be largely self-perpetuating in Britain, as some studies have suggested (Layard 1986). Proportions intending to vote for the incumbents vary in a seemingly autonomous fashion but also depend on past unemployment, in keeping with the arguments of most political economists (Alt 1979; Hibbs 1982; and Hudson 1985). It is reasonable to assume then that the six-equation VAR model captures the general contours of British political economic reality.[11]

The *F*-statistics do not establish the superiority of any single theoretical perspective. As regards the predictions in Table 5.1, Panel B, about half of each perspective's claims are refuted. Typically, the first and third perspectives predict causal relationships that did not appear in the

Table 5.2. *F-statistics for six-variable vector autoregressive model: Britain, 1956-III thru 1984-II*

	Causes (right-hand-side variables)					
Consequences (left-hand-side variables)	*C*	*U*	*P*	*PRV*	*PUB-GOVT*	*VOTE*
C	12.2**	1.6	2.8†	2.0†	1.0 II, ~III	.9
U	1.0	68.6**	.5	.8	.5 ~I, II	.8
P	2.0†	2.0†	138.0**	1.4	1.2 ~I, II	1.8
PRV	2.2†	2.6†	1.4	3.6**	2.3† III	.7
PUB-GOVT	3.9** ~II, III	3.3** I, ~II	5.0** I, ~II	.6 ~III	18.8** II, III	1.9†
VOTE	.6	2.8† I	.2 II	.8	.7 II, III	19.8** I

Note: Six lags of each variable were used in this case; constants were included in all the equations. The Roman numerals under the *F*-statistics indicated whether the statistics confirm or disconfirm (~) the causal claims of the respective theoretical perspectives as summarized in Table 5.1, Panel B.
†$p < .10$; *$p < .05$; **$p < .01$.

fitted model; in contrast, relationships appeared to exist where the second perspective predicted none.

The too little control perspective offers the most accurate account of the welfare and electoral consequences of public investment. It correctly predicts that public investment is not causally prior to consumption, unemployment, or prices. This result is inconsistent with the too much control claim about the distributive effects of public investment and also with the technocratic perspective's expectation that public investment produces significant consumption gains. The too little control perspective's claim that expressions of support for incumbents do not depend on patterns of public investment is confirmed as well. The *F*-statistic in the bottom cell of the fifth column of Table 5.2 is quite small and statistically insignificant. The finding that public investment is not causally prior to vote intention is inconsistent with the idea that elections reveal citizens' preferences for executing collective ownership rights on behalf of particular welfare outcomes. There simply is little evidence that public investment directly affects voting intentions.[12]

The *F*-statistics indicate that public investment is motivated by trends in societal welfare. The statistics in the fifth row of Table 5.2 contradict the second perspective and offer mixed verdicts on the first and third perspectives. The results suggest that public investment varies in response to changes in consumption, unemployment, and inflation.[13] This shows that public investment is not purely an outgrowth of its own past history; it does not vary in a purely bureaucratic, incremental fashion. The results also show that public investment is not motivated purely by vote intentions, as some proponents of the first perspective claim. But neither is public investment motivated solely by consumption, nor is private investment causally prior to public investment, as some proponents of the third perspective suggest (but see the upcoming discussion).

In sum, the *F*-tests do not tell us which perspective best accounts for the effects of electoral politics on public investment. The fact that both unemployment and inflation are causally prior to public investment is noteworthy because it indicates that public investment is motivated, in part, by a concern for outcomes whose effects are not distributed evenly across groups of partisan supporters. This result coupled with the finding of marginally significant *F*-statistics for the direct effect of vote intention on public investment might lead us to conclude that the first perspective (too much popular control) best accounts for the British experience. However, the fact that public investment depends on societal consumption supports the technocratic perspective. The *F*-statistics contradict the claims of the second perspective (too little popular control) that the determinants of public investment are purely bureaucratic, but they are consistent with its predictions about the welfare consequences of public investment. Clearly then we need to analyze the British system further before we can establish the superiority of one or more of the perspectives.

Politicoeconomic eras and stability: the effects of changes of government

The results are historically meaningful in the sense that our system of equations are stable across major political and economic events. Table 5.3 reports the modified likelihood ratio test statistics for relevant

Table 5.3. *Tests for homogeneity across major political and economic eras and administrations: six variable vector autoregressive models*

	Likelihood ratio test statistics		Critical χ^2 values	
	C, U, P, PRV, PUB-GOVT, VOTE	*C, U, P, PRV, PUB-CORP, VOTE*	.10 level	.05 level
Eras				
Morrisonian; pre-first white paper on the Nationalized Industries (1956-III thru 1964-II)	$\chi^2(192) = 138.7$	$\chi^2(192) = 168.8$	217.5	225.3
Post-third White Paper on the Nationalized Industries (1978-II thru 1984-II)	$\chi^2(150) = 145.9$	$\chi^2(150) = 130.2$	172.6	179.6
Party administrations				
Eden-MacMillan (1956-III thru 1959-IV)	$\chi^2(84) = 57.1$	$\chi^2(84) = 69.1$	101.0	106.4
MacMillan-Home (1960-I thru 1964-III)	$\chi^2(114) = 94.0$	$\chi^2(114) = 91.4$	133.7	139.9
Wilson I (1964-IV thru 1970-II)	$\chi^2(138) = 133.2$	$\chi^2(138) = 135.9$	159.7	167.2
Health (1970-III thru 1974-I)	$\chi^2(90) = 77.3$	$\chi^2(90) = 69.6$	107.6	113.1
Wilson II (1974-II thru 1976-I)	$\chi^2(48) = 82.4$	$\chi^2(48) = 81.7$	60.9	65.2
Callaghan (1976-II thru 1979-II)	$\chi^2(78) = 81.1$	$\chi^2(78) = 85.6$	94.4	99.6
Thatcher (1979-III thru 1984-II)	$\chi^2(120) = 128.4$	$\chi^2(120) = 115.4$	140.3	146.6
All Labour governments (1964-IV thru 1970-II and 1974-II thru 1979-II)	$\chi^2(264) = 248.4$	$\chi^2(264) = 244.6$	293.8	302.9
Post-oil shock (1974-I thru 1984-II)	$\chi^2(252) = 225.2$	$\chi^2(252) = 216.1$	281.2	290.0

Note: Specifications identical to those that apply for Table 5.2. Test statistics are calculated according to the formula given in Sims (1980, p. 17). Critical χ^2 values are calculated with the formula given in Dixon and Massey (1969).

political and economic eras. First, there is practically no evidence that subsamples differed for any party administration or, more generally, for periods of Labour Party governance (see the tenth row). This lack of change in public investment corresponding to changes in partisan incumbency is inconsistent with the too much control perspective. The only exception is the period in which the second Wilson government was in office. Since some comparatively radical ministers served in this administration and it adopted some seemingly new policies with regard to public investment (e.g., the National Enterprise Board and the Accelerated Projects Scheme), one might attribute the unusual character of this subsample to the investment decisions that this particular government made. However, the second Wilson government was in office in the years immediately following the oil price increase of late 1973. Hence, the unusual character of this part of our sample also could be due to the occurrence of that external economic event. Either way, this subsample is a small part of the entire sample; it constituted only 7 of the 118 observations in our time series.[14]

Moreover, subsamples for all other administrative and partisan eras are not different from the entire sample, and the subsample for the whole remaining period after the oil price increase is also not different from the sample as a whole (see the eleventh row of Table 5.3). In particular, the first 5 years of the Thatcher administration are not discrepant from a model estimated over the previous 24 years. Apparently asset sales involving public corporation have not (yet) been accompanied by significant structural changes in the relationships between public investment and the rest of the macroeconomy, echoing a point made by Alt (1987b). Finally, the statistics indicate that the samples for the periods before the first and third White Papers are not different from the sample for the entire period and that the efforts to change the accounting procedures for the nationalized industries did not alter the structure of the relationships in our models. There are good reasons to believe then that parameters of our VAR models are relatively stable and hence that our results about causal relationships are historically meaningful.

Innovation accounting: size and direction of relationships

The results of the innovation accounting are inconsistent with some of the theoretical predictions of the first perspective (too much control). They are more consistent with the predictions of the third (technocracy) than with the second perspective (too little control). Table 5.4 contains the decomposition of forecast error variance for the estimated British model under the "economics of politics" ordering. The decomposition

Table 5.4. ***Percentages of forecast error variance k quarters ahead produced by each innovation: Britain 1956-III thru 1984-II. Economics of politics ordering***

		Innovation in					
Forecast error in	*k*	*C*	*PRV*	*PUB-GOVT*	*U*	*P*	*VOTE*
C	1	100.0	0.0	0.0	0.0	0.0	0.0
	5	91.7	0.8	1.0	0.6	3.1	2.8
	15	85.6	3.8	2.2	2.6	4.1	1.2
	25	84.8	5.2	4.5	1.5	2.7	1.1
PRV	1	29.6	70.3	0.0	0.0	0.0	0.0
	5	62.2	30.8	1.6	3.7	0.9	0.6
	15	74.8	11.1	5.3	1.7	0.9	0.7
	25	79.2	9.4	6.0	1.3	2.1	2.0
PUB-GOVT	1	5.2	2.0	92.6	0.0	0.0	0.0
	5	23.9	1.2	58.6	5.7	2.0	8.4
	15	41.6	3.2	31.0	5.5	12.2	6.3
	25	32.6	3.3	27.4	11.6	17.3	7.7
U	1	10.0	1.4	1.1	87.4	0.0	0.0
	5	9.6	2.6	0.2	79.6	6.4	1.4
	15	23.4	3.6	2.2	63.5	7.9	1.2
	25	31.8	4.8	1.0	53.4	7.2	1.5
P	1	12.6	3.6	0.7	1.8	81.2	0.0
	5	56.2	0.4	0.4	5.8	37.0	0.2
	15	71.0	3.2	1.6	10.7	13.2	0.1
	25	75.8	4.8	3.3	7.0	8.6	0.3
VOTE	1	1.4	0.1	4.4	3.5	9.2	81.2
	5	1.0	5.7	4.2	6.2	7.6	75.0
	15	1.8	6.2	3.3	14.8	9.0	64.6
	25	2.6	6.0	3.2	18.6	8.6	60.8

Note: Six lags of each variable were used in this case; constants were included in all of the equations. Due to rounding, the numbers in each row do not add to 100. The ordering of variables is *C*, *PRV*, *PUB-GOVT*, *U*, *P*, and *VOTE*.

is derived from subjecting the model to a set of orthogonalized shocks in the variables. Reading down the table and looking at 15-quarter effects, we see that the forecast error variance in consumption depends on shocks in that same variable; the forecast error variance in private investment depends on shocks in consumption and, to a lesser extent, shocks in itself; the forecast error variance in public investment depends on shocks in consumption, shocks in itself, and to a lesser extent, shocks in the price level; the forecast error variance in unemployment depends primarily on shocks in itself and, to some degree, on shocks in consumption; the forecast error variance in prices depends primarily on shocks in consumption; and the forecast error variance in voting intentions depends primarily on shocks in that same variable but also, to some degree, on shocks in unemployment.

Contrary to what the too much control perspective claims, public investment does not depend on shocks in vote intention or, to a great degree, on shocks in unemployment; surges in vote intention and unemployment account for (at very different lags) at most 8.4 percent and 11.6 percent of the forecast error variance in public investment, respectively. In contrast, the effect of inflation on public investment is larger, at least if one is prepared to wait long enough. There is no evidence that vote intention depends on surges of public investment, which accounts for no more than 4.4 percent of the forecast error variance in vote intention. Finally, note that at most 2 percent of the forecast error variance in private investment is attributable to shocks in vote intention. To the extent that these typical shocks capture the uncertainty in the workings of the British electoral system, this result contradicts the final implication of the first perspective. The relatively small percentage of forecast error variance in private investment attributable to a shock in vote intention implies that political uncertainty does not have a major direct impact on private investors' willingness to undertake new investments. The fact that shocks in vote intention have only a minor impact on public investment and shocks in public investment have only a minor impact on consumption implies that political uncertainty also has no major indirect effects on private investment. In sum, our innovation accounting provides little support for the central tenets of the too much control perspective.[15]

These same results are consistent with the claims of both the second and the third theoretical perspectives, which predict most of the just-mentioned findings. Where they differ is in their accounts of the interrelationships between consumption, private investment, and public investment. The results in Table 5.4 are unfortunately not definitive in this regard. The decomposition of error variance indicates that in explaining the forecast error variance in public investment, the impact of

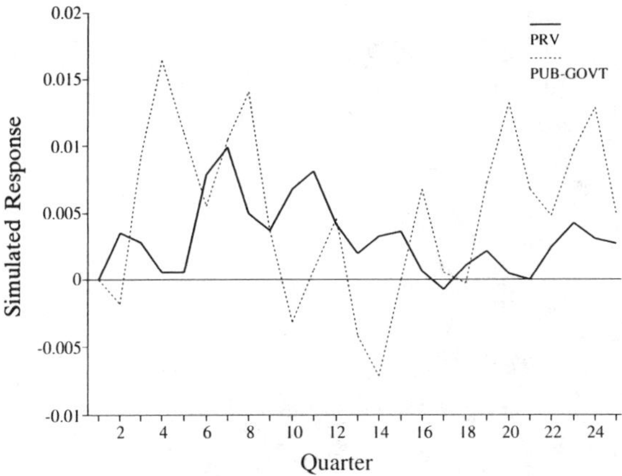

Figure 5.1. Simulated responses of the moving-average representation of the six-variable British political economic system to a one standard deviation, orthogonalized, positive surge or shock in the proportion of the electorate expressing an intention to vote for the incumbent government (*VOTE*); specifications identical to those on which Tables 5.2 and 5.4 are based.

shocks in consumption eventually exceeds that of shocks in public investment itself. In fact, by 15 quarters almost 41.6 percent of the forecast error variance in public investment is attributable to shocks in consumption. This contradicts the idea that managers pursue their self-interest, a central claim of the too little control perspective. However, there is no evidence that public investment is motivated by shocks in private investment or that unexpected surges of public investment have major impacts on private investment or consumption. Shocks in private investment account for at most 3.3 percent of the forecast error variance in public investment; shocks in public investment account for no more than 6.0 percent and 4.5 percent of the forecast error variance in private investment and consumption, respectively. These results contradict the technocratic control perspective.[16]

A closer look at these results reveals several additional patterns that bear on the direction of relationships. While they are not unambiguous, these patterns strengthen support for the technocratic perspective and, on balance, weaken the case for the too much control perspective. First, Figure 5.1 depicts the response of both public and private investment to a "historically grounded," positive, orthogonalized surge (shock) in vote intention. The cyclical nature of the responses makes them difficult to interpret.[17] However, an unexpected surge in support for incumbents

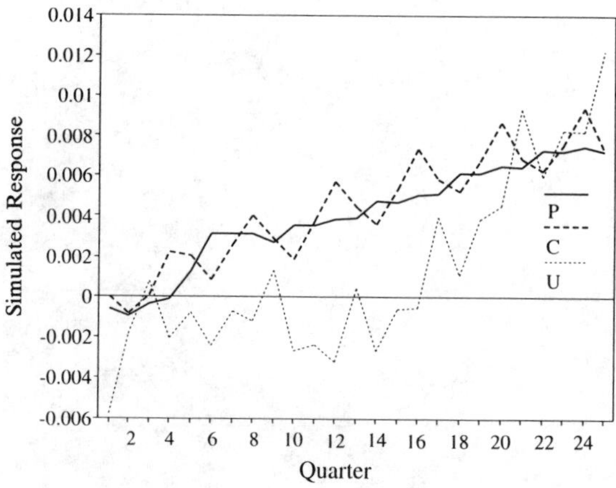

Figure 5.2. Simulated response of the moving-average representation of the six-variable British political economic system to a one standard deviation, orthogonalized, positive surge or shock in the log of combined government investment (*PUB-GOVT*); specifications identical to those on which Tables 5.2 and 5.4 are based.

actually spawns more public investment over the short term. This is consistent with the first, but not the other, perspectives. A surge in support also spawns more private investment over the medium term; by implication, a negative shock in vote intention would produce a decline in private investment. While this is at first glance consistent with the first perspective, recall that overall these shocks in vote intention have little impact on private investment (Table 5.4).

Next, turning to the welfare consequences of public investment, Figure 5.2 shows that a positive innovation in public investment produces, after a short delay, sustained increases in societal consumption and in the index of retail prices. The same shock produces a small decline in unemployment over the medium term; unemployment eventually increases after about four years have passed. In other words, positive surges of public investment augment personal consumption and hold down unemployment over the medium term. These "innovations" also produce an increase in retail prices, however. The result regarding the impact of shocks in public investment on consumption is important. It indicates that while the relative magnitude of this impact is small, the dynamic character of the impact of a shock in public investment on consumption is different from what the second theoretical perspective (too little control) predicts.

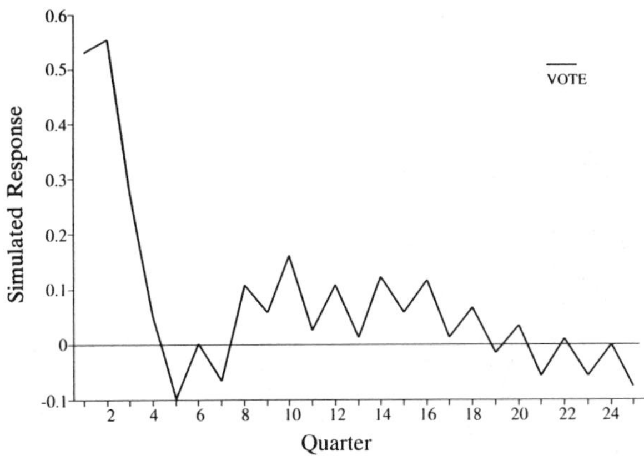

Figure 5.3. Simulated response of the moving-average representation of the six-variable British political economic system to a one standard deviation, orthogonalized, positive surge or shock in the log of combined government investment (*PUB-GOVT*); specifications identical to those on which Tables 5.2 and 5.4 are based.

Figures 5.3 and 5.4 also cast light on the debate about elections and investment, that is, on how seemingly unexpected changes in public investment affect voting intentions and private investment. The former displays the effects on vote intention of a surge in public investment. It shows that a positive surge of public investment produces an immediate increase in the proportion of the citizenry intending to vote for the incumbent party. But this effect is not sustained. Within three to four quarters the vote intention variable settles back to its initial value (i.e., zero in the simulation exercise). This is consistent with the idea that British citizens only *temporarily* reward incumbents for unexpected, positive surges of public investment, a tenet of both the second and third perspectives.

Figure 5.4 displays the responses of the investment variables to a positive innovation in public investment. It shows that a positive (negative) shock in public investment produces an increase (decrease) in private investment after a short delay, and this increase (decrease) is sustained over time. This is inconsistent with the claim that government's willingness to undertake new investment discourages private investors from doing the same. Just the opposite seems to be true: unexpected surges of government investment elicit increases in private investment. Beyond this, the medium- and longer-term response of the

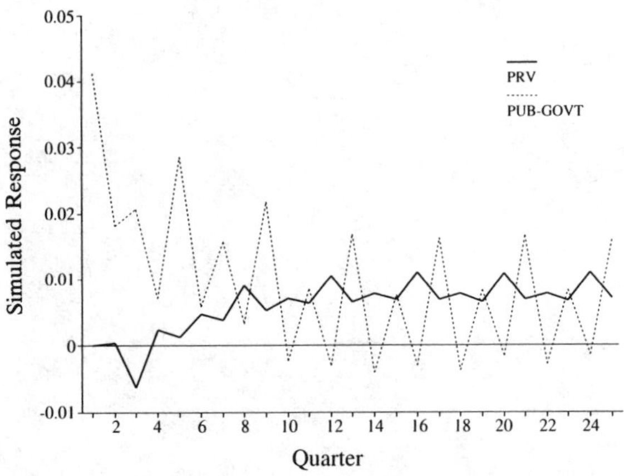

Figure 5.4. Simulated response of the moving-average representation of the six-variable British political economic system to a one standard deviation, orthogonalized, positive surge or shock in the log of combined government investment (*PUB-GOVT*); specifications identical to those on which Tables 5.2 and 5.4 are based.

variables in Figure 5.4 suggests that public investment is designed to bring about a relatively stable pattern of private investment or that public administrators use public investment to control private investment. This might explain why the *F*-statistic in the fourth cell of the fifth row of Table 5.2 is statistically insignificant, that is, because the causality tests we are using generally fail to detect the situation in which one variable is used to control another variable (see Sims 1981, p. 289; or Freeman 1983b, p. 337).

CONCLUSION

Putting everything together, our results offer the least support for the too much control perspective. True, public investment responds to economic conditions with significant distributional aspects, but there is little evidence for the central claim that electoral (party) politics has major direct or indirect effects on public and private investment. The idea that political shocks (uncertainty about either the course of public investment or the electoral fortunes of governments) have socially deleterious effects on private investment is not supported by the data. Because we used the VAR approach, these results do not depend on strong a *priori* model restrictions.

Our results are less definitive with respect to the second and third theoretical perspectives. They appear more consistent with the technocratic perspective. However, this perspective is flawed in some respects. For example, there is little evidence that public investment substantially improves collective welfare. There is evidence that innovations in public investment increase consumption and hold down unemployment (over the medium term). But there is also evidence that public investment innovations are inflationary. While these results support the view that elections allow too little popular control of public investment, this second perspective fails in other specific ways to provide as good an account of the British experience as the technocratic perspective. In particular, the findings about the sources of investment activity in Britain (that consumption, unemployment, and prices affect public investment) imply that public investment decisions are made by state managers and planners who are willing but unable to enhance collective welfare substantially. Finally, the second perspective performs best only under sympathetic causal-ordering assumptions, while the technocratic perspective performs quite well under several different causal orderings (see note 16).

It may seem unfortunate that the data do not choose more decisively between the second and third perspectives. On the contrary, we have discriminated clearly among three broad claims, and we have seen a good deal of evidence about exactly which of the more specific claims of each perspective did and did not find support in the data. This means we have taken a major step toward determining which variables and relationships must be included in any satisfactory structural equation model of public investment (e.g., the macroeconomic determinants of public investment, namely, consumption, unemployment, and prices) and which variables and direct relationships can be ignored (e.g., the lack of effect of all economic variables except unemployment on vote intention, and of public investment on most other variables). As we have shown, the results reported here are robust and historically meaningful.[18] They are generally consistent with economic analyses of consumption (Hall 1978) and private investment (Bean 1981a, b). However, they indicate that any structural equation model consistent with our reduced-form VAR model would have a high degree of endogeneity and include a large number of lagged variables, which will present obstacles to both identifying and estimating such a model.

What contribution do the results make to the debates about democracy and investment? As regards the British experience, the results do not indicate that political uncertainty is responsible for shortfalls in private investment. They show that technocratic control of public investment decisions is a feasible, enduring feature of the British political economy that survived the first Thatcher administration.[19] Nor is there any reason to believe that the uncertainties that the electoral (party) system presently produces have any major effects on private investment in Britain.

While our results are restricted to the workings of British institutions, they have broader implications. One is that electoral politics, even in countries in which there is deep dissensus about public investment, need not undermine the authority of the officials who manage the public's shareholdings and fiscal affairs.[20] At the same time, the results leave little doubt that technocrats face difficult tasks. They indicate that despite their good intentions, British state managers and planners are unable to bring about major changes in consumption or unemployment, or to avoid inflationary costs.

Yet citizens presumably want public investment to enhance social welfare. And, as common owners of public enterprises and of public property generally, they have a right to encourage, if not compel, governments to promote social welfare. Our results suggest that expressions of voting intention (and of approval) are at best ineffective means of exerting this kind of control or of executing public ownership rights. Put another way, positing the existence of a multiparty system and elections for large, publicly owned firms or for society as a whole will not guarantee that state managers and administrators will be held accountable to public owners. Rather the indications are that some new kind of democratic and/or economic institutions must be created for this purpose. Welfare state advocates who promote public enterprise must find better channels through which citizens can execute their public ownership rights than through electoral politics. Or they must provide a greater role for enlightened technocrats.[21]

NOTES

1. This section refers to liberal theories of political economy. Some radical thinkers like Nove (1983) and Dahl (1982, 1985) make many of the same assumptions that liberals make about the workings of democratic institutions and investment.
2. The argument that in a democracy public ownership facilitates the pursuit of particular or partisan interests at the expense of collective interests is not new; see e.g., Breton (1964). Writers like Aharoni (1986) treat the validity of that argument as given. On the idea that the managers of public and private firms behave in fundamentally different ways – the former maximize votes while the latter maximize profits – is explored in such works as Peltzman (1975).
3. Hart (1986) describes Conservative promises (and subsequent delivery) of public investment to British Leyland in the 1979 election campaign. He argues that this helped carry several important Midlands constituencies.

For additional evidence of the Thatcher governments' intervention in the nationalized industries, see Redwood and Hatch (1982, p. 34). On early, disguised episodes of governmental intervention in the decisions of nationalized industries, see Garner (1985) or Millward (1976). Examples of partisan intervention in specific decisions of the nationalized industries include hiring (Pryke 1981, p. 87), wage policy (Pryke 1981; Silberston 1982), pricing (Millward 1976), investment decisions (Rowley 1982; Pryke 1981, esp. chap. 10). The case against democratic management of publicly owned firms is made by Eltis (1979), Pryke (1981), and Redwood and Hatch (1982).

4. Because lengthy time series on income distribution and other indicators of intragenerational equity are not available, we focus here on unemployment and inflation as indicators of a concern for the welfare of particular groups (see Hibbs 1982). Detailed analysis of the distributional effects of changes in the investment mix in Britain can be found in Freeman (1989, chap. 7).
5. Clearly, there are other arguments that could be tested, apart from those for which we have no data. We restrict our attention to a small set of variables most central to the competing perspectives, for which the expectations of positive, negative, or zero effects are clearest. For example, we could see whether the harmful effects of elections show up in lasting negative effects on aggregate indicators like consumption, but this effect is indirect and seems less firmly grounded in the first perspective than those effects we have included. Clearly, we also expect statistically significant relationships among some of the macroeconomic variables in the model. However, the various perspectives do not make different predictions about what relationships we should find.
6. Like the first perspective, the second holds that trends in private and public investment are not necessarily related. Because elections exert too little popular control over state managers and these managers are unwilling or unable to act as public guardians, there need be no causal relationship between the two types of investment. Again, we would not regard the perspectives as being contradicted if such a relationship were to appear.
7. Note that this implication is a matter of *degree*. The technocratic perspective implies a *relatively greater* emphasis on consumption than on unemployment, as compared with the first perspective, for example. Of course, the third perspective also assumes that techniques of macromanagement are effective.
8. Note that in this paper "consumption" means nominal consumption. Seasonally adjusted data were available only for the mid-1960s on. Rather than discard the earlier data or impose a seasonal adjustment on this part of our series, we used the complete seasonally unadjusted series and tested for lag length.
9. We used the modified likelihood ratio statistic described in Sims (1980) to determine an appropriate lag length. The respective statistics for the test of four versus six lags and six versus eight lags were $\chi^2(72) = 114.1$ ($p < .001$) and $\chi^2(72) = 72.2$ ($p < .470$). The robustness checks involved analyses of models in which GDP and real disposable income were substituted for consumption, the implicit GDP deflator was used for prices, and/or *APP* and *LEAD* were used in place of *VOTE*. The checks also involved estimation of models with different lag lengths and trend terms included in the equations. All estimates were carried out using the Regression Analysis of

Times Series (RATS) package, version 1.12. Results are available from the authors.

10. As a check on the robustness of our results under alternative assumptions about the primacy of politics, we also employed a second ordering: *VOTE, PUB-GOVT, C, PRV, U, P*. This ordering assumes that market processes are immediately disturbed by unexpected changes or shocks in political variables but not vice versa. That is, shocks in *VOTE* and *PUB-GOVT* have immediate effects on *C, PRV, U,* and *P*, but shocks in *C, PRV, U*, and *P* affect *VOTE* and *PUB-GOVT* only with a lag. Since the shocks that originate in the polity have immediate effects on all economic variables, we call this alternative ordering "politicized economics." Results for this ordering are reported in note 16.
11. The results of the *F*-tests for alternative systems containing *APP* and *LEAD* were essentially the same as those reported in Table 5.2. In the innovation accounting that will be described, a positive surge in *U* causes a decline in the moving-average response of *VOTE*, as one would expect. The same is true of a positive surge in prices.
12. There also is no evidence of indirect effects on vote intention since public investment has no impact on unemployment, and although public investment is motivated by consumption, it has little impact on consumption, and consumption has little impact on vote intention. Regarding the welfare consequences of public investment, the results hold up in models containing the variable for public corporate investment alone, *PUB-CORP*. These results also hold up in models composed of *LEAD* and *APP* variables and/or of the GDP and GDP deflator variables. In all these models, small proportions (2–8 percent) of the forecast error variance in C, GDP, unemployment, and prices are accounted for by innovations in public investment, *PUB-GOVT*.
13. A parallel analysis of public corporate investment produces a statistically significant effect only for inflation. This suggests that the investment decisions of the British public corporations are intended to fight inflation more than to enhance consumption and/or to reduce unemployment (see, e.g., Millward 1976).
14. The modified likelihood ratio test statistics for the models containing *APP* are essentially the same as those reported in Table 5.3. We believe that the results for the period of the second Wilson government are a sign of "nonnormality" or of usually large residuals between 1974–II and 1976–I (see Sims 1980a, p. 20).
15. Analyses of alternative models consistently indicate that *VOTE, LEAD*, and *APP* are not causally prior to public investment. Rather, *PUB-GOVT* always depends on its own past history and on *C* (GDP), *U*, and *P* (GDP deflator). *PUB-CORP* depends on its past history, *C* (GDP), and *P* (GDP deflator). In the corresponding innovation accountings, shocks in *C* (GDP) explain the largest shares of the forecast error variances in *PUB-GOVT* and *PUB-CORP*. Shocks in *U* and *P* (GDP deflator) explain moderate amounts of the forecast error variance in the two investment variables. Shocks in *VOTE, APP*, and *LEAD* do not account for any more than 7–8 percent of the forecast error variance in *PUB-GOVT, PUB-CORP*, or *PRV*.
16. The innovation accounting under the alternative "politicized economics" ordering similarly disconfirms the first perspective. Even here, after 15 quarters, shocks in consumption explain more of the forecast error variance

in public investment than do shocks in vote intention. Moreover, the moving-average response under this ordering is qualitatively identical to that for the "economics of politics" ordering. Since this ordering maximizes the scope for political variables to have such effects, this is a strong contradiction of the first perspective. Less surprisingly, a majority of the second perspective's specific predictions fail under the "politicized economics" ordering. The technocratic perspective clearly does best of all. Only two of its predictions are disconfirmed under this alternative ordering: vote intention in fact does and private investment in fact does not affect public investment.

17. The jagged character of the time paths in the figures derive from the fact that the time series are seasonally unadjusted (note 8). The results reported in this section were qualitatively unaffected by the choice of ordering.
18. Clearly one can make further robustness checks with alternative adjustments to and measures of certain of the time series. The model itself can be enlarged to include other economic variables like interest rates and aspects of monetary and fiscal policy, or indeed of international economic activity. Preliminary indications are that the incorporation of an exchange rate variable leaves the results reported in this paper qualitatively intact, though stability checks for the seven-variable model indicated some heterogeneity for both the second Wilson and Thatcher governments, exactly as one would predict from Alt (1987a). For the latter government the modified likelihood ratio statistic was $\chi^2(140) = 171.2$ ($p < .03$). However, for this same seven-variable model the periods of Labour governance and after the oil price increase appeared stable. The two statistics were $\chi^2(308) = 286.2$ ($p < .81$) and $\chi^2(294) = 299.3$ ($p < .41$), respectively.
19. Admittedly, with its restrictions on investment financing and reprivatization program, the Thatcher government could have changed the structure of the British political economy. Hence, data from the remainder of the 1980s may yield different results. However, note that the test statistics for the era of the first Thatcher government in the six-variable model are quite small and insignificant. See the ninth row of Table 5.3.
20. For example, Dahl is unclear on this point inasmuch as he sees legislative, executive, and bureaucratic intervention in state enterprise as inevitable under most conditions. Yet he equates this intervention with a drift to bureaucratic socialism (1985, p. 144). Our results show that bureaucratic control is likely, but it is not necessarily socially malign.
21. The same is true for advocates of "feasible socialism." For instance, in his guidelines for feasible socialism, Nove assigns numerous tasks to democratic institutions, and he provides for a substantial state enterprise sector (1983, pp. 50, 91, 207). However, Nove does not explore the deeper problems of holding state managers (and planners) accountable through such institutions as elections. Nor does he acknowledge any need for a benign technocracy.

REFERENCES

Aharoni, Y. 1986. *The Evolution of State-Owned Enterprises*. Cambridge, Mass.: Ballinger.

1988. "The United Kingdom: Transforming Attitudes." In R. Vernon (ed.), *The Promise of Privatization*, pp. 23–56. New York: Council on Foreign Relations.

Alt, J. E. 1979. *The Politics of Economic Decline: Economic Management and Political Behavior in Britain Since 1965.* Cambridge University Press.

1987a. "Crude Politics: Oil and the Political Economy of Unemployment in Britain and Norway." *British Journal of Political Science* 17(2):149–200.

1987b. "New Wine in Old Bottles: Thatcher's Conservative Economic Policy." In B. Cooper, A. Kornberg, and W. Mishler (eds.), *The Resurgence of Conservatism in Anglo-American Democracies*, pp. 217–57. Durham, N.C.: Duke University Press.

Alt, J. E., B. Sarlvik, and I. Crewe. 1976. "Partisanship and Policy Choice: Issue Preferences in the British Electorate, February 1974." *British Journal of Political Science* 6(3):273–90.

Arrow, K., and M. Kurz. 1970. *Public Investment, the Rate of Return and Optimal Fiscal Policy*. Baltimore: Johns Hopkins University Press.

Bean, C. R. 1981a. "A New Approach to the Empirical Investigation of Investment Expenditures: A Comment." *Economic Journal* 91:104–5.

1981b. "An Econometric Model of Manufacturing Investment in the U.K." *Economic Journal* 91:106–21.

Breton, A. 1964. "The Economics of Nationalism." *Journal of Political Economy* 72(4):376–86.

Brittan, S. 1983. *The Role and Limits of Government: Essays in Political Economy*. Minneapolis: University of Minnesota Press.

Cohen, L., and R. Noll. 1984. "The Electoral Connection to Intertemporal Policy Evaluation by a Legislator." Stanford University, Stanford, Calif. Mimeo.

Dahl, R. 1982. *Dilemmas of Pluralist Democracy: Autonomy vs. Control*. New Haven, Conn: Yale University Press.

1985. *A Preface to Economic Democracy*. Berkeley: University of California Press.

Dixon, W. J., and F. J. Massey, Jr. 1969. *Introduction to Statistical Analysis*, 3d ed. New York: McGraw-Hill.

Eltis, W. 1979. "The True Deficits of the Public Corporations." *Lloyd's Bank Review* 1:1–20.

Freeman, J. R., 1983a. "The Politics of Mixed Economies." Proposal submitted to the National Science Foundation. University of Minnesota, Minneapolis. Mimeo.

1983b. "Granger Causality and the Time Series Analysis of Political Relationships." *American Journal of Political Science* 27(2):327–58.

1989. *Democracy and Markets: The Politics of Mixed Economies*. Ithaca, N.Y.: Cornell University Press.

Freeman, J. R., J. T. Williams, and Tse-min Lin. 1989. "Vector Autoregression and the Study of Politics." *American Journal of Political Science* 33(4):842–77.

Frey, B., and F. Schneider. 1978. "A Political-Economic Model for the United Kingdom." *Economic Journal* 88:243–53.

Garner, M. R. 1979. "The White Paper on the Nationalized Industries: Some Criticisms." *Public Administration* 57:7–20.

1985. "The Governmental Control of Public Corporations in Britain: A History and an Evaluation." Paper presented at the 13th World Congress of the International Political Science Association, Paris.

Hall, R. 1978. "Stochastic Implications of the Life Cycle-Permanent Income Hypothesis: Theory and Evidence." *Journal of Political Economy* 86(6):971–87.

Hart, J. 1986. "British Industrial Policy." in C. E. Barfield and W. A. Schambra (eds.), *The Politics of Industrial Policy*, pp. 128–60. Washington, D.C.: American Enterprise Institute.

Heurtibise, A. 1978. "The Place of Public Enterprise in the Economy." *Annals of Public and Cooperative Economy* 49:309–43.

Hibbs, D. A., 1977. "Political Parties and Macroeconomic Policy." *American Political Science Review* 71(4):1467–87.

1982. "Economic Outcomes and Political Support for British Governments Among Occupational Classes: A Dynamic Analysis." *American Political Science Review* 76(2):259–79.

Hudson, J. 1985. "The Relationship Between Government Popularity and Approval for the Government's Record in the United Kingdom." *British Journal of Political Science* 15:165–86.

Knight, A. 1983. "Ideas and Action: How to Improve Industrial Performance?" The Fairburn Lecture. Delivered at Lancaster University, January 28.

Layard, R. 1986. *How to Beat Unemployment*. Oxford University Press.

Millward, R. 1976. "Price Restraint, Anti-Inflation Policy and Public and Private Industry in the United Kingdom, 1949–1973." *Economic Journal* 86(June):226–42.

Millward, R., and D. Parker. 1983. "Public and Private Enterprise: Comparative Behavior and Relative Efficiency." In R. Millward, M. T. Summer, and G. Zis (eds.), *Public Sector Economics*, pp. 199–274. London: Longman.

Moore, J., MP. 1986. "Why Privatise?" In J. Kay, C. Mayer, and D. Thompson (eds.), *Privatisation and Regulation: The UK Experience*, pp. 78–93. Oxford University Press.

Nove, A. 1983. *The Economics of Feasible Socialism*. London: Allen & Unwin.

Peltzman, S. 1975. "Pricing in Public and Private Enterprises: Electric Utilities in the United States." *Journal of Law and Economics* 14:109–47.

Pierce, D. A., and L. D. Haugh. 1977. "Causality in Temporal Systems: Characterizations and Survey." *Journal of Econometrics* 5:265–93.

Pryke, R. 1981. *The Nationalized Industries: Policies and Performance Since 1968*. Oxford: Martin Robertson.

Redwood, J. 1980. *Public Enterprise in Crisis: The Future of the Nationalized Industries*. Oxford: Blackwell Publisher.

Redwood, J., and J. Hatch. 1982. *Controlling Public Industries*. Oxford: Blackwell Publisher.

Rowley, C. 1982. "Industrial Policy in the Mixed Economy." In E. Roll (ed.), *The Mixed Economy*, pp. 35–57. London: Macmillan Press.

Shonfield, A. 1965. *Modern Capitalism: The Changing Balance of Public and Private Power*. New York: Oxford University Press.

Silberston, A. 1982. "Steel in a Mixed Economy." In E. Roll (ed.), *The Mixed Economy*, pp. 94–113. London: Macmillan Press.

Sims, C. 1980. "Macroeconomics and Reality." *Econometrica* 48(1):1–48.

1981. "An Autoregressive Index Model for the U.S., 1948–1975." In J. Kmenta and J. B. Ramsey (eds.), *Large Scale Macroeconomic Models: Theory and Practice*, pp. 233–329. New York: North Holland.

1987. "Comment [on Runkle]." *Journal of Economic and Business Statistics* 5:443–9.

Usher, D. 1981. *The Economic Prerequisite to Democracy*. Oxford: Blackwell.

PART II

Pooled time-series and cross-sectional analysis

6

Introduction to pooling

ALEXANDER M. HICKS

Imagine that you wish to investigate the macroeconomic impacts of government wage–price controls. However, you have data for only a dozen years on each of a handful of nations, and you fear that you have insufficient observations for competent analysis. Or imagine that you wish to test a model of voluntary wage restraint that stresses impacts of inflation and proportional representation (a bulwark of the consensual mode of governance). Unfortunately, you think, inflationary dynamics that must be studied over time and proportional representation, which varies only across nations during years of interest, seem incompatible with a single study. Neither cross-sectional nor time-series data seem adequate to the task of studying both inflationary dynamics and proportional representation at one and the same time.

Pooled data, which range across time and space, may enable you to overcome your difficulties. Pooled data are arrayed across both cross-sectionally differentiated entities like nations and temporally differentiated ones like years. Thus, they tap variance both in temporally inert variables such as proportional representation and in more temporally lively ones like inflation rates. Intersections of time and space such as the "nation–year" serve as units of analysis in pooled data arrays. Such "place–time" marriages of data multiply numbers of observations. Thanks to pooling, it may be possible after all to find data with the axes of variation and the numbers of observations that you need.

Pooled data are becoming central to quantitative studies of the political economy of democratic welfare states, especially in studies of income maintenance spending, benefits, and "rights" (Pampel and Williamson 1988, 1989; Korpi 1989; Palme 1990; Huber, Ragin, and Stephens 1991; and Hicks and Swank 1992). They are also becoming notable resources for studies of macroeconomic policy and performance – the macroeconomic route to enhanced public welfare (Weede 1986; Alvarez, Garrett, and Lange 1991; Hicks 1991; and Swank 1992).

Technically, "pooled" arrays of data are ones that combine cross-sectional data on J spatial units (e.g., nations) and T time periods (e.g., years) to produce a data set of $J \times T = N$ observations. When the distinct cross-sectional units that contribute to a pool are more numerous than temporal units that contribute to it (e.g., 60 nations over 5 time periods), the pool is often conceptualized as a "stack" of temporally distinct time periods, regarded as a "cross-sectionally dominant" pool, and termed a "time series of cross sections" (TSCS). When the temporal units in a pooled array of data are more numerous than the spatial units (e.g., 40 years with 10 countries), the array is then regarded "temporally dominant" and called a "cross section of time series" (CSTS). Indeed, the literature on pooling is replete with its own esoteric jargon (see Judge et al. 1985, chap. 13). In an effort to stay in touch with this volume's focus on the macropolitical economy of advanced welfare states, I shall keep my terminology, as well as my examples, close to this substantive literature. For example, I shall usually refer to "nations" instead of "units" and to "years" instead of "time periods."

A PRELIMINARY OVERVIEW: PURPOSES, PROBLEMS, PROCEDURES, AND TWO EXAMPLES

There are several reasons for the increasing centrality of pooled data in the quantitative literature on the political economy of democratic welfare states. One reason is a great increase in the econometric sophistication of the sociologists and political scientists studying the welfare state since the late 1970s (see Hibbs 1987; Pampel and Williamson 1989). Increasing econometric sophistication certainly allows an increasing number of scholars to analyze pooled data. Indeed, it probably spurs on increasing numbers to actually do so. However, it also warrants caution in the use of pooled data.

A second reason for the increasing centrality of pooled data in quantitative studies of the political economy of democratic welfare states is the "small-N" problem. Not only is the number of democratic welfare states limited to about 20, give or take a few. Relevant econometric data for these nation-states are largely confined to the past three or four decades (i.e., to about 40 annual observations). Viewed in conventional cross-sectional or time-series terms, the degrees of freedom needed for reasonably precise estimates and reasonably powerful statistical tests are very restricted among democratic welfare states. Yet the nation–year (or $J \times T$) definition of pooled observation can greatly relax this restriction (see Judge et al. 1985, chap. 13).

A third reason for the increasing use of pooled data is that they permit inquiry into "variables" that elude study in simple cross-sectional or time-series arrays because their variability is negligible, or nonexistent, across either time or space. In particular, many characteristics of national systems and institutions tend to be temporally invariant. For example, the federal or unitary character of political systems tends toward invariance for decades or centuries, while degrees of labor union centralization and monopoly, political party reformism and discipline, and the like tend to be nearly invariant for as long as decades at a time (Cameron 1984; Lijphart 1984). Moreover, some characteristics of nations tend to be relatively invariant across time (as opposed to nation) because they are prone to inertia (like age structure) or tend toward large cyclical movements (like the utilization of productive capacity). Regression analyses of pooled data can combine both types of variables. For example, they may combine the centralization of labor union structure and the degree of capacity utilization as regressors predicting aggregate growth (Chenery and Syrquin 1975).

In extending axes of comparison across both time and space, pooled data do not only expand degrees of freedom. They also do not solely permit simultaneous consideration of both temporal and cross-national dimensions of variability (and axes of comparison). As vehicles for the concurrent study of both cross-sectional and longitudinal variability, pooled data also open the door to a number of analytical refinements. Thus, to state a fourth boon of pooled data, they permit systematic comparisons of cross-sectionally and longitudinally varying causal forces (Pollard 1983). For example, pooled data permit effects of such temporally variable characteristics of nations as changes in partisan government and such temporally inert traits as types of electoral systems (e.g., proportional representation) to be estimates and compared within single analyses (Hicks and Swank 1992).

To identify a fifth reason for the use of pooled data, they permit cross-national (or intertemporal) shifts in statistical parameters and underlying changes in causal processes to be studied in terms of temporally invariant traits of nations or cross-sectionally stolid characteristics of periods. For example, in Chapter 8 of this volume O'Connell examines the differential consequences of strikes on earnings across nations marked by neocorporatist or pluralist modes of policy formation. In Chapter 7, Hicks models economic growth effects of Left-party government as functions of union centralization.

Unfortunately, the ordinary least squares (OLS) regression estimates that social scientists most commonly use to link potential causes and effects are likely to be inefficient, biased, or both when they are applied to pooled data. This is so because the errors for regression equations estimated from pooled data using OLS formulas and pooled data tend to behave in a number of ways that violate OLS assumptions.

First, errors tend to be nonindependent from one time period to the next. This is because observations and the traits that characterize them tend to be interdependent across time. (For example, temporally successive values of many national traits such as population size, many individual traits such as body weight, and so on, tend not to be independent over time.) In turn, unspecified characteristics of observations that are omitted from specific regression equations and thus are reflected in their residuals often are interdependent or nonindependent as well. Moreover, interdependent errors tend to be linearly as well as more generally interdependent. As a result, regression errors in pooled data tend to be *autocorrelated or autoregressive*, as in most time series.

Second, errors tend to be *heteroskedastic*; that is, they tend to have differing variances across ranges or subsets of nations or years. For example, nations with higher values on variables tend to have less restricted and, hence, higher variances on them. For example, the United States tends to have more volatile as well as higher unemployment rates than does Switzerland. Third, errors tend to be *correlated across nations*. For example, omitted explanatory factors in a model of economic growth will tend to be similar, and thus correlated, across propinquitous nations (Chenery and Syrquin 1975, chap. 10). As these propinquitous factors tend to be reflected in errors for propinquitous nations, these errors tend to be correlated.

Fourth, *errors may well contain both temporal and cross-sectional components* (reflecting both temporal "period" effects and cross-sectional "unit" effects), although this is inconsistent with their expression as single (unidimensional) vectors (Judge et al. 1985). In particular, the structure of interdependencies among cross-sectionally varying errors may differ from that for temporally varying errors (and *vice versa*). Fifth, errors also may tend to be *nonrandom across spatial and/or temporal units* because parameters – like the underlying causal processes that they reflect – are *heterogeneous* across subsets of units (Maddala 1977, chap. 14). For example, processes linking strike rates to earnings levels may vary considerably across subsets or dimensions of nations as O'Connell and Hicks suggest in Chapters 8 and 7, this volume, respectively. (See Hannan and Young 1977; Judge et al. 1985; and Stimson 1985 for overviews.)

In summary, errors for regression equations estimated from pooled data with OLS procedures tend to be (1) temporally autoregressive, (2) cross-sectionally heteroskedastic, and (3) cross-sectionally correlated, as well as (4) conceal unit and period effects and (5) reflect some causal heterogeneity cross space, time, or both. As a result of these complications, defining mathematically tractable, empirically realistic models with good (e.g., best linear unbiased estimator) estimator properties can be problematic. (See Johnston 1985, chaps. 2, 5, on BLUE.)

Next, I present two useful models of pooling that help illustrate the nature of regression assumptions and procedures needed for good estimates. Finally, I turn to a more technical mode of exposition in my effort to map out the principal options available for regression with pooled data. If my language and content seem to get rather specialized, note that a degree of expertise is necessary for competent use, indeed even for competent consumption, of pooling. Furthermore, the variety of pooling options that the bird's-eye view offered by a "map" can provide is essential to a moderately sophisticated use of pooled regression.

TWO MODELS OF POOLED REGRESSION

The Parks–Kmenta model

Kmenta ([1971] 1988) elaborates a regression model for the analysis of pooled data that is probably the one most commonly used by sociologists and political scientists during the past decade. (See e.g., Hibbs 1987, chap. 1; Pampel and Williamson 1989; Alvarez, Garrett, and Lange 1991; and Hicks and Swank 1992. See also Kmenta [1971] 1988 Hicks and Misra, in press). Because the model is an elaboration of Parks (1966), I shall refer to it as the Parks–Kmenta model. The regression equation for the model may be written as

$$Y_{it} = B_1 + \sum_{k=1}^{K} B_k X_{kit} + e_{it}. \qquad \text{(PK.1)}$$

This equation has a single intercept B_1 and slopes B_k that are constant across units and time periods, as well as an error structure that attempts to accommodate the realities of pooled data.[1]

As regards the model's error structure, recall that pooled data has a time-series dimension. In data with such a dimension, errors can be expected to be serially dependent and, thus, serially autocorrelated and autoregressive over time. A common model for serial autogressiveness is the so-called AR(1) (i.e., first-order autoregressive) model that can be written as follows:

$$E_{it} = \rho_i E_{it-1} + U_{it} \qquad \text{(PK.2)}$$

(autoregression), where

$$U_{it} \sim N(0, \phi_{it}),$$

and ρ_i is a coefficient of first-order autoregressiveness, that is, a slope for the regression of E_{it} on E_{it-1}. Kmenta (1971 [1988], p. 619) nicely describes a simple two-step procedure whereby ρ_i can be estimated so that it varies by nation. The AR(1) model of errors is a simple but fairly robust (and widely employed) one wherein all effects of past errors on a contemporaneous one are channeled through the immediately previous error for the same unit (Stimson 1985).[2] With the incorporation of a conception of error *autoregressiveness*, the Parks–Kmenta model addresses problem (1).

Pooled data arrays with notable cross-sectional variability are likely to have errors with cross-sectionally heterogeneous variances. In more technical terms, they are apt to be *heteroskedastic*, (i.e., they are likely to be troubled by problem (2)). For example, variances in unemployment rates will tend to be greater for bigger nations with large heterogeneous labor forces than for small, homogeneous nations. As a result, errors in predictions from our models of such phenomena will tend to be larger and, in turn, more volatile in the larger nations. A simple regression specification that allows for such cross-sectionally unequal error variances to be written is the following:

$$E(\varepsilon_{it}^2) = \delta_{ij}^2 \text{ (heteroskedasticity)}, \qquad \text{(PK.3)}$$

for $(i \neq j)$. Kmenta (1971 [1988], pp. 619–22) nicely describes how such cross-sectionally unequal variances can be incorporated into the actual formulas and generalized least squares (GLS) estimation procedures for the Parks–Kmenta model.

It might be injudicious to expect errors for particular nations to be independent. In particular, we might seriously doubt that geographically propinquitous nations characterized by shared heritages, intensive commercial and diplomatic relations, and the like would have mutually independent causal processes or errors in prediction. We would not expect errors for Belgium to lack some resemblance to those for the Netherlands or errors for Canada and the United States to be altogether independent. Instead, we would expect disturbances for such nations to be *cross-sectionally correlated* (problem (c)). Algebraically, such contemporaneous correlation of errors across particular pairs of nations can be expressed as follows:

$$E(\varepsilon_{it}\ \varepsilon_{jt}) = \delta_{ij}^2 \text{ (cross-unit correlation)}. \qquad \text{(PK.4)}$$

Implementation of this aspect of the Parks–Kmenta model is elaborated in Kmenta (1971 [1988], pp. 623–5). Formulas for slopes, standard error, and other aspects of the Parks–Kmenta model are reported in Kmenta (1971 [1988], pp. 623–5).[3]

Practically, it is most important to stress that this model not only addresses estimator problems (1), (2), and (3) directly. It can be made to address the *unit and period effects* (problem (4)) through the ad hoc addition of dummy variables for nations, time periods, or both (see Castles and Dowrick 1990).

The Parks–Kmenta model also can address problem (5) – that of heterogeneous slopes – by means of a number of ad hoc elaborations. First, diagnoses can be employed to establish whether heterogeneity is a problem. Chow's *F*-tests for significant deterioration of model goodness-of-fit with the jump from J nation-specific time-series equations to one $J \times T$ pool are perhaps most useful (Chow 1960; Maddala 1977, chap. 14). These warrant pooling if model deterioration in the form of increasing model error variance (or "sum of squares") is not significant. However, in evaluating results some consideration must be given to the extent to which the individual time series are informative. For example, one set of time series may have ample degrees of freedom (per nation), yield precise estimates, and contain variables that are all longitudinally meaningful in theoretical terms. A second set of time series might have few degrees of freedom per time series; it might yield no precise parametric information; and it might exclude variables because they lack temporal variation or degrade their estimates because theory for these refers to consequences of cross-sectional variations.[4] In the first case, an insignificant Chow's *F* could provide no warrant for pooling, for any gain in parsimony due to pooling would be the fruit of gross averaging of parameter estimates and entail a major loss of information. In the second case, a significant Chow's *F* might not preclude pooling. Although it would imply some averaging of heterogeneous national results in the pooled model, this pooled model might still be more informative than the individual time series: clear average patterns in the pool might tell us more than barely perceptible nation-specific ones.[5]

Unfortunately, to date, no one has formulated precise rules of thumb on how much averaging is tolerable in exchange for theoretical precision and statistical power. However, assuming the diagnostic decision that pooling is not warranted, two main options are available. One is to focus on the less aggregated, unpooled findings (e.g., nation-specific time series), including "seemingly unrelated regressions" (Kmenta 1971, pp. 620–30). The second is to respecify one's pooled model with an eye to upgrading its goodness-of-fit relative to the disaggregated model(s). This may include additions to the pooled model of mediating or interactive variables that are explicitly aimed at modeling cross-sectional (or cross-temporal) heterogeneity. For example, one might model the effects of partisan government on economic growth as a function of the strength of unions (Hicks, Chapter 7, this volume) or model variable impacts of labor militance on worker earnings as a function of the post-OPEC economic troubles (O'Connell, Chapter 8, this volume).

Overall, the Parks–Kmenta model is a highly useful one for the analysis of "temporally dominant" models in which T exceeds J and we are, in effect, pooling time series (Stimson 1985; Hicks, Chapter 6, this volume).

The "error components" model

This approach takes off from a direct confrontation with the units effect problem. It addresses the problem by means of the simple assumption that cross-sectional and time-series variations have distinctive properties that may ground distinctive aspects, or components, of an overall effect and be analyzed in terms of two "error components." One is a "between unit" component that draws on cross-sectional variations in unit-specific over-time averages. The second is a "within unit" component based on over-time variations of cross-sectional averages. Each of these components is treated as a (between- or within-unit) error whose properties are important for final estimator properties. The so-called error component (or "variance component") equation can be written as

$$Y_{it} = B_1 + \sum_{k=1}^{K} B_k X_{kit} + E_{it}. \tag{EC.1}$$

This specification has an "error structure" that addresses problem (4) by decomposing the summary error into three mutually independent terms. These are (1) a cross-sectionally varying one, U_i, that is invariant over time, (2) a temporally varying one, V_t, that is invariant across units, and (3) a third residually defined term, W_{it}, equal to $Y_{it} - U_i - V_t$ (see Judge et al. 1985, pp. 521–6).

The procedure's solution to the "unit" problem takes the form of systematic incorporation of two error components (and the residually defined third error component) into its (generalized) least squares formulas for intercepts and slopes. The overarching GLS formulas aside, the model may be described in terms of the precise assumptions about the equation error that help specify the GLS formula for the estimation of B via the minimization of least squares residuals. This specification of "error structure" (for *three* error components!) is as follows (Kmenta 1971 [1988], pp. 625–30).

First, at the cost of some repetition:

$$\varepsilon_{it} = U_i + V_t + W_{it} \ (i = 1, 2, \ldots, J;\ t = 1, 2, \ldots, T) \tag{EC.2}$$

E_i has three components, each normally distributed with a constant variance denoted by some variant of sigma squared. The separate components of the error are kept simple: each, one may notice, has properties like those assumed for OLS regression. Each *component* also has a constant, or homoskedastic, error variance such that the variance for the summary error ε_{it} is constant or homoskedastic. Thus, despite its differentiation of errors and error variances, the model cannot be said to thoroughly address problem (2).

Each error component has a zero mean and is normally distributed, that is,

$$U_i \sim N(0, \sigma_u^2);\; V_t \sim N(0, \sigma_v^2). \qquad \text{(EC.3)}$$

Each component is also free of autocorrelation. That is,

$$\begin{aligned} &E(U_iV_t) = E(U_iW_{it}) = E(V_tW_{it}) = 0; \qquad \text{(EC.4)}\\ &E(U_iU_j) = 0; \quad = E(V_tV_s) = 0;\\ &E(W_{it}W_{is}) = E(W_{it}W_{jt}) = E(W_{it}W_{js}) = 0. \qquad (i \neq j;\ t \neq s) \end{aligned}$$

However, despite this apparent neglect of problem (1) concerning error autoregressiveness, a nonzero, over-time correlation of ε_i is implied by this formulation. This autocorrelation is described by

$$\frac{Cov(\varepsilon_{it}, \varepsilon_{is})}{Var(\varepsilon_{it})Var(\varepsilon_{is})} = \frac{\sigma_u^2}{\sigma_u^2 + \sigma_v^2 + \sigma_w^2}. \qquad \text{(EC.5)}$$

This feature of the model means that for each nation the correlation of disturbances remains unchanged, no matter how far apart the disturbances may be. This assumption contrasts sharply with the usual assumption of a first-order autoregressive (AR(1)) process. Indeed, AR(1) and similar autoregressive processes imply a geometric decline in the degree of autocorrelation as the temporal distance of one error (e.g., ε_t) increases from the other (e.g., $\varepsilon_{t+1}, \varepsilon_{t+2}, \ldots, \varepsilon_{t+T}$). Despite the theoretical elegance of expression (EC.5), this problem is a serious one that I shall return to later.

The problem of contemporaneous, cross-national correlation between pairs of errors ε_{it} and ε_{jt} – here $t = t$ but $i \neq j$, that is, time points are equivalent, but nation does not equal nation – is addressed in a manner described by the following expression:

$$\frac{Cov(\varepsilon_{it}, \varepsilon_{jt})}{Var(\varepsilon_{it})Var(\varepsilon_{jt})} = \frac{\sigma_v^2}{\sigma_u^2 + \sigma_v^2 + \sigma_w^2} \quad (i \neq j). \qquad \text{(EC.6)}$$

Overall, the error component model is a very useful one for spatially dominant models in which J exceeds T and we are, in effect, pooling cross sections (Stimson 1985; Hicks, Chapter 7, this volume). It is most realistic where the X_{kit} register purely cross-sectional effects and are temporally invariant (i.e., constant across t). This situation, a very interesting one resembling that postulated by Coleman's (1968) formulation of differential equation models, is not inconceivable (see Hannan and Young 1977; Judge et al. 1985). For example, it might be realized for a model of long-term economic growth explained in terms of such systemic traits of national economies as free market or command modes of allocation (Pryor 1985). Nevertheless, a situation that is even approximated by a set of explanatory variables that only vary cross-sectionally is quite unlikely, and error component assumptions are very strong. Very simply, most regressors are likely to vary over time. Moreover, Y and errors in its prediction are likely to reflect this. Under such circumstance, the weight of past modeling efforts and empirical experience suggests that relatively propinquitous errors (say, errors at $t-1$ and t) are likely to be more highly autogressive than are more temporally distant errors (say, ε_{t-10} and ε_t).[6] Perhaps the best that can be said about the variance components model of autoregressiveness is that the damage done by its lack of autoregressive realism diminishes as the share of longitudinal variance in total model variance diminishes; that is, the specification's lack of realism diminishes as the share of the variance of the summary error ε_{it} that is taken up by the "temporal" component U_i diminishes (Judge et al. 1985). In short, the objection to the model's specification of error autocorrelation fades in importance as the model becomes "spatially dominant" (Stimson 1985). At least we have here a model whose disadvantage fades in heavily cross-sectional data arrays.

A MAPPING OF POOLING OPTIONS

A look at the most general form of a multiple regression equation for a pooled data array can help put the range of available regression models of pooled arrays into perspective. This general form (Judge et al. 1985, pp. 515–16) is the following:

$$Y_{it} = \sum_{i=1;\, t=1}^{J,T} B_{it} + \sum_{k=1}^{K} B_{kit} X_{kit} + e_{kit}, \qquad (1)$$

where $i = 1, 2, \ldots; J$ refers to a cross-sectional "individual," $t = 1, 2, \ldots; T$ refers to a time period, and $k = 1, 2, \ldots; K$ readers to a specific explanatory variable. Thus, Y_{it} and X_{kit} refer, respectively, to dependent and independent variables for unit i and time t; e_{kit} is a random error; and the B_{kit} and B_{kit} refer, respectively, to matrices of intercept parameters B_{kit} and the matrix of slope parameters B_{kit}. These unknowns, although free in principle to differ across particular "individual-time" observations, must usually be constrained. For example, empirical estimation without constraints would entail more parameter values than observations (< 0 degrees of freedom!) and be impossible to estimate.

Although Equation 1 has insufficient degrees of freedom for estimation and direct empirical usefulness, it provides a helpful baseline for descriptions of more practical multiple regression models and a vantage point from which the thicket of regression models of pooled data can be put in some perspective.

A simple constrained variation of equation (1) is

$$Y_{it} = B_1 + \sum_{k=1}^{K} B_k X_{kit} + e_{kit}. \tag{A.1}$$

This has a single intercept B_1 and slopes B_k that are constant across units and time periods. It would, if its error were to meet OLS assumptions for efficient and unbiased estimates, provide a very succinct function of Y_{it}. However, it is unlikely to be very realistic. Whatever process is being modeled, it is unlikely to be so perfectly specified or so unaffected by cultural and historical particulars that neither its slopes nor intercepts vary across time and place. However, a slight elaboration of Equation (A.1) is likely to be more realistic.

This variation, more commonly utilized than (A.1), is

$$Y_{it} = \sum_{i=1}^{J} B_i + \sum_{k=1}^{K} B_k X_{kit} + e_{kit}, \tag{A.2}$$

with cross-sectionally heterogeneous intercepts. This variant is called a least squares dummy variable (LSDV) regression. It is a variant of (1) that addresses potential problems of "unit" effects (problem "4") in a simple, rather broadly appealing manner. Assuming strong theory and "temporal dominance" (or a preponderance of cross-temporal to cross-spatial variances and covariances), this model allows for a set of nation-specific unit effects. That is, a different mean value of Y_{it} is designated by B_i for each i. (These are most easily captured by inclusion of $J - 1$ dummies for J nations.) However, it assumes that the causal process operating within each nation is a homogeneous one common to each nation and uncomplicated by "period" effects. It elaborates (A.1) to address problem "4" and, as a by-product of that, problem "2."[7] However, a perhaps more realistic and utilized equation than (A.2) is

$$Y_{it} = B_1 + \sum_{k=1}^{K} B_k X_{kit} + e_{kit}, \tag{B.1}$$

with GLS error structure elaborated by Parks (1966) and Kmenta (1971 [1988], pp. 619–25). This is the Parks–Kmenta model of Equation (PK.1) that adjusts for temporally autoregressive errors ("a" above), contemporaneously heteroskedastic errors ("b"), and, in one elaboration, contemporaneously correlated cross-national errors ("c"). This model provides a rather realistic treatment of error autoregressiveness over time. By doing this, the model provides a basic expression for situations of "temporally dominance" in which $I > J$ and we reasonably assume processes that are dominated by over-time covariances. The model, however, also assumes that these processes are relatively homogeneous across units. This is an assumption that depends for the making (as we shall see) on more than temporal dominance. It depends, in effect, on strong theory, congenial diagnostic tests, or in the worst case, optimism or a willingness to accept coarse averages as useful findings.

The Parks–Kmenta model can be refined into the following equation:

$$Y_{it} = \sum_{i=1}^{J} B_i + \sum_{k-1}^{K} B_k X_{kit} + e_{kit}, \tag{B.2}$$

which is simply the Parks–Kmenta model of Equation (B.1) *with the addition of cross-sectionally distinct intercepts*. This elaboration of Parks–Kmenta addresses problem (4) just as Equation (A.2) did, that is, by allowing intercepts to vary by nation (i.e., by different values of Y_{it} for $B_k X_{kit} = 0$ for each i). Here again is a model for temporally dominant situations in which time points exceed cross-sectional units, and causal processes are well described by longitudinal data, indeed by common within-unit slopes. This specification allocates all strictly cross-sectional variance to the fixed unit effects of a series of dummy variables for nations. Thus, it yields parameters for the X_{kit} values that are purged of cross-sectional variation. By so doing it provides an extreme expression of a temporally dominant model: a model for which all cross-sectional variation in explanatory and dependent variables may be relegated to a set of fixed unit effects.

For all their merits, the OLS specifications of Equations (A.1) and (A.2) give insufficient attention to some likely departures of pooled errors from OLS assumptions about them. In turn, GLS specifications (B.1) and (B.2) either neglect unit effects (B.1) or treat them in a manner that appropriates *all* cross-unit variance to a set of fixed unit effects for nations (B.2), thereby downwardly biasing the $B_k X_{kit}$ values (Judge et al. 1985). Fortunately, loose variants of the (B) equations that take some account of the units problem without cross-sectionally vitiating the X_{kit} values have been developed. One such specification is

$$Y_{it} = B_1 + \sum_{k=1}^{K} B_k X_{kit} + E_{it}. \tag{C.1}$$

This is the error component specification of Equation (EC.1), indeed of equations (EC.1) through (EC.6), that I have already described at length. A variation of Equation (C.1) is introduced by the following equation:

$$Y_{it} = \sum_{t=1}^{T} B_t + \sum_{k=1}^{K} B_k X_{kit} + E_{it}. \tag{C.2}$$

This is a variant of (C.1) for which temporal variability in Y_{it} and the X_{kit} values is entirely allocated to fixed effects of a set of $T - 1$ dummies for the T time periods (or to expression of regressors and regressands as deviations from their with-unit means. This is a dummy variable variant of the error components model for which intercepts are allowed to vary across periods, while temporal variations in Xs and in the temporally varying error component (V_t in EC. 2) are assumed away.

Additional models may, of course, be specified. One might be

$$Y_{it} = \sum_{t=1}^{T} B_t + \sum_{k=1}^{K} B_k X_{kit} + e_{kit}, \tag{D.1}$$

a fixed-time-effects model specified with unrealistic OLS assumptions and estimated via OLS.

Of particular interest is a series of models in which *slope* coefficients are allowed to vary across units, most commonly such cross sections as nations. Such models explicitly allow for the kind of historical and cross-cultural differences in parameters that many nation specialists and historians suspect. Especially interesting among such flexible (but mathematically daunting) models are the random coefficient models, which yield average as well as unit-specific slope estimates (Swamy 1970; Hsiao 1975; and Judge et al. 1985). Also of some interest, despite virtual retreat from a pooled to a multiple time-series format, is the "seemingly unrelated regression" model, interpretable as a series of nation-specific regressions that utilizes contemporaneous cross-equation error correlations among the errors of a system of equations to improve the efficiency of the equations' estimates (Zellner 1962). These models, involving theoretical complications and practical shortcomings that place them beyond the scope of this introduction to pooling, are well summarized in Judge et al. (1985, chaps. 12–13.)

For a systematic mapping of relations among some principal procedures for the analysis of pooled data, the reader is referred to Table 6.1. As we have noted, one can, fortunately, adjust to the deficiencies of each of the models highlighted. As regards the Parks-Kmenta model, researchers may make fixed adjustments for fixed unit effects by means of unit (e.g., time period and/or cross-sectional) dummies; one may model heterogeneous slopes by means of statistical interactions; and so on. As regards variance component models, time-invariant autoregressiveness may be fully realistic where it coincides with time-invariant *explicantia* and may be realistic enough where models are spatially dominant.

Table 6.1. *Modes of pooled analysis*

	Simple OLS estimators		Simple GLS estimators		
Simple OLS (A.1 and D.1)	"Individual" effects (or cross-sectionally differing intercepts) (A.2)	"Time" effects (or "temporally" differing intercepts) (D.1)	"Individual" and "time" effects	Constant slope coefficients	Heterogeneous slope coefficients (e.g., Swamy, Hsiao, and "seemingly unrelated regressions")
	Realistic GLS models of autoregressiveness		GLS models of constant autoregressiveness		
Parks-Kmenta (PK) model of errors (B.1)	PK model of errors with fixed "unit" effects for "individuals"	PK model with fixed "unit" effects for "time"	PK model with fixed "unit" effects for "time" and "individuals"	"Error components" (EC.1, C.1)	"Error components" with fixed "unit" effects for "time"
i.e., AR(1) or AR(T)[a] autoregressiveness; heteroskedasticity; contemporaneously correlated errors	(B.2)				(C.2)
	Time-dominant models		Spatially dominant models		

[a] AR(T) refers to an autoregressive model covering periods 1, 2, ..., T.

Moreover, some cross-sectional or temporal stylization or averaging of effects may be tolerable, for we may have insufficient theoretical means for generalizing about, or even interpreting, an accumulation of small cross-national (or cross-period) deviations of parametric findings from a more general pattern.

Where such deviations are large and where efforts to slur over them with statistical averages and theoretical stylizations seem more obfuscatory than enlightening, pools may be disaggregated into relatively homogeneous subsets of observations. Indeed, in the extreme they may be disaggregated into nation- or period-specific patterns, even into temporally varying nation-specific patterns (Isaac and Griffin 1989). Again, rejection of pooling on the basis of heterogeneous parameter estimates is clearly warranted where Chow's *F*-tests indicate a definite degradation of model fit due to the pooling together of time series or cross sections (Chow 1960; Maddala 1977), while more impressionistic scrutiny indicates that less disaggregated models indeed offer enough information so that the "averaged" estimates offered by pooled analyses have some alternative meaningful enough to be judged "degraded." Again, relaxations of constraints on nations or years may be expressed by means of "random coefficient" or "seemingly unrelated regression" models that estimate heterogeneous parameters without relinquishing the use of pooled data arrays (see Judge et al. 1985, chap. 13; Hsiao, 1985). Or pooling may be abandoned altogether in exchange for the specificity of separate time series or cross sections.

Very often, pooling will be worthwhile because available observations are insufficient for disaggregated estimation and/or because available theory is insufficient for worthwhile interpretation of small or unstable national idiosyncracies. At other times, pooling will provide us with both the means and the incentive for theoretical and statistical elaborations in which general patterns accommodate and incorporate the nuances of structure and process, place and epoch (see O'Connell, Chapter 8).

FUTURE PROSPECTS

Again, the analysis of pooled data is becoming central to quantitative studies of the political economy of democratic welfare states. Impressive literatures employing pooled data have emerged on welfare rights and expenditure and on state macroeconomic performance.

Regression analysis of pooled data predominates because regression offers a means for the solution of more problems than those posed by small *N*s alone or the mere need to concurrently tap cross-sectional and temporal variability. Pooled regression analyses provide potent vehicles for many avenues of research. With them we can generalize models from accumulations of time-series (and comparative time-series) analyses. We can assess the cross-case homogeneity of multination models. Indeed, by means of "statistical interactions" that systematically elaborate cross-national differences in parameters, we can estimate models of heterogeneity (Sayrs 1989; Alvarez et al. 1992; and O'Connell, Chapter 8). By so doing, we can explicitly distinguish among systemic and processual facets of reality and between spatially and temporally focused modes of analysis. We can articulate and research relations between these. For example, we may compare political-economic processes across institutional contexts (O'Connell, Chapter 8). We may parameterize cross-national differences in the impacts of partisan government on growth in national product or social wage (Alvarez et al. 1991). We may compare relatively long- and short-run models of aggregate economic policy and performance (see Hicks, Chapter 7). Overall, multiple regression analysis of pooled data provides us with a powerful lens for scrutinizing the political-economic processes and structures of the welfare state.

ANNOTATED BIBLIOGRAPHY

Entrée point books/articles

Alvarez, Michael, R. Geoffrey Garrett, and Peter Lange. 1991. "Government Partnership, Labor Organization and Macroeconomic Performance, 1967–1984." *American Political Science Review* 85:539–56.

This research paper provides an elegant example of pooling and entrée to some diagnostic procedures for assessing the robustness of estimates across small changes in one's cases.

Pampel, Fred C., and John B. Williamson. 1988. "Welfare Spending in Advanced Industrial Democracies, 1950–1980." *American Journal of Sociology* 50:1424–56.

An influential application of pooling to the welfare state.

Stimson, James A. 1985. "Regression in Space and Time: A Statistical Essay." *American Journal of Political Science* 29:915–47.

This "workshop" paper, despite its dearth of mathematical expressions, probably remains the best introduction to pooling for the sociologist or political scientist.

Methodological and statistical texts

For the case of regression analyses of pooled data, the following texts may provide fine introductory as well as technical treatments of pooling.

Introduction to pooling

Judge, George, and W. D. Griffith, R. C. Hill, H. Lutkepohl, and T. C. Lee. 1985. *The Theory and Practice of Econometrics.* 2d ed. New York: Wiley.
Chap. 13 provides a remarkably comprehensive and lucid overview of the methods of regression analysis of pooled (and kindred) data arrays.

Kmenta, Jan. 1971/1988. *Elements of Econometrics.* New York: Macmillan.
Chap. 12, sec. 2, of this excellent text (including its 2d edition) contains classic technical treatments of both Parks–Kmenta and error component procedures for the regression analysis of pooled data.

Maddala, George S. 1977. *Econometrics.* New York: McGraw-Hill.
This text contains a good overview of pooling and a systematic discussion of the use of Chow's *F*-test and other tests and diagnostic procedures for the assessment of parameter homogeneity.

Computer programs

SAS. 1986. *SUGI Supplemental Library User's Guide, Version 5.* Carey, N.C.: SAS.
The "Time Series Cross Section Regression" component of SAS's *Supplemental Library* provides useful software for implementation of the Parks–Kmenta and error component procedures. However, the procedures are short on descriptive and diagnostic statistics (e.g., apt coefficients of determination, tests for error autocorrelation) and ancillary capabilities for data transformation and management (e.g., generation of predicted values and residuals); and isolation of this "supplemental" procedure from convenient access to many SAS capabilities rigidifies these limitations.

Shazam. 1988. *Shazam Econometrics Computer Program: User's Reference Manual, Version 6.1.* New York: McGraw-Hill.
The "Pooled Cross-Section Time-Series" component of this time-series program provides an excellent means for the estimation, description, diagnosis, and elaboration of Parks-Kmenta regression models.

NOTES

1. "Error structure" refers to statistical properties of errors (variances, covariances, etc.) that are relevant to the quality of estimators.
2. Both stipulation and observation of the dependence of an error at time t on relatively propinquitous errors, especially the error for the immediately preceding time period ($t - 1$), are very prevalent in analyses and models of

error structure. This dependence may occur on a linear combination of a number of relatively propinquitous preceding errors or on a moving average of such errors. Dependence of an error on earlier errors may also be cyclical (following diurnal or annual patterns as might occur with predictions of sleep or Christmas shopping). However, it is nearly always variable across errors at different distances from each other within a particular cross-sectional context (Belsley, Kuh, and Welsh 1980).

3. Some other important assumptions stressed in Kmenta (1971 [1988], pp. 222–5) are

$$E(\varepsilon_{i,t=1}, U_{it}) = 0,$$
$$E(U_{it}) = \phi_{ij},$$
$$E(U_{it}, U_{jt}) = 0 \qquad (t \neq s),$$
$$\sigma_{ij} = \phi_{ij}(1 - \rho_i^2), \text{ and}$$
$$\sigma_{ij} = \phi_{ij}/(1 - \rho_i \rho_j).$$

4. Tests for cross-temporal heterogeneity may also be implemented and may also include such complications as models specifying cross-period interactions (see O'Connell, Chapter 8, for one such model).
5. As multicollinearity degrades the precision of intercept and slope estimates in multiple regressions but does not degrade the predicted values of regressands, it may render crucial parameter estimates in a model quite useless, even while permitting the model more predictive power than a second model with relatively precise parameter estimates. For example, parameter estimates for a set of short time-series models with limited degrees of freedom may be seriously blurred due to multicollinearity; the set of time series may yield more accurate predictions of Y values than a pooling of the time series; yet the more precise parameter estimates from the pool may, despite averaging of nation-specific slopes, be more informative than those destabilized by multicollinearity within each national regression (Belsley, Kuh, and Welsh 1980). In the extreme, where comparison is between noise and a gross average, the average is preferable.
6. Recall that error interdependence is nearly always variable across errors at different distances from each other within a particular cross-sectional context (Belsley, Kuh, and Welsh 1980). Also note that Freedman and Peters (1984) report that estimated standard errors for the class of "seemingly related regression" models originated by Zellner (1962) are underestimated and that t statistics or this class of models are, thus, overestimated where N is large relative to T (as for example in the case with $N = 10$ and $T = 18$, which they elaborate). This result is attributed to the large (i.e., $N(N - 1)/2$) number of contemporaneous covariances that must be estimated on scant (NT) observations with formulas that have only asymptopic, or "large sample," justification. The full blown Parks-Kmenta model that adjusts for contemporaneous, cross-national correlation of errors estimates the same $N(N - 1)/2$ number of covariances – one for each pair of "nations." Thus, we should, pending information on the small sample properties of standard errors and t statistics in the Parks-Kmenta model, be wary of downward bias in standard errors and upward bias in t statistics to the extent that $N(N - 1)/2$ "approaches" NT in Parks-Kmenta models, which adjust for contemporaneous, cross-national correlation of errors. More generally, although it is commonplace to regard samples of a few hundred as "large" enough for reliance upon asymptotically established estimator, we should

be wary of estimators that have only asymptotic justification and aware that simpler models may be preferrable to more complex ones where assumptions for the former are more credible than those for the latter.

7. The nation-specific intercepts designated by B_i address the "unit" effect facet of problem "4." As these intercept effects soak up all cross-national variance, cross-nationally heteroskedastic errors are precluded, obviating occurrence of problem "2."

REFERENCES

Alvarez, Michael, R. Geoffrey Garrett, and Peter Lange. 1991. "Government Partnership, Labor Organization and Macroeconomic Performance, 1967–1984. *American Political Science Review* 85:539–56.

Belsley, David, and Edwin Kuh, and Roy Welsh. 1980. *Regression Diagnostics*. Cambridge, Mass.: MIT Press.

Cameron, David R. 1984. "Social Democracy, Corporatism and Labor Quiescence. In John H. Goldthorpe (ed.), *Order and Conflict in Contemporary Capitalism*, pp. 143–78. New York: Oxford University Press.

Castles, Francis G., and Steve Dowrick. 1990. "The Impact of Government Spending on Medium Term Economic Growth in the OECD, 1960–85." *Journal of Theoretical Politics* 2:00–00.

Chenery, Hollis, and Moises Syrquin. 1975. *Patterns of Development, 1950–70*. Oxford University Press.

Chow, C. G. 1960. "Tests for Equality Between Sets of Coefficients in Two Linear Regressions." *Econometrica* 28:591–605.

Coleman, James S. 1968. "The Mathematical Study of Social Change." In H. M. Blalock Jr. (Ed.), *Methodology in Social Research*, pp. 428–78. New York: McGraw-Hill.

Freedman, David A., and Stephen C. Peters. 1948. "Bootstrapping a regression equation: some empirical results." *Journal of the American Statistical Association* 79:97–106.

Hibbs, Douglas A. Jr. 1987. The Political Economy of Industrial Demacracies. Cambridge, Mass.: Harvard University Press.

1989. *The Political Economy of Industrial Democracies*. Cambridge, Mass.: Harvard University Press.

Hicks, Alexander, 1991. "Unions, Social Democracy, Welfare and Growth." *Research in Political Sociology* 5:209–34.

Hicks, Alexander and Joya Misra. In Press. "Political Resourses and the Expansion of Welfare Effort." *American Journal of Sociology*.

Hicks, Alexander, and Duane Swank. 1992. "Politics, Institutions and Welfare Spending in Industrialized Democracies, 1960–1982." *American Political Science Review* 86:658–74.

Hsiao, C. 1975. "Some Estimation Methods for a Random Coefficient Model." *Econometrica* 43:305–25.

1986. Analysis of Panel Data. Cambridge University Press.

Huber, Evelyn, Charles Ragin, and John Stephens. 1991. "Quantitative Studies of Variation Among Welfare States: Toward a Resolution of the Controversy." Paper presented at the Workshop on Comparative Studies of State Development of the International Sociological Association, Vuoranta, Finland, August 29 to September 1.

Isaac, Larry W., and Larry J. Griffin. 1989. "Ahistoricism in Time-Series Analyses of Historical Processes." *American Sociological Review* 54:873–90.
Johnston, John, 1985. *Econometric Methods*, 3d ed. New York: McGraw-Hill.
Judge, George, W. D. Griffith, R. C. Hill, H. Lutkepohl, and T. C. Lee. 1985. *The Theory and Practice of Econometrics*, 2d ed. New York: Wiley.
Kmenta, Jan. 1971/1988. *Elements of Econometrics*. New York: Macmillan.
Korpi, Walter. 1989. "Power, Politics and State Autonomy in the Development of Social Citizenship." *American Sociological Review*, 54:309–28.
Maddala, George S. 1977, *Econometrics*. New York: McGraw-Hill.
Palme, Joakim. 1990. *Pension Rights in Welfare Capitalism*. Stockholm: Swedish Institute for Social Research.
Pampel, Fred C., and John B. Williamson. 1988. "Welfare Spending in Advanced Industrial Democracies, 1950–1980." *American Journal of Sociology* 50:1424–56.
1989. *Age, Class, Politics and the Welfare State*. Cambridge University Press.
Parks, Robert W. 1966. "Efficient Estimation of a System of Regression Equations When Disturbances Are Both Serially and Contemporaneously Correlated." *Journal of the American Statistical Association* 62:500–9.
Pollard, Walker A. 1983. "Presidential Elections: Cyclical and Distributional Effects." *Public Finance Quarterly* 11:217–36.
Pryor, Frederick L. 1985. *A Guidebook to the Comparative Study of Economic Systems*. Englewood Cliffs, N.J.: Prentice-Hall.
Sayrs, Lois W. 1989. *Pooled Time Series Analysis*. Newbury Park, Calif.: Sage.
SAS. 1986. *SUGI Supplemental Library User's Guide, Version 5*. Carey, N.C.: SAS.
SHAZAM. 1988. *Shazam Econometrics Computer Program: User's Reference Manual, Version 6.1*. New York: McGraw-Hill.
Stimson, James A. 1985. "Regression in Space and Time: A Statistical Essay." *American Journal of Political Science* 29:915–47.
Swamy, P. A. V. P. 1970. "Efficient Inference in a Random Coefficient Regression Model." *Econometrica* 32:313–23.
Swank, Duane H. 1992. "Structural Power and Capital Investment in the Capitalist Democracies." *American Political Science Review* 86:38–54.
Weede, Erich. 1986. "Sectoral Reallocation: Distributional Coalitions and the Welfare State as Determinants of Economic Growth Rates in Industrialized Democracies." *European Journal of Political Research* 14:501–14.
Zellner, A. 1962. "An Efficient Method of Estimating Seemingly Unrelated Regressions and Tests for Aggregation Bias." *Journal of the American Statistical Association* 57:348–68.

7

The social democratic corporatist model of economic performance in the short- and medium-run perspective

ALEXANDER M. HICKS

Interest in political and institutional explanations of macroeconomic performance has burgeoned during the past two decades. The explosion of relevant works has been particularly impressive for the case of the industrialized democracies. From the early 1970s through the 1980s, political scientists and economists extensively elaborated Schumpeter's and Kalecki's early forays into the electoral rhythms of macroeconomic performance in these nations (Kalecki 1943; Schumpeter 1943 and Hibbs 1987a, b). In the late 1970s, Hibbs's (1977) "Political Parties and Macro-economic Policy" inaugurated a similar boom in studies of the macro-economic impacts of partisan differences in government (see Hibbs 1987a, b). In the early 1980s, works by Schmitter (1981) and Olson (1982) spurred new study of macroeconomic consequences of modes of interest organization, already a notable topic since Shonfield's (1965) landmark publication of *Modern Capitalism*.

The literatures on macroeconomic impacts of elections, government partisanship, and interest organization have branched out beyond my ability to comprehensively trace, much less integrate, them here (see Bruno and Sachs 1985; Friedland and Sanders 1985; Katzenstein 1985;

This is a revision of a paper prepared for conference on The "New Compass of the Comparativist conference," Duke University, Durham, N.C., April 26–8, 1991. The author would like to acknowledge the indispensable assistance provided by Richard Lee, Joya Misra, and John Pitt with the collection and management of data used in this paper and to thank Geoffrey Garrett, Fred C. Pampel, Robin Stryker, Adam Przeworski, and (most especially) Duane H. Swank for their generous contributions to the data set used here. The author acknowledges the very useful comments of John Freeman, David Patterson, Charles Ragin, John Stephens, and Derek Scissors on the Duke University, and earlier, precursors to this chapter.

Hibbs 1987a, b; Calmfors and Driffil 1988; Hage, Garnier, and Fuller 1988; Przeworski and Wallerstein 1988; Golden, Lange, and Wallerstein 1991; and Swank 1992). Nevertheless, these strands of scholarship have been drawn together in what I shall call the "social democratic corporatist" (SDC) model of national economic performance. This stresses the following Janus-faced proposition: union organizational strength yields improved macroeconomic performance to the extent that Left parties participate in government; moreover, Left-party rule enhances economic performance to the extent that unions are strong. In the short time since its initial conception, the model has been intensively researched (Lange 1984; Lange and Garrett 1985, 1986; Garrett and Lange 1986, 1989; Hicks 1988, in press; Hicks and Patterson 1989; Alvarez, Garrett, and Lange 1991; and for criticism, Jackman 1986, 1989). However, until Alvarez et al. (1991), evidence for its core proposition had been confined to 15-nation, 1972–83 cross sections.[1] Even including Alvarez et al. (1991), analyses have lacked temporally variable measures of unionization rates, which are key indicators of union strength. Furthermore, they have failed to specify the model to the short-run and longer-term time frames that economists have established for the analyses of economic performance, even though these importantly differentiate theories of economic growth.

My primary goal in this paper is to elaborate and test the social democratic model of economic performance across short-run and medium-run time frames. To do so I review the social democratic theory and then elaborate it in several regards. In elaborating the theory, I (1) sketch a conventional, economic conception of time frames, (2) hypothesize variations in policy instruments across time frames, (3) discuss some prominent econometric estimation procedures for appropriate "pooled" data arrays, and (4) match instruments to time frames and time frames to estimators. I then test the theory across both annual and six- to seven-year time frames using pooled data. Results of my tests clarify the relevance of time frame to the social democratic model of economic growth, illustrate some estimation procedures for the analysis of pooled data, and largely support the social democratic theory.

The social democratic corporatist model

Once again, this formulation argues that strong Left-party government and strong unions (i.e., extensive, centralized union confederations) enhance economic performance. More specifically, it argues that union organizational strength enhances performance insofar as Left parties rule and, vice versa, that Left parties' participation in government improves performance insofar as unions are strong. The theory or model has two facets, a "union" facet and a "party" one, each spelled out in a trio of equations in Table 7.1 (Panel II).

The union facet of the model focuses on variable effects a^* of U (unions), which are conditional on values of L, Left-party strength. The underlying idea is, first, that the union policies of labor quiescence and wage restraint bolster profits, investment, and the like, as well as augment growth. *Crucially*, their ability to do this is advanced by Left governments, which sustain high employment, help restrain prices, guarantee labor rights and deals, and so on.[2] Algebraically, a^* varies with L. In the extreme, when L is low, a^* may be negative, because the party-independent component of a^* – that is a – may be negative (e.g., unions may operate as short-sighted special interests). The party facet focuses on variable effects b of Left governments. These effects vary with U, or union organizational strength. The stress here is on Left government policies – high employment, incomes, investment policies, and so on. The benevolent effects of these policies are contingent on union strength – wage restraint that makes high-employment policy sustainable, support for economy-wide long-term growth policies, and so on. (Importantly, cohesive, encompassing unions advance these policies because they have constituencies too homogeneous and too extensive to escape poor national economic performance.) Here b may be negative, and b^* may be negative, in turn, as U falls below some threshold. Equations (A3) and (B3) are actual estimation equations. One can obtain (A3) by substituting from (A2) for a^* in (A1) and, similarly, get (B3) from (B1) and (B2) (see Cohen and Cohen 1975).

The SDC propositions are usefully elaborated in terms of the four cells of Table 7.1, Panel II. In Cell A, the presence of an organizationally strong labor movement enhances performance. Powerful central union confederations, the argument goes, deliver wage restraint from their constituents, who have an interest in pursuing a "collective gain strategy" of noninflationary wage, profit, and investment growth. Such a strategy, however, is rational only where the uncertainty that restraint will result in favorably distributed economic growth is low. Leftist control of government reduces that uncertainty because state stabilization and investment policies provide both "strong incentives for capital to reinvest" and safeguards that future increases in societal product will be distributed favorably to workers (Lange and Garrett 1985, p. 795). Thus, union wage restraint, complemented by labor's industrial cooperation or quiescence, is central for growth. By these means, strong ("encompassing") unions "contribute to greater profits, a more favorable investment environment and higher rates of economic growth" (Olson 1982; Lange and Garrett 1985, p. 795). Crucially, realization of such goals is contingent on Left control of government, which reduces labor's uncertainty

Table 7.1. *Social democratic corporatist, interactive model of economic performance*

Panel I. Algebraic presentation of two facets of SDC model

(A) Union facet	(B) Party facet
(A1) $G = i + a^*U + bL + Xf + e$	(B1) $G = i + b^*L + aU + Xf + e$
(A2) $a^* = a + cL$	(B2) $b^* = ab + cU$
(A3) $G = i + aU + bL + c(LxU) + Xf + e$	(B3) $G = i + aU + bL + c(LxU) + Xf + e$

Panel II. Heuristic presentation of relationships between labor union strength (U), Left strength (L), and economic growth (G)

	Union organizational strength (U)	
Left-party strength (L)	High	Low
High	A. High growth (Austria)	B. Low growth (United Kingdom)
Low	C. Low growth (Netherlands)	D. High growth (United States)

and connotes "Keynes-plus" policies of fiscal stabilization augmented by labor-market, policies, investment incentives, incomes policies, and the like.

When labor is organizationally strong but politically weak (Cell B) or vice versa, politically strong but organizationally weak (Cell C), high rates of economic growth are less likely. However, in the former situation of union but not Left-party strength, Lange and Garrett stress that labor, in the absence of governmental guarantees and compensations, would be "more likely to exploit their organizational strength in the market" through wage militancy than to follow wage restraint (1985, p. 800). (Individual unions would separately pursue their special interests, free riding where labor-wide policy options arose.) One might also stress that Left governments are not available to implement "Keynes-plus" policies, much less to reinforce union labor market ones. Societal gains from union restraint and/or Left macroeconomic stewardship will be marginal at best. In the situation of union weakness and Left governmental strength that is described by Cell C, uncertain Left-party societal support is likely to undermine Left confidence and decisive action. Union militancy (now scattered by union fragmentation) is likely to bar effective incomes policies and to partially offset any beneficial Keynes-plus policies (1985, pp. 800–1).

Finally, if labor is organizationally and politically weak as in Cell D, something approaching "the pure play of market forces" obtains (Lange and Garrett 1985, p. 801). Labor's organizational and political weakness would reduce its "ability to disrupt the capitalist growth process" (p. 801) and, presumably, to disrupt relatively free-market-driven growth.

Note that Lange and Garrett stress the causal agency of union wage and lobbying restraint (see also Garrett and Lange 1986; Lange 1984). To this they add the function of guarantor for union collective gain policies that a Left government exercises by means of its demand management, incomes, investment, and social wage policies. Hicks (1988) places his emphasis on the pro-growth functions of government policies, which he views as reinforced by union policies.

In this formulation, cooperation via wage restraint, cooperation with incomes policies, and the like limit inflationary threats to sustained high-employment policies. Cooperation thereby buoys capacity utilization, anticipated demand, investment, and profits while forgoing inflationary market distortion and, finally, enhancing productivity, income growth, and high employment.

Although very strong union-plus-party labor movements are expected to promote economic growth, the implications of Cell D in Table 7.1 should not be neglected. Below some level of union (or Left-party) strength, their effects turn *negative*. The negative effects beyond that point may be reinterpreted as *positive* effects of labor (or Left) *weakness* and, in turn, the *positive* effects of business (or non-Left) strength. Thus, in an important twist of the SDC formulation, positive conservative (or non-Left) effects on economic performance can be expected where Left parties (or unions) are weak. It is cases of inconsistent (or intermediate) union and Left strength like the British and Dutch that contrast most poorly with the Left corporatist ones.

The SDC model is generally consistent with Scharpf's (1987, chap. 9) model of voluntary wage restraint and national economic performance. Scharpf stresses the political viability and economic effectiveness of combined social democratic fiscal and monetary expansiveness and union wage restraint where norms of long-term cooperation are institutionalized by unions (chap. 9, esp. pp. 170–2, 182–93). Scharpf's model is more fine-grained, implicating more nuanced and nation-specific institutional conditions for performance than mere Left-Keynesian government and large/centralized unions in its design. For example, Scharpf (pp. 189–93) judges the Austrian Commission for Prices and Wages and the extension of proportional representation into the far reaches of governmental administration to be notable pillars of long-term union cooperativeness. In addition, he views Keynesian coordination as checked by the very high real interest rates imposed on Europe by the U.S. budget deficits since 1981 (pp. 244–7). An SDC response to the last problem is attempted in Hicks and Patterson (1992).

Time frame, macroeconomic instruments, and economic performance

Time frames. Of course, causal processes appear different and may actually be so over different time horizons. Changing interest rates, like, say, social cuts ("He or she really meant that!") may have different consequences on first impact than when their effects are all played out. Likewise, some factors operate differently over various time frames, like the weather fluctuating from day to day, seasonal cycles, and trending only over the very long run.

Actually, distinctions among processes of differing durations are rather well developed by economists who differentiate among short-, medium-, and long-run processes and models (Christ 1966). The short run hovers about the shortest relevant spans for registering effects of one factor on another: periods of a few days to a few years needed for impacts of variables (of money market borrowing rates on transactions or a new capital depletion allowance on productivity). The medium term may extend from time that is needed for the cumulative, "equilibrium" effect of a short-term factor (a tax cut) to be exhausted to the length of a business cycle phase (Castles and Dowrick, 1990). The long term is more an uncapped residual category (capitalism since Bretton Woods – or Speenhamland) in the economic accounting of time.

This chapter examines short-run periods of a year each (i.e., annual time series) and the three medium-run periods of 1966–71, 1972–7, and 1978–83 (i.e., three 6-year panels). It eschews the truly long term because, although the 20 or 25 years that could bear on it might be sufficient, merely 17 national cases would impair robust estimation of long-run causal patterns.[3]

Instruments, intermediary targets, and performance. Distinctions among causal processes specific to particular time frames are relatively well developed in macroeconomics (Christ 1966). For example, monetarists deny long-term impacts of monetary expansion on "real" economic outcomes like production and employment rates, while Keynesians stress the short-run efficacy of fiscal policy for moderating economic fluctuations in the same outcomes about their secular growth paths (Barry 1985).[4]

Indeed, the distinction applies to most of the policy instruments and intermediate goals stipulated and/or implied by the SDC model of real outcomes such as aggregate product growth and (un)employment. *Investment* in capital plant and equipment should enhance the quality and quantity of capital over the longer haul, thus augmenting growth and employment across all but the shortest time frames (Dornbusch and Fischer 1978). Conventional *fiscal and monetary stabilization instruments*, in contrast, principally stimulate growth by mobilizing underutilized productive capacity, which drives longer-term growth. True, fiscal and monetary stimulation may exert some upward pressure on longer-run growth paths by averting resource underutilization. For the most part, economists have been wary of postulating longer-term consequences of stabilization policy (Dornbusch and Fischer 1978). Those who have drawn most attention to adverse longer-run consequences of stabilization policy have been its "new classical" critics. These critics stress the allocative efficiency of undistorted competitive markets as the key to growth and have singled out *inflation* as a principal distorter of market signals, market efficiency, and sustainable real growth and high employment (Brenna and Buchanan 1981).[5]

Labor quiescence should contain inflationary and profit-squeezing work stoppages, while buoying worker morale and business confidence, and should thereby stimulate economic growth and employment in both the shorter and longer run. Of course, short-term wage *increases* will, by augmenting consumer demand, augment growth, at least to the extent that productive capacity is not yet fully utilized; but to that extent they are compatible with a policy of wage restraint. Together, the instruments and outcomes just discussed exhaust most of those underlying the SDC case. As a result, SDC theory's predictive power should erode as it is put to longer-run uses. Our principal purpose here is to see whether already documented short-run effects of SDC theory's core political variables erode over time. However, it is also interesting to examine whether or not our differential short- and long-run predictions about the specific instruments underlying governmental macroeconomic policy effectiveness bear up under empirical scrutiny. In order to do so we examine some representative measures of these "instruments."

The exact policy manipulanda that we shall use in our analyses of aggregate economic growth and (un)employment rates include both direct policy instruments and policy targets such as inflation that policymakers manipulate with at least one eye to buoying growth and minimizing unemployment. The specific policy manipulanda, more fully detailed in the Appendix, include the following:

two instruments of stabilization policy as it is conceived within the Keynesian–neoclassical synthesis, namely, public-sector budget deficits, operationally normed on GDP, and the percentage rate of change in the money supply (i.e., M1);

inflation, conceived in new classical terms as a source and indicator of market distortion, allocative inefficiency, and poor macroeconomic performance;

the investment rate, operationally the share of gross fixed investment in GDP, the core explanatory variable in orthodox growth theory; and

three indicators of labor quiescence/militance, namely, the strike rate, the share of worker compensation in GDP, and the annual rate of change in this "wage share."

Expected effects of the policy manipulanda on aggregate economic growth and, for direct comparison, changes in high employment (operationally unemployment) are outlined in Table 7.2.

Some major thrusts of the propositions merit more detail than the table provides. One is that the stimulative effects of fiscal and monetary stabilization instruments are expected to vanish in the medium run. (Recall that I have skirted consideration of the really long term and that this medium run refers to our seven-year chunks of time.) A second thing to stress is that effects of investment are expected to be sustained, perhaps to predominate, in the medium run. I make no prediction for labor militancy in the medium run. Patterns of effects across time frames are the same for growth and employment. A third key point is that effects of Left/union variables are expected to weaken in the medium run as effects of underlying instruments weaken. Further, effects of

Table 7.2. *Policy instruments for achievement of aggregate economic growth and high unemployment: short- and medium-run effects*

	Aggregate growth		High employment[a]	
	Short run	Medium run	Short run	Medium run
Gross investment (% GDP)	Stimulation	Stimulation	Stimulation	Stimulation
Inflation	Erosion	(Erosion)	Erosion	(Erosion)
Percent change money supply	Stimulation	Zero	Stimulation	Zero
Public deficits (% GDP)	Stimulation	Zero	Stimulation	Zero
Labor quiescence[b]				
Wage share of GDP	Erosion		Erosion	
Wage increase	Stimulation		Stimulation	
Strike rate	Erosion		Erosion	

[a]Operationalized with measures of unemployment in Tables 7.4, where effects should be reverse of those in these columns as stated in note 2, (e.g., negative or "erosion" effects of monetary expansion on short-run unemployment).
[b]Operationalized in Table 4.5 with an inverse indicator of quiescence, (i.e., the strike rate) a measure of labor militancy.

inflation are expected to operate in the long run as well as in the short run, although this is anticipated with some trepidation given the monetarist denial of long-term consequences of "nominal" quantities on "real" ones. Although effects of year-to-year increases in wages (normed on national product) are expected to be expansionary – and to denote a valuable instrument of strong, cohesive unions – less transitory aspects (and measures) of labor militancy are expected to erode economic performance over the short as well as the long run. That is, the less transitory aspects of labor quiescence are expected to have stimulative effects. In particular, the wage *share* of GDP, a measure of more durable wage restraint than the rate of change in wages, is expected to depress economic growth and, in turn, employment rates. As past levels of economic growth figure among our controls in models of high employment, the strike rate is used as an alternative measure of labor militance in (un)employment models.

Pooled estimators and time frames

Pooled data arrays lend themselves nicely to the study of economic performance. They may combine temporally lively sources of growth such as investment rates with temporally inert (systemic) factors such as the centralization of union confederations, and they can augment otherwise scarce observations. Furthermore, they are useful for analyses of data both on short periods such as years and on longer, more highly aggregate periods such as phases of business cycles.

However, pooled data like that on nation-years that I will use here complicate estimation. Within a multiple regression framework, the analyses of pooled data require careful selection and implementation of one class of specialized GLS estimators. As the methodological introduction on pooling noted, OLS estimators of pooled data such as ours are plagued by problemactic regression errors: (1) error autoregressiveness over time, (2) error correlation across nations, (3) error heteroskedasticity over nations, (4) temporal or cross-sectional unit effects, and (5) temporally or cross-nationally heterogeneous parameters (and underlying causal processes) (see Judge et al. 1985; Stimson 1985; and Kmenta, 1971 [1988]). As a result of these complications, defining mathematically tractable, empirically realistic, good, best linear unbiased estimators (BLUE) is problematic.

Fortunately, two models or procedures for estimation of substantive formulation like those at issue here were identified in the methodological introduction. First, the Parks–Kmenta model combines simple, conventional solutions to the problems of autoregressive errors, cross-sectionally dependent errors and cross-sectional heteroskedastic errors, and is tailored to fit "temporally dominant" data. Second, error variance or error components model, elegantly addresses error-related complication, most realistically for "spatially dominant" data arrays (Parks 1966; Kmenta 1971).

With longer-term models that require temporal aggregation of information, spatial dominance is typical. It obtains for my medium-run model. In other words, in temporally dominant data arrays (in which the number of time periods T exceeds the number of cross sections J) the variance component model's lack of autoregressive realism is a decisive liability (Stimson 1985). However, in such models the Parks–Kmenta procedural autoregressive realism is a strength. In cross-sectionally dominant data arrays (in which the number of cross sections J notably exceeds the number of time periods T), the variance component model's shortfall from autoregressive realism may be tolerable. Indeed, the flexibility of the error components model with regard to unit effects, contemporaneous cross-sectional error correlation, and the like begins to come into play as a strong virtue.

Importantly, relatively short-run models tend toward temporal dominance (see Table 7.3). Because the number of cross-sectional units for which social scientists have comparable time series is usually limited, when we preserve relatively short time periods (instead of collapsing them into longer ones), we tend to favor temporal dominance – despite the temporally truncated character of most time series. Furthermore, causality, essentially a longitudinal process that unfolds over time, is best reflected in longitudinal covariations. Therefore, we seldom turn to cross-sectional data except as a last resort and, even then, use it only as a "proxy" for the time-series data that we lack. Conversely, temporally dominant models tend to be short term because we seldom have long series of long time periods. My short-term model, not surprisingly, turns out to be temporally dominant. The Parks–Kmenta model suits it well (Stimson 1985).

Similarly, relatively long-run models tend toward spatial dominance. Indeed, relative spatial dominance pressures us to conceptualize long-run models. Either spatially dominant models reflect conscious aggregations of time done in the effort to construct relatively long-run models or they reflect a dearth of time points pressuring us toward short-term conceptualizations. Good examples of necessity mothering long-term (or medium-term) theory are the strictly cross-national models of income equality and like phenomena for which time-series data are lacking, and which gain causal interpretability from the assumption that they capture processes "in equilibrium," that is, processes that have played themselves out and for which our *explananda* are fully realized outcomes. Serviceable examples of temporal aggregation done in an effort to build long-term models resulting in cross-sectionally dominant models are provided later. Not surprisingly my medium-term model is spatially dominant. The error components procedure suits it well.

DATA AND METHODS

Our SDC model's estimation equations are of the form

$$P = i + aU + bL + cUL + f(1)X(1) + \ldots f(K)X(K) + e. \qquad (1)$$

Here, $K = 3$, for models of economic growth, running across controls for "catch-up," lagged growth, and "import price inflation"; $K = 4$, when it includes an additional control for lagged unemployment rates

Table 7.3. *Congenial estimation models/techniques for combinations of theoretical time frame, temporal/spatial dominance in variance of data array, and stress of error structure model*

		Error structure emphasis	
Theoretical time frame	Time-space dominance (in variation)	Stress on realistic timewise autocorrelation	Stress on flexible (random) unit effects
Short-run period-to-period impacts (and cumulation)	Time dominant ($T > N$)	Parks-Kmenta	Random coefficient models
Longer-run temporally aggregated and/or intermittent observations	Space dominant ($N > T$)	—[a]	Variance components with time-variable regressors

[a]No clearly preferred model/technique.

in models of unemployment rates. Here i is an intercept; and a, b, and c are estimates for core SDC parameters.

To add to the information on measures already provided and available in the Appendix, economic growth is measured as real percentage growth with data from Summers and Heston (1988). This is done from time $t - 1$ to t in short-run models and for $t - 5$ to t (within each panel) for medium-run models. (Further information on measurement, lag specifications, and data sources for growth of another variables used in this chapter are described in the Appendix.) For comparability with Alvarez et al. (1991), unemployment performance is measured in terms of *changes* in unemployment rates, specifically, percentage changes in unemployment rates. (See Appendix.)

Measurement of the core SDC variables follows the lead of Garrett and Lange (1986) in all but two respects. First, the Garrett–Lange measure of centralization is extended to Ireland and Switzerland via a replication of the procedures indicated in Garrett and Lange (1986); and centralization scores are divided by 10 to bring their range into line with the 0.0–1.0 range of union density measures. (This yields "centralization" scores of 0.6 for Ireland and Switzerland, scores that tap information on union-confederation concentration as well as centralization.) Second, annually varing measures of union density are used (see Misra and Hicks 1991).

Control variables are limited to conserve degrees of freedom in the medium-run models, which have *N*s of only 51, and to avert effacing core SDC effects by controlling for the very instruments and pathways by which they operate. I do not wish to go so far in my efforts to control for environmental disturbances that I end up like the man who wore earplugs to cut out the chatter at the opera. In addition, specification of "domestic" models of economic performance is complex, ideally entailing multiple equation models beyond the scope of this paper (Alvarez et al. 1991). As a result my controls are of a preliminary and, where possible, catchall variety.

"Catch-up" controls are used to tap effects of lagged values of per capita income or product. Theoretically, these are interpreted as effects of the level of technological advancement at the beginning of a period. These effects capture a Janus-faced process in which there is one tendency for technological leaders, hamstrung by the difficulty of sustained innovation, to "fall back" and a corresponding tendency for technological laggards, aided by the relative ease of tehnological adoptions, to "catch up." Empirically, researchers typically operationalized technological level in terms of lagged level of per capita national product. They typically gauge such effects in terms of the presence and strength of negative effects of lagged per capita national product. Their expectations have been impressively supported (e.g., see Olson 1982; Choi 1983; Pryor 1985; Baumol 1986; and Hicks 1988). Methodologically, the theoretical distinctiveness of catch up effects is clouded, but their empirical robustness is enhanced, by their close resemblance to "regression toward the mean" phenomena endemic to models of change (see Meyer and Hannan, 1979). Catch-up controls are included in models of unemployment rates as well as of production growth, because technological catch-up and fall-back effects seem applicable to as close a correlate of economic growth as unemployment. (See X_1 in the Appendix.)

Lagged measures of economic growth are included in aggregate growth models. This is done following the lead of Alvarez et al. (1991), who employ lagged growth as a measure of recent growth performance (and, by implication, capability). Lagged aggregate growth is also included in unemployment models as economic expansion generates demand for labor, which reduces unemployment (Dornbusch and Fischer 1978). (Faced with a choice between specification of highly collinear measures of lagged unemployment growth and lagged economic growth we chose the latter because of its stronger theoretical links to current changes in unemployment rates (Dornbusch and Fischer 1978).) Lagged values of (levels of) unemployment rates are included in unemployment models in order to adjust for "regression toward the mean" phenomena in processes driving unemployment.

Examination of international economic factors was confined to inflation and volatility in the cost of imports, perhaps the most dramatic international influence during the period of petroleum cartels and volatile harvests under study here (see, e.g., Dornbusch and Fischer 1978; Gourevitch 1985; and Alvarez et al. 1991). Following Alvarez et al. (1991), we control for an index of the value of a nation's imports that is weighted by a measure of the nations' sensitivity to increases in such prices. (See Tables 7.4 and 7.5 for more details on these controls, especially lag structures.) We have no hypotheses about the operation of the controls for past performance across short- and medium-run models.

Measures of the policy instruments, highlighted in Table 7.2, are further detailed in the Appendix. Before turning to our short- and medium-term tests of the SDC formulation, we turn to tests of our hypotheses regarding effects of these instruments on economic performance. Regressions for these analyses of changes in aggregate economic product and unemployment rates include the same control variables just introduced with the SDC models of economic performance.

Analyses were executed using the Parks–Kmenta GLS procedure for short-run models and the Fuller–Battesse variance component model for medium-run models (see Shazam 1988; SAS 1988).

Table 7.4. *Short- and medium-run GLS analyses of percent growth in real GDP, 1966-83, with a focus on policy instruments (raw metric slope estimates with t-statistics beneath them)*

	Cross section of time series (CSTS) GLS (Parks)	Panel of periods (TSCS) GLS (variable component)	Panels of periods (TSCS) GLS (variable component) pruned
Real GDP/ pop (t - 1)[a]	-0.032** (13.27)	-0.020** (3.88)	-0.022** (4.08)
Change in real GDP (t - 1/ t - 2)	0.111** (4.40)	0.223** (6.50)	0.279** (7.23)
Import price inflation (t - 1/t - 2)	-0.0009** (12.34)	-0.0005 (0.82)	—
Gross investment/ GDP (t - 1)	0.063** (7.12)	0.053 (1.29)	0.062** (1.88)
Consumer price inflation (t - 1/t - 2)	-0.151** (10.83)	-0.110** (2.00)	-0.063** (1.93)
Deficit GDP (t - 1)	0.088** (8.86)	0.054 (0.95)	—
Percent change M1 (t - 1/t - 2)	0.0005** (9.61)	-0.0004 (1.09)	—
Wage share (t - 1)	-0.778** (8.12)	-0.003 (0.54)	—
Change in wage share (t - 1)	-0.022** (3.19)	-0.002 (0.39)	—
Constant	0.236** (12.94)	0.252** (3.12)	0.206** (4.21)
R^2	0.960	0.539	0.540
Df	298	43	46
D.W.d.	1.900	NR	NR

[a]Lag and aggregation structures for medium-run models are presented in the Appendix.
**$p < .05$ (one-tailed).

Table 7.5. *Short- and medium-run GLS analyses of percent growth in unemployment rates, 1966-83, with a focus on policy instruments (raw metric slope estimates with t-statistics beneath them)*

	Cross section of time series (CSTS) GLS (Parks)	Panel of periods (TSCS) GLS (variable component)	
	Percent change	Percent change	Percent change (pruned)
ln (unemployment) $(t - 1)^a$	-1.311^{**} (14.38)	-1.350^{**} (3.13)	-1.854^{**} (4.04)
GDP/population $(t - 1)$	-0.46^{**} (4.42)	-0.157^{**} (2.94)	-0.161^{**} (3.29)
Change in real GDP $(t - 1/t - 2)$	-4.19^{**} (45.37)	-1.203 (1.35)	-1.348 (1.60)
Import cost inflation $(t - 1/t - 2)$	0.002^{**} (3.09)	0.009^{*} (1.78)	0.009^{**} (2.02)
Capital investment share GDP $(t - 1)$	0.211^{**} (2.35)	-1.066 (2.26)	-1.256^{**} (2.72)
Inflation $(t - 1)$	0.985^{**} (3.37)	1.111^{*} (1.61)	1.187^{**} (2.76)
Deficit/GDP $(t - 1)$	-0.403^{**} (3.37)	-0.012 (0.02)	— —
Change in money $(t - 1/t - 2)$	-0.194^{**} (4.97)	-0.013^{**} (2.83)	-0.013^{**} (3.24)
Strike rate	0.006^{**} (4.03)	0.005^{**} (3.47)	— —
Constant	0.630^{**} (6.69)	0.007^{**} (3.62)	0.016^{**} (3.24)
R^2	0.930	0.740	0.710
Df	296	41	42
D.W.d	1.720	NR	NR

[a]Lag and aggregation structures for medium-run models are presented in the Appendix.
$^{*}p < .10$ (one-tailed); $^{**}p < .05$ (one-tailed); NR not relevant.

FINDINGS

Models of policy instruments

Findings for policy instruments for aggregate growth models conform to expectations (see Table 7.4). Investment rates, budget deficits, and money-supply expansion all have stimulative effects in the short run, while inflation has a negative effect in the short run. The wage share of GDP has the predicted dampening effect on year-to-year aggregate growth, but the change in the wage share, a more transitional measure of labor militancy, has the predicted stimulative effect. In line with expectations, effects of stabilization variables (deficits and money supply growth) and "nominal" quantities (money supply and inflation) erode drastically – as we move into the medium run. True, inflation, consistent with new classical economic views of price increases as a facet of distortions of otherwise efficient market allocative processes, has a continued dampening effect in the medium run, but this is less than half of its short-run effect (i.e., –.063 vs. –.153). Consistent with expectations, effects of capital investment are sustained, at least in the pruned model from which variables "irrelevant" to aggregate growth (i.e., with absolute *t* statistics below 1.0) have been removed. Effects of the "controls" are strong and carry anticipated signs in the short run, but only the catch-up control has notable medium-run effects. In brief, consequences of all of the policy *manipulanda* and conduits for SDC effects that are investigated here, except those of investment rates , erode in magnitude as well as in significance over the long term. In addition, catch-up effects prove robust in the longer run, while effects of recent growth precedents and international price inflation do not. Growth precedent effects, although positive, do not indicate, as some have conjectured, that the recently sluggish "bounce back", but rather that faster growers tend to sustain a good pace. Effects of import costs are not sustained beyond the short run. (See Table 7.4.)

Overall, both labor quiescence and demand stabilization lose their effectiveness over time. Yet high investment and low inflation remain conducive to aggregate growth over the longer haul. As a result, both decay and persistence of SDC effects can be expected as we move from the short to medium run.

Turning to percent changes in unemployment rates, findings for policy instruments roughly conform to expectations for measures of fiscal and monetary policy, inflation, and strike rates *in short-run models* (see Table 7.5). Consistent with past theorizing, stabilization policy reduces unemployment; inflation has the negative effect hypothesized by new classical economists, who stress its reflection and exacerbation of distorted price signals and clearing; and labor militancy worsens unemployment. Our measure of investment, however, yields a positive, short-term effect that, though weak, is anomalous for the short run. Perhaps short-run stimulations of demand are picked up by the effects of inertia and stabilization policy leaving investment to double as a catch-up measure and an index of labor-displacing innovations.

In any case, investment effects have the correct sign for the medium term, for which effects of fiscal, if not monetary, policy are muted. (Perhaps, monetary expansiveness, as a means for the accommodation of fiscal expansiveness, is the more proximate source of high employment and, thus, the more robust variable in a "structural" model of strictly "direct" effects such as ours. As in models of GDP growth, pernicious effects of inflation remain in the longer run; indeed, inflation's undermining of employment increases with the move to a longer-term time frame.) Labor militancy, for which we have no strong long-run expectations, ceases to significantly affect unemployment rates over the longer haul. Among control variables, findings for lagged growth and import costs were predictable in the short run: growth reduces unemployment while import costs augment it. Catch-up effects turned out to be negative, indicating that high levels of development buoy *employment* in the short run. Not surprisingly, lagged unemployment turned out to have extremely significant but substantively small "regression toward the mean" impacts on short-run changes in unemployment: a 1 percent level at "$t-1$" dampens growth in unemployment from $t-1$ to t by 1.83 percent. (Partial autocorrelation in levels of unemployment rates is about .90.)

As regards unemployment, the policy foundations for the SDC effects investigated here are called into some question over the longer terms. Fiscal policy and labor quiescence (the latter less unequivocally) both lose effectiveness over the longer term. Yet monetary expansion remains effective and, as was the case for aggregate growth, both high investment and low inflation rates remain important preconditions for high employment in the medium run.

Across both growth and employment models, then, policy foundations for short-term effects appear to be extensive, while those for longer, medium-run effects appear to be largely confined to manipulations of investment and price stability.

Models of social democratic corporatism

As regards aggregate growth in real GDP, the SDC model remains substantially supported in the short run, despite the addition of Switzerland to our cases, the addition of time-varying data on union member

Table 7.6. *Short- and medium-run GLS analyses of percent growth in real GDP, 1966-83, with a focus on SDC factors (raw metric slope estimates with t-statistics beneath them)*

	Cross section of time series (CSTS) GLS (Parks)	Panel of periods (TSCS) GLS (variable component)	Panel of periods (TSCS) GLS (variable component) pruned
Real GDP/population	-0.035**	-0.043**	-0.053**
(*t* - 1)[a]	(15.76)	(5.50)	(8.14)
Change in real GDP	0.197**	0.058	—
(*t* - 1/*t* - 2)	(7.77)	(0.60)	—
Import price	-0.0012**	-0.0004	—
inflation (*t* - 1/*t* - 2)	(19.96)	(0.85)	—
Union strength	-0.010**	-0.007	-0.012*
(*t* - 1)	(3.97)	(0.88)	(1.52)
Left government	-0.026**	0.033*	0.035*
(*t* - 1)	(11.35)	(1.52)	(1.52)
Union x Left	0.427**	0.026*	0.028*
(*t* - 1)	(10.27)	(1.48)	(1.52)
Constant	0.349**	0.420**	0.513**
	(17.24)	(5.96)	(8.80)
R^2	0.940	0.501	0.606
Df	299	44	46
D.W.d	1.910	NR	NR

[a]Lag and aggregation structures for medium-run models are presented in Table 7.4.
*$p < .10$ (one-tailed); **$p < .05$ (one-tailed); NR not relevant.

density in the measure of union strength to our measures and innovative statistical controls (see Table 7.6, first and second columns).[6] I write "substantial" because results are confined to strong additive effects of union strength and Left government. The SDC interaction is statistically insignificant as well as perversely signed.[7] Support for the model is sustained over the longer run, albeit at a marginal level of statistical significance. Apparently, SDC policies that operate by means of capital investment rates, the only ones examined by us that did not erode fully over the longer run, are sufficient to sustain an effective SDC policy configuration with respect to medium-run aggregate real growth in GNP.

As regards models of changing unemployment, short-run results conform to SDC predictions.[8] However, results for these models, despite correct signs, collapse into statistical insignificance in the medium run. As multicollinearity is high in our small-*N* regressions and may be responsible for the collapse, I ran regressions on additional regressions predicting *levels* of unemployment. These regressions, although plagued by stubborn error autocorrelation, support SDC predictions (see Table 7.7, third and fourth columns). Those for annual data, indeed, support the full SDC model, complete with a negative (antiunemployment) union–Left interaction. Those for medium-run models indicate a persistence of *anti*unemployment effects of union strengths (but not of Left government or the SDC interaction) over the longer haul. These results are consistent with the persistence of investment and inflation effects in our longer-run models of policy instruments.

Overall, then, interactive effects of strong unions and Left governments occur in the short run and appear to persist into the medium run. Turning to models of short-run unemployment, it is unclear whether the SDC interaction of unions and Left strength obtains for unemployment but clear that, if it does not, strong unions and Left governments do, at least, act additively to reduce unemployment. In the medium run, results provide weaker support for SDC predictions. Results for the model of percent changes in unemployment rates provide no sign of union or Left effects. However, a model of levels of unemployment indicates that strong unions, if not Left governments, curtail unemployment in the medium run.

CONCLUSIONS

In the short run of year-to-year economic fluctuations, the social democratic corporatist (SDC) theory of economic performance is distinctly upheld for the case of economic growth. This is so despite our additions of case, annual measurement of union density, and innovative use of statistical controls relative to previous studies. The argument, in brief, that is amply born out is that union organizational strength is conducive to growth insofar as Left parties rule and that Left-party participation in government is conducive to growth insofar as unions are strong. However, the SDC thesis is less clearly upheld for the case

Table 7.7. *Short- and medium-run GLS analyses of percent growth and levels of unemployment rates, 1966-83, with a focus on SDC factors (raw metric slope estimates with t-statistics beneath them)*

	Cross section of time series (CSTS, Parks)	Panel of periods (TSCS, variable components)	Cross section of time series (CSTS, Parks)	Panel of periods (TSCS, variable components)
	Percent change	Percent change	Level	Level
Real GDP/population $(t-1)^a$	-0.008 (0.62)	0.075 (1.01)	0.060** (44.23)	0.023 (0.82)
Change in real GDP $(t-1/t-2)$	-4.83** (66.70)	4.521 (0.38)	-0.269** (94.77)	-0.254 (0.76)
ln (unemployment) $(t-1)$	-1.603** (24.14)	0.019 (0.07)	— —	— —
Import price inflation $(t-1, t-2)$	0.007** (12.65)	-0.028 (0.40)	0.003** (22.32)	0.066** (3.81)
Union strength $(t-1)$	-0.210** (12.64)	-0.075 (0.08)	-0.063** (35.24)	-0.058** (2.29)
Left government $(t-1)$	-0.070* (-3.64)	0.090 (0.43)	0.019** (24.99)	0.037 (0.71)
Union x Left $(t-1)$	0.065* (1.34)	-0.100 (0.41)	-0.063** (41.58)	0.037 (0.71)
Constant	0.528** (4.56)	-0.093 (0.56)	-0.414** (36.58)	-0.094 (0.37)
R^2	0.963	0.313	0.987	0.501
Df	299	43	300	44
D.W.d	1.740	NR	1.320	NR

[a]Lag and aggregation structures for medium-run models are presented in Table 7.4.
*$p < .10$ (one-tailed); **$p < .05$ (one-tailed); NR not relevant.

of unemployment rates. For changes in unemployment, the model's core union–Left product term has an anomalous, albeit statistically insignificant, estimated effect, although union and Left strength do appear to decelerate unemployment rates separately, and the union–Left product term does strongly support SCD theory when levels of unemployment are predicted.

Some policy instruments that provide the policy foundations for the SDC model of economic performance appear to be effective only in the short run and to be ineffective in the medium run. The short-run instruments in question involve both short-run stabilization (i.e., fiscal and monetary instruments) and aspects of labor quiescence, whose effects on economic performance only appear to be sustainable in the short run. Consistent with the Keynesian–neoclassical synthesis with regard to economic growth, it appears that high capital investment rates translate into effective economic performance in the medium as well as the short run. Consistent with some new classical formulations, it appears that inflation rates, controlling for fiscal and monetary instruments, do function as indicators of market distortions that inhibit growth in both the short and medium runs. Deprived of some of its policy instruments, most especially fiscal and monetary instruments, SDC theory would seem likely to prove less applicable in the medium run.

This, in fact, proves to be the case. As regards SDC formulations about aggregate economic growth, medium-run evidence on the SDC formulation is supportive if a .10 significant level is allowed. However, medium-run evidence is weaker than short-run evidence. As regards high-employment performance, the initial SDC operationalization is not at all sustained. In particular, there is no evidence of medium-run Left-party effectiveness in decreasing growth in unemployment. However, there is some evidence that strong unions do help reduce unemployment over both the short and medium runs. Reduction of *joint* Left–union macroeconomic efficacy to simple *union* efficacy is consistent with our discussion and findings regarding policy instruments. Fiscal and monetary instruments long stressed as instruments of short-term stabilization are those that most require government for implementation and that most fully and assuredly decay over time. One of the policy *manipulanda* that remains most robust with the passage of time is the capital investment rate, which union policies of wage restraint presumably enhance where unionization is relatively comprehensive and centralized. The second is inflation, which, under SDC theory, strong unions and Left governments collaborate to restrain. Nonetheless, support for the interactive core of SDC theory is lacking where medium-run unemployment is concerned.

These conclusions not only modify our knowledge of neocorporatist economic policy and performance, they also illustrate the relevance of varied time frames to political-economic theory, of pooled data analysis to the study of such theories, and of varied data arrays and estimation techniques to the flexible analysis of pooled data. They call for more extensive examination of SDC theory across time frames – for example, the modeling of policy instruments as functions of core SDC variables. They also call for the extention of SDC analyses into the truly long run.

APPENDIX: MEASURES AND DATA SOURCES

Y_1: Real percentage Growth (G). Defined as the natural logarithm of the ratio of GDP (see OECD, selected years a) at t to that at $t - 1$ for short-run models and of the average of the same ratio for the preceding five years of each of the following periods for medium-run ones: 1966–71, 1972–7, 1978–83. Data from Summers and Heston (1988).

Y_2: Unemployment rate. Measured conventionally with OECD (selected years b) data: at t in short-run models; averaged across the preceding five years of each of three data panels for medium-run ones.

Y_3: Percentage of change in unemployment rate. Defined as the natural logarithm of the ratio of unemployment at t to that at $t - 1$ for short-run models and of the average of the same ratio for the first five years of each of the following periods for medium-run ones: 1966–71, 1972–7, 1978–83.

U: Union organizational strength index. Summing a measure of union centralization and a measure of union density (from Lange and Garrett 1985). The measure of centralization (which varied from 3 to 9) has been rescaled to vary from 0.3 to 0.9 for better comparability with the measure of union density. This now varies across all years (see Misra and Hicks 1991).

L: Left-party strength. Percentage of cabinet portfolios held by Left parties (Left parties defined by Castles and Mair, 1984; data are from Mackie and Rose 1982), and their 1982–5 entries in *European Journal of Political Research*. Measured at $t - 1$ for short-run models; averaged across first five years of each of three panels for medium-term ones.

$U \times L$: Multiplicative interaction of U and L.

X_1: Natural logarithm GDP per capita (Catch-up). Real GDP (Summers and Heston 1988) divided by population (also from Summers and Heston, 1988) and measured at $t - 1$ for short-run models; averaged across the preceding five years of each of three panels for medium-term ones.

X_2: Natural logarithm of unemployment rate. Measured (as Y_2) at $t - 1$ in short-run models; in 1966, 1972, and 1978 in medium-run ones.

X_3: Import price inflation shocks (I). The product of openness and import-price change, where openness is the sum of exports and imports as a proportion of GDP and import-price change is the annual percentage of change in an index of import prices (OECD 1987) measured at $t - 1$ for short-run models; averaged across the first five years of each of three panels for the medium-run ones.

X_4: Investment (gross) in capital stock as proportion of GDP. (OECD Selected years C) measured at $t - 1$ for short-run models; averaged across first five years of each of three panels for medium-run ones.

X_5: Surplus/deficit as share of GDP (Surp.). Surplus/deficit (in millions from International Monetary Fund, 1965–88) measured at $t - 1$ in the short-run models; averaged across first five years of each of three panels for medium-run ones.

X_6: Annual percentage of Change in the M_1 Money supply. From International Monetary Fund (1965–88) measured at $t - 1$ for the short-run models; averaged across first five years of each of three panels for medium-run ones.

X_7: Wage share in GDP. Wage and salary compensation of workers as a proportion of GDP (from Griffin, O'Connell, and McCammon 1989, courtesy of Larry J. Griffin). Measured at $t - 1$ for short-run models; averaged across first five years of each of three panels for medium-run ones.

X_8: Strike rate. Natural logarithm of strike rate (man-days as proportion of work time) with data from Hicks, Swank, and Ambuhl (1989) and courtesy of D. H. Swank. Measured at $t - 1$ for short-run models; averaged across first five years of each of three panels for medium-run ones.

NOTES

1. Alvarez et al. (1991) adds Ireland to the typical 15 suspects, but not Switzerland, which is viewed as insufficiently competitive with regard to partisan rule. Our population of affluent, durably democratic, postwar societies consists of Australia, Belgium, Canada, Denmark, Finland, France, the GFR, Ireland, Italy, Japan, the Netherlands, Norway, Sweden, Switzerland, the United Kingdom, and the United States. Iceland and Luxemberg are excluded because of their populations of less than 1 million each, Israel because of its war economy and restrictions on Palestinian franchise, and Spain, Portugal, and Venezuela because of short or spotty democratic records. New Zealand would have figured in present analyses but for its lack of international trade data and neglect in extant codings of union confederations (see Cameron 1984; Lange and Garrett 1985). Also, the robustness of results in small-sample, cross-sectional research on social democratic corporatist theory has been debated in Jackman 1986, 1989; Hicks 1988; Hicks and Patterson, 1989; and Lange and Garrett 1986; Garrett and Lange 1989).
2. "High employment" is used here in the sense in which it is used in stabilization theory, i.e., as unemployment at a sufficently "high" or "full" level to denote full short-term utilization of labor resources (Blinder and Solow 1974). It is

not used in the sense of high levels of employment *as opposed to low levels of unemployment* that has become increasingly commonplace in the wake of the great 1980s growth in the economically active population of the United States.

3. Moreover, while some attribute notable long-term enhancement of output to efficient utilization of resources, others claim that no long-run benefits of fiscal policy are possible (Alt and Chrystal 1983).
4. We are close to distinct cycles for 1966–71 and 1972–7 but merely capture one minicycle plus the beginning of a second cycle with 1978–83. Still, even here, we bridge two "peaks" with the first two periods and get from one peak into a (second) subsequent expansion with the third period. The three time aggregates are reasonably comparable.
5. True, for neoclassical economists of both Keynesian and monetarist persuasions, inflation is one causal mechanism in the transmission of fiscal and monetarist stimuli. However, to the extent that such stimuli translate into inflation, *existing productive capacity is being exhausted*; and to this extent, inflation within the neoclassical synthesis entails fiscal and monetary excess rather than stabilization (Dornbusch and Fischer 1978).
6. Although a full account of the effects of SDC variables on the policy instruments and the (intermediate) targets underlying SDC effects on ultimate economic performance is beyond the scope of this chapter, some consideration of such effects may be illuminating. To provide this, zero-order correlations (each adjusted for AR(1) autocorrelation of errors) have been run between union strength and Left government and each of the instruments/targets. For union strength, correlations are predictively positive with deficits (0.727), investment rates (0.235), inflation rates (0.194), and changing wage shares (0.361); negative with levels of wage shares (–.134) and strike rates (–.625); and close to zero (0.001) for money supply expansion. For Left government, correlations are predictively positive with deficits (0.244), money supply expansion (0.131), inflation rates (0.792), and increases in wage shares (0.623) and are negative with levels of wage shares (–.131) and strike rates (–.672).
7. My models of instruments are merely illustrative and exploratory. They do buttress the plausibility of my arguments about instrumental causal mechanisms for the SDC model. However, it would be presumptuous in the face of the massiveness of relevant macroeconomic writings to expect them to be fully and precisely enough specified to be stable (and more than roughly average parameters) across time and space. The SDC model, which builds directly on a growing literature, may be more robust. To test for the homogeneity of its slopes and intercepts across nations and years, Chow *F*-tests were computed for the model's core equation (Table 7.6, first column). These test the null hypothesis that the error sum of squares from a "constrained" pooled regression with cross-temporally or cross-sectionally uniform slopes and intercepts is equal to (no larger than) the error sum of squares from a set of nation- or period-specific regressions with unconstrained estimates that are free to vary across nation or period (Chow 1960; Maddala 1977, chap. 14). Furthermore, where regressors are identically specified across all disaggregated and pooled equations, these *F*s test for the equivalence of all parameters for analogous variables (e.g., union strength). The Chow *F*s were computed for short-run SDC models of growth. That for parameter homogeneity across years equaled 1.75, allowing a rejection of null at the .05

level. (Period interactions are considered in Hicks and Patterson, 1992.) Those for homogeneity across nations were complicated by the temporal invariance or virtual invariance of my measures of Left strength within several nations (i.e., Canada, Italy, Japan, Switzerland, and the United States). They were, in turn, plagued by the nonestimability of union–party interaction terms for these nations. Nevertheless, testing for model homogeneity after excluding the party strength and union–party interaction terms yields an F (90, 204) = 1.192. I also tested for equality of the error sum of squares from 17 unconstrained national regressions, excluding these variables, to the error sum of squares for the fully specified pooled model, obtaining an F (95, 204) = 1.252. The null hypotheses of overall homogeneity of slopes and intercepts across nations were not rejected. However, it should be noted that cross-national homogeneity does not bar the possibility of period differences for specific parameters across specific subsets of nations. (Analogously, a significant effect of a Baptist dummy variable may be found in an equation predicting social liberalism where the overall "effect" of a set of religious and denominational dummies is not significant.) It also bears noting that my small samples may not provide sufficient statistical power for rejections of null hypotheses. Indeed, homogeneity tests were precluded for long-run models because of the scarce degrees of freedom and scant statistical power available for such tests.

8. Chow's F-test for longitudinal homogeneity was computed for my short-run SDC model of levels of unemployment, yielding an insignificant 1.33. Tests for cross-national homogeneity of parameters yielded significant Fs of 2.89 and 2.55. This indicates that the unemployment model is not homogeneous across nations and suggests a need for future unemployment models that capture cross-national heterogeneity by means of interactions or for a respecification of models at the national level with longer time series.

REFERENCES

Alt, James E., and K. Alec Chrystal. 1983. *Political Economic*. Berkeley: University of California Press.

Alvarez, Michael, R. Geoffrey Garrett, and Peter Lange. 1991. "Government Partnership, Labor Organization and Macroeconomic Performance, 1967–1984." *American Political Science Review* 89:539–56.

Barry, Brian. 1985. "Does Democracy Cause Inflation? Some Political Ideas of Some Economists." In Leon Lindberg and Charles S. Maier (eds.) *The Politics of Inflation and Economic Stagnation*, pp. 280–317. Washington, D.C.: Brookings Institution.

Baumol, William J. 1986. "Productivity Growth, Convergence, and Welfare: What the Long-Run Data Show." *American Economic Review* 76:1073–85.

Blinder, Alan S., and Robert M. Solow. 1974. "Analytical Foundations of Fiscal Policy." In Alan S. Blinder and Robert M. Solow (eds.), *The Economics of Public Finance*, pp. 3–115. Washington, D.C.: Brookings Institution.

Brenna, George, and James Buchanan. 1981. "Implications of Money Creation Under Leviathan." *American Economic Review: Papers and Proceedings*, pp. 347–51. Nashville, Tennessee: American Economic Association.

Bruno, Michael, and Jeffrey D. Sachs. 1985. *The Economics of Worldwide Stagflation*. Cambridge, Mass: Harvard University Press.

Calmfors, L., and J. Driffil. 1988. "Bargaining Structures, Corporatism and Macroeconomic Performance." *Economic Policy* 6:14–61.

Cameron, David. 1984. "Social Democracy, Corporatism and Labor Quiescence: The Representation of Economic Interests in Advanced Capitalist Societies." In John H. Goldthorpe (ed.), *Order and Conflict in Contemporary Capitalism*. New York: Oxford University Press.

Castles, Francis, and Steve Dowrick. 1990. "The Impact of Government Spending Levels on Medium-term Economic Growth in the OECD, 1960–1965." *Journal of Theoretical Politics* 4:173–204.

Castles, Francis, and Peter Mair. 1984. "Left–Right Political Scales: Some Expert Judgements." *European Journal of Political Research* 12:73–88.

Choi, Kwang. 1983. *Theories of Comparative Economic Growth*. Ames: Iowa State University Press.

Chow, C. G. 1960. "Tests for Equality Between Sets of Coefficients in Two Linear Regressions," *Econometrica* 28:591–605.

Christ, C. F. 1966. *Econometric Models and Methods*. New York: Wiley.

Cohen, Jacob, and Patricia Cohen. 1975. *Applied Multiple Regression Correlation Analysis*. Hillside, N.J.: Erlbaum.

Dornbusch, Rudiger, and Stanley Fischer. 1978. *Macroeconomics*. New York: McGraw-Hill.

Friedland, Roger, and Jimy Sanders. 1985. "The Public Economy and Economic Growth in Western Market Economies." *American Sociological Review*, 50:421–37.

Garrett, Goeffrey, and Peter Lange. 1986. "Performance in a Hostile World: Economic Growth in Capitalist Democracies, 1974–1982." *World Politics* 38:517–45.

1989. "Government Partisanship and Economic Performance." *Journal of Politics* 51:676–93.

Golden, Miriam, Peter Lange, and Michael Wallerstein. 1991. "Union Centralization in Advanced Industrial Democracies." Research Proposal. Mimeo. Department of Political Science, U.C.L.A.

Gourevitch, Peter A. 1985. *Politics in Hard Times*. Ithaca, N.Y.: Cornell University Press.

Griffin, L., P. O'Connell, and H. McCammon. 1989. "National Variation in the Context of Class Struggle." *Canadian Review of Sociology and Anthropology* 25:37–68.

Hage, Jerald, Maurice Garnier, and Bruce Fuller. 1988. "The Active State: Investment in Human Capital and Economic Growth." *American Sociological Review* 53:824–37.

Hibbs, Douglas A., Jr. 1977. "Political Parties and Macroeconomic Policy." *American Political Science Review* 71:1467–87.

1987a. *The American Political Economy: Macroeconomics and Electoral Politics in the United States*. Cambridge, Mass.: Harvard University Press.

1987b. *The Political Economy of Industrial Democracies*. Cambridge, Mass: Harvard University Press.

Hicks, Alexander. 1988. "Social Democratic Corporatism and Economic Growth." *Journal of Politics* 50:677–704.

In press. "Unions, Social Democracy, Welfare and Democracy." *Research in Political Sociology*.

Hicks, Alexander, and W. David Patterson. 1989. "On the Robustness of the Left Corporatist Model of Economic Growth." *Journal of Politics* 51:169–81.

1992. "Waning Socialist Fortunes? Social Democratic Corporatism and Economic Growth in the Affluent Capitalist Democracies, 1964–1985." Paper presented at the 1991 annual meeting of the Midwest Political Science Associations, April, Chicago.

Hicks, Alexander, Duane Swank, and Martin Ambuhl. 1989. "Welfare Expansion Revisited: Policy Routines and Their Mediation by Party, Class and Crisis, 1957–1982." *European Journal of Political Research* 17:401–30.

International Monetary Fund. Selected years. *International Financial Statistics*. New York: IMF.

Jackman, Robert. 1986. "The Politics of Economic Growth in Industrial Democracies, 1974–1980: Leftist Strength or North Sea Oil." *Journal of Politics* 48:242–56.

1989. "The Politics of Economic Growth, Once Again." *Journal of Politics*, 51:646–61.

Judge, George, and W. D. Griffith, R. C. Hill, H. Lutkepohl, and T. C. Lee. 1985. *The Theory and Practice of Econometrics*, 2d ed. New York: Wiley.

Kalecki, Michael. 1943. "Political Aspects of Full Employment." *Political Quarterly*. 14: 322–41.

Katzenstein, Peter J. 1985. *Small States in World Markets: Industrial Policy in Europe*. Ithaca. N.Y.: Cornell University Press.

Kmenta, Jan. 1971/1988. *Elements of Econometrics*. New York: MacMillan.

Lange, Peter. 1984. "Unions, Workers and Wage Regulation: The Rational Bases of Consent." In John H. Goldthorpe (ed.), *Order and Conflict in Contemporary Capitalism*, pp. 98–123. New York: Oxford University Press.

Lange, Peter, and Geoffrey Garrett. 1985. "The Politics of Growth." *Journal of Politics* 47:792–827.

1986. "The Politics of Growth Reconsidered." *Journal of Politics* 48:257–74.

Mackie, Thomas, and Richard Rose. 1982. *The International Almanac of Electoral History*. 2d ed. London: Macmillan Press.

1982–5. "General Elections in Western Nations." *European Journal of Political Research*.

Maddala, George S. 1977. *Econometrics*. New York: McGraw-Hill.

Meyer, John, and Michael Hannan. 1979. *Development in the World System*. Stanford, Calif: Stanford University Press.

Misra, Joya, and Alexander Hicks. 1991. "Catholicism and Unionization" Paper presented at the annual meeting of the American Sociological Association, August, Cincinnati.

Olson, Mancur. 1982. *The Rise and Decline of Nations: Economic Growth Stagflation and Social Rigidities*. New Haven, Conn.: Yale University Press.

Organization for Economic Cooperation and Development. Selected years a. *National Accounts Statistics, Main Aggregates*. Paris: OECD.

Selected years b. *Labor Force Statistics*. Paris: OECD.

Selected years c. *Quarterly National Accounts*. Paris: OECD.

1987. *Economic Outlook: Historical Statistics, 1960–1985*. Paris: OECD.

Parks, Richard W. 1966. "Efficient Estimation of a System of Regression Equations When Disturbances Are Both Serially and Contemporaneously Correlated." *Journal of the American Statistical Association* 62:500–9.

Przeworski, Adam, and Michael Wallerstein. 1988. "Structural Dependence of the State on Capital." *American Political Science Review* 82:11–31.

Pryor, Frederick L. 1985. *A Guidebook to the Comparative Study of Economic Systems*. Englewood Cliffs, N.J.: Prentice-Hall.

SAS. 1988. *SUGI Supplemental Library User's Guide, Version 5*. Carey, N.C.: SAS.

Scharpf, Fritz. 1987. *Crisis and Choice in European Social Democracy*. Ithaca N.Y.: Cornell University Press.

Schmitter, Phillipe C. 1981. "Interest Intermediation and Regime Governability in Contemporary Western Europe and North America." In Suzanne Berger (ed.), *Organizing Interests in Western Europe*, pp. 285–327. Oxford University Press.

Schonfield, Andrew. 1965. *Modern Capitalism*. Oxford University Press.

Schumpeter, Joseph. 1943. *Capitalism, Socialism and Democracy*. London: Allen & Unwin.

Shazam. 1988. *Shazam Econometrics Computer Program: User's Reference Manual, Version 6.1*. New York: McGraw-Hill.

Stimson, James A. 1985. "Regression in Space and Time: A Statistical Essay." *American Journal of Political Science* 29:915–47.

Summers, Robert, and Alan Heston. 1988. "Improved International Comparisons of Real Product and Its Components, 1950–1984," *Review of Income and Wealth* 30:207–62.

Swank, Duane S. 1992. "Politics and the Structural Dependence of the State in Capitalist Democracies." *American Political Science Review* 92:30–52.

8

National variation in the fortunes of labor: a pooled and cross-sectional analysis of the impact of economic crisis in the advanced capitalist nations

PHILIP J. O'CONNELL

The last decade and a half was a critical period for the working class in the advanced capitalist countries. Beginning in the early 1970s, the rate of economic growth declined throughout the advanced capitalist world, while unemployment and inflation increased dramatically. The crisis marked the end of the long postwar boom of the 1950s and 1960s, in which sustained and rapid economic growth combined with relatively full employment and price stability, and during which workers in most advanced capitalist societies succeeded in extracting rising real wages and increasing shares of national income.

While labor unions and the political movements of the working class made impressive economic and political gains during the boom, there is general consensus that the crisis has turned the tide against labor; labor unions and working-class political parties have been placed on the defensive, their bargaining power has been eroded, and the movements themselves have become fragmented and isolated (Bowles 1982; Armstrong, Glyn, and Harrison 1984; and Griffin, O'Connell, and McCammon 1989). It has also been observed, however, that while all of the advanced capitalist countries shared in the experience of sluggish growth and inflation since the early 1970s, nations responded to the crisis in very different ways, resulting in a greater degree of variation between countries in macroeconomic performance than could have been observed during the previous expansionary period (Cameron 1984; Goldthorpe 1984). In an era of international recession and stagflation, some countries were able to contain inflationary pressures and maintain their commitment to nearly full employment while others "were able to stabilize prices only by bludgeoning labor with sharp increases in unemployment to levels that had not been seen since the 1930s" (Cameron 1984, p. 143). This chapter examines cross-national differences in labor's capacity to extract real wage gains from the labor market (i.e., incomes adjusted for changes in prices). More specifically, it investigates the impact of (1) macroeconomic conditions and (2) state corporatist institutions for regulating industrial conflict on the determination of workers' incomes in the advanced capitalist countries.

Wages and fringe benefits together represent the single most important dimension of labor's market-generated economic well-being. While state transfer payments to households increased over the post-war period, labor market compensation of workers, including both wages and fringe benefits, remains the single largest source of income, accounting for almost two-thirds of total workers' living standards (i.e., aggregating market compensation plus total government transfer payments to households) averaged across 18 advanced capitalist countries over the years 1975–80 (Griffin et al. 1989). Worker compensation, moreover, is the major component of costs for individual capitalists and is crucial to the conditions for profitability. Averaged across the advanced capitalist countries, real compensation per worker increased at a rate of 4.35 percent per annum between 1960 and 1973. Over the next decade, average annual increases amounted to only 0.47 percent, and over the five years from 1979 to 1983, real compensation per worker *fell* by 0.76 percent per annum. These trends indicate a dramatic decline in workers' labor market returns during the period of crisis. A study commissioned by the Organization for Economic Cooperation and Development concluded that "high unemployment has brought down wage inflation in almost every country to, in many cases, rates lower than seen before the early 1970s" (1989, p. 30). The crisis thus represented a dramatic downturn in the fortunes of labor, and since the late 1970s workers have experienced a marked decline in living standards.

One way of appreciating the changes wrought by the crisis is to examine the social structure of accumulation of the postwar boom and contrast it with conditions obtaining during the crisis. Two related arrangements are argued to have been central to the maintenance of rapid growth, prosperity, and stability in the early postwar period. First was the restructuring of class conflict in most liberal democracies with the acceptance of a "capital–labor accord." In Bowles's (1982, p. 52) formulation, the postwar capital–labor accord "represented, on the part of labor, the de facto acceptance of the logic of profitability and markets as the guiding principles of resource allocation, international exchange, technological change, product development, and industrial location, in return for an assurance that minimal living standards, trade union rights, and liberal democratic rights would be protected, that massive unemployment would be avoided, and that real incomes would rise approximately with labor productivity, all to be guaranteed by the intervention of the state, if necessary."

Second was the expansion of the Keynesian welfare state. Keynesian policies entailed the use of state fiscal policies to regulate aggregate demand and thus to curb the booms and slumps of the business cycle and to maintain low levels of unemployment. The expansion of the welfare state meant that an increasing share of workers' living standards were channeled through the state in the form of the "social wage" (i.e., state provision of education, health, income maintenance, and housing services) (Korpi and Shalev 1980; Stephens 1979; Bowles 1982; Offe 1985). The expansion of the Keynesian welfare state partially decommodified labor insofar as it reduced workers' dependence on the market for economic security (Bowles 1982; Offe 1984; and Myles 1989).

The combined effects of the capital–labor accords and the general expansion of the Keynesian welfare state were, according to most observers, first, to foster the unprecedented and sustained period of economic growth and stability of the 1950s and 1960s and, second, to deradicalize industrial and class conflict and to reorganize such conflicts into increasingly economistic and institutionalized forms (Bowles 1982; Offe 1984). The latter transformation was manifest in shifts in the sites of industrial conflicts during the boom from firm- to industry- and national-level collective bargaining, the spread of national policies of wage restraint (Flanagan, Soskice, and Ulman 1983), and the diversion of distributional conflicts from the economic to the political realm (Hibbs 1978; Korpi and Shalev 1980).

Numerous commentators from both the Left and the Right have argued that the Keynesian welfare state undermined the postwar social structure of accumulation. Bowles (1982) and Offe (1984) argue that while the Keynesian welfare state proved remarkably effective in resolving the problem of macroeconomic demand stabilization, it impeded capital accumulation. The expansion of the welfare state released labor from the disciplinary force of the market, thus strengthening its bargaining position. The realization of nearly full employment had a similar effect. Labor's share of national income increased throughout the capitalist democracies between the 1950s and the 1970s (Bowles 1982). Distributional conflicts intensified in the late 1960s as labor unions pressed their new found advantage (Cox 1987). Profitability declined (Armstrong et al. 1984) and with it went the incentive to invest, the lifeblood of a capitalist economy. To compound these difficulties, international competition intensified and the advanced capitalist countries were confronted by rising costs of raw materials and energy due to the pressure from the less developed peripheral countries for more favorable terms of trade (Keohane 1984; Cox 1987; and Crotty 1989). Averaged across the member nations of the OECD, economic growth rates, adjusted for inflation, dropped to 0.8 percent in 1974 and averaged 2.2 percent per annum over the following decade, less than half the rate of growth enjoyed during the previous decade. Unemployment soared, increasing from an average of 3 percent during the 1960s to over 8 percent in 1982–3. The international economy, which had transmitted growth and prosperity during the boom years, now began to transmit stagnation, inflation, and unemployment. From the mid-1970s, workers found it increasingly difficult to achieve increases in real incomes and, as the crisis deepened in the 1970s, experienced real declines in living standards.

This characterization of postwar trends captures the common experiences of the advanced capitalist countries, but it overstates the degree of convergence among this group of countries. Numerous studies have pointed to the diversity of class relations and state policies among the advanced capitalist countries. Thus, while the concept of the capital–labor accord may depict a general phenomenon in which the intensity of industrial conflict declined across the system between the interwar and postwar periods, there remains substantial national variation in the level of strike activity (Hibbs 1978, 1987; Korpi and Shalev 1980). While the Keynesian welfare state expanded in most advanced capitalist countries, important differences remain in the level of state welfare expenditures and in the institutional structures of public welfare policies (Korpi 1980; Castles 1982; Schmidt 1982; and Hicks and Swank 1984). And while all advanced capitalist nations shared in the common experience of international economic crisis since the early 1970s, they responded in very different ways to that crisis (Cameron 1984; Schmidt 1983; and Alvarez, Garrett, and Lange 1991).

In accounting for national differences in class relations and state policy making, analysts have emphasized the importance of the balance of power between organizations of labor and capital, and on state institutional arrangements for the regulation of class relations. In this respect the concept of corporatism has become a central focus in the study of state–society relationships. "Corporatism" refers to cooperation between the state and the organizations of capital and labor in the formulation and implementation of public policies (Lehmbruch 1984; Marks 1986). In essence, corporatism entails an exchange between the organizations of capital and labor, frequently organized under the auspices of the state, in which wage restraint is traded for increased state intervention to promote economic growth and high employment, extensive welfare systems, and the integration of unions in the formulation of state economic and social policies (Panitch 1980; Lehmbruch 1984; and Marks 1986). The strength of corporatist institutions and policies has been argued to be closely related both to the strength and centralization of labor unions and to social democratic party control of government (Cameron 1984; Marks 1986; and Griffin et al. 1989). Corporatism thus entails a system of institutionalized income policies in which governments underwrite labor quiescence and restraint with commitments to maintain low unemployment, and high welfare spending, as well as some assurance that capital will reinvest profits to maintain economic growth. We can expect, therefore, that corporatist countries should be characterized by low levels of strike activity and, to the extent that corporatist policies are successful in delivering wage restraint, by more modest increases in money wages than found in noncorporatist countries where distributional conflicts are more contentious. The implications of corporatist structures for changes over time in workers' compensation have not, however, been subjected to rigorous empirical examination.

MEDIATING CONTEXTS

The foregoing discussion suggests the difficulty of attempting to examine broad generalizations across differing historical and national contexts regarding causal processes determining the outcomes of market-generated conflicts. First, the literature suggests that the processes determining workers' incomes changed in the early 1970s as stagnation and unemployment eroded the bargaining position of workers. This suggests an interaction process in which the determinants of changes in workers' incomes are differentially shaped by macroeconomic conditions. Thus, for instance, we need to examine whether the effects of strike activity on changes in real compensation were similar during both expansionary and crisis periods. Second, the import of the corporatist literature is to suggest that precisely because of the trade-off between labor quiescence and state commitments on the social wage and on unemployment, the processes of income determination differ between nations in which corporatist institutions are prominent and those in which such arrangements are absent. Again, to return to the preceding example, we need to examine whether, and to what extent, the returns to strike activity (in the form of increases in compensation) are mediated by state corporatist institutions.

Conventional empirical approaches do not help us in exploring these potential interactions. Cross-national approaches suffer from limited degrees of freedom because of the small size of the population of advanced capitalist nations. Neither do they represent a satisfactory method of examining dynamic relationships (Griffin, Walters, O'Connell, and Moore 1986; Griffin et al. 1989). However, country-specific time-series analyses allow us to examine causal processes over time but do not allow us to compare processes across nations. (For one solution to this problem of comparing time-series relationships across countries, see Griffin et al. 1989.) Moreover, when we are concerned with the mediating effects of corporatism, we find that where such institutions have been important (e.g., Austria and Sweden), they have also proved enduring; there has been little if any variation in corporatism over time (i.e., we lack sufficient "policy-off" periods).

The present study seeks to exploit the advantages of a research design that pools cross-sectional and time-series observations for the 18 relatively large capitalist democracies for the years from 1960 to 1983. Pooling time-series and cross-sectional data substantially mitigates the problems of restricted degrees of freedom associated with conventional cross-sectional analyses of this population, and it permits the analysis of both cross-sectional and temporal processes. Incorporated into this design is consideration of two mediating factors using a modified version of a research design employed by Hicks, Swank, and Ambuhl (1989) in their analysis of the postwar expansion of state welfare expenditures. The two mediating factors are corporatism and macroeconomic conditions, both of which are operationalized as dichotomous variables. Separate equations are estimated for expansionary and crisis periods. The differential effects of corporatist institutions are explored by investigating interactions between corporatism and the other explanatory variables within each of the macroeconomic-context-specific equations.

In distinguishing between corporatist and noncorporatist countries, I draw primarily on two closely related conceptualizations of corporatism. Schmitter (1981) argues that "societal corporatism" refers to the "institutional structure of interest intermediation." His concept of corporatism encompasses (1) the aggregation of individual interests into collective decision making and representative associations (as well as the capacities of such collective bodies to exert social control over individual members) and (2) the extent to which such associations "are incorporated within the process of authoritative decision making and implementation" (p. 295). Lehmbruch's (1984) classification scheme measures corporatism by reference to both the degree of centralization of collective bargaining and the extent of union participation in state policy formation. Both conceptualizations assume that corporatist concertation of macroeconomic policies in general, and incomes policies in particular, is more likely, but by no means guaranteed, where workers' associations are both centralized and monopolistic and that where workers' associations are so organized, other interests, particularly employers, will be correspondingly organized in peak associations.

Lehmbruch classifies Austria, the Netherlands, Norway, and Sweden as highly corporatist, characterized by the effective and relatively enduring participation of highly centralized unions and organized business in national policy formation and implementation. In Belgium, Denmark, Finland, Germany, and Switzerland, collective bargaining is less centralized, and there is greater variation in the extent of union participation in policy, and Lehmbruch classifies them as "medium" on his scale of corporatism. These nine "strong" and "medium" corporatist countries are the top nine countries in Schmitter's classification, although the rank ordering of countries differs between the two schemas, and I have classified all of them as corporatist.

I also classify Japan as corporatist following Pempel and Tsunekawa (1979) and Schmidt (1983), although collective bargaining there is decentralized, and corporatism appears to operate at the level of the firm rather than the nation-state (Paloheimo 1984). Lehmbruch regards both Japan and France as cases of "concertation without labor," reflecting the weakness of labor unions in both countries, their lack of participation in state policy formation, and the exclusive nature of the relationships between business and the state. Japan appears sufficiently more similar to the other corporatist countries than to the noncorporatist countries with respect to an important underlying dimension of corporatism, the level of economic consensus (Paloheimo 1984) (although this is arguably an effect, rather than a dimension, of corporatism), to warrant inclusion in the corporatist category.[1] In France, however, with its unilateral, centralized state planning and an exceptionally weak and fragmented union movement, "incomes policy is not a major instrument of economic policy" (Marks 1986, p. 65), so France is classified as noncorporatist.

Australia, Britain, Canada, Ireland, Italy, the United States, and New Zealand, as well as France, are all characterized by either weak corporatist institutions or by fragmented and competing interest groups and are classified as noncorporatist. This classification of Ireland departs from Lehmbruch's categorization because corporatist institutions there have been of relatively recent origin and were largely organized by the state, and because the fractionalization of the union movement renders corporatist concertation exceedingly difficult (Hardiman 1988; O'Connell 1989). My classification of both Ireland and France is consistent with Schmidt (1983) and Schmitter (1981).[2] My measure of corporatism therefore dichotomizes Schmitter's (1981) ranking of "societal corporatism" for the Western European and North American countries – my corporatist countries are the top nine in his ranking – with the special case of Japan added, the appropriateness of which is empirically tested in the analysis.

Differentiating between periods of macroeconomic expansion and contraction is rather more straightforward. The year 1973 marks the end of the postwar boom. Thereafter, economic growth slowed and Keynesian macroeconomic policy proved incapable of managing the business cycle (Crotty 1989). Moreover, the novel coincidence of high inflation with high unemployment during the subsequent decade suggests a change in the relationship between unemployment and money wages. I thus classify the years from 1960 to 1973 as an expansionary period and the years from 1974 to 1983 as one of economic crisis.

THE DETERMINATION OF WORKERS' COMPENSATION

Existing theories are not sufficiently well developed to generate precise propositions regarding the processes determining wages within the mediating contexts framing the analysis. The analyses that follow are therefore necessarily exploratory. Some tentative expectations regarding the relationships between market distribution and class organization and conflict may, however, be derived from past research (Korpi and Shalev 1980; Przeworsky 1985; Hibbs 1987; and Griffin et al. 1989).

This study regards as axiomatic that the working class has an interest in maximizing worker compensation (market-generated wages plus fringe benefits) within the constraints established by the imperatives to maintain capital accumulation and profitability, because the largest share of workers' material well-being is determined by the sale of their labor power. Capitalists are also interested in workers' incomes because the wage bill represents the major component of the costs of production and because profits, at least in the short term, are inversely related to wage costs (Armstrong et al. 1984). Distributional conflict is therefore inherent to the exchange between capital and labor.

Workers pursue their interests in capitalist societies through collective action organized primarily in unions and political parties. Unions represent perhaps the most important form of collective organization available to workers to pursue their material interests in the market (Griffin, Wallace, and Rubin 1986). Unions fight for higher wages and fringe benefits and seek to maintain employment for their members. We can expect, therefore, that unionization generally should stimulate real compensation per worker, other things being equal. That general effect, however, is contingent on macroeconomic and institutional contexts. Unions generally should enable workers to defend their living standards during the crisis, suggesting that the effect of unionization during that period is positive and stronger than during the expansionary period. In countries where centralized unions participate in national policy formation, that is, in corporatist countries, union leaders may be more disposed to bargain over a wider range of issues, including the security and conditions of employment, and even to offer wage restraint in exchange for such other benefits. However, given the close correlation between union strength and corporatism, it is not a *priori* clear whether unionization should account for any additional differences between corporatist and noncorporatist nations – this is a question addressed empirically in the upcoming analyses.

Organized workers possess an additional tactic to pursue their market interests – the strike. Strikes disrupt production and threaten to impose hardship on capital. The strike weapon may be used defensively, to resist pay cuts and threatened job losses or deskilling, or offensively, to achieve higher incomes or to gain greater influence in corporate decision making (Edwards 1979; Hibbs 1987; and Griffin et al. 1989). Generally, then, strikes should stimulate increases in real compensation. That effect should be stronger during the expansionary period, when economic growth rendered real wage gains attainable, and strongest in the noncorporatist countries, because of the absence of institutional arrangements to foster wage restraint.

Working-class political parties, where they successfully mobilize sufficient electoral support to contend seriously for state power, either alone or in coalition, are held to pursue policies favorable to the material interests of the working class (Hibbs 1987). It is not clear, however, whether social democratic party control of government directly affects market-generated incomes (net of commitments by social democrats to maintain high unemployment, which in turn enhances the bargaining position of workers). In corporatist countries, strong and stable social democratic governments, particularly those enjoying cooperative relationships with strong encompassing labor unions, may seek to hold wages down, offering inducements such as increased social wage payments in order to maintain price stability (Hicks, Swank, and Ambuhl 1989). This effect, moreover, may be stronger during the crisis. Among the noncorporatist countries, in contrast, social democratic strength may stimulate real wages, since, in those countries, the political wing of the labor movement cannot expect to extract any benefits to its constituents from wage restraint.

Unemployment is expected to undermine the bargaining power of labor. Unemployment should retard real compensation during both expansionary and crisis periods, as well as in both corporatist and noncorporatist countries. Given, however, state commitments to high-employment policies and the maintenance of high social wage levels in corporatist countries, the effect of unemployment during the crisis should be lower than in the noncorporatist countries where deflationary policies led to sharp increases in unemployment and imposed severe costs on workers.

Other macroeconomic conditions are unlikely to have differentiated between institutional contexts. Economic growth expands the social product available for distribution and should, therefore, stimulate real increases in compensation. The stimulative effects of economic growth are likely to have been less pronounced during the crisis, however, both because of the declining bargaining power of workers and because the benefits of economic growth are likely to have been devoted to restoring corporate profitability. Inflation is expected to erode real wages and is specified as a control variable.

Keynesian fiscal policies, designed to stimulate demand through increased state spending to counteract cyclical downturns, are held to promote economic growth and reduce unemployment but are also believed to stimulate inflation. Whether Keynesian fiscal policies have an additional impact on real wages, beyond their effects on employment, growth, and inflation, remains to be empirically investigated.

Finally, the entire postwar period was one of increasing international economic interdependence. As countries increased their dependence on external markets, the issue of competitiveness loomed increasingly large. Accordingly, increases in trade dependence are expected to have retarded real wage increases. During the crisis, international competition intensified. This suggests that trade dependence should have had a larger negative effect on real compensation during this period.

DATA AND METHODS

The empirical investigation is conducted using multiple regression analyses on a pooled time-series cross-sectional matrix of data for 18 advanced capitalist countries for each of the years between 1961 and 1983. Variables, their operationalization, and data sources are described in Table 8.1.

Pooling time-series and cross-sectional data yields a substantially larger number of observations than is possible with either individual country time-series or cross-national analyses. This allows the inclusion of a much larger number of regressors than is possible with the other comparative regression designs. Resulting regression estimates, moreover, will have smaller sampling variability, thereby increasing the statistical significance of the coefficients. Pooling cross-section and time-series data also entails statistical problems, however. If ordinary least squares (OLS) assumptions are not fulfilled, OLS parameter estimators are unbiased

Table 8.1. *Variables, operationalization, and data sources*

1. Compensation per worker. The dependent variable. Annual percent change in the ratio of aggregate employee compensation (i.e., wages plus fringe benefits), expressed in constant (1980) dollars, to the total number of wage-dependent workers. Compensation is from OECD, National Accounts. Dependent labor force is from OECD, Labor Force Statistics; Bain and Price 1980; and Visser 1984.

2. Union density. Annual percent change in the ratio of total union membership to the wage-dependent labor force. Union membership is from Bain and Price 1980; Kjellberg 1984; Visser 1984; and various national sources.

3. Strike days. Total number of strike days per 100,000 wage-dependent workers. Number of strike days are from International Labor Office, Yearbook of Labor Statistics.

4. Social democratic control of government. Number of votes received by left parties participating in cabinet expressed as a percentage of total votes received by all parties with cabinet representation. Votes are from Mackie and Rose 1982, 1990, 1991. Cabinet composition is from Europa Yearbook. Party program is from McHale 1983.

5. Unemployment. Annual magnitude of change (first difference) in the number unemployed expressed as a percentage of the civilian labor force. Number unemployed is from OECD, Labor Force Statistics. Civilian labor force is from OECD, Labor Force Statistics.

6. Economic growth. Percent change in Gross Domestic Product, in constant units of national currencies, from OECD, National Accounts.

7. Budget deficit. Total general government expenditures less revenues, expressed as a percentage of GDP, from OECD, National Accounts.

8. Inflation. Rate of change in the consumer price index, from International Monetary Fund, International Financial Statistics.

9. Trade dependence. Rate of change in the ratio of imports plus exports to GDP, from OECD, National Accounts.

10. Corporatism. Coded 1 for Austria, Belgium, Denmark, Finland, West Germany, Japan, the Netherlands, Norway, Sweden, and Switzerland, and 0 for Australia, Britain, Canada, France, Ireland, Italy, New Zealand, and the United States (see text for rationale underlying classification).

11. Economic expansion period. Coded 1 for 1961-73, 0 for 1974-83.

12. Economic crisis period. Coded 1 for 1974-83, 0 for 1961-73.

and consistent but are no longer efficient, and error variances of parameter estimates are biased. Violation of OLS assumptions is likely for two reasons. First, specification errors can be expected because of the difficulties in including all relevant causal variables in analyses of comparative-historical data sets, not least because the data requirements for this procedure are very exacting (requiring annual data for each country over an extended period of years). Second, time-series data tend to exhibit autocorrelation among the residuals, and error variances may differ among cross-sectional units (countries in the present instance).

A number of solutions have been developed to deal with these problems (Kmenta 1971; Hannan and Young 1977; and Judge et al. 1985). One common solution has been to assume that while slope coefficients are constant across countries, intercepts may vary due to between-country differences in the level of the dependent variable. If cross-sectional units differ on the level of the dependent variable, then the assumption of constant intercepts would entail misspecification, resulting in high serial correlations that are stable over successive time lags. The least squares dummy variable (LSDV), or covariance, model allows intercepts to vary across countries by specifying $N - 1$ dummy variables for countries. The LSDV model, using only within-unit (i.e., time-series) variance and relegating between-country variance to the intercept dummies, is thus expected to account for unmeasured factors that are cross-nationally variant but temporally invariant. In the LSDV model, the residuals are expected to conform to OLS assumptions. Where autocorrelation remains a problem – detected by examining the residuals – it is possible to introduce generalized least squares (GLS) estimators to correct for autocorrelation (Kmenta 1971; Hannan and Young 1977). An alternative strategy, the error components (GLSE) model, assumes that intercepts are random variables, the average of which is the common intercept. In the GLSE model, spacial error, temporal error, and error systematic to both time and space contribute independently to the total error. This model uses the covariance structure to derive unbiased and efficient estimates and requires no assumptions about where the variance should be fixed. GLSE models may therefore be particularly appropriate in the absence of theoretical expectations guiding assumptions and specification.

Neither of these approaches seems appropriate to this study because both of them entail a loss of cross-national information and both forgo the opportunity to take account of systematic differences between countries. In the present context we have strong theoretical reasons to expect that differences between countries are systematically related to the institutional context surrounding class relations in labor markets. If theories about the importance of corporatism are correct, then we should expect that national variation in both the levels of the dependent variable and in the processes determining changes in workers' income over time should differ by institutional context. This suggests (1) that intercept differences should be minimal between corporatist countries and greater between corporatist and noncorporatist countries and (2) that slope coefficients should differ between corporatist and noncorporatist countries.

These considerations suggest two modifications of the LSDV model for the pooled times-series estimation of workers' compensation. First, we specify a common intercept for corporatist countries (effectively a dummy variable coded 1 for corporatist countries), assuming minimal differences among them, while allowing the intercepts for noncorporatist countries to vary (by specifying country dummies for this group) on the expectation of greater variation among the latter group of countries. We can investigate the appropriateness of this grouping strategy by inspecting the residuals from the estimated model. If the residuals for a particular country do not sum to (close to) zero, or if they exhibit high levels of autocorrelation that fail to decay with increasing time lags, then we have reason to suspect that the country is not well represented by the group dummy (i.e., that the country differs from the "average" corporatist experience) and that the model is misspecified (Stimson 1985). If the residuals are well behaved, however, then we can conclude that corporatist countries constitute a distinctive subpopulation of the advanced capitalist democracies, and we have gained parsimony in substituting 1 substantively meaningful dummy variable for 10 theoretically vacuous dummies.

The second modification to the standard LSDV model is to estimate multiplicative interaction terms between corporatism and the other explanatory terms in the equation. This allows us to investigate whether the effects of our explanatory variables differ across institutional contexts. The appropriateness of specifying interaction terms can be investigated with standard tests of increments to explained variance.

FINDINGS

Table 8.2 shows means and standard deviations for the major variables in the analysis in both corporatist and noncorporatist countries and in both expansionary and crisis periods. Mean annual change in real compensation per worker fell precipitously between the two periods. Among the corporatist countries, the mean percentage of change dropped from 4.8 percent in 1961–73 to 0.56 percent in 1974–83. The decline was similar in the noncorporatist countries, from 3.78 to 0.35 percent. Rates of economic growth in both corporatist and noncorporatist countries were similar, about 5.5 percent between 1961 and 1973, but declined

Table 8.2. *Means and standard deviations (in parentheses) of major variables by institutional and macroeconomic context*

	Corporatist countries		Noncorporatist countries	
	Expansionary period 1961-73	Crisis period 1974-83	Expansionary period 1961-73	Crisis period 1974-83
Real compensation per worker (percent change)	4.80 (2.50)	0.56 (2.84)	3.78 (2.56)	0.35 (3.43)
Union density	50.94 (14.93)	56.44 (18.93)	37.25 (10.62)	39.74 (12.93)
Strike days per 100,000 workers	119.84 (302.22)	100.94 (212.60)	591.91 (1047.33)	592.22 (449.06)
Social democratic control of government	42.18 (39.41)	53.05 (40.70)	11.34 (27.34)	21.31 (37.31)
Unemployment	1.22 (0.74)	3.54 (2.88)	3.32 (7.15)	6.40 (14.18)
Economic growth (% change in real GDP)	5.55 (2.68)	1.71 (2.78)	5.53 (2.79)	2.87 (4.64)
Inflation	4.70 (2.10)	7.62 (3.60)	4.31 (2.27)	11.59 (3.93)

to 1.17 percent in the corporatist countries and to 2.87 percent among the noncorporatist countries during the crisis years. On average, corporatist countries are characterized by higher levels of union density and social democratic control of government, as well as by substantially lower levels of strike activity and unemployment. These country differences persist over time. Although unemployment increases considerably during the crisis years in both groups of countries, the level of unemployment among corporatist countries is substantially lower than in the noncorporatist countries.

Table 8.3 reports the analysis of the determinants of changes in real compensation per worker for the expansionary period 1961–73. Column 1 shows the results of the OLS model. Strikes stimulate compensation during this period, as expected, but organization in neither the labor market (union density) nor in the political sphere (as represented by social democratic party control of government) appears to have any direct impact on workers' incomes. The effect of unemployment is negative, a result that is consistent with our expectation that unemployment should weaken the bargaining position of labor. The positive effects of economic growth and budget deficits are also in accordance with our theoretical expectations. Increases in trade dependence have negative effects on workers' compensation, an effect that reflects the restraining impact of exposure to international competition. The results from the OLS model are therefore in general conformity with theoretical expectations, although the adjusted R^2 (.33) is rather low. Inspection of the residuals, however, suggests the possibility of serial correlation among them, and there is clear evidence that for several countries the intercept differs from the common intercept (unit residuals are greater than zero and serial correlation is high).

In the first modified LSDV model (Column 2), country dummies are included for the noncorporatist countries, with the corporatist dummy as the reference category. The modified LSDV model yields a substantial increment to R^2 (from .33 to .52). The coefficients of the country dummies suggest that increases in compensation are significantly greater among the corporatist countries and that there is substantial variation among the noncorporatist countries in the level of the dependent variable. Inspection of the residuals suggests that the assumption of a common intercept for the corporatist countries is warranted (the sum of residuals for each case is close to zero, with no evidence of high and stationary serial correlation). The pooled Durbin–Watson statistic[3] (2.04) indicates that serial correlation has been eliminated. The modified LSDV model introduces no major reinterpretation of the effects of the explanatory variables. It increases the efficacy of strikes, economic growth, and

Table 8.3. *Unstandardized regression coefficients for models of real compensation per worker during expansionary period, 1961-73 (standard errors in parentheses)*

	OLS	Modified LSDV	Modified LSDV	
			Linear	Interaction
	(1)	(2)	(3a)	(3b)
Union density (% change)	0.05 (0.05)	0.02 (0.04)	0.08* (0.06)	-0.09 (0.08)
Strike days per 100,000 workers	0.29** (0.19)	0.39** (0.17)	0.29* (0.18)	1.41** (0.55)
Social democratic government	0.20 (0.39)	-0.13 (0.36)	0.97* (0.72)	-1.52* (0.83)
Unemployment (annual change)	-1.42** (0.37)	-1.41** (0.32)	-1.23** (0.40)	0.49 (0.64)
Economic growth (% change, GDP)	0.44** (0.06)	0.59** (0.05)	0.49** (0.09)	-0.03 (0.11)
Budget deficits	0.08* (0.06)	0.14* (0.06)	-0.13 (0.15)	0.33* (0.16)
Inflation	0.02 (0.08)	-0.12* (0.07)	0.13 (0.12)	-0.42** (0.15)
Trade dependence (% change)	-0.05* (0.04)	-0.05* (0.03)	0 (0.04)	-0.10* (0.06)
Time trend	0	0.04	0.07	
Intercept	1.68			
Corporatist		2.42	3.27	
Australia		-1.68	-2.81	
Canada		-4.45	-5.44	
France		-0.82	-2.06	
Ireland		-0.50	-0.78	
Italy		0.46	-0.05	
New Zealand		-1.75	-3.11	
United Kingdom		-0.79	-2.07	
United States		-2.78	-3.16	
R^2	0.33	0.52	0.56	

$*p < .10$, $**p < .01$.

budget deficits in stimulating real compensation, and the effect of inflation becomes negative and significant.

The estimation reported in Column 2 suggests that corporatist countries are distinctive but cannot indicate whether the effects of the explanatory variables differ across institutional context. Inclusion of interaction terms between corporatism and the other explanatory variables allows us to explore this possibility in Equation 3. Column 3a reports additive effects and Column 3b reports the coefficients of the corporatist interaction terms. The increment to explained variance in Equation 3 is small but nevertheless significant ($p < .01$), and the residuals remain well behaved both with respect to serial correlation and the specification of the common corporatist intercept.

Five of the interaction terms are significant, and the new model substantially alters our interpretation of the determinants of changes in real compensation. Increases in union density have a positive and significant effect in the noncorporatist countries. The interaction term is negative but not significant, suggesting that the corporatist countries do not differ significantly as a group from the other countries with respect to the effects of increases in unionization. Both additive and interactive effects of strike activity are positive and significant. This suggests that strikes generally lead to increases in workers' compensation but are substantially more efficacious in the corporatist countries. These effects should be interpreted in light of the differences between the two groups of countries: the volume of strike activity is considerably lower among the corporatist countries than the noncorporatist countries (see Table 8.2). The extent of social democratic party control of government stimulates workers' compensation in the noncorporatist countries, but it retards income growth among the corporatist countries. Budget deficits, however, have no impact on compensation in the noncorporatist countries, but they stimulate incomes in the corporatist countries. Inflation and increases in trade dependence retard wage growth only in corporatist countries. Finally, there is no evidence to suggest that the effects of either economic growth or unemployment differ between corporatist and noncorporatist countries.

The results of Equation 3 suggest that corporatism did indeed represent a distinctive context for the determination of workers' compensation during the expansionary period 1961–73. The analyses in Table 8.4 replicate the previous models for the period of macroeconomic crisis, 1974–83. The pattern of effects in the additive equations (Columns 1 and 2) is generally consistent with the findings from the corresponding models estimated for the earlier period. Economic growth continues to stimulate workers' compensation; unemployment, trade dependence, and inflation in the LSDV model have negative effects.

Table 8.4. *Unstandardized regression coefficients for models of real compensation per worker during crisis period, 1974-83 (standard errors in parentheses)*

	OLS	Modified LSDV	Modified LSDV		Modified LSDV	
			Linear	Inter-action	Linear	Inter-action
	(1)	(2)	(3a)	(3b)	(4a)	(4b)
Union density (% change)	-0.06 (0.08)	-0.04 (0.57)	-0.16* (0.11)	0.36* (0.18)	-0.16* (0.11)	0.30* (0.17)
Strike days per 100,000 workers	0 (0.00)	0.25 (0.72)	1.58* (0.94)	-2.59* (1.46)	1.58* (0.92)	-3.20* (1.44)
Social democratic government	0.15 (0.48)	-0.44 (0.48)	1.30* (0.83)	-2.59** (1.02)	1.30* (0.81)	-2.52** (1.01)
Unemployment (annual change)	-1.50** (0.21)	-1.22** (0.21)	-1.32** (0.31)	0.25 (0.42)	-1.32** (0.31)	0.42 (0.41)
Economic growth (% change, GDP)	0.19** (0.05)	0.29** (0.06)	0.23** (0.09)	0.02 (0.13)	0.23** (0.09)	0.10 (0.13)
Budget deficits	0.04 (0.05)	-0.06 (0.06)	-0.46** (0.17)	0.45** (0.19)	-0.46** (0.17)	0.42** (0.18)
Inflation	-0.02 (0.05)	-0.09* (0.06)	-0.19* (0.10)	0.06 (0.13)	-0.19* (0.10)	0.12 (0.13)
Trade dependence (% change)	-0.06** (0.02)	-0.06** (0.02)	-0.12** (0.04)	0.10* (0.05)	-0.12** (0.04)	0.09* (0.05)
Time trend	-0.45	-0.46	-0.47		-0.45	
Intercept	3.49					
Corporatist		4.33	4.74		4.58	
Australia		0.03	0.86		1.01	
Canada		-3.32	-2.09		-1.93	
France		1.50	2.02		2.17	
Ireland		1.55	5.93		6.09	
Italy		1.58	5.03		5.19	
New Zealand		-0.87	0.22		0.37	
United Kingdom		0.97	2.12		2.28	
United States		-1.84	-1.04		-0.89	
Netherlands					-1.56	
Norway					-1.76	
R^2	0.45	0.52	0.55		0.57	

* $p < .10$; ** $p < .01$

Strikes, apparently, no longer drive up workers' incomes, however. The country-specific intercepts indicate greater variation in the level of the dependent variable among the noncorporatist countries during this period of economic crisis. These models would suggest the interpretation that controlling for national differences in levels of the dependent variable, the processes driving workers' compensation during the crisis period are broadly similar to those during the preceding expansionary period but that the efficacy of strikes has receded. Thus, during a period of general macroeconomic downturn the main determinants of changes in compensation per worker are macroeconomic, rather than political, in nature.

The LSDV models estimated by Equations 3 and 4 challenge this macroeconomic interpretation. Equation 3 adds the corporatist interaction terms to the modified additive LSDV model in Column 2. Inspection of the residuals suggested that the intercepts for two corporatist countries, the Netherlands and Norway, deviate from the common corporatist intercept.[4] Equation 4 adds dummy variables for the Netherlands and Norway to correct for this misspecification. The residuals from Equation 4 are well behaved under the new specification. The pooled Durbin–Watson statistic (1.92) indicates the absence of serial correlation. Inclusion of the two additional country dummies, moreover, does little to alter either the additive or interaction coefficients.

The effects of unemployment and economic growth remain similar to their effects during the 1961–73 period. Unemployment retards compensation, economic growth stimulates compensation, and these effects do not differ across institutional contexts. As unemployment rises, the cost of militancy increases and the bargaining position of labor is weakened. The regression results for both periods suggest that unemployment unequivocally weakens labor's bargaining position across all mediating contexts.

Economic growth, in contrast, generally increases workers' incomes across all mediating contexts. The coefficients for economic growth are considerably lower for the later period, however, suggesting that workers benefited less from economic growth during the crisis than during the expansionary period, perhaps because of the shift in the balance of power between labor and capital due to declining growth and rising unemployment.

Keynesian fiscal policies are designed to boost aggregate demand and promote economic growth. The operationalization adopted here – budget deficits, defined as the difference between total government spending and revenue – is admittedly crude. If deficits have any effects on workers' incomes, net of their effects on unemployment and growth, these should be to stimulate wages. The regression results suggest that deficits retard wage growth in the noncorporatist countries, but their impact is substantially reduced among the corporatist countries during the crisis. This is in contrast to the earlier period, when deficits stimulated compensation among the corporatist countries. The negative effect means that larger deficits (or smaller surpluses) are associated with real declines in compensation – an effect that appears to run counter to our understanding of Keynesian fiscal policy. The effect may, however, be due to the operationalization employed, or it may be spurious; declining rates of growth and increases in unemployment may have simultaneously slowed wage growth and increased state budget deficits.

Perhaps the most interesting effects in Equation 4 are the differential effects of the measures of class organization and conflict. Working-class organization and struggle in the economic arena (union density and strike activity) and perhaps in the political arena (social democratic party mobilization) generally should stimulate increases in workers' real compensation, other things being equal. The regression results suggest, however, that controlling for the effects of other relevant variables, the effects of class organization and struggle are mediated by both institutional and macroeconomic contexts. The additive models suggested that these variables contributed little to the explanation of changes in workers' compensation. Equation 4 suggests that the additive models conceal important interactions between class organization and conflict and corporatism.

First, social democratic control of government stimulates compensation among the noncorporatist countries, but it has a negative effect among the corporatist countries. These effects continue the pattern found for the expansionary period and suggest the capacity of stronger social democratic parties to utilize corporatist structures to secure union cooperation in wage restraint during the period of crisis in order to promote price stability and economic growth – as occurred, for instance, in the voluntary exercise of restraint by the Austrian Trade Union Federation in the late 1970s (Flanagan et al. 1983).

Second, increases in union density are associated with declines in real compensation among the noncorporatist countries. This negative effect was not anticipated, but it may be due to the capacity of organized workers to continue to extract real wage increases despite *falling* membership in a number of countries (Bowles 1982; Griffin, McCammon, and Botsko 1990). Among the corporatist countries, however, increases in union strength have a positive effect, suggesting that in those countries increases in union strength served to defend workers' living standards even during the period of macroeconomic downturn.

Strike activity remains efficacious among the noncorporatist countries in pushing up incomes. The strong negative effect of the corporatist – strikedays interaction coefficient suggests, however, that strikes retard wage growth in the corporatist countries. Strikes generally have positive effects on real compensation; they do so during both periods in the noncorporatist countries and during the expansionary period in the corporatist countries. In the latter countries, however, strike activity has a negative effect, due, arguably, to the capacity of corporatist arrangements to foster wage restraint in return for guarantees of low unemployment and higher social wage payments; corporatism appears to punish militancy, at least during the period of economic crisis.

Finally, increases in trade dependence, by increasing the exposure of national economies to international competition, are expected to retard real increases in workers' incomes. The regression results provide general confirmation of this expectation. Among the corporatist countries, where external economic vulnerability is itself argued to be an important factor in the creation and maintenance of corporatist institutions (Katzenstein 1985), increases in external trade dependence are associated with real incomes restraint throughout the postwar era, although that effect is attenuated during the crisis. Among the noncorporatist countries, the negative effect of trade dependence emerges only during the crisis period – a period in which international competitive pressures intensified (Cox 1987; Crotty 1989).

CONCLUSION

The empirical analysis suggests that while class organization and struggle generally serve to increase labor's market returns, these effects are mediated by institutional and macroeconomic contexts. Among the corporatist countries, where both unions and social democratic parties were generally strong, union organization had no discernible impact on market compensation during the expansionary period, although the returns to strike activity were substantially higher than in the noncorporatist countries. During the crisis, however, union organization proved successful in extracting real wage gains, but union militancy was punished, and stronger social democratic party governments were more likely to secure wage restraint. These findings reflect the paradoxical effects of corporatism. Corporatism may be a consequence of working-class organizational power (Panitch 1980), but the benefits of incorporation (state commitments to maintain high social wages and low unemployment) come at the expense of quiescence and wage restraint, particularly during periods of systemic crisis.

National variation in the fortunes of labor

This paper has argued and demonstrated that the processes determining workers' real compensation in the advanced capitalist countries since World War II are mediated by institutional and macroeconomic factors. The analysis suggests that this is particularly true of the differential effects of class organization and conflict. The effects of macroeconomic conditions show less variation across macroeconomic and institutional contexts, although we did find that the positive effects of economic growth on workers' compensation was attenuated in the crisis period. The analysis thus implies that there is no general historical time trend governing the effects of class organization and struggle, as well as objective macroeconomic conditions, on changes in workers' material well-being. If countries differ in the strength and direction of temporal relationships, then this suggests the inappropriateness of conventional static cross-sectional analyses of political-economic processes – precisely because such designs ignore the fact that historical processes vary across countries. Moreover, if historical relationships are themselves contingent on structural and temporal contexts, then such contexts need to be acknowledged and incorporated into the analysis of those relationships.

Acknowledgment of historical contingency does not, however, necessarily preclude comparative research across nations and over time. In this chapter, I have argued that there are systematic differences between countries in the organization, conduct, and effects of class struggles in the market. I have also argued that one important set of factors that structure class struggle in the market are state institutional arrangements; the processes determining changes in workers' incomes differ between corporatist and noncorporatist countries. Equally, I have argued that historical relationships are not necessarily stable over time and that the postwar era can be understood as two distinct periods, one expansionary, one of crisis, representing differing structural contexts for class struggle. Thus, the crisis period not only entailed a deterioration in workers' living standards; it also entailed a shift in the effects of class organization and struggle on market returns.

NOTES

1. Whether Japan should be classified with the corporatist countries might be regarded as an empirical question. I replicated the analyses reported in Tables 8.3 and 8.4, omitting Japan. The coefficients were not appreciably different from those reported for the analysis of all 18 countries, suggesting that the model for Japan is not different from the other corporatist cases.
2. My classification of both Ireland and France is consistent with Schmitter (1981), who ranks both countries toward the bottom of his corporatism index, and with Schmidt (1983).

3. The regular Durbin–Watson statistic, *d*, yields an estimate of the autoregression in a single time series. The pooled Durbin–Watson statistic is calculated for each cross section and then averaged, yielding an estimate of the autoregression, on average, in all the time series in the pool.
4. Both the Netherlands and Norway departed from consensual corporatist arrangements in the late 1970s and early 1980s, opting instead for statutory wage controls and, in the case of Norway, for reductions in income taxation in order to encourage wage restraint. These statutory incomes policies may explain why the estimated intercepts are lower for both countries than the common corporatist intercept.

REFERENCES

Alvarez, R., G. Garrett, and P. Lange. 1991. "Government Partisanship, Labor Organization, and Macro-Economic Performance, 1967–1984." *American Political Science Review* 86(2): 539–56.

Armstrong, P., A. Glyn, and J. Harrison. 1984. *Capitalism Since World War II: The Making and Break-up of the Great Boom*. London: Fontana

Bain, G., and R. Price. 1980. *Profiles of Union Growth: A Comparative Statistical Portrait of Eight Countries*. Oxford: Blackwell Publisher.

Bowles, S. 1982. "The Post-Keynesian Capital–Labor Stalemate." *Socialist Review* 65:45–72.

Cameron, D. 1984. "Social Democracy, Corporatism, Labor Quiescence, and the Representation of Economic Interest in Advanced Capitalist Society." In J. Goldthorpe (ed.), *Order and Conflict in Contemporary Capitalism*, pp. 143–78. Oxford University Press.

Castles, F. (ed.). 1982. *The Impact of Parties: Politics and Policies in Democratic Capitalist States*. (ed.) Newbury Park, Calif.: Sage.

Cox, R. 1987. *Production, Power and World Order: Social Forces in the Making of History*. New York: Columbia University Press.

Crotty, J. 1989. "The Limits of Keynesian Macroeconomic Policy in the Age of the Global Marketplace." In A. MacEwan and W. Tabb (eds.), *Instability and Change in the World Economy*, pp. 82–100. New York: Monthly Review Press.

Edwards, R. 1979. *Contested Terrain: The Transformation of the Workplace in the Twentieth Century*. New York: Basic.

Europa. Various years. *The Europa Yearbook*. London: Europa Publications.

Flanagan, R., D. Soskice, and L. Ulman. 1983. *Unionism, Economic Stabilization, and Incomes Policies: European Experience*. Washington, D.C.: Brookings Institution.

Goldthorpe, J. 1984. "Introduction." In J. Goldthorpe (ed.), *Order and Conflict in Contemporary Capitalism*, pp. 1–14. Oxford University Press.

Griffin, L., H. McCammon, and C. Botsko. 1990. "The 'Unmaking' of a Movement? The Crisis of U.S. Trade Unions in Comparative Perspective." In M. Hallinan, D. Klein, and J. Glass (eds.), *Change in Social Institutions*, pp. 56–81. New York: Plenum.

Griffin, L., P. O'Connell, and H. McCammon. 1989. "National Variation in the Context of Struggle: Postwar Class Conflict and Market Distribution in the Capitalist Democracies." *Canadian Review of Sociology and Anthropology* 26:37–68.

Griffin, L., M. Wallace, and B. Rubin. 1986. "Capitalist Resistance to the Organization of the New Deal: Why? How? Success?" *American Sociological Review* 91(2):147–167.

Griffin, L., P. Walters, P. O'Connell, and E. Moore. 1986. "Methodological Innovations in the Analysis of Welfare-State Development: Pooling Cross Sections and Time Series." In N. Furniss (ed.), *Futures for the Welfare State*, pp. 101–38. Bloomington: Indiana University Press.

Hannon, M., and A. Young. 1977. "Estimation in Panel Models: Results on Pooling Cross-Sections and Time-Series." In D. Heise (ed.), *Sociological Methodology*, pp. 52–83. San Fransisco: Jossey-Bass.

Hardiman, N. 1988. *Pay, Politics, and Economic Performance in Ireland, 1970–1987*. Oxford University Press.

Hibbs, D. 1978. "On the Political Economy of Long-Run Trends in Strike Activity." *British Journal of Political Science*, 8:153–75.

1987. *The Political Economy of Industrial Democracies*. Cambridge: Mass.: Harvard University Press.

Hicks, A., and D. Swank. 1984. "On the Political Economy of Welfare Expansion: A Comparative Analysis of 18 Advanced Capitalist Democracies, 1960–1971." *Comparative Political Studies* 17(1):81–119.

Hicks, A., D. Swank, and M. Ambuhl. 1989. "Welfare Expansion Revisited: Policy Routines and Their Mediation by Party, Class and Crisis, 1957–1982." *European Journal of Political Research* 17:401–30.

International Labor Office. Various years. *Yearbook of Labor Statistics*. Geneva: ILO.

Judge, G., W. Griffiths, R. Hill, H. Lutkepohl, and T-S. Lee. 1985. *The Theory and Practice of Econometrics*. 2d ed. New York: Wiley.

Katzenstein, P. 1985. *Small States in World Markets: Industrial Policy in Europe*. Ithaca N.Y.: Cornell University Press.

Keohane, R. 1984. "The World Political Economy and the Crisis of Embedded Liberalism." In J. Goldthorpe (ed.), *Order and Conflict in Contemporary Capitalism*, pp. 15–38. Oxford University Press.

Kjellberg, A. 1984. *Facklig Organisering i tolv lander*. Lund: Arkiv.

Kmenta, J. 1971. *Elements of Econometrics*. New York: Macmillan.

Korpi, W. 1980. "Social Policy and Distributional Conflict in the Capitalist Democracies: A Preliminary Comparative Framework." *Western European Politics* 4:296–316.

Korpi, W., and M. Shalev. 1980. "Strikes, Power and Politics in the Western Nations, 1900–1976." In M. Zietlin (ed.), *Political Power and Social Theory*, 1:301–34. Greenwich, Conn.: JAI.

Lehmbruch, G. 1984. "Concertation and the Structure of Corporatist Networks." In J. Goldthorpe (ed.), *Order and Conflict in Contemporary Capitalism*, pp. 60–80. Oxford University Press.

Marks, G. 1986. "Neocorporatism and Incomes Policy in Western Europe and North America." *Comparative Politics* 17:253–77.

McHale, V. 1983. *Political Parties of Europe*. Westport, Conn.: Greenwood Press.

Myles, J. 1989. *Old Age in the Welfare State*. Laurence: University of Kansas Press.

O'Connell, P. 1989. *Transnational Economic Relations, Class Politics, and the Fiscal Crisis of the State*. Ph.D. diss., Indiana University, Bloomington.

OECD. 1989. *Economic in Transition: Structural Adjustment in OECD countries*. Paris: OECD.

Various years. *Labor Force Statistics*. Paris: OECD.
Various years. *National Accounts*. Paris: OECD.

Offe, C. 1984. *Contradictions of the Welfare State*. London: Hutchinson.

Paloheimo, H. 1984. "Distributive Struggles and Economic Development in the 1970s in Developed Capitalist Countries." *European Journal of Political Research*. 12:179–201.

Panitch, L. 1980. "Recent Theorizations of Corporatism: Reflections on a Growth Industry." *British Journal of Sociology* 31(2):159–87.

Pempel, T., and K. Tsunekawa. 1979. "Corporatism Without Labor: The Japanese Anomaly." In P. Schmitter and G. Lehmbruch (eds.), *Trends Towards Corporatist Intermediation*, pp. 249–87. Newberry Park, Calif.: Sage.

Przeworski, A. 1985. *Capitalism and Social Democracy*. Cambridge University Press.

Schmidt, M. 1982. "The Role of the Parties in Shaping Macroeconomic Policy." In F. Castles (ed.), *The Impact of Parties*, pp. 97–176. Newbury Park, Calif.: Sage.

1983. "The Welfare State and the Economy in Periods of Economic Crisis: A Comparative Analysis of Twenty-Three OECD Nations." *European Journal of Political Research*, 11:1–26.

Schmitter, P. 1981. "Interest Intermediation and Regime Governability in Contemporary Western Europe and North America." In S. Berger (ed.), *Organizing Interests in Western Europe*, pp. 285–327. Cambridge University Press.

Stephens, J. 1979. *The Transition from Capitalism to Socialism*. London: Macmillan Press.

Stimson, J. 1985. "Regression in Time and Space: A Statistical Essay." *American Journal of Political Science* 29(4):914–47.

Visser, J. 1984. *Dimensions of Union Growth in Western Europe*. EUI Working Paper no. 89. Florence: European University Institute.

PART III

Event history analysis

9

Introduction to event history methods

DAVID STRANG

Event history analysis is a set of techniques for the study of the timing of various kinds of events. Events may take the form of either state transitions or event recurrences (Hannan 1989). State transitions are changes in a discrete variable, such as movement from married to unmarried, from colonial dependency to sovereignty, or from a command to a market economy. Event recurrences are distinct happenings such as the outbreak of civil or international wars. Most event history methods assume that the process operates in continuous time (i.e., that an event can occur at any time). Parallel methods exist for the discrete-time case, where events can only occur at particular points in time (see Allison 1982).

The aim of event history analysis is to describe and model the underlying stochastic process that generates events. This goal is usually translated into a regression-like examination of how explanatory variables accelerate or slow the rate at which the event occurs. These variables may characterize the environment or the case "at risk" and may be measured on a categorical or interval level.

The potential applications of event history analysis are very broad. Contemporary methods have roots in actuarial and medical settings (where "survival" analyses examine human mortality) and in industrial engineering (where "failure time" analyses examine product durability). Event history analysis has more recently found wide application in the social sciences, where most work has studied demographic and institutional shifts occurring to people and organizations: the classical trio of birth, death, and marriage – or merger.[1]

There is a growing empirical literature that uses event history methods to study public policy making and change in political structures. Within the United States, researchers have examined change in government structures (Knoke 1982; Tolbert and Zucker 1983), legislative decisions (Pavalko 1989; Berry and Berry 1990), and collective action (Olzak

1989). Cross-national comparisons include the study of shifts in regime type (Hannan and Carroll 1981), the passage of national legislation (Soysal and Strang 1989; Usui, Chapter 10, this volume), executive succession (Bienen and van den Walle 1989), and decolonization (Strang 1990). But the potential applications of event history analysis to macrosociological and political concerns has just begun to be tapped.

METHODOLOGICAL BASICS

An *event history* is a record of the sequence and timing of events occurring to an individual case during some observation period. For example, an event history of the regime changes for a country would consist of a record of changes in political regime together with the dates of these changes.

Event history data could be analyzed with standard regression techniques – for example, by modeling the length of time between events. But this strategy presents two difficulties. First, some durations are incomplete or "censored"; observation periods may end with a case waiting to experience an event, and the analyst does not know if and when the event will occur. In fact, some cases may experience no events during the period under observation. Second, causal factors are often time varying; their values change over time. Standard regression methods can accommodate neither censoring nor time-varying explanatory factors. Event history methods are designed to do so.

The statistical theory underlying event history analysis characterizes the distribution of the random variable T, the time of the event. While most distributional theory works in terms of the cumulative density function and the probability density function, event history models are usually developed in terms of the *instantaneous transition rate*, or rate for short. The rate is defined as

$$r_{jk}(t) = \lim(dt \rightarrow 0)\ Pr(t, t + dt)/dt,$$

where $Pr(\cdot)$ is the limiting probability that a case moves from state j to state k (i.e., an event occurs) at t, given that the event does not occur before t. The rate is analogous to (and can be approximated by) the proportion of cases that experience an event over some interval of time, divided by the length of the interval.

Nonparametric methods permit the description of temporal patterns in the frequency of events. Standard techniques provide graphic displays of the survivor function, the integrated hazard, and the hazard. These techniques are valuable in helping the analyst assess how transition rates vary over time, which is crucial to the development of parametric models. They are also useful when the analyst wishes to compare differences in event timing across groups – for example, to compare susceptibility of democratic or socialist regimes to coups d'état.

Parametric methods seek to model the underlying process as a function of covariates and time. It is common to specify the rate as an exponential function of covariates multiplied by some function of time:

$$r_{jk}(t) = \exp(BX_{it})q(t).$$

The log-linear form for the covariates is chosen to help ensure that predicted rates are nonnegative, as implied in the rate's definition. X is indexed by i to indicate heterogeneity by case and by t to make clear that the values of explanatory variables may change over time.

Parametric models are generally distinguished by different choices of $q(t)$. Adequate representation of time dependence in the rate helps the analyst obtain reasonable estimates of the effects of measured covariates. Time often serves as a proxy for basic causal factors that are difficult to measure – for example, the effects of age on human mortality. In addition, unobserved heterogeneity (i.e., variation in rates uncaptured by measured covariates) produces systematic forms of time dependence. Popular parametric approaches for modeling time dependence include Gompertz, Weibull, and log-logistic formulations. Cox models employ a partially parametric technique that controls for an unspecified $q(t)$.

Parametric models are generally estimated by the method of maximum likelihood. A model for the transition rate permits the analyst to write down the probability of sample observations. Maximum likelihood estimation seeks the values of parameters that maximize this (model-specific) joint probability. Maximum likelihood estimation also gives estimates of parameter standard errors and permits tests of improvement in goodness-of-fit (where more complex models are compared to simpler nested models). While maximum likelihood estimation relies on asymptotic theory, Monte Carlo studies have demonstrated a strong resolving power at the sample sizes that comparative researchers typically work with (Tuma and Hannan 1984).

DATA MANIPULATION

The data demands of event history analysis are on the order of those of dynamic analyses of continuous outcomes. The researcher needs data on both dependent and independent variables over time. These demands are of course much greater than those of cross-sectional analysis, where data at only one point in time are needed. Where many events occur to a single case (perhaps terrorist acts in Lebanon), the analysis may be limited to that case, much like time-series analysis. More commonly, researchers compare the timing of events across cases, making event history analysis most comparable to multiwave panel (i.e., pooled cross-section and time-series) analysis.

From the user's point of view, the most confusing aspect of event history analysis often involves data organization. Of course, formatting schemes vary across estimation programs. But generally the basic set-up is to divide the time each case is at risk into intervals that can be unambiguously characterized in terms of the known timing of events and the values of explanatory variables. These time intervals, often called "spells," can be thought of as the units of analysis. A spell may terminate with an event, or not; but by definition an event cannot occur during a spell. For example, consider a country studied from 1965 to 1975 that experienced coups in 1967 and 1971. This case could be recorded in three spells: from 1965 to 1967 (ending in a coup), from 1967 to 1971 (ending in a coup), and from 1971 to 1975 (ending without a coup).

Explanatory covariates are attached to spells. For example, one might attach the (temporally appropriate) values of national income and regime type to the spells as defined. If the values of covariates are observed to change at times so they cannot be unambigously attached to spells, spells can be subdivided to permit synchronization. For example, with decennial data on national income we might divide the spell from 1967 to 1971 into spells from 1967 to 1970 (now censored, with the national income value for the 1960s) and one from 1970 to 1971 (ending in an event, with the national income value for the 1970s).

There is no standard way to describe the *N* involved in an event history analysis. The problem is similar to the difficulty of describing the *N* in a time-series analysis at *t* time points; whether one has an *N* of one, *t*, or something in between depends on how serious autocorrelated error is, and error is always unobserved. The amount of information in event history data depends on the number of events and on variability in explanatory factors across cases and within cases over time. As indices of the size of the problem, it is informative to report the number of observed events, the number of cases studied, and the frequency of observation on exogenous covariates.

RESEARCH STRATEGY

In a general sense, good research strategy for an event history problem is completely parallel to good research strategy in any explanatory enterprise. It involves sensible conceptualization, measurement, and so on. Some of the distinctive choices involved in an event history analysis can be outlined, however.

A first concern is with the conceptualization and measurement of the "dependent variable," the event whose timing the analyst wants to study. Event history analysis operates under the assumption that individual events form instances of some abstract class of events. The researcher needs to conceptualize and operationalize the definition of the events to make this assumption acceptable and ignore (in the data analysis) residual idiosyncracy in the actual events.

Event history analysis also generally assumes that the event is precisely dated to a point in time. While researchers always work in terms of intervals of time (years, months, days, etc.), one wants to be "precise enough" given the variability in event times, the frequency of change in explanatory factors, and the frequency of measurement of explanatory factors. Accuracy to the year may be adequate for legislative events occurring over a century or more, while accuracy to the month or day may be necessary when modeling job shifts within an organization.

Because event history analyses study change over time, it is necessary to define the observation period, that is, the period when susceptibility to the event is being examined. This decision should be theoretically motivated; the analyst needs to consider over what interval causal relationships may usefully be considered invariant. Of course, practical issues come into play: it may be impossible or too expensive to collect data on relevant variables over a very long period. In comparative research, analysts most often define their observation period by historical era. Where the event is a relatively new social construction, the starting point of the study is sometimes taken to be the first event (e.g., the first instance of a national workmen's compensation law).

Research strategy also involves consideration of whether and how transition rates depend on time. A first question is, what way of measuring time is relevant? Commonly used "clocks" are historical time (which tends to reflect the impact of external conditions), age (which tends to reflect the impact of internal processes), and time since the last event (which tends to represent the way previous events either suppress or facilitate additional ones). Of course, all of these may be operating at once: the rate of social revolution is probably a function of historical era (some eras are more revolutionary), age (older polities may be more or less flexible in handling challenges), and duration (revolutions often pave the way for counter-revolutions). Event history analysis provides many tools for describing and controlling for time dependence, but it is up to the researcher to conceptualize the possibilities.

Finally, a research strategy involves an observation scheme for the explanatory variables. Ideally, one would like to know the exact values of the explanatory variables at all times when the case is at risk of an event. For some variables this is quite possible: only one measurement is needed on time-invariant characteristics like an individual's gender and race. Repeated measurement is needed to approximate the values of variables that change erratically over time, as most national characteristics do. More frequent observation is advisable when the variable changes more quickly and unpredictably; when change is slow and/or steady, a smaller number of observations can capture its time-path in a satisfactory way.

THE PROMISE OF EVENT HISTORY ANALYSIS

Event history analysis provides a powerful set of tools that fit well with the interest in qualitative change that marks both macrosociology and political science. Its greatest advantages, relative to alternative methodological approaches to the same problems, lie in its superior resolving power. Event history analysis permits a simultaneous examination of the individual-, network-, and system-level factors that affect the propensity to experience events. Event history analysis also helps the analyst synchronize causes and effects, so outcomes are connected to contemporaneous conditions. Alternative approaches generally average over both outcomes and explanatory variables and are less well equipped to deal with the temporal basis of social processes.

A second promise is shared between event history analysis and other forms of dynamic methods, such as time-serial methods for continuous outcomes as well as methods for the study of event counts and event sequences (which may be viewed as special cases of event history analysis). Dynamic methods explicitly model change in outcomes over time, rather than the level of a variable at a point in time. This shift often provides a different and substantively important perspective on old problems. For example, we may learn something different when we ask why and how command economies turn into market economies than when we ask why some economies are organized by command and others by the market.

A GUIDE TO THE LITERATURE

Books and articles

Applications of event history analysis to macrosociological and macropolitical research have been cited. There are a number of excellent methodological overviews that explain the basic statistical concepts involved in event history analysis, and provide examples from sociology, including:

Allison, Paul D. 1984. *Event History Analysis: Regression for Longitudinal Data Analysis*. Newbury Park, Calif.: Sage.

Introduction to event history methods

Blossfeld, Hans-Peter, Alfred Hamerle, and Karl Ulrich Mayer. 1989. *Event History Analysis.* Hillsdale, N.J.: Erlhausen.

Especially strong on software examples and applications.

Carroll, Glenn R. 1983. "Dynamic Analysis of Discrete Dependent Variables: A Didactic Essay." *Quality and Quantity* 17:425–60.

Lawless, J. F. 1982. *Statistical Models and Methods for Lifetime Data.* New York: Wiley.

Extended treatment of parametric techniques and types of censoring.

Miller, Rupert G. 1981. *Survival Analysis.* New York: Wiley.

Focuses on nonparametric and semiparametric methods.

Tuma, Nancy B. In press. "Event History Analysis: An Introduction." In A. Dale and R. Davies (eds.), *Analyzing Social and Political Change.* Newbury Park, Calif.: Sage.

More advanced presentations include the following:

Tuma, Nancy B., and Michael T. Hannan. 1984. *Social Dynamics: Models and Methods.* New York: Academic Press.

Presentation oriented to regression-like analysis, coupled with substantive discussion of the application of event history modeling to the social sciences.

Computer software

There is a large and growing set of statistical packages that perform event history analysis. Event history modules within general purpose statistical packages inlude SURVIVAL in SPSSX, LIFEREG and LIFETEST procedures in SAS, and 1L and 2L in BMDP. The routines in SPSSX are quite limited, while BMDP and SAS provide more features. Dedicated programs provide additional flexibility, but are relatively difficult to use. RATE permits parameters and covariates to vary over time in more general ways. CTM provides expanded routines for the analysis of repeated events. See Goldstein et al. (1989) for an extensive review of software options for personal computers.

BMDP. 1985. *BMDP Statistical Software.* Berkeley: University of California Press.

SAS. 1985. *SAS User's Guide: Statistics, Version 5 Edition.* Cary, N.C.: SAS.

SPSSX. 1990. *SPSSX Reference Guide.* Chicago: SPSS.

Tuma, Nancy B. 1980. *Invoking RATE.* Menlo Park, Calif.: SRI International.

Yi, Kei-Mu, Bo Honore, and James Walker. 1987. *CTM: A Program for the Estimation and Testing of Continuous Time Multi-State Multi-Spell Models.* Chicago: ERC/NORC, University of Chicago Press.

NOTE

1. Recent collections of these sorts of applications include Hannan and Freeman (1989) and Mayer and Tuma (1990).

REFERENCES

Allison, Paul D. 1982. "Discrete Time Methods for the Analysis of Event Histories." In S. Leinhardt (ed.), *Sociological Methodology*, pp. 61–98. San Francisco: Jossey-Bass.

1984. *Event History Analysis: Regression for Longitudinal Data Analysis*. Newbury Park, Calif.: Sage.

Berry, Frances Stokes, and William D. Berry. 1990. "State Lottery Adoptions as Policy Innovations: An Event History Analysis." *American Political Science Review* 84:395–416.

Bienen, Henry S., and Nicholas van den Walle. 1989. *Of Time and Power*. Stanford, Calif.: Stanford University Press.

Blossfeld, Hans-Peter, Alfred Hamerle, and Karl Ulrich Mayer. 1989. *Event History Analysis*. Hillsdale, N.J.: Erlbaum.

BMDP (1985). *BMDP Statistical Software*. Berkeley: University of California Press.

Carroll, Glenn R. 1983. "Dynamic Analysis of Discrete Dependent Variables: A Didactic Essay." *Quality and Quantity* 17:425–60.

Goldstein, Richard, Jennifer Anderson, Arlene Ash, Ben Craig, David Harrington, and Marcello Pagano. 1989. "Survival Analysis Software on MS/PC-DOS Computers." *Journal of Applied Econometrics* 4:393–414.

Hannan, Michael T. 1989. "Macrosociological Applications of Event History Analysis: State Transitions and Event Recurrences." *Quality and Quantity* 23:351–83.

Hannan, Michael T., and Glenn Carroll. 1981. "The Dynamics of Formal Political Structure: An Event-History Analysis." *American Sociological Review* 46:19–35.

Hannan, Michael T., and John Freeman. 1989. *Organizational Ecology*. Cambridge, Mass.: Harvard University Press.

Knoke, David. 1982. "The Spread of Municipal Reform: Temporal, Spatial, and Social Dynamics." *American Journal of Sociology* 87:1314–39.

Lawless, J. F. 1982. *Statistical Models and Methods for Lifetime Data*. New York. Wiley.

Mayer, Karl Ulrich, and Nancy B. Tuma (eds.). 1990. *Event History Analysis in Life Course Research*. Madison: University of Wisconsin Press.

Miller, Rupert G. 1981. *Survival Analysis*. New York: Wiley.

Olzak, Susan. 1989. "Labor Unrest, Immigration, and Ethnic Conflict: Urban America, 1880–1915." *American Journal of Sociology* 94:1303–33.

Pavalko, Eliza K. 1989. "State Timing of Policy Adoption: Workmen's Compensation in the United States, 1909–1929." *American Journal of Sociology* 95:592–615.

SAS. 1985. *SAS User's Guide: Statistics, Version 5 Edition*. Cary, N.C.: SAS.

Soysal, Yasemin Nuhoglu, and David Strang. 1989. "Construction of the First Mass Educational Systems in Nineteenth Century Europe." *Sociology of Education* 62:277–88.

SPSSX. 1990. *SPSSX Reference Guide*. Chicago: SPSS.

Strang, David. 1990. "From Dependency to Sovereignty: An Event History Analysis of Decolonization." *American Sociological Review* 55:846–60.

Tolbert, Pamela, and Lynne Zucker. 1983. "Institutional Sources of Change in the Formal Structure of Organizations: The Diffusion of Civil Service Reform." *Administrative Science Quarterly* 28:22–39.

Tuma, Nancy B. 1980. *Invoking RATE*. Menlo Park, Calif.: SRI International.

In press. "Event History Analysis: An Introduction." In A. Dale and R. Davies (eds.), *Analyzing Social and Political Change*, Newbury Park, Calif.: Sage.

Tuma, Nancy B., and Michael T. Hannan. 1984. *Social Dynamics: Models and Methods*. New York: Academic Press.

Yi, Kei-Mu, Bo Honore, and James Walker. 1987. *CTM: A Program for the Estimation and Testing of Continuous Time Multi-State Multi-Spell Models*. Chicago: ERC/NORC, University of Chicago Press.

10

Welfare state development in a world system context: event history analysis of first social insurance legislation among 60 countries, 1880–1960

CHIKAKO USUI

The modern welfare state emerged first in Germany when Bismarck introduced income security measures for industrial workers in 1883.[1] It then spread to the rest of the Continent and England. Welfare states in Europe achieved steady growth, adding new programs periodically and extending coverage to additional segments of their populations. In North America, however, comparable social insurance legislation was not enacted until 1927 in Canada and 1935 in the United States. These countries achieved partial development of major income maintenance programs such as national health insurance, sickness and maternity insurance schemes for workers, family allowances, and housing. In the 1970s Canada took steps toward a public provision of all these measures, leaving the United States the only advanced nation that has not adopted a package of comprehensive national insurance plans.

Efforts to explain these broad variations in the adoption and development of modern welfare programs have taken many forms. Most explanations consider a combination of domestic socioeconomic and political factors among Western countries. They maintain the view that national welfare programs were the result of domestic changes in economic relations and political forces. More recently there has been growing recognition of the importance of the world context shaping the course of welfare state development. This position suggests that national welfare programs were not only a product of unique domestic conditions of each country, but also the outcome of a process of state transformation in a larger world context.

This chapter examines whether domestic socioeconomic and political as well as world system factors, separately or jointly, can appropriately explain the development of welfare states among 60 autonomous nations for the period 1880 and 1960.

THE DEVELOPMENT OF THE WELFARE STATE DOMESTIC FACTORS

This position contains many schools of thought. What they share is their emphasis on features internal to the countries they examine. They consider the development of welfare states an autonomous outcome of a combination of domestic socioeconomic and political factors. While the relative importance attributed to each of these factors differs among various authors and schools, all agree that no single factor sufficiently explains why and how the welfare state developed as it did. A number of authors have presented cogent descriptions of these theoretical views (Esping-Andersen 1989; Collier and Messick 1975; Flora and Alber 1981; Orloff and Skocpol 1984; Uusitalo 1984; Skocpol and Amenta 1986; Quadagno 1987; Pampel and Williamson 1988; and Hicks, Swank, and Ambuhl 1989; Korpi 1989). I will therefore summarize the substantive themes and the shortcomings of the previous research as they relate to this study.

Socioeconomic factors

Socioeconomic forces potentially affecting welfare state development stem from changes in the technological, economic, social, or demographic structure of a society. The "Logic of Industrialism" (Kerr et al. 1964), for example, suggests that nations will increasingly converge in social structures and social policies as they are transformed to modern industrial societies (see also Cutright 1965; Aaron 1967; Mishra 1977). The process of industrialization creates contingencies that could seriously jeopardize individual and family lives (e.g., unemployment, old age). State intervention in the realm of labor protection, health care, and social welfare is thus called for. Also, financial capacity of the state in meeting these needs comes only with industrial advancement (Wilensky 1975; Hage and Hanneman 1980; and Issac and Kelly 1981).

Political factors

Authors emphasizing political factors have taken two general positions: those emphasizing societal political forces and those emphasizing political forces internal to the state. The first group of scholars has emphasized the importance of political factors in the development of the welfare state, such as political mobilization of the working class, strength of unions, mass party organizations, electoral turnout, and characteristics of government (e.g., "strategies of social demand anticipation"). The "social democratic model of welfare development" (also known as the working-class strength theory in Shalev (1983), or the "power resources" approach in Korpi (1989)) considers the welfare state as a product of class-based political struggles over state intervention to benefit the working class. Others emphasize non-class-based interests' demand for welfare programs. Pampel and Williamson (1988) point out how economic and demographic changes lead to the emergence of diversified groups of people (e.g., the retired), which compete with other non-class-based groups for public resources. These models focus on the process in which welfare demands are articulated to affect the government through electoral participation of workers (see also Korpi 1978; Korpi and Shalev 1980). For example, the working class exerts political power through elections to implement social policies in its interests. However, when employer associations, corporations, and right-wing parties are powerful, welfare development is minimal and slow.

A second group of researchers also focuses on political factors but emphasizes those factors related to government. They maintain that it is not just class-based political struggles but also government administrators that affect welfare state development. They argue that government representatives, politicians, and political parties seek to obtain electoral support by pursuing social legislation. These government representatives are dependent for their power on electoral support. Welfare programs promote electoral support. Thus, government representatives mediate the relationship between societal interests and government welfare policy (Block 1977; 1980; Orloff and Skocpol 1984; Skocpol 1985; and Skocpol and Amenta 1986). In this view, social insurance legislation cannot be adequately explained by the demands of societal interest groups, class conflicts, and unions but reburies recognition of the self-interest of government officials and their independent roles in welfare policy-making processes.

Research findings

Large-scale empirical studies testing internal socioeconomic and political explanations of the emergence of the modern welfare state offer mixed results. Among those testing the influence of both economic and political factors, Pryor (1968) reports empirical support for the importance of unionization in his analysis of 19 countries in 1913. Schneider (1982) shows that voter participation had the most significant and consistent effects for all five types of social insurance programs among 18 countries between 1919 and 1975. Kuhnle's (1981) analysis of four

Scandinavian countries for the period 1880–1913, however, suggests that *both* socioeconomic and political mobilization forces influenced the adoption of social insurance programs. In contrast, Flora and Alber (1981), who examined 12 European nations for the period 1880–1970, report mixed results about the roles of socioeconomic development and political mobilization. A more recent study (Korpi 1989) of the origins of sickness insurance policies among 18 OECD nations during 1930–80 provides strong evidence that Left-party government participation had the more significant effects on the legislation of social insurance policies than any other variables, such as the rate of economic growth, the state autonomy, and social unrest.

Case studies examining the role of government representatives have produced detailed, historical, qualitative analyses of few nations. Heclo (1974), for example, examines the development of unemployment and old-age assistance programs in Britain and Sweden and points out that civil service administrators in both countries played more important roles than political parties or interest groups in that they engaged in the intellectual activities of diagnosing societal problems and framing policy alternatives, thereby going through "collective puzzlement" on behalf of society.

WORLD CONTEXTUAL FACTORS

Those authors focusing on world context as an explanation of welfare state development demonstrate two variations: economic and ideological emphasis corresponding to world system and world polity (or "cultural" school of world system) arguments. Rather than viewing the world as a collection of individual, self-sufficient nations and then seeking domestic causes of welfare expansion, these models stress the important linkages between individual nations and the world system and explain the growth of the welfare state by looking at world-level variables.

In describing the rise of capitalism in sixteenth-century Europe, Wallerstein (1974) distinguished two types of world system: world economy (a territorial division of labor encompassing a set of political entities) and world empire (a territorial division of labor encompassed by a single political structure) (Chase-Dunn and Rubinson 1971, p. 454). The former is distinguished from the latter because a world economy involves competition for market sale and access to resources, which in turn gives rise to a geographical division of labor across three main zones: core (Northwestern Europe), semiperiphery (Mediterranean Europe including Portugal and Spain), and periphery (Eastern Europe and Latin America). Each zone is united with the world economy for the exchange of everyday consumption and is distinguished from the others in its economic structure. In this process the state emerges as a regulator of the world market by means of noneconomic devices. The prime function of the state arises in conjunction with the interests of the dominant capitalist class and leads to strong states in the core and weak ones in the periphery. Moreover, these differences in the strength of state mechanisms lead to unequal exchange between core and peripheral states. This happens precisely because the states in the core could achieve strong coalitions with capitalist classes and gain plentiful economic resources from capital through taxation. Scholars argued that the development of welfare state policies must be examined in relationship to a country's location in the world economy – for instance, government strategies for managing trade links to the global economy (Cameron 1978; Katzenstein 1984) or government strategies for economic development among peripheral countries (Spalding 1980).

One variation on the world system perspective suggests the importance of ideological or cultural transmission. They maintain that the important features of world systems are not limited to economic linkages. According to John Meyer and others (see Meyer and Rowan 1977; Meyer et al. 1976; Bergesen 1980; Thomas and Meyer 1984; Meyer 1987; Thomas and Lauderdale 1988), the world is an "organizational and cultural milieu that penetrates virtually all countries and places rigorous demands on them". Certain values and beliefs become institutionalized in the world system and give rise to world cultural rules. These "rulelike" forces affect nation-states as subunits of the world system, since compliance with them is an important source of legitimacy and resources. National social insurance programs have become one of the institutions of modernity, and state provision of such services has been incorporated into the definition of a modern nation-state. The world ideology of modernization and progress has legitimized the active involvement of the state in the organization, financing, and delivery of welfare services.

Empirical findings on world system factors

World system arguments have been useful in empirical analyses of the economic growth of nations (Chase-Dunn 1975; Snyder and Kick 1979), the post–World War II welfare state (Cameron 1978), national systems of education (Meyer et al. 1976; Ramirez and Boli 1987), and regime changes (Krasner 1983; Kratochwil and Ruggie 1986). More recent work (Strang 1990) shows that the process of decolonization for the period 1870–1987 is best explained by the shifts in the world context, as exemplified by the 1960 pronouncements of the United Nations.

Although some authors suggest that a world-level networking of nations in the promotion of social welfare legislation started since the turn of the century, few studies on the origin of the modern welfare policies have considered the world cultural or ideological context.[2] Laroque (1969) reports that international collaboration among nations started in 1891 when the Permanent International Committee on Social Insurance (PICSI) first addressed the problems of industrial accidents and, later, of sickness, unemployment, and old age through the creation of international treaties by governments. The work of the PICSI continued until 1914 and was succeeded by the International Labor Organization (ILO) in 1919. Rys (1964, p. 64) and Lund (1972) notes that technical assistance and regional seminars offered by the ILO in matters of social insurance/security had a large impact on the development of social insurance policies in Asia and Africa. Similarly, Collier and Messick (1975) and Alber (1981) point out that these international conferences and treaties exerted considerable influence on the development of social insurance policies from the 1910s to the 1930s.

There is evidence that these mechanisms of ideological transmission in the world context were more than just technical assistance and data collection. Usui (1988) argues that the ILO was not merely a source of technical assistance or a data collecting agency, but that it brought workers, employers, and governments together at its annual conferences. For example, 40 out of 49 member states attended the conference in 1919, and of those 40, 24 states were represented by the complete delegations. During the period 1919–60, there were 11 meetings that were directly related to the international promotion of social insurance policies (Usui 1988, pp. 40–54). The ILO's activities – especially the establishment of international labor legislation – indicate political discourse in support of welfare programs through government legislation. Although the ILO had no legal power on the enforcement of international legislation, its international conferences, agreements, and recommendations exerted a demonstrable influence over participating nations toward their own social insurance legislation.[3] These international meetings might well have generated world standards to which nations are expected to conform.

The present study will develop measures of global networking and examine the hypothesized impact of world polity on the actions of individual states.[4] Then these measures will be compared with standard measures of domestic socioeconomic and political factors to assess their explanatory values.

OBJECTIVE AND METHOD

Why did some countries succeed in introducing social insurance policies earlier than others? I examine both adoptions and nonadoptions over the 80-year period. The sample consists of 60 countries that were autonomous in their domestic policies. This criterion excludes those colonial countries that may have experienced imposed welfare development. The data cover the period 1880–1960. These 80 years involve the period of substantial welfare state generation and development. This sample selection is consistent with the rationale used in the previous research (Collier and Messick 1975).[5]

Data were collected from U.S. Department of Health and Human Services (1984). The period of study is from 1880 to 1960 – the first consolidated social insurance legislation took place in Germany in 1883, and of the 60 countries, the last adoption took place in 1960.

Dependent variable: the events

Social insurance legislation, as the initial starting point of the modern welfare state, is well established in the literature (Rimlinger 1971; Malloy 1979; Flora and Heidenheimer 1981; and Orloff and Skocpol 1984; Skocpol and Amenta 1986). This study examines the rate at which the first social insurance programs – compulsory legislation involving a substantial segment of the population – were adopted. Social insurance laws that were legislated but not implemented or those laws that covered only limited segments of the population (e.g., civil servants) are not considered. As a rule, nations introduced work injury programs first. However, in some cases, a sickness or old-age insurance program was introduced first. Thus, the unit of the analysis initially consisted of *two events per country*: (1) the date of first adoption in any of five categories of social insurance programs and (2) the date when work injury insurance laws were legislated. Preliminary analysis of these two events, however, yielded nearly identical results, so analysis of only the first is reported here.[6]

Independent variables

All independent variables were measured repeatedly for the time period 1880–1960 to capture temporal variation within cases.

Domestic variables. The first domestic variable is the degree of *industrialization and urbanization* as measured by the percentage of the labor force employed in agriculture (*LFA*). Industrialization and urbanization are recognized as creating population dislocations and expanding the tax base, which promote the adoption of social insurance legislation. Data were collected from four sources: Cipolla (1975), Kuznets (1957, 1971) (publications on long-term changes in the structure of labor force),

(Flora et al. 1983–7, vol. 1), and the annual publications of the ILO (1951, 1989). I considered other measures of industrialization and urbanization (e.g., the percentage of labor force in industry, income per capita, the percentage of the population in cities), but data for early historical years were less complete.

A second domestic variable related to social insurance adoption is the percent of the population that is aged, measured here as the *percentage of persons 65 and older* in the total population (*AGEDPOP*). Data were obtained from the annual publications of the ILO. The size of an aged population might be considered more important for the adoption of old-age pensions rather than for the first adoption. However, I included this variable for three reasons. First, the growth of an aged population comes about when a society achieves low death rates and low fertility rates. Thus, this variable taps noneconomic changes that are associated with the process of industrialization and urbanization, such as improvement in public health and changes in the structure of the family. Second, 10 of the 60 countries examined in this study enacted either sickness or old-age programs as their first piece of social insurance legislation. Thus, the inclusion of the percentage of population that is aged seemed reasonable. Third, historical data for the aged population were available for a large number of nations.

The third domestic variable is the extension of the voting franchise (*VOTING*), which is understood as a key mechanism for mobilizing mass demands for social legislation. Existing studies (Pryor 1968; Flora and Alber 1981; Kuhnle 1981; and Korpi 1989) of the adoption of social insurance programs employ such variables as the extension of the franchise, the distribution of votes by party, type of regime, and the strength of labor unions, social unrest, and state autonomy. However, these measures do not exist for earlier time periods and less developed countries. Banks's (1975) data provided the most complete historical information on the extension of the franchise.

World polity variables. Three variables were used to measure the world polity factors contributing to adoption of social insurance legislation. I examined the ILO and its member states, as well as their promotion of international social legislation, and indexed the information by three measures. First is the *percentage of countries attending the international labor conference* in a given year (*INTCON*), which measures the strength of the world polity concerning the importance of social welfare legislation. It reflects the degree of integration of the nation system as a whole. Data for world polity variables were gathered in several steps. First, I counted the number of nations attending ILO conferences in each of 12 meetings between 1906 and 1960. Second, based on the annual reports for these 12 meetings, I identified the member countries of the International Association for Labor Legislation and counted countries that attended each meeting with a complete set of delegates. Third, for each year I counted the total number of nations that attended the conference and expressed the number as a percentage of independent nations that existed in the world in that year. Before 1906, there were no large-scale international gatherings concerned with the promotion of social insurance laws. I thus coded this as zero – the nonexistence of a world nation system. The data for the international meeting in 1906 were collected from ILO (1906). For the period 1919–60, data were obtained from the *International Labor Conference*, the annual publication of the ILO in Geneva. Data on the number of countries that existed in a given year were collected from Banks's (1975) "List of Independent States: 1815–1973."[7]

The second world polity variable is the *number of countries that had already legislated their first social insurance laws* 10 years prior to the observation point (*NUMBER*), which is a lagged variable that measures the degree to which state intervention in the form of social policy legislation had become institutionalized at the world level. The data for this variable were available for the entire observation period, 1880–1960.

The third measure of the world polity argument is whether or not a country had *direct involvement in international labor legislation and world communication* prior to its national social insurance legislation (*COMLINK*), which is also a lagged variable measuring a more direct linkage between a country and the world nation system. It is a dummy variable that reflects whether a country was in any way involved or had contact with the nation state system of international labor and social legislation.[8] *COMLINK* indicates whether each nation attended each of the 12 conferences. For the period 1880–1905, zero was entered for each country since there was no international conference directly related to the promotion of social insurance programs in that period. For the period 1906–18, the forerunner of the ILO existed and held annual meetings; however, data specifying which countries attended what year are unavailable. Thus, I also assigned the value of zero for 1906–18, but in reality, the nation-state system existed then in ways that the present study fails to capture. This data problem becomes evident later in the analysis, and therefore results are reported with and without *COMLINK*. In both cases, however, the main results are largely the same.

Method of analysis

Many of the studies of welfare state development use static conventional methods of analysis, even though this process is a continuous

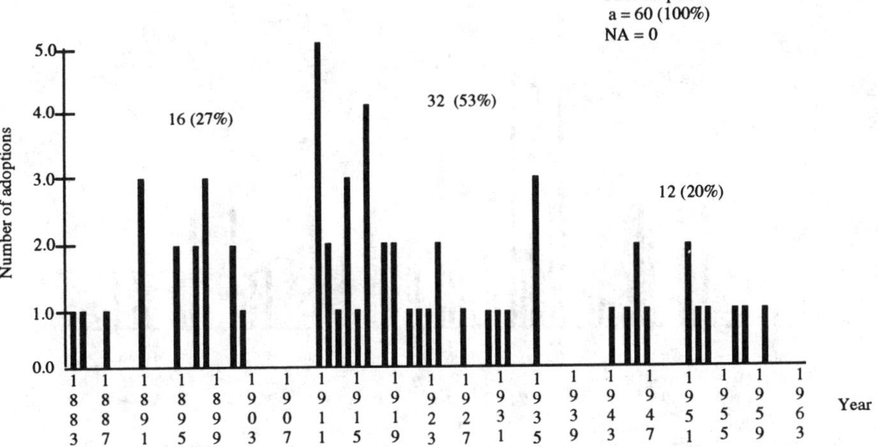

Figure 10.1. Events in social insurance adoption by programs ($N = 60$): first adoption; number of adoptions = 60(100 %); number of non-adoptions = 0.

process having discrete outcomes (i.e., adoption or nonadoption of a social insurance program). It is therefore more appropriate to employ dynamic methods that explicitly incorporate time, such as event history analysis (Carroll 1983; Tuma and Hannan 1984). Tuma's (1980) "RATE" utilizes the Gompertz model and maximum likelihood estimation. It offers more universal applications of the procedure to the study of the timing of social insurance legislation. For this multivariate analysis, the logarithm of the rate could be a linear accumulation of the variables:

$$\ln r(t) = L_0 + L_1X_1(t) + L_2X_2(t) + \ldots + L_nX_n(t),$$

where $r(t)$ is the instantaneous rate at time t, L_0 is a constant coefficient, L_n values are the coefficients to be estimated, and X_n values are the independent variables. The log-linear specification is chosen because the logarithm of the rate of adoption is considered to be a function of the linear addition of independent variables. Once this function is established, the RATE program clarifies, in addition to overall statistical significance, the best approximation for each coefficient L_n and its range of statistical error.

RESULTS

The distribution of events

Figures 10.1 and 10.2 depict how the two events of interest occurred over the 80-year period. Each country's event is identified as a unit

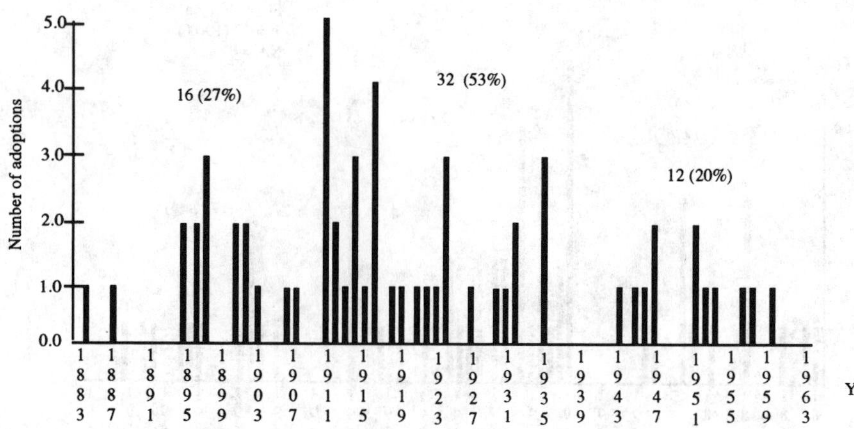

Figure 10.2. Events in social insurance adoption by programs ($N = 60$): work injury programs; number of adoptions = 60(100%); number of non-adoptions = 0.

vertical bar, and the overall patterns of events for 60 countries are drawn. Figures 10.1 and 10.2 also report the number of total events (adoptions) over time. During the period 1880–1960, all 60 countries completed the initial (first) adoption of a social insurance program, though the specific dates of legislation varied considerably among countries.

A closer examination of the curves reveals that the pattern of events for work injury insurance programs is strikingly similar to that of first adoption. These two figures indicate that there is a significant break in "first adoption" and "work injury" around 1905–10. Prior to the establishment of the ILO in Basel in 1906 and the ILO in Geneva in 1919, a small group of nations took initiatives to enact social insurance laws; but shortly after the first international meeting in 1906, a large number of countries followed suit.

Survival analysis

In order to detect the trend and to learn more about the relationship between nonadoption of social insurance policy and the rate of social insurance adoption, I produced the survival function in log-scale for a total of 60 countries from 1880 to 1960 using SURVIVAL (SPSS, 1983).

In survival analysis, special attention should be directed to the change of the slope. In Figure 10.3, change in the slope indicates change in the rate of social insurance legislation. When the rate of transition from the initial state to destination state (i.e., adoption) is independent of

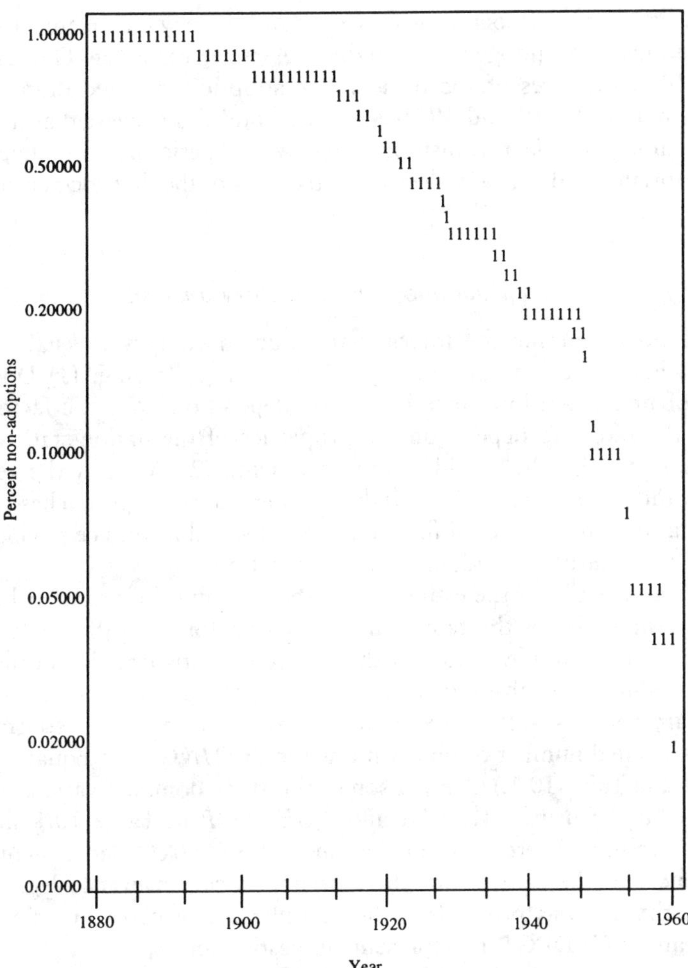

Figure 10.3. First adoption of social security system – all countries (log scale graph of survival function; survival variable time)

the duration in the state of "social insurance nonadoption," the rate has a linear relation to the logarithm of the survivor function. If the plot is nonlinear, the transition rate will be dependent on the duration of initial state. This change in the rate may be caused by pure time dependence or by independent variables that are time dependent.

The slope of the survival function in Figure 10.3 is not linear, indicating some form of time dependence. In addition, the two "shoulders" present in the plot suggest that the observed temporal variation in transition rates of social insurance adoption may be related to both exogenous and endogenous variables. As seen earlier in Figures 10.1 and 10.2, the rates of social insurance adoption changed dramatically at around 1905–10 and 1935–40. These findings suggest that a model with time-dependent transition rates with "periodization" might be appropriate for describing the overall patterns of the first social insurance adoption.

First adoption: event history analysis

I will now examine the forces that induce a country to enact a first social insurance law. Specifically, I asked the following: (1) Does the rate of first social insurance legislation depend on domestic factors, or does the rate also depend on the properties of the nation-state system as suggested by the world polity argument? (2) What is the relative magnitude of effects of the variables under the two approaches in predicting the timing (rate) of first adoption of social insurance policies? (3) Does the rate of first adoption vary over time?

Table 10.1 shows the estimated coefficients and their standard errors (in parentheses) for the rate of first adoption for five different models. Positive or negative values and the degree of statistical significance are more telling than absolute values in interpreting the coefficients. Preliminary analysis of the three domestic variables was overly constrained by the limited number of observations for *VOTING*. (See Equations 1.1 and 1.2 in Table 10.1.) Comparison of this three-domestic-variable model with a model using only *LFA* and *AGEDPOP* in Table 10.1 showed similar results. There is no indication that *VOTING* had a significant influence on the rate of adoption of first social insurance legislation. Thus, the analysis proceeds with the fuller set of cases by using only *LFA* and *AGEDPOP* to represent domestic factors.

Equation 1 in Table 10.2 consists of only two domestic variables, *LFA* (percent labor force in agriculture) and *AGEDPOP* (percent aged population):

$$\ln r(t) = L_0 + L_1\ LFA(t) + L_2\ AGEDPOP(t).$$

Equations 2.1 and 2.2 in Table 10.2 include different combinations of the three world polity variables in addition to the two domestic variables. These two equations are built on the same number of covariates, but they differ in the combination of world polity variables. Equation 2.1 contains *INTCON* and *COMLINK*; Equation 2.2 includes *NUMBER* and *COMLINK*. *INTCON* and *NUMBER* are highly correlated ($r = .93$) and are entered in two separate equations to avoid multicollinearity.

Table 10.1. ***Effects of domestic and world variables on the rate of first social insurance legislation, 1880-1960***

Independent variables	Coefficients for equations (1.1)	(1.2)
Constant	-5.391* (2.072)	-5.310* (1.754)
LFA	-1.754 (2.384)	-5.177 (2.898)
AGEDPOP	61.170 (34.62)	83.740 (38.14)
VOTING	-5.087 (4.241)	-4.762 (3.900)
INTCON	10.910** (3.568)	—
NUMBER	—	0.163* (0.051)

Note: LFA: % labor force in agriculture; *AGEDPOP*: % aged population; *VOTING*: the extension of the franchise; *INTCON*: % nations attending the international labor conference (a measure of integration of the nation-state system); *NUMBER*: the number of countries that already enacted a program in question 10 years prior to the observation year (a measure of institutionalization of the social insurance programs).
$^*p < .10$; $^{**}p < .05$.

The chi-square (χ^2) statistic in Table 10.2 indicates the goodness-of-fit for each equation. The chi-square statistic is 1.06 for Equation 1 and is statistically insignificant. It indicates that with the two domestic variables alone, we cannot make reasonable estimates of the rate of first program adoption. The addition of world system variables improves the model considerably, as is indicated in the increased chi-squares from 1.06 to 24.74 (Equation 2.1) and to 19.13 (Equation 2.2), both

Table 10.2. *Effects of domestic and world variables on the rate of first social insurance legislation, 1880-1960*

Independent variable	Coefficients for equations (1)	(2.1)	(2.2)	(3.1)	(3.2)
Constant	-3.347* (0.849)	-3.986** (0.878)	-3.512** (0.866)	-4.036** (0.901)	-3.680** (0.854)
LFA	0.244 (0.925)	-2.718* (1.123)	-2.328 (1.229)	-2.644* (1.235)	-2.395 (1.238)
AGEDPOP	9.997 (9.868)	36.060* (13.10)	27.140* (12.33)	35.930** (13.35)	27.790* (12.47)
INTCON	—	6.554** (1.452)	—	7.019** (1.756)	—
NUMBER	—	—	0.063** (0.016)	—	0.133** (0.038)
COMLINK	—	-1.374 (0.762)	-1.327 (0.762)	—	—
Period 2: 1919-35	—	—	—	0.56 (0.893)	-0.218 (0.967)
Period 3: 1936-60	—	—	—	-0.671 (0.835)	-3.364* (1.621)
χ^2	1.06	24.74***	19.13***	21.27***	20.95***
df	2	4	4	5	5

Note: LFA: % labor force in agriculture; *AGEDPOP*: % aged population; *INTCON*: % nations attending the international labor conference (a measure of integration of the nation-state system); *NUMBER*: the number of countries that already enacted a program in question 10 years prior to the observation year (a measure of institutionalization of the social insurance programs); *COMLINK*: a lagged dummy variable measuring whether a country attended the international labor force conference prior to its national legislation of a program in question (a measure of direct linkage between a nation and the world system).

*$p < .10$; **$p < .05$; ***$p < .01$.

significant at the .01 level. Thus, models containing both domestic and world system variables provide a better fit.

Equations 2.1 and 2.2 also show that the effects for *LFA* are negative. As expected, this indicates that the legislation of first insurance laws is more likely as countries shift from an agricultural to a more industrial economy. The effect is statistically significant at the .10 level in Equation 2.1 but not in Equation 2.2.

The coefficient for *AGEDPOP* is positive and statistically significant at the .10 level in both equations. Thus, the larger the percentage of the population that is aged and the more industrially advanced the country is, the earlier that country adopts its first social insurance program. The results for *LFA* and *AGEDPOP* are clearly consistent with the existing view of welfare state development that emphasizes the importance of domestic socioeconomic conditions of society.

Equations 2.1 and 2.2 also indicate that the effects of *INTCON* and *NUMBER* are positive and significant at the .05 level. Thus, the rate of first adoption increases as more nations are incorporated into the world polity. The rate also increases as the idea of social insurance legislation becomes more institutionalized. These results suggest that the global institutional environment was clearly important in the first adoptions of social insurance programs. The historical development of social insurance appears to be strongly related to the development of the nation-state system.

In both Equations 2.1 and 2.2, the coefficient for *COMLINK* is negative, meaning that the rate of first adoption was faster among countries that had no direct connection to the ILO prior to the first adoption of a social insurance program. This result may probably be a measurement artifact. As mentioned, specific names of countries attending international labor conferences were missing for 1906–18. Sixteen nations enacted their first social insurance laws prior to 1906. Thus, 27 percent of the 60 countries introduced their first social insurance laws on their own initiatives well before being integrated into a world nation-state system. Another 18 countries adopted their first program during 1906–18, but we do not know which of these nations attended international labor conferences during that period. Thus, 34 countries (57 percent) that enacted their first social insurance program prior to 1919 entered the equation with a score of zero on *COMLINK*. It is not surprising that *COMLINK* has a negative coefficient in Equations 2.1 and 2.2.

In Equations 3.1 and 3.2, I reestimated coefficients by replacing *COMLINK* with dummy variables reflecting three periods: 1880–1918, 1919–35, and after 1936. These periods were chosen for theoretical and empirical reasons.[9] I used the first period (1880–1918) as the baseline period (omitted category) because it is more logical to interpret the effects of the second and third periods relative to the effects of the first.[10]

The chi-square statistics are 21.27 and 20.95 for Equations 3.1 and 3.2, respectively, and are significant at the .01 level. Consistent with the previous results, both the domestic variables and the world system variables show strong effects on the rate of first adoption.

Equations 3.1 and 3.2 also show that the effects of the second period (1919–35) are insignificant. That is, the rate in the second period did not differ much from the rate in the initial period (1880–1918). The coefficients for the third period proved negative in both equations, meaning that the rate slowed down after 1936, compared with the periods before 1936. However, the coefficient is significant in only one equation. The most prudent conclusion is that the rate of adoption was nearly constant across all three periods.

The results indicate that equations containing both the domestic and the world polity variables fit the data fairly well. They suggest that the emergence of the welfare state is determined by these two sets of forces. These forces stem from the processes of industrialization and urbanization within a nation, as well as from the development of world system and global norms that are shared among nations regarding state intervention in the promotion of social security and welfare for its workers.

The present findings indicate that modern welfare states evolved as a result of societies' change from agricultural economies to industrially and technically advanced ones. The results also show that the development of state-sponsored social insurance policies was strongly associated with the rise of a world nation system. In fact, the estimates of effects of the domestic variables and world polity variables are quite robust in describing the rate of adoption of the first social insurance program. Despite social, cultural, and historical differences affecting national attitudes toward national social insurance programs, nations conform to a uniform pattern of social structure as they develop socioeconomically and as the nation-state system expands in the world. The emerging uniformity among nations is not solely the result of a single set of forces but the product of both societal and global institutional forces.

DISCUSSION

This macrosociological dynamic analysis of modern welfare state development among 60 countries for the period 1880–1960 leads to the conclusion that the origin and development of modern welfare states was affected both by internal socioeconomic factors and by the larger world context. Rhythmic patterns such as those found in Figures 10.1 and 10.2 cannot be explained without considering worldwide influences on each country. These two figures show, for example, that there are significant breaks in social insurance adoption around 1905–10 and 1935–40. In other words, prior to the establishment of the ILO in Basel in 1906 and in Geneva in 1919, a group of nations took initiatives to enact social insurance laws; but shortly after the first pre-ILO meeting in 1906, a large number of countries followed suit. This indicates that variables measuring the global network of nations and world ideology must also be examined.

While the potential importance of world polity factors has been suggested by others, no previous studies on the origin and development of welfare states have delineated and tested the hypothesized mechanisms. The present results suggest that the world institutional environment is a strong force in the universalization of social welfare policies in the past 80 years.

Given the ambiguity in the literature concerning the roles of industrialization and urbanization on the timing of social insurance programs, it is perhaps surprising to find significantly large effects for the economic development variables. This finding runs counter to some studies (e.g., Schneider 1982; Korpi 1989) that report very weak effects for economic variables. One reason for the difference in results may be methodological in nature. Previous studies based their analyses on data sampled from the outcome. These studies selected only the legislation of social insurance policies and then examined the determinants of these events, while not paying attention to conditions that kept countries in the state of non-legislation. Also, most prior studies focused on the Western welfare states, employing a smaller set of Western countries for a specific time period.

The present study also shows weak and mixed results concerning the analysis of variation in the rate of adoption over time. The analyses in Figures 10.1 and 10.2 indicate changes in the rate of adoption over the three periods. The patterns depicted in these figures follow world polity arguments, with the second period showing the highest rates of adoption and the third period slower rates. Testing for these effects in Table 10.2, however, shows no significant increase in the rate of adoption for the second period, providing weak support. Only Equation 3.2 in Table 10.2 indicates that rate of adoption slowed in the third period. World polity arguments would suggest that this is a saturation effect. This effect is, however, not significant in Equation 3.1, providing mixed results. Further analysis of these period effects would be appropriate.

Finally, more qualitative and quantitative analyses are needed to address the question of why some nations become integrated to the world system earlier and why some nations conform to its dictates more readily than others. Whether or not similar forces operated for the subsequent adoption of other types of social insurance policies also remains to be seen.

NOTES

1. The welfare state is generally defined as a state in which the government promotes social welfare through the collection of resources and the distribution of goods and services to its citizens. There is agreement in the literature that the creation of government-sponsored social insurance programs initiated the modern welfare state because it represented a clear "institutional breakthrough" from the previous poor relief method (Rimlinger 1971; Malloy 1979; Flora and Heidenheimer 1981; Skocpol and Amenta 1986; and Orloff and Skocpol 1984). The term "welfare state" emerged after World War II when British intellectuals distinguished "welfare" conceptions from the old poor law solutions in which social protection was given to persons at the sacrifice of their citizenship rights.
2. Modernization theorists have developed a "diffusion" model, proposing that modern features (such as social insurance policies) diffuse from "modern" to "traditional" societies through regional or international travel, trade, political influence, migration, and telecommunications. Empirical studies of diffusion in the adoption of social insurance programs (e.g., Collier and Messick 1975), however, have not been successful owing mainly to difficulties in modeling the paths of diffusion. Although the initial transmission of policy ideas may take relatively simple, fixed movements from one leader country to a number of potential adopters, with the passage of time, countries that adopt a policy innovation become "source" countries that can exert influences over other countries. Thus, the paths of diffusion adds complexity as a number of source countries increases over time. Like modeling a transmission of virus in a population, the exact route of diffusion becomes intractable. It is even harder to assess the relative magnitude of influence for different types of diffusion (e.g., political influence vs. trade).
3. The ILO takes the following procedures to enforce the rules of international legislation: when international legislation is adopted (called "convention"), each member state is then required to bring the convention before the authority of its country for the enactment of legislation within one and a half years. When the member state obtains the consent of the authority, it registers the ratification of the convention to the ILO. If the member state fails to obtain the consent of its national authority, there is no further obligation on the member state.
4. One may argue that establishing the statistical association between the adoption of a certain social insurance program and the nation's participation in the ILO's conference prior to its legislation of that program does not necessarily demonstrate that the social insurance legislation was influenced by the ideology of world community. It should be noted, however, that the international meeting involved representatives from the government and the organizations of employees and employers from 40 or 50 countries. The direct involvement with and exposure to these international discussions

must have made each participating state more aware of the thinking of other countries toward social insurance legislation. These influences are clearly external to the individual society; they are influences stemming from the global nation-state system.

5. The 60 countries are (in chronological order of their first social insurance legislation) Germany, Belgium, Austria, Denmark, Hungary, Sweden, Finland, Norway, Ireland, the United Kingdom, France, Italy, New Zealand, the Netherlands, Luxembourg, Australia, El Salvador, Japan, Peru, Switzerland, the United States, Romania, the Union of Soviet Socialist Republic, Portugal, Greece, South Africa, Uruguay, Argentina, Chile, Colombia, Cuba, Panama, Bulgaria, Canada, Brazil, Spain, Ecuador, Yugoslavia, Venezuela, Bolivia, Costa Rica, Paraguay, Nicaragua, Mexico, the Dominican Republic, Iran, Iraq, Egypt, Liberia, Turkey, Afghanistan, Guatemala, Saudi Arabia, China, Haiti, Honduras, South Korea, Thailand, Libya, and Ethiopia. One may object to the inclusion of Hungary, Ireland, Norway, Finland, Yugoslavia, Australia, and New Zealand. However, these countries are also included in the previous empirical studies that covered the early historical period of social insurance legislation. Collier and Messick (1975) included all but Ireland. Flora and Alber (1981), Kuhnle (1981), and Alber (1981) included Norway and Finland. Schneider (1982) included all but Hungary and Yugoslavia. Countries that were under colonial rule during the observation period (1880–1960) were not considered because of the possibility that the inclusion of "imposed" social insurance legislation may distort the analysis.
6. Fifty of the 60 countries legislated work injury programs as their first piece of social insurance legislation. Thus, the analysis of "first adoptions" is *basically* the analysis of work injury programs. It may seem appropriate to limit the analysis to only those 50 countries that adopted work injury programs. However, I analyzed the first adoption *in general* for two reasons. First, sample size prohibits a separate event history analysis for those 10 countries that adopted sickness or old age programs as their first programs, because the sample of 10 countries is too small. Second and more important, this study focused on all the instances of the first piece of social insurance legislation, whatever the type was, not just on countries that introduced work injury laws as their first legislation. A restricted sample of 50 countries would have excluded some very important nations, including Germany, Belgium, Denmark, Sweden, New Zealand, and Luxembourg.
7. The present study examined 60 countries that were *autonomous in their domestic policies* during the period 1880–1960. Banks's data, however, provide the *independent* states for the period 1815–1973. Accordingly, the number of independent states in his count is less than 50 up to 1900, rather than 60. In order to be consistent with the criteria I adopted in selecting countries, I adjusted Banks's count by adding those countries that were not independent but were autonomous with their domestic policies.
8. Whether *COMLINK* should be thought of as a world polity variable or as a nation characteristic is not clear. This study employed *COMLINK* to measure the degree of a nation's connectedness to the nation-state system following the work by Boli, Ramirez, and Meyer (1985) and Snyder and Kick (1979). Moreover, it differs from Wallerstein's conception of structural positions (or locations) of nations in the world system in that *COMLINK* captures a nation's interaction or bonds to the system that may change

from year to year. In Wallerstein's treatment, the nations are classified into three zones that are more or less fixed over time. *COMLINK*, however, is a more sensitive measure of interactions between the nation and the system.

9. The earlier inspection of Figures 10.1 and 10.2 suggested that the expansion of a social insurance program involved three phases of development. Also, the role of the ILO in the promotion of social insurance was greatly broadened in the 1930s due to an increased need of providing technical information on various types of social insurance approaches. For example, its capacity was enlarged by appointing 102 experts from a total of 27 countries in 1930 from the former committee composed of 15 experts. This can be interpreted as indicating the expansion of the nation-state system or the institutionalization of social insurance legislation as part of national development. Thus, it seemed reasonable to distinguish periods around 1935 at which point the second surge of events was completed and the third began to rise. To construct the second period, I chose the beginning year 1919, when the ILO was established, rather than the year 1906, when the forerunner of the ILO was established in Basel and its first conference was held. The selection of 1906 might have been ideal, but data were missing more in the 1880–1905 than the 1880–1918 period. I therefore used 1919, when the ILO was established, as a dividing point between the first and the second periods.
10. It is possible to use the second or the third period as the baseline. If the second period is used as the baseline period, the effects of the first and third periods would be compared with the rate in the second period. If the third period is used as the baseline, then the effects of the first and the second periods could be determined in relation to the third period. For similar application of this technique, see Hannan and Freeman (1987).

REFERENCES

Aaron, Henry. 1967. "Social Security: International Comparisons." In O. Eskstein (ed.), *Studies in the Economics of Income Maintenance*, pp. 13–49. Washington, D.C.: Brookings Institution.

Alber, Jens. 1981. "Government Response to the Challenge of Unemployment: The Development of Unemployment Insurance in Western Europe." In P. Flora and A. Heidenheimer (eds.), *The Development of Welfare States in Europe and America*, pp. 15–83. New Brunswick, N.J.: Transaction Books.

Banks, Arthur. 1975. *Cross-National Time-Series Data Archive*. Binghamton: State University of New York, Center for Comparative Political Research.

Bergesen, Albert (ed.). 1980. *Studies of the Modern World System*. New York: Academic Press.

Block, F. 1977. "Beyond Corporate Liberalism." *Social Problems* 24:352–61.

1980. "Beyond Relative Autonomy: State Managers as Historical Subjects." In R. Miliband and J. Saville (eds.), *The Socialist Register*, pp. 227–62. London: Merlin.

Boli, John, Francisco Ramirez, and John Meyer. 1985. "Explaining the Origins and Expansion of Mass Education." *Comparative Education Review* 29(2):145–70.

Cameron, David. 1978. "The Expansion of the Public Economy: A Comparative Analysis." *American Political Science Review* 72:1243–61.

Carroll, Glen. 1983. "Dynamic Analysis of Discrete Dependent Variables: A Didactic Essay." *Quality and Quantity* 17:425–60.

Chase-Dunn, Christopher. 1975. "Effects of International Economic Dependence on Development and Inequality: A Cross-National Study." *American Sociological Review* 40:720–38.

Chase-Dunn, Christopher, and Richard Rubinson. 1971. "Toward a Structural Perspective on the World System." *Politics and Society* 7(4):453–76.

Cipolla, Carlo. 1975. *The Economic History of World Population.* Baltimore, Md.: Penguin.

Collier, David, and Richard Messick. 1975. "Prerequisites Versus Diffusion: Testing Alternative Explanations of Social Security Adoption." *American Political Science Review* 69:1299–1315.

Cutright, Phillips. 1965. "Political Structure, Economic Development and National Social Security Programs." *American Journal of Sociology* 70:537–50.

Esping-Anderson, Gøsta. 1989. "The Three Political Economies of the Welfare State." *Canadian Review of Sociology and Anthropology* 26(1):10–36.

Flora, Peter, and Jens Alber. 1981. "Modernization, Democratization, and the Development of Welfare States in Western Europe." In P. Flora and A. Heidenheimer (eds.), *The Development of Welfare States in Europe and America*, pp. 37–80. New Brunswick, N.J.: Transaction.

Flora, Peter, et al. 1983–7. *State, Economy, and Society in Western Europe, 1815–1975.* 2 Vols. Germany: Campus.

Hage, Jerald, and Robert Hanneman. 1980. "The Growth of the Welfare State in Britain, France, Germany, and Italy: A Comparison of Three Paradigms." *Comparative Sociological Research* 3:45–70.

Hannan, Michael, and John Freeman. 1987. "The Ecology of Organizational Founding: American Labor Unions." *American Journal of Sociology* 92(4):910–43.

Heclo, Hugh. 1974. *Modern Social Politics in Britain and Sweden.* New Haven, Conn.: Yale University Press.

Hicks, Alexander, Duane Swank, and Martin Ambuhl. 1989. "Welfare Expansion Revisited: Policy Routines and Their Mediation by Party, Class and Crisis, 1957–1982." *European Journal of Political Research* 17:401–30.

Isaac, Larry, and William Kelly. 1981. "Racial Insurgency, the State, and Welfare Expansion: Local and National Level Evidence from the Postwar United States." *American Journal of Sociology* 86:1348–86.

International Labor Office. 1906. *Bulletin of the International Labor Office. Vol. 1, 1906.* Basel: ILO.

1951. *Yearbook of Labor Statistics, 1949–50.* Geneva: ILO.

1984. *Yearbook of Labor Statistics, 1984.* Geneva: ILO.

Katzenstein, Peter. 1984. *Small States in World Markets: Industrial Policy in Europe.* Ithaca, N.Y.: Cornell University Press.

Kerr, Clark, John. Dunlop, Frederick Harbison, and Charles Myers. 1964. *Industrialism and Industrial Man.* New York: Oxford University Press.

Korpi, Walter. 1978. *The Working Class in Welfare Capitalism.* London: Routledge & Kegan Paul.

1989. "Power, Politics, and State Autonomy in the Development of Social Citizenship: Social Rights During Sickness in 18 OECD Countries Since 1930." *American Sociological Review* 54:309–28.

Korpi, Walter, and Michael Shalev. 1980. "Strikes, Power and Politics in the

Western Nations, 1900–1976." *Political Power and Social Theory* 1:301–34.

Krasner, Stephen D. (ed.). 1983. *International Regimes*. Ithaca, N.Y.: Cornell University Press.

Kratochwil, Friedrich, and John Gerard Ruggie. 1986. "International Organization: A State of the Art on the Art of the State." *International Organization* 40:753–75.

Kuhnle, Stein. 1981. "The Growth of Social Insurance Programs in Scandinavia: Outside Influences and Internal Forces." In P. Flora and A. Heidenheimer (eds.), *The Development of Welfare States in Europe and America*, pp. 37–80. New Brunswick: Transaction.

Kuznets, Simon. 1957. *Quantitative Aspects of the Economic Growth of Nations*. Economic Growth of Nations. Vol. 5, no. 4. Cambridge, Mass.: Harvard University Press.

1971. *Economic Growth of Nations*. Cambridge, Mass.: Harvard University Press.

Laroque, Pierre. 1969. "The International Labor Organization of Social Security." *International Social Security Review* 20(4):469–79.

Lund, Michael. 1972. *Comparing the Social Politics of Nations: A Report on Issues, Methods, and Resources*. Chicago: Center for the Study of Welfare Policy, University of Chicago.

Malloy, James. 1979. *The Politics of Social Security in Brazil*. Pittsburgh: University of Pittsburgh Press.

Meyer, John. 1987. "The World Polity and the Authority of the Nation-State." In G. M. Thomas, J. W. Meyer, F. O. Ramirez, and J. Boli (eds.), *Institutional Structure: Constituting State, Society, and the Individual*, pp. 00–00. Newsbury Park, Calif.: Sage.

Meyer, John, and Brian Rowan. 1977. "Institutionalized Organizations: Formal Structure as Myth and Ceremony." *American Journal of Sociology* 83:340–63.

Meyer, John, Francisco Ramires, Richard Rubinson, and John Boli-Bennett. 1976. "The World Educational Revolution, 1950–1970." Paper presented at the annual meeting of the American Sociological Association, August.

Mishra, Ramesh. 1977. *Society and Social Policy: Theoretical Perspectives on Welfare*. London: Macmillian Press.

Orloff, Ann, and Theda Skocpol. 1984. "Why Not Equal Protection? Explaining the Politics of Public Social Spending in Britain, 1900–1911, and the US, 1880–1920." *American Sociological Review* 49:726–51.

Pampel, Fred, and John Williamson. 1988. "Welfare Spending in Advanced Industrial Democracies, 1950–1980." *American Journal of Sociology* 93(6):1424–56.

Pryor, Fredric. 1968. *Public Expenditures in Communist and Capitalist Nations*. Homewood, Ill.: Irwin.

Quadagno, Jill. 1987. *Theories of the Welfare States*. Annual Review of Sociology, Vol. 13, W. R. Scott, and J. F. Short, Jr. (eds.). Palo Alto, Calif.: Annual Reviews.

Ramirez, Francisco, and John Boli. 1987. "The Political Construction of Mass Schooling: European Origins and Worldwide Institutionalization." *Sociology of Education* 60:2–17.

Rimlinger, Gaston. 1971. *Welfare Policy and Industrialization in Europe, America, and Russia*. New York: Wiley.

1966. "Comparative Studies of Social Security." *Bulletin of the International Social Security Association* 7–8:242–68.

Schneider, Saundra. 1982. "The Sequential Development of Social Programs in Eighteen Welfare States." *Comparative Social Research* 5:195–219.

Shalev, Michael. 1983. *The Social Democratic Model and Beyond: Two Generations of Comparative Research on the Welfare State.* Comparative Social Research, Vol. 6. Greenwich, Conn.: JAI.

Skocpol, Theda, and Edwin Amenta. 1986. "States and Social Policies." *Annual Review of Sociology* 12:131–57.

Snyder, David, and Edward Kick. 1979. "Structural Position in the World System and Economic Growth, 1955–1970: A Multiple-Network Analysis of Transnational Interactions." *American Journal of Sociology* 84(5):1096–1126.

Spalding, Rose. 1980. "Welfare Policymaking: Theoretical Implications of a Mexican Case Study." *Comparative Politics* 12:419–38.

Strang, David. 1990. "From Dependency to Sovereignty: An Event History Analysis of Decolonization, 1870–1987." *American Sociological Review* 55(6):846–60.

Thomas, George, and John Meyer. 1984. "The Expansion of the State." *Annual Review of Sociology* 10:461–82.

Tuma, Nancy. 1980. Invoking Rate. Menlo Park, Calif.: SRI International.

U.S. Department of Health and Human Service. 1984. *Social Security Programs Throughout the World, 1983.* Washington, D.C.: U.S. Government Printing Office.

Usui, Chikako. 1988. "The Origin and the Development of Modern Welfare States: A Study of the Societal Forces and World Influences on the Adoption of Social Insurance Policies Among 63 Countries, 1880–1976. Ph.D. diss., Stanford, Calif.: Stanford University.

Uusitalo, Hannu. 1984. "Comparative Research on the Development of the Welfare State: the State of the Art." *European Journal of Political Research* 12(4):403–23.

Wallerstein, Immanuel. 1974. *The Modern World-System.* New York: Academic Press.

Wilensky, Harold. 1975. *Welfare State and Equality.* Berkeley: University of California Press.

11

British and French political institutions and the patterning of decolonization

DAVID STRANG

While the literature on twentieth-century decolonization occasionally ventures into comparison across empires (Emerson 1960; Smith 1978; von Albertini 1982; and Holland 1985), there is little quantitative research into the processes producing imperial collapse. This chapter presents an event history analysis of the precipitants of decolonization in the two major Western empires: the British and the French. It contrasts the way British and French political institutions shaped the pattern of imperial breakdown.

Elsewhere, I argue that metropolitan political institutions organized around expanded forms of citizenship promote decolonization (Strang 1990, 1991a, 1992). The rise of the nation-state produces a tension between the political theories and structures of the metropolis (where rights are expanded) and the colony (where they are not). New models of the state diffuse to the colonies and inform peripheral nation building. And metropolitan powers organized as nation-states can neither accommodate nor easily repress such nationalisms. They are unwilling to extend full membership to the colonized and find it unappetizing to crush movements constructed around Western models.

Expanded incorporation may be conceived in the terms Marshall (1964) made famous: legal, political, and social citizenship. Of the three, disparities in legal status are the least obviously pertinent to decolonization. Disputes between "natives" were often referred to indigenous law, but this mainly reflected the administrative weakness of the colonial state. It was the growing gulf between the political and social citizenship of Europeans and colonized peoples that produced distinctive tensions.

Broadened political rights within the metropolitan population sharply differentiated imperial center and colonial possession in a new way.

In dynastic systems, all populations were subjects of the crown, and peripheral elites could rise to the imperial center. The political incorporation of the middle and working classes in the metropolis and the spread of theories of popular sovereignty helped stimulate political mobilization within colonial dependencies. With full incorporation into the metropolis blocked, colonized peoples sought sovereignty and full citizenship within their own communities.

The growth of social citizenship within the metropolis had a similar meaning and consequence. The notion of social citizenship provides a platform on which peripheral nationalists could build; national liberation was seen as replacing exploitative colonial arrangements with a national state dedicated to the social and economic needs of the people. And metropolitan politicians and populations were unwilling to enlarge the social definition of national welfare to include the colonized.[1]

Previous work examines the effects of metropolitan institutions on decolonization across a broad range of settings. An event history analysis of twentieth-century decolonization (Strang 1990) shows that the rate of decolonization increases with the breadth of metropolitan suffrage. Qualitative examination of the major Western empires in both the first and second waves of decolonization (Strang 1992) finds that metropoles organized around expanded citizenship witnessed relatively rapid decolonization grounded in internal tensions, while metropoles organized around limited forms of incorporation faced slower decolonization grounded in external pressures.

This chapter takes a closer look at British and French decolonization. One limitation of a broadly comparative approach (i.e., the analysis of dependencies in many empires) is that political systems must be located along a few simple metrics. On a general level, French and British citizenship expanded at about the same time. If anything, the radical republican tradition of France suggests that it should have experienced more rapid decolonization than should Britain, which retained the symbols of dynastic empire in a constitutional monarchy. Yet Britain is generally seen as having weathered decolonization more quickly and easily than France (see Smith 1978). In particular, France fought wars to retain Indochina and Algeria while Britain negotiated Indian independence.

Examined more closely, the two political systems furnish a strong contrast. France provides the preeminent instance of a centralized bureaucracy insulated from society. In Birnbaum and Badie's words, "the French state has steadily expanded its control over civil society and constituted itself as an autonomous power, an immense and hermetic administrative machine capable of dominating all peripheral power centers" (1983, p. 105). Formally, the French state is a unitary republic whose departments are administrative conveniences, not constituent elements. While theoretically the instrument of the popular will, the French state is better described as having constructed the French people (Weber 1976).

Great Britain has much less that one can describe as a "state," if by the term we mean an organization set apart from and directing civil society. Core British political traditions have to do with the autonomy and rights of the individual, seen as prior to and constitutive of the state. The core British political institution is Parliament, a representative assembly. In practice, British government is decentralized and open to influence from civil society.

The common rule that imperial structures mirror metropolitan institutions holds true for both France and Britain. French colonial administration was centralized and bureaucratic, with little attention paid to local diversity. The British constructed a differentiated and decentralized empire, with self-governing institutions in the settler Dominions and indirect rule in most of Africa.

Similarly, the way the British and the French made sense of their imperial activity was linked to each society's political traditions. The logic of French empire was assimilation, the drive culturally to Gallicize the colonized and politically to enlarge France. This aim fit the bureaucratic and centralized structure of the French state, which was capable of elaborating to rule a larger territory and population. And the French concept of a nation defined by will rather than ancestry could be extended to Asians and Africans in a way that the ancient rights of Englishmen could not.

By contrast, Britain's empire was legitimated as the white man's burden: schooling non-Western peoples in British traditions. It aspired to the construction of autonomous replicas of the United Kingdom, where a family resemblance and common ties would sustain political association. These aims fit with Britain's liberal tradition of individual rights and with its conservative tradition of a political community grounded in common descent and culture. And the cultivation of local autonomy limited the administrative strain of empire.

Contrasts in imperial aims suggest two hypotheses:

Hypothesis 1: Political incorporation into the metropolis should be attained more rapidly by French colonies than by British colonies.
Hypothesis 2: Political independence should be attained more rapidly by British colonies than by French colonies.

British and French political institutions should also mediate the impact of internal and external factors differently. The localized structure of the British empire should expand the impact of dependency characteristics on decolonization. In particular, British political traditions should enhance the role of colonial assemblies and metropolitan settlers. In British eyes, the former could legitimately claim national authority, while the latter could claim the rights of Englishmen.

The same governmental traditions should diminish the impact of external factors on decolonization. The absence of a unified institutional structure reduced opportunities for imitation and cooperation among British dependencies. And Britain's stated aim to govern until the individual dependency was "ready" to stand on its own should reduce the impact of contextual effects (such as the global delegitimation of imperialism after 1960).

The French empire should display the opposite tendency. France's administrative centralization promoted uniformity of outcomes across its dependencies. In seeking systemic solutions to political demands, the French were driven to grant the same rights and opportunities to all dependencies, even those where demands were less strongly voiced. For example, all sub-Saharan colonies had the same institutional roles in the abortive French Union and French Community. Given this uniformity, French decolonization should exhibit reduced sensitivity to variations across dependencies in scale, indigenous political traditions, and economic development.

In contrast, French decolonization should be strongly affected by the larger imperial and world systemic context. By seeking administrative standardization, the French facilitated imitation and cooperation within the French empire. And by aiming at a coherent response to colonial pressures, the French increased the role that systemic conditions might play in decolonization. In short:

Hypothesis 3: British decolonization should be more strongly affected by colonial characteristics than should French decolonization.
Hypothesis 4: French decolonization should be more strongly affected by the imperial and global context than should British decolonization.

FUNDAMENTAL DEFINITIONS

The study of decolonization requires explicit a conceptual scheme distinguishing colonial dependencies, outlying metropolitan territories, and sovereign states. The scheme employed in this chapter is elaborated at length elsewhere (Strang 1991b) and is briefly summarized here.

Dependency is defined as a formal relationship of ownership or subordination tying one polity to another. It includes both "crown colony" rule, where the imperial power directly administers a territory as its possession, and various forms of partial sovereignty such as the protectorate. "Decolonization" is defined as the acquisition of recognized sovereignty within the Western state system. Recognition by the imperial power is the operational criterion, unless metropolitan recognition has no meaning or is widely opposed within the international community. In the analysis of the twentieth-century empires of Britain and France, Algeria is the one case to which the latter restriction was applied. It is coded as a French dependency from 1879 to 1962, despite France's internal definition of Algeria as an integral part of the metropolitan state (a political definition which did not change the legal, political, or welfare status of the mass of the Algerian population).

Movement from dependency to sovereignty can take one of three forms. The dependency may become sovereign as a new independent state; it may be fully incorporated as an integral part of the national territory; or it may be integrated into some other state. The third possible form of decolonization is not of central interest here, since it is relatively unaffected by metropolitan policy. The first two are of interest and should be kept theoretically and analytically distinct.

This paper examines the period 1870 to 1987. The data examined here are taken from a larger project on Western imperialism from 1500 to the present. The basic sources for data on the creation, dissolution, and decolonization of British and French dependencies are Henige (1970) and Banks (1987). Research into secondary materials was used to supplement these sources.

Modeling framework

Event history analysis provides an appropriate methodology for the quantitative analysis of decolonization, which involves an event (movement from dependency to sovereignty) that may occur at any time. Within this framework, it is conventional to consider the process in terms of the *instantaneous transition rate* at which the event occurs. Event history methods include nonparametric analyses examining how the rate varies with time and parametric analyses that model the impact of measured covariates. Both forms of analysis are useful here. Nonparametric analyses explore differences in the larger temporal pattern of British and French decolonization. Parametric analyses gauge the differential impact of specific conditions on British and French decolonization.

NONPARAMETRIC ANALYSES

As argued, a primary distinction between British and French colonial traditions has to do with the disparate aims of association and assimilation. These alternative goals were to some degree realized in the actual pattern of imperial breakdown.

Table 11.1. ***Decolonization counts by empire, 1870-1987***

	France	Great Britain
Cases of metropolitan incorporation	5	0
Cases of nonmetropolitan incorporation	1	2
Cases of independence	26	61
Transition rate to independence	0.0152	0.0142
Dependencies remaining in 1987	10	5

Table 11.1 gives the number of decolonization events occurring within each empire during the 1870 to 1987 period. Great Britain, which boasted the largest Western overseas empire, saw 63 dependencies decolonize. All but two became new independent states. Newfoundland joined Canada; Weihaiwei (a treaty port leased to the British in 1898) was returned to China. No British colonies became integral parts of the United Kingdom. By contrast, 5 of the 32 French dependencies reaching sovereign status were incorporated into the metropolis. The dependencies involved were the remnants of France's eighteenth-century empire: Guadeloupe, Martinique, French Guinea, Reunion, and Sainte Pierre and Miquelon. These small, culturally Gallicized dependencies were made overseas departments, assuming legal, political, and administrative continuity with continental France. The first four were integrated in 1944, with Sainte Pierre and Miquelon following in 1976.[2]

France was clearly more ready to integrate her colonies into the metropolis than was Britain, which could have assimilated analogous colonies like Bermuda and Saint Croix. But the difference should not be exaggerated. Less than a sixth of all French colonies were integrated into the French nation. While French imperialism was initially legitimated in terms of the assimilation of overseas possessions, the great majority eventually became new independent states.

The transition rate to independence given in Table 11.1 indicates that French colonies became independent more rapidly than did British colonies. But this difference is small and statistically insignificant. It may also be misleading, since it does not control for compositional differences across the two empires. As a first approximation, however, it would appear that independence occurred at roughly the same rate in the British and French empires.

Similarity in the overall rate of decolonization may hide differences in the patterning of event times. To gauge such patterns, Figures 11.1 and 11.2 plot the integrated hazard of decolonization in the British and French empires. The transition rate equals the slope of the graph in

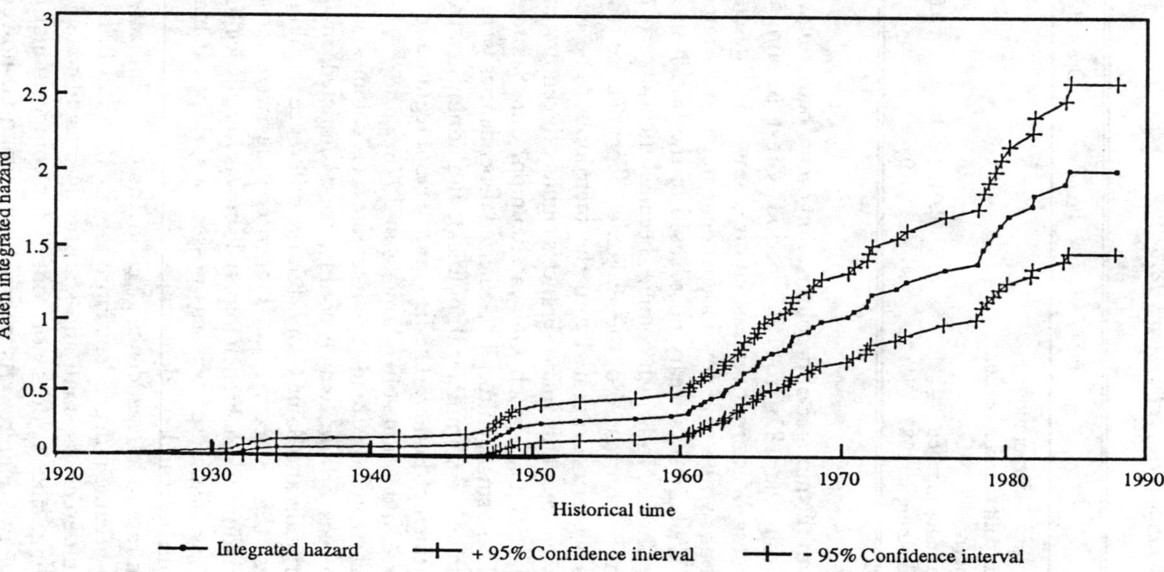

Figure 11-1. British decolonization

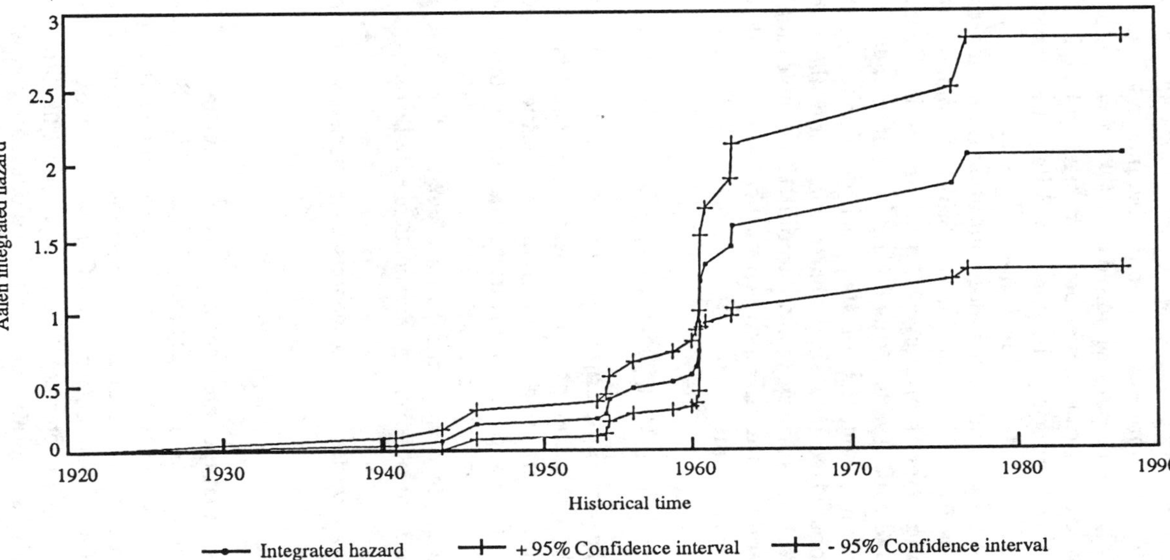

Figure 11.2. French decolonization

these figures. The historical sequences of decolonization are broadly similar across the two empires. No colonies became independent until after World War I. Both empires witnessed relatively slow decolonization between the world wars (the curves are quite flat) and rapid rates of decolonization after World War II. For both Britain and France, most decolonization occurred during the 1960s.

The pattern of British and French decolonization differs most in how concentrated it is over time. The rate of British decolonization held steady at a high level for about 20 years, from African independence in the late 1950s and early 1960s through Caribbean independence in the late 1970s. By comparison, half of all French decolonization through independence took place in a single burst. Note how the integrated hazard in Figure 11.2 is nearly vertical around 1960, indicating a very rapid transition rate. Thirteen French dependencies became independent during that one year alone.

PARAMETRIC ANALYSES

In addition to the kind of descriptive portraits of decolonization shown in Figures 11.1 and 11.2, event history methods permit regression-like analysis of conditions affecting the underlying stochastic process. There are too few events to support multivariate analyses of the process of metropolitan incorporation – in fact, the process is utterly unidentified in the British case. But it is practical to ask what factors facilitated or slowed the attainment of sovereign independence by British and French colonies.

I assume the rate varies with exogenous characteristics but not with time per se:

$$r_{jk}(t) = exp(B\ X_t).$$

The assumption that the rate does not vary as a function of historical time may seem surprising, given Figures 11.1 and 11.2. But prior work on decolonization suggests that temporal variation in the covariates examined here are sufficient to capture the observed trend. The inclusion of explicit time dependencies (via a Gompertz or Cox formulation) has little effect on parameter coefficients and model fit (Strang 1990). Exploratory analyses of British and French colonies are consistent with this conclusion.

Independent variables

This chapter applies the models presented in Strang (1990), with one exception. Ironically, a direct focus on the effects of British and French metropolitan institutions is not easily approached by measuring features of each political system. Many institutional characteristics are time invariant and thus serve the same function as a binary variable for empire. The strategy employed here is to treat metropolitan political institutions as contextual variables whose effects are revealed through differences in causal factors at the dependency and system level.

Two dependency characteristics that should reflect British traditions of local autonomy are the presence of representative institutions and the scale of metropolitan settlement. "Representative institutions" is coded as a binary variable equaling one when a colonial legislature is elected on a broad suffrage (taken from Cook and Paxton 1979; and annual volumes of the *Statesman's Yearbook*). Metropolitan settlement forms two binary variables. "Settler minority" equals one when more than 5 percent but less than 50 percent of the dependency's population are Europeans or their descendants, while "settler majority" equals one when more than half of the dependency's population are settlers. Data were taken from Barrett (1982) and the *Statesman's Yearbook*.

Additional dependency characteristics include dependency population and foreign trade per capita. Both measures are logged to reduce skewness and are taken from the *Statesman's Yearbook*. In some analyses I also employ a measure of urbanization, for which data are only available in the post–World War II period.

Diffusion processes provide one important index of sensitivity to the larger global context. Diffusion is modeled by using the number of prior cases of decolonization occurring within some relevant category as covariates. (This strategy's motivation is discussed in Strang 1991c.) Empire (British or French) and geographic region (North Africa and the Middle East, sub-Saharan Africa, the Americas, Asia, or the Pacific) are examined as two channels of diffusion. The variable "regional diffusion" equals the amount of number of prior decolonization events occurring within the dependency's region, while "imperial diffusion" counts the number of prior events within the empire.

Two binary variables for historical period are examined. "U.S. hegemony" equals one from 1945 to 1967, the period when the United States was the unchallenged economic power (Wallerstein 1983). Theorists of the world economy have argued that the presence of a hegemonic power should loosen political bonds between core and periphery by decreasing the level of competition within the core (Chase-Dunn and Rubinson 1979). "UN declaration" equals one after the United Nation's 1960 "Declaration on the Granting of Independence to Colonial Countries and Peoples." This declaration reflects the delegitimation of imperialism within global political discourse.

Descriptive statistics for all exogenous variables are given in Table

Table 11.2. *Descriptive statistics: colonial dependencies, 1870-1987*

Variable	France Mean	France S.D.	Great Britain Mean	Great Britain S.D.
Dependency characteristics				
Population	6.07	2.13	5.40	2.03
Trade	2.65	3.03	4.30	1.61
Settler minority	0.18	0.38	0.15	0.36
Settler majority	0.10	0.30	0.08	0.28
Representation	0.29	0.45	0.33	0.47
Systemic characteristics				
U.S. hegemony	0.56	0.49	0.54	0.47
U.N. declaration	0.25	0.43	0.42	0.49
Diffusion variables				
Empire	9.52	10.29	16.52	15.80
Region	5.30	7.01	7.97	8.21

11.2. Variables are measured repeatedly over time, generally at intervals of 10 years or less, and are assumed constant between observations. Systemic and diffusion variables are measured continuously. I should note that there are substantial missing data for variables capturing dependency: population, trade, and metropolitan settlement. Twenty-three percent of British and 20 percent of French dependency years cannot be analyzed due to missing observations. This loss of data occurs mainly for the smaller and less economically developed dependencies, as well as for dependencies at earlier points in time. The ability of the study to make inferences about these kinds of dependencies and contexts is diminished as a result.

Results

Table 11.3 presents results from multivariate analyses of the transition from colonial dependency to sovereign state. The first equation examines the French empire in isolation, while the second examines the British. Estimates may be interpreted as multipliers of the rate for an infinitesimal change in the covariate, with positive coefficients indicating a faster rate of decolonization.

A first difference between the two equations is the substantially larger constant term in the analysis of British dependencies. This difference is

Table 11.3. ***Maximum likelihood estimates for transitions to independence, 1870-1987***

	French dependencies	British dependencies
β_0	-20.80**	-10.22**
Dependency effects		
Population	1.67**	0.48**
Trade	-0.08	-0.12
Settler minority	-2.57*	-0.69
Settler majority	-0.80	1.39**
Representation	0.54	0.78**
Diffusion effects		
Empire	0.02	-0.08
Region	0.16**	-0.007
Systemic effects		
U.S. hegemony	2.57**	1.53**
U.N. declaration	3.42**	1.47**
χ^2	153.4	185.7
Observed events	25	56

*$p < .05$; **$p < .01$

statistically significant.[3] Once compositional differences in dependency and systemic conditions are taken into account, it appears that independence came more rapidly to British colonies than to French colonies. Hypothesis 2 is thus supported.

Table 11.3 provides some evidence that British decolonization works through the acquisition of local autonomy and citizenship rights, while French decolonization does not. The rate of British decolonization is significantly higher where dependencies have representative political institutions and where metropolitan settlers form a majority of the population. French decolonization is unrelated to either of these factors. The difference in coefficients is not significant for either variable, primarily because the estimates for French colonies are quite unstable.

But Hypothesis 3 does not seem borne out in the large. More populous dependencies become independent faster in both empires, with French colonies showing a significantly larger impact of population size. French decolonization is slowed by the presence of a substantial settler minority, while British decolonization is not.[4] Dependency urbanization bears no relation to British or French decolonization (analyses not reported). Only dependency trade has a marginally stronger effect for British dependencies than for French dependencies.

While differences in sensitivity to dependency characteristics do not vary consistently across empires, differences in sensitivity to the larger global context are substantial and in the expected direction. Most important, the independence of French colonies exhibits strong signs of spatial diffusion, while British colonies are unaffected by the decolonization of other dependencies within the region. The difference between these coefficients is statistically significant.[5]

The best example of French regional diffusion is the rapid burst of decolonization occurring in 1960. All 13 French colonies attaining sovereignty in that year were African. While the colonies of French West and Equatorial Africa became independent in such quick succession that their independence might be supposed to have been centrally legislated, each colony voted its independence by plebiscite. These dependencies varied in levels of economic development and had very different kinds of economic ties to France in 1960 (Berg 1960). But the identical institutional position of the French African colonies made for rapid diffusion.

Both French and British decolonization are significantly accelerated by U.S. hegemony and the delegitimation of imperialism in global discourse (as signaled by the United Nations' 1960 declaration). The impact on French colonies is larger, though. The rate of decolonization in French dependencies is multiplied by 13 during the period of U.S. hegemony and by 30 after the United Nations' declaration; for Britain the comparable multipliers are 4.6 and 4.3.

More rapid French decolonization during the period of U.S. hegemony casts doubt on Tony Smith's (1978) analysis of the impact of international political alliances on decolonization. Smith argues that postwar Britain was willing to accept colonial independence because its status as a great power was maintained through a close relationship to the United States, while France clung to her empire as a symbol of former greatness. This notion seems undermined by the finding that French decolonization was accelerated more during the period of U.S. global dominance than was British decolonization. It is possible that British linkages to the United States helped hold the empire together, while France's desire to steer an independent course led to faster disintegration.

DISCUSSION

Analysis of British and French decolonization suggests some strong contrasts. French decolonization sometimes resulted in metropolitan incorporation, was concentrated in a short period of time, was relatively slow once dependency and systemic variables are taken into account, and was strongly linked to larger contextual factors. British decolonization never resulted in incorporation, occurred at a steady pace over three decades, was relatively rapid given dependency composition, and was strongly linked to local grants of autonomy.

These differences make sense in terms of the contextual effects of metropolitan institutions. The centralized French state sought to assimilate colonial dependencies and resisted colonial independence, while the decentralized British polity did the opposite. The French drive for colonial uniformity created the basis for explosions of independence, as each colony gained the same institutional opportunities at the same time. Britain's makeshift empire made common responses to global conditions and imitation of prior decolonization unlikely. Its traditions of self-government provided a more local route to independence.

While differences across the British and French empires are substantial, it should also be noted that they are far from overwhelming. The French goal of assimilation was seldom realized, and colonial demands generally led to independence in both French and British colonies. French decolonization was not unrelated to dependency characteristics, as it would be if Gallic administrative standardization was entirely successful. And the rate of decolonization in British colonies was significantly affected by global conditions like U.S. hegemony and the growing dominance of an anticolonial discourse.

I would suggest two factors that attenuate the distinctiveness of national decolonization patterns. The first is the one-sidedness of any Eurocentric explanation of imperial outcomes. It is well to recall that the motive force behind decolonization was fundamentally located in the action of indigenous populations, not metropolitan states. While I have emphasized the way metropolitan political models and institutions helped to shape colonial demands, indigenous peoples and elites were empowered by more than the ideas, opportunities, and concessions offered by imperial powers. They drew on their own political traditions and social organization, as well as on the successes of national independence movements elsewhere. For these reasons, French centralization was unable to stamp out local differences, and British decentralization was unable to isolate colonial experiences from each other.

It is also important to recall the fundamental similarity of British and French political institutions: their organization around expanded forms of metropolitan citizenship. In a political system grounded in popular sovereignty, assimilation requires a real sharing of political and economic power. For example, French incorporation of the *colonies anciens* involved not only the extension of France's legal code and administrative arrangements, but also the extension of French electoral and welfare rights. This was not problematic for a few small island territories; but to do the same for all French colonies was to extend full political and economic rights to a population larger than France itself.

As a result, French recipes for union fell far short of full political and social equality for the colonized (Marshall 1973). Under these conditions indigenous elites abandoned their early willingness to assimilate (von Albertini 1982), and the French state was forced to substitute local autonomy for full metropolitan participation. Confronted with the real meaning of assimilation into a polity grounded in citizenship, France was led to reinvent the British policy of association.

The results of decolonization

This chapter has emphasized the effects of metropolitan institutions on British and French decolonization, with an eye to both their distinctive effects and their underlying similarities. It may be useful to go a step further and consider the reverse process. How did massive decolonization affect British and French political institutions?

The loss of overseas empire fundamentally altered the political landscape in both countries. As the foci of huge empires, Britain and France were the global superpowers of their day. With massive decolonization, Britain and France were reduced to second-rate powers and forced to turn inward. This inward turn may have facilitated the further expansion of metropolitan political, social, and especially welfare rights.

The argument is straightforward at the level of available resources. In the aggregate, British and French colonies were run at a net loss, costing more to administer than they provided in additional tax revenue (Clark 1936). Further, France and Britain had devoted considerable resources to maintaining a global military capability that not only defended the empire but projected power beyond it. This capability was unnecessary and impractical after decolonization. Imperial breakdown thus freed resources for domestic programs.

Work in international political economy suggests why welfare programs might be especially likely to capture social resources in postimperial societies. Katzenstein (1985) argues that high levels of openness to world markets produces determined attempts to limit class conflict, with large-scale welfare systems as one by-product. Cameron (1978) argues that trade dependence heightens industrial concentration, which in turn facilitates centralized labor federations, corporatist bargaining, and high levels of welfare-related public expenditure. And Evans (1985) suggests that transnational capitalists press for a domestically passive state;

conversely, the loss of empire (and opportunities for capital export) should permit a more active, interventionist state policy.

Decolonization brought the political economy of France and Britain closer to that of the Scandanavian, Alpine, or Benelux countries. Though colonial dependencies were seldom the critical targets of foreign trade and investment, the British and French empires represented politically controllable trading systems that could buffer the metropolis against world markets. The loss of empire may have increased the need and opportunity for capital and labor to make social peace at home. As a working hypothesis, I would thus suggest not only that the expansion of metropolitan citizenship promotes decolonization, but that decolonization promotes the further expansion of metropolitan citizenship.

CONCLUSIONS

This chapter has built on the traditional opposition of British association and French assimilation, stressing the way metropolitan institutions structure colonial opportunities. The contrast between British and French political institutions helps account for important differences in their decolonization experiences. British traditions of individual rights and administrative localism blocked colonial assimilation and made the loss of empire a steady, incremental process. French centralization permitted some assimilation and helped make decolonization an explosive affair more sensitive to the larger imperial, regional, and global context. Attention to differences in metropolitan political institutions complements an understanding of the commonalities in the British and French colonial experience.

NOTES

1. The politics of immigration provides useful insights here. Immigration from colony to metropolis was generally restricted. And British citizenship has recently been reorganized on a two-tier system to block immigration from existing and prior colonies. Resident aliens (who form a much smaller and better-off group than colonized populations) generally enjoy an intermediate form of citizenship including social but not ultimate political rights (Brubaker 1989; Soysal in press). Even this status may be fragile, however, given growing nativist opposition.
2. Sainte Pierre and Miquelon is one of the few dependencies to be recolonized after attaining sovereign status. In 1985, the population of Sainte Pierre and Miquelon voted to return to dependent status to avoid the burdensome taxes imposed on them as full participants in the French state. See Strang (1991b) for a discussion of the infrequency of this kind of event.
3. The significance of differences in coefficients across equations is determined through analyses simultaneously examining all dependencies in a model

including a full set of interactions by empire. Significant differences are those where the interaction term is statistically significant.

4. Settler minorities (e.g., in Algeria and Southern Rhodesia) fought decolonization to protect their privileged status within the colonial framework.
5. Diffusion within the empire seems unimportant in Table 11.3. This occurs because these analyses examine only one empire at a time, which means that intraimperial diffusion exhibits temporal but not cross-sectional variation. Analyses examining decolonization across multiple empires consistently show effects of intraimperial diffusion (Strang 1990, 1991a).

REFERENCES

Banks, Arthur S. (ed.) 1987. *Political Handbook of the World: 1987.* Binghamton, N.Y.: CSA Publications.

Barrett, David B. (ed.) 1982. *World Christian Encyclopedia.* Oxford University Press.

Berg, Elliot J. 1960. "The Economic Basis of Political Choice in French West Africa." *American Political Science Review* 55:391–405.

Birnbaum, Pierre, and Badie, P. 1983. *The Sociology of the State.* Chicago: University of Chicago Press.

Brubaker, W. Rogers. 1989. "Membership Without Citizenship: The Economic and Social Rights of Noncitizens." In W. R. Brubaker (ed.), *Immigration and the Politics of Citizenship in Europe and North America*, pp. 145–62. Washington, D.C.: University Press of America.

Cameron, David R. 1978. "The Expansion of the Public Economy: A Comparative Analysis." *American Political Science Review* 72:1243–61.

Chase-Dunn, Christopher, and Richard Rubinson. 1979. "Toward a Structural Perspective on the World-System." *Politics and Society* 7:453–76.

Clark, G. 1936. *The Balance Sheets of Imperialism.* New York: Columbia University Press.

Cook, Chris, and John Paxton. 1979. *Commonwealth Political Facts.* New York: Facts on File.

Emerson, Rupert. 1960. *From Empire to Nation.* Cambridge, Mass.: Harvard University Press.

Evans, Peter B. 1985. "Transnational Linkages and the Economic Role of the State: An Analysis of Developing and Industrialized Nations in the Post–World War II Period." In P. B. Evans, D. Rueschmeyer, and T. Skocpol, *Bringing the State Back In*, pp. 192–226. Cambridge University Press.

Henige, David. 1970. *Colonial Governors.* Madison: University of Wisconsin Press.

Holland, R. F. 1985. *European Decolonization, 1918–1981: An Introductory Survey.* New York: St. Martin's.

Katzenstein, Peter. 1985. *Small States in the World Economy.* Ithaca, N.Y.: Cornell University Press.

Marshall, D. Bruce. 1973. *The French Colonial Myth and Constitution-Making in the Fourth Republic.* New Haven, Conn.: Yale University Press.

Marshall, T. H. 1964. *Class, Citizenship, and Social Development.* Garden City, N.J.: Doubleday.

Smith, Tony. 1978. "A Comparative Study of French and British Decolonization." *Comparative Studies in Society and History* 10:70–102.

Soysal, Yasemin. (In press). "Limits of Citizenship: Post–National Membership in the Contemporary Nation-State System." Chicago: University of Chicago Press.

Statesman's Yearbook. 1864–87. Vols. 1–123. London: St. Martin's.

Strang, David. 1990. "From Dependency to Sovereignty: An Event History Analysis of Decolonization." *American Sociological Review* 55:846–60.

1991a. "Global Patterns of Decolonization, 1500–1987." *International Studies Quarterly* 35:429–54.

1991b. "Anomaly and Commonplace in European Political Expansion: Realist and Institutional Accounts." *International Organization* 45:143–62.

1991c. "Adding Social Structure to Diffusion Models: An Event History Framework." *Sociological Methods and Research* 19:324–53.

1992. "The Inner Incompatibility of Empire and Nation: Popular Sovereignty and Decolonization." *Sociological Perspectives* 35:367–84.

von Albertini, Rudolf. 1982. *Decolonization: The Administration and Future of the Colonies, 1919–1960*. New York: Holmes & Meier.

Wallerstein, Immanuel. 1983. "The Three Instances of Hegemony in the History of the Capitalist World-Economy." *International Journal of Comparative Sociology* 24:100–8.

Weber, Eugen. 1976. *Peasants into Frenchmen*. Stanford, Calif.: Stanford University Press.

PART IV

Boolean analysis

12

Introduction to qualitative comparative analysis

CHARLES C. RAGIN

Qualitative comparative analysis (QCA) is a new analytic technique that uses Boolean algebra to implement principles of comparison used by scholars engaged in the qualitative study of macrosocial phenomena (Ragin 1987). Typically, qualitatively oriented scholars examine only a few cases at a time, but their analyses are both *intensive* – addressing many aspects of cases – and *integrative* – examining how the different parts of a case fit together, both contextually and historically. By formalizing the logic of qualitative analysis, QCA makes it possible to bring the logic and empirical intensity of qualitative approaches to studies that embrace more than a handful of cases – research situations that normally call for the use of variable-oriented, quantitative methods. While quantitative methods are powerful data reducers, they embody strong assumptions about social phenomena that are often at odds with the interests of investigators. QCA avoids these troublesome assumptions. This chapter develops the contrast between qualitative (or case-oriented) research and quantitative (or variable-oriented) research as a way to introduce QCA and then presents a brief overview of the technique.

CASE-ORIENTED AND VARIABLE-ORIENTED RESEARCH STRATEGIES

In the study of macrosocial phenomena there are two basic research strategies, case-oriented and variable-oriented. While many different types of strategies have been described (e.g., Przeworski and Teune 1970;

I thank Mary Driscoll, Alexander Hicks, and Thomas Janoski for their many useful comments on various versions of this chapter.

Bonnell 1980; Skocpol and Sommers 1980; Tilly 1984; Kohn 1989; and Janoski 1991), the continuum represented by the distinction between case-oriented and variable-oriented work forms the primary axis of variation among strategies.

The case-oriented strategy starts with the simple idea that there are distinct and singular entities (major features of countries, world regions, cultures, etc., or their histories) that parallel each other sufficiently to allow comparing and contrasting them (e.g., social revolutions in France, Russia, and China, as in Skocpol 1979, or national revolts in the Philippines, Colombia, and Kenya, as in Walton 1984). The case-oriented strategy sees cases as meaningful but complex configurations of events and structures, and treats cases as singular, whole entities purposefully selected, not as homogeneous observations drawn at random from a pool of equally plausible selections. While comparative analysis of cases is advocated, the analyst must proceed cautiously because much may be lost when cases are decomposed into their component parts.

In variable-oriented work, by contrast, investigators begin research not by asserting the existence of comparable entities, but by positing general dimensions of macrosocial variation. In this approach, empirical instances are viewed as partial, jumbled, or impure representations of underlying theoretical concepts or principles. Instances vary in the degree to which they express these underlying properties, and researchers view their task as one of uncovering basic patterns of covariation among essential properties. Investigators initiate their research by defining the issue to be explored in a way that allows examination of many cases (conceived as substitutable empirical observations). For example, instead of studying three social revolutions, a researcher might proclaim an interest in variation in levels of political unrest. Next, researchers specify relevant causal and outcome variables, matched to theoretical concepts, and then collect information on these variables. From this point on, the language of variables and the relations among them dominates the research process. The resulting understanding of empirical relations is shaped by examining patterns of covariation in the data set, observed and averaged across many cases, not by studying how different features or causes fit together in individual cases.

There are several ways to label these two strategies; each labeling suggests a different but complementary characterization of their contrasting features. The most common way to characterize their difference is to describe the first as qualitative and the second as quantitative. This dichotomy overlaps significantly with the case-oriented versus variable-oriented distinction, but the fit is imperfect. For example, a researcher might use a quantitative method such as time-series analysis to extend his or her knowledge of individual countries and then conduct a case-oriented comparative analysis of these countries using the new knowledge generated by the separate time-series analyses. Alternatively, a researcher might use qualitative historical methods to code features of countries and then analyze covariation among these features using quantitative methods. While a variety of divergent strategies can be identified in this manner (see Janoski 1991), case-oriented work is predominantly qualitative, and variable-oriented work is predominantly quantitative.

A second characterization of the two strategies is to describe the first as a small-*N* strategy and the second as a large-*N* strategy. This characterization is based on recognition of the practical difficulties of careful, case-oriented analysis of many cases. To treat each case as a singular entity and understand it on its own terms is time consuming. Empirical intimacy with cases comes at a very high price. Not only is it exhausting to become well acquainted with many cases; it is difficult to analyze all the relevant similarities and differences that exist among many cases, especially when these similarities and differences are understood as configurations (the usual situation in small-*N* research). One source of the difficulty is the simple fact that the number of comparisons that can be addressed increases geometrically as the number of cases increases (number of comparisons = $[N(N-1)]/2$). The unraveling of the web of similarities and differences that exist among eight cases – a feat attempted by Barrington Moore, Jr., in *Social Origins of Dictatorship and Democracy* (1966) – is cause for great acclaim in comparative sociology. With large *N*s, researchers must use more powerful techniques to reduce data and complexity. The methodological device of variables and correlations offers an attractive reduction strategy.

A third, related characterization of the differences between the two strategies comprehends the first as an intensive strategy and the second as an extensive strategy. Those who do case-oriented work try to provide answers that are intensively correct, embracing one or a small number of observations in a detailed and integrative way; those who do variable-oriented studies try to provide answers that are extensively correct, embracing many observations. The extensively oriented researcher justifies findings by demonstrating their generality in a very direct and visible way; the intensively oriented researcher justifies findings by showing their correctness or completeness relative to other aspects of the case or cases in question. Further, those who do small-*N*, intensive studies sometimes go to great lengths to argue that the few cases examined in an investigation are the best cases to study for a given question, that these cases are the most representative of the general process in question, or that they are the most decisive relative to the theoretical issues at hand (see, e.g., Smelser 1959; Lipset 1963; Moore 1966; Bendix 1978; and Skocpol 1979).

Table 12.1. *Case-oriented and variable-oriented research strategies*

Case-oriented	Variable-oriented
1. View of cases	
Singular entities	Observations of variables
Small number of cases	Large number of cases
Intensive-integrative examination	Extensive analysis of variation
2. Understanding of causation	
Multiple conjunctural causation	Uniform causation
Historical or genetic causation	Structural causation
Temporal order studied directly	Static analysis/inferred temporality
Invariant relationships	Probablistic relationships
3. Explanation	
Integrative accounts	Radically analytic
Interpretive explanations	Parsimonious explanations
Historically specific	Universal/nomothetic
4. Goals	
Knowledge of cases	Theoretically relevant knowledge
Understand patterned diversity	Explain variation
Use/apply/advance theory	Test/adjudicate theories

Table 12.1 offers a summary presentation of the differences between case-oriented and variable-oriented research strategies and elaborates the characterizations just discussed. The two strategies are contrasted with respect to their views of cases, their views of causation, their orientations toward explanation, and their goals. Essentially, this table presents the two approaches as ideal typic methodological strategies. In practice, most researchers combine some elements of the two strategies in the course of their research because good comparative research should balance case-oriented and variable-oriented discourse (see Ragin 1991).

The two approaches differ dramatically in their understanding of cases. In case-oriented work, cases are singular entities selected for their significance, and they are studied intensively and contextually. In variable-oriented work, cases are simply observational units – sites for the measurement of variables. The greater the number of such units, the better, because individual cases are unreliable representations of general, theoretical processes.

Their views of causation also diverge dramatically. In the case-oriented approach, causes are viewed in the context of the case and its history. Temporal order matters, and there is no expectation for a given historical outcome (e.g., democratic institutions) to emerge in the same way in all cases. In fact, the usual argument is that similar outcomes may result from any one of a number of causally equivalent combinations of conditions ("multiple conjunctural causation"; see Ragin 1987, pp. 42–9 for a detailed discussion). In the variable-oriented approach, causation is understood in more structural terms; correlations between variables measured across cases usually signal the operation of causal processes. Because cases are impure representations of theoretical processes, the expectation is that relations between variables are probabilistic and error laden; thus, cases will vary considerably in the degree to which they conform to a theoretically specified causal model. Because of this expectation of imperfect fit, the tendency in variable-oriented work is to construct a single causal model that fits most cases best and to conceive of deviations from that model as error.

Explanations offered by case-oriented and variable-oriented researchers also differ greatly. In case-oriented work, explanations are interpretive accounts of how conditions come together in historically specific ways to produce outcomes in specific cases. Causal conditions are approached inclusively; that is, a causal condition is included in an explanation if it helps makes sense of the evidence. For example, even though the strength of the bourgeoisie is very strongly associated with democratic outcomes in Moore (1966) (suggesting a tidy, univariate causal explanation), this did not stop him from discussing other causal factors (e.g., those relevant to peasants and large landowners) in his explanation of the differences among the eight countries he studied. In variable-oriented work, by contrast, explanations strive toward economy and parsimony. Variables are pitted against each other in a contest to explain variation; the variables that uniquely explain the largest proportion of variation in the dependent variable usually win. This feature of variable-oriented work often gives precedence to generic features of social units in explanatory statements (e.g., economic development as an explanation of democratic political institutions; see Rueschemeyer 1991).

Finally, the two strategies also differ dramatically in their goals. The goals of the first approach are case-oriented – to advance knowledge of cases and to use this knowledge to advance theoretical understanding. As noted, cases are considered singular entities and are purposefully selected for examination and explanation. The goals of the second are to test general theoretical propositions and to adjudicate between competing explanations of general social phenomena by determining which best accounts for observable variation.

BRIDGING THE TWO STRATEGIES WITH QCA

The methodological gulf between intensive, case-oriented research and extensive, variable-oriented research is wide. Case-oriented work typically examines many causal and outcome conditions in different configurations in a limited number of cases, while extensive, variable-oriented work typically examines only a few variables across a large number of cases. To bridge the methodologies of different kinds of comparative social science it is necessary to develop tools that preserve the intensity of the case-oriented approach, especially its attention to combinations and configurations of causes and conditions, when examining many cases. This synthesis combines the strengths of the two approaches and provides as well a way to travel the middle road between generality and complexity (Ragin and Zaret 1983).

Is it possible to be broadly comparative without disaggregating countries into variables and then focusing almost exclusively on relations among variables? Is there a methodology appropriate for analyzing systematic similarities and differences among many cases (i.e., more than a mere handful) that allows preservation of the integrity of cases as separate, meaningful, and interpretable? The basic problem is to implement methods and strategies that bring the logic of intensive, case-oriented research to investigations with large numbers of cases. Relevant features of case-oriented research that should be preserved in large-*N* comparative studies include the following:

1. Attention to cases as configurations. In case-oriented studies the different parts of a case (e.g., different characteristics of a country) are defined in relation to each other – in terms of the whole they form. For example, an aspect of a country's political system (say, its multiparty character) is understood in the context of other features of the country (say, its ethnic diversity). This way of approaching cases is not the same as using one aspect to account for another (e.g., as in using degree of ethnic diversity to explain why a multiparty system exists in some countries but not in others). It is a matter of interpretation: having a multiparty system conveys and signifies different things about a political system depending on whether or not significant ethnic diversity exists.

2. Attention to causal conjunctures. In intensive investigation, explanations of outcomes typically cite combinations of conditions – causal conjunctures and configurations. The classic example of this kind of

explanation is Weber's (1978) explanation of the conditions that combined to give rise to rational capitalism in the West. John Stuart Mill (1967) called this type of causation "chemical" because the outcome, a qualitative change, emerges from a combination of causal agents. In social science attention is directed toward understanding how the different causes combine to produce an outcome.

3. Attention to causal heterogeneity. In small-*N* research a typical finding is that different causes combine in different and sometimes contradictory ways to produce roughly similar outcomes in different settings. Barrington Moore, Jr. (1966), for example, showed how different but comparable conditions combined to produce democratic institutions in Great Britain, France, and the United States. There is no presumption that the same causal factors operate in the same way in all contexts. The effect of any particular causal condition depends on the presence and absence of other conditions, and several different conditions may satisfy a general causal requirement – they may be causally equivalent at a more abstract level. For example, according to Moore (1966) either a civil war or a social revolution may constitute a revolutionary break with the past, one of the conditions necessary for the emergence of democratic institutions in the cases he studied.

4. Attention to deviating cases and concern for invariance. There is no such thing as error in small-*N* studies; investigators account for every case in their attempt to uncover patterned diversity. Cases often deviate from common patterns, but these deviations are identified and addressed as historically specific deviations. Thus, conclusions typically are not stated in probabilistic terms. The goal of unraveling patterned diversity mandates careful attention to cases that deviate from common patterns and gives these cases a special place in the investigation (e.g., as exceptions that challenge general patterns and provide a means for elaborating theory).

5. Attention to qualitative outcomes. Small-*N* studies typically address specific qualitative changes in specific contexts. In some studies the qualitative changes are dramatic (e.g., countries with social revolutions; see Skocpol 1979); in others the changes emerge very slowly through time (e.g., countries experiencing similar historical transformations of certain institutional arrangements; see Bendix 1978). Often the boundaries of an investigation are set by the universe of relevant qualitative changes (e.g., a study of the emergence of national educational systems in Third World countries).

6. Attention to outcome complexity – to diversity across a range of comparable outcomes. Interest in outcome heterogeneity complements interest in causal heterogeneity in case-oriented research. The usual practice in intensive research is to grasp diversity in outcomes across a

range of cases as different configurations of ideal typical outcomes. This way of conceiving outcomes allows examination of qualitative differences among similar cases. For example, while Great Britain, France, and the United States all developed democratic political institutions (the common qualitative outcome), these institutions differ in important ways from one country to the next, both in formal structure and in stability over time (Moore 1966). These differences in political outcomes are related to the different conditions of their historical emergence. In other words, there is interpretable diversity in outcomes within the set of democratic countries studied by Moore. Furthermore, the conditions that are relevant to explaining this within-category diversity are similar to those that distinguish these three countries from those in other categories (communist and fascist).

Most of these features of case-oriented, qualitative research are antistatistical. This is obvious for the fourth feature just listed, which argues that probabilistic statements and error vectors usually are avoided. The other five features are antistatistical in the more limited sense that they structure a research dialogue that is relatively hostile to the world of statistical methodology.

The first feature, for example, argues in essence that no value on any variable (categorical or interval) can be understood in isolation, but only in the context of the values of other relevant variables. This principle wreaks havoc on most analytic procedures because it suggests that apparent similarities (e.g., the category "countries with multiparty political systems") may be epiphenomenal. Most statistical analyses assume that the meaning of a category or a value on a variable is the same across all cases.

The second argues that causes rarely operate in a simple additive fashion; rather, they usually combine and intersect to produce change. In the world of statistical methods, causal combinations are assessed through analysis of statistical interaction. But the most used and most popular statistical techniques are additive, and quantitative researchers are often warned to remove interaction from their models by transforming variables. Interaction models present difficult estimation and specification issues, especially when the number of observations is modest, as is usually the case in macrosocial research.

The third feature extends the idea of causal conjunctures by arguing that different combinations of causes may produce the same outcome. That is – in statistical terminology – there may be several relevant interaction models for a given outcome. The only way to uncover this kind of causal complexity is through techniques that assume maximum causal complexity (i.e., saturated interaction) at the outset and then work backward toward simpler models. Most tests for interaction, however, work from the bottom up – testing second-order interactions, then third-order interactions if second-order interactions were found, and so on. If many causal conditions are relevant, saturated interaction creates an indecipherable cacophony of collinearity. Also, in most cross-national investigations there are simply too few cases to permit starting with saturated interaction and then working backward toward simpler models.

The fifth feature, which asserts an interest in unraveling how causes fit together to generate qualitative change, presents problems for statistical methods to the extent that negative instances of qualitative change are difficult to identify. How large is the set of negative cases of social revolutions? In case-oriented research it is common to study causal similarities and differences among only positive instances. In statistical parlance this amounts to selecting on the dependent variable (a sin to be avoided) or, worse yet, to using a dependent variable with no variation (a practical impossibility).

Finally, the sixth feature suggests that each case's outcome may be a unique configuration – a situation that complicates representing outcomes in terms of variation from a central tendency. While it is possible to measure the departure of a case from an ideal type (see, e.g., Ragin 1983) and use this measure as a variable, the study of configurations of outcomes is in its infancy. Researchers may specify types of outcomes in advance (with the aid of theory) and then assign cases to types, but this is not the same as studying outcomes configurationally. A study of general strikes, for example, might identify eight key qualitative features of strikes and further assert that these eight features should be understood contextually. (For example, "leadership of coal miners" might mean different things depending on whether or not the general strike first took root in that industry.) Allowing this much complexity in outcomes is difficult in statistical models because each case may exhibit a qualitatively unique outcome configuration, yielding as many categories on the dependent variable as there are cases.

While these features of case-oriented research are hostile to the world of statistics, many of them can be overcome if the analysis embraces a sufficient number of cases. It is possible, for example, to test complex interaction models involving multiple conjunctural causation and multiple outcomes if the number of cases is very large. Consider, for example, an analysis involving 5 dichotomous independent variables and 3 dichotomous outcome variables, where the goal is to assess the effects of all logically possible combinations of the independent variables on the different combinations of the outcome variables. There are 32 logically possible combinations of the independent variables and 8 logically possible combinations of the outcome variables. If each cell in the analysis contains 5 cases (a recommended minimum for log-linear analysis), then a minimum of 5 × 32 × 8 = 1,280 cases would be required. (Of course, for each cell to contain a minimum of 5 cases, the average cell might need to embrace 10 or more cases.) This is not a large *N* for researchers who use census data, but for most other social scientists, it is gargantuan. An *N* of "only" 1,280 is rare for social scientists who use macrosocial units. In fact, in comparative social science the typical case-oriented study has an *N* of less than 5; the typical variable-oriented study has an *N* of 50 to 100.

Clearly, the empirical intensity of the case-oriented strategy is difficult to recreate with conventional quantitative methods. The question that is explored in the remainder of this chapter concerns the nature of the analytic operations that recreate basic features of case-oriented research in investigations with larger *N*s (i.e., in studies with more than a handful of cases). Many of the basic features of intensive research can be preserved once it is recognized that the logic of the comparative method used in case-oriented research can be formalized. The formalization I will present uses Boolean algebra, the algebra of logic and sets. Most statistical techniques use linear algebra, a system that is less compatible with the logic of comparative methodology.

Boolean methods of logical comparison represent each case as a combination of causal and outcome conditions. These combinations can be compared with each other and then logically simplified through a bottom-up process of paired comparison. Computer algorithms developed by electrical engineers in the 1950s provide techniques for simplifying this type of data (see e.g., Mendelson 1970; Roth 1975). The data matrix is reformulated as a "truth table" and reduced in a way that parallels the minimization of switching circuits (see Ragin 1987). These minimization procedures mimic case-oriented comparative methods but accomplish the most cognitively demanding task – making multiple comparisons of configurations – through computer algorithms (see Drass and Ragin 1989).

QUALITATIVE COMPARATIVE ANALYSIS: A BRIEF OVERVIEW OF THE TECHNIQUE

In QCA each case is conceived holistically, as a configuration of conditions, not a collection of scores on variables. The simplest type of analysis involves dichotomous causal and outcome variables, but more complex variable types can be examined. As in statistical analysis, the most decisive part of a qualitative comparative investigation involves the selection of outcome variables and the specification of causal conditions. In QCA, however, the causal variables define the different configurations that are possible within the confines of the analysis. For example, the specification of seven dichotomous causal variables provides for 128 (i.e., 2^7) logically possible, qualitatively distinct configurations of causes. Causal variables are not examined one at a time or in terms of their unique contribution to explained variation as in statistical analyses, but as basic elements that define configurations. In other words, combinations of values take precedence over individual variables in QCA.

Once causal conditions have been selected, cases conforming to each combination of causal conditions are examined to see if they agree on the outcome variable (or variables). If there are many causal combinations with cases that disagree on the outcome variable, the investigator takes this as a sign that the specification of causal variables is incorrect or incomplete. (Alternatively, the investigator may use probabilities to construct the truth table; see Ragin, Mayer, and Drass 1984; Ragin 1987; and Ragin and Bradshaw 1991.) The close examination of cases that have the same values on the causal variables yet display contrasting outcomes is used as a basis for selecting additional causal variables. The investigator moves back and forth between specification of causal variables (using theory, substantive knowledge, and substantive interests) and examination of cases to build a combinatorial model with a minimum number of cases having the same combination of values on the causal conditions but contrasting outcomes.

Once a satisfactory set of causal conditions has been identified, data on cases can be represented as a truth table, and then the truth table can be logically minimized. A truth table lists the different combinations of causal conditions and the value of the outcome variable for the cases conforming to each combination. An analysis with 3 dichotomous causal conditions yields a truth table with 8 rows; 4 causal conditions produce a truth table with 16 rows; and so on.

Consider, for example, the simple truth table presented in Panel A of Table 12.2. This truth table lists the different combinations of values for four dichotomous causal conditions and a single outcome variable. In this hypothetical table, the outcome is the adoption of universal public pensions (labeled *U*). The four causal conditions are presence/absence of a corporatist system of wage negotiations (*C*), a coding of whether or not the country had been ruled by Left or Center-Left political parties for at least 5 years prior to the adoption of universal pensions (*L*), a dichotomous code distinguishing countries with greater ethnic-cultural homogeneity (e.g., Sweden) from those with less homogeneity (*H*), and a coding of whether or not the country had experienced at least 10 years of sustained economic growth prior to the adoption of universal pensions (*G*). All codes are Boolean: 1 indicates that a condition or outcome is present; the value 0 indicates it is absent. Alternatively, uppercase

Table 12.2. *Simple example of QCA using hypothetical data*

A. Truth Table

C	*L*	*H*	*G*	*U*	No. of Cases
0	0	0	0	0	4
0	0	0	1	0	3
0	0	1	0	0	6
0	0	1	1	1	2
0	1	0	0	1	3
0	1	0	1	1	4
0	1	1	0	0	3
0	1	1	1	1	5
1	0	0	0	0	7
1	0	0	1	0	8
1	0	1	0	0	1
1	0	1	1	1	7
1	1	0	0	1	3
1	1	0	1	1	2
1	1	1	0	0	7
1	1	1	1	1	6

B. Reduced to prime implicants (for $U = 1$)

-10- (or *Lh*: Left rule with ethnic diversity)[a]
-1-1 (or *LG*: left rule with economic growth)
--11 (or *HG*: ethnic homogeneity with economic growth)

C. Prime implicant chart

Terms to be covered ($U = 1$)

Prime implicants	0100	1100	0101	1101	0011	1011	0111	1111
-10-	x	x	x	x				
-1-1			x	x			x	x
--11					x	x	x	x

Table 12.2. *(cont.)*

D. Reduced equation: true = -101 + --11 or
$U = Lh + HG$

Verbal restatement: Universal pensions were adopted in ethnically diverse countries after a period of at least 5 years of Left or Center-Left rule and in ethnically homogeneous countries after at least 10 years of sustained economic growth.

Notes: C = Corporatist wage negotiations; L = At least 5 years of rule by Left or Center-Left parties; H = Ethnic-cultural homogeneity; G = At least 10 years of sustained economic growth; U = Adoption of universal pension system. [a]Uppercase is used to indicate presence; lowercase is used to indicate absence.

letters are used to indicate presence, and lowercase letters are used to indicate absence. The last column shows the number of cases with each causal combination and is included simply to remind the reader that each row may contain any number of cases (including no cases; see Ragin 1987; pp. 104–13). As presented, this truth table is ready to be logically reduced (minimized) because there are no causal combinations (rows of the truth table) that embrace cases with contradictory outcomes (i.e., rows with and without universal pensions).

The goal of the logical minimization is to represent – in a logically shorthand manner – the information in the truth table regarding the different combinations of conditions that produce a specific outcome. In the example in Table 12.2, the goal is to specify the different combinations of *C, c, L, l, H, h, G,* and *g* that produce *U* (lowercase is used to signal the absence of a condition). The first step in the minimization process is to compare rows with each other and simplify them through a bottom-up process of paired comparison. These paired comparisons follow a simple rule that mimics experimental design: combine rows that differ on only one causal condition but produce the same outcome. The fifth and sixth rows, for example, differ on only the fourth condition (*G* vs. *g*) and both produce *U*. Thus, they can be combined to produce a single, simpler expression. This simpler expression states that if *C* (corporatism) and *H* (ethnic-cultural homogeneity) are absent and *L* (Left rule) is present, *U* (universal pensions) results; the value of *G* (presence/absence of sustained economic growth) is irrelevant. The reduced expression can be represented as *cLh* or as 010-, where the dash indicates that the fourth term (*G*) has been eliminated as a cause. By contrast, the fourth and sixth rows, which both result in *U*, cannot be combined to form a simpler expression because they differ on more than one causal condition. The process of paired comparisons continues until no further simplifications are possible. The reduced expression *cLh* (010-), for example, is later combined with *CLh* (110-) to produce *Lh* (-10-).

The process of paired comparisons culminates in the production of prime implicants, shown in Panel B of Table 12.2. Often there are more prime implicants than are needed to embrace or cover all the causal combinations for a particular outcome. This pattern obtains in Table 12.2, as is shown in Panel C. This panel shows the next phase of logical minimization, which involves constructing a chart (called the prime implicant chart) that shows the correspondence between the prime implicants (just derived from the process of paired comparisons) and the original causal combinations for the outcome of interest drawn from the truth table (i.e., all the rows where $U = 1$). It is apparent from simple inspection of this chart (Panel C) that only two prime implicants are needed to cover the eight causal combinations for the presence of *U* from the truth table. The second prime implicant does not uniquely cover any of the eight causal combinations from the truth table. From a strictly logical point of view, it is redundant.

Use of the prime implicant chart is the final phase of logical minimization and culminates in a logical equation for the outcome of interest. The final, reduced equation for the presence of *U* is reported in Panel D of Table 12.2. The equation states simply that there are two main combinations of causal conditions that result in the presence of *U*: universal pensions were adopted in (1) ethnically diverse countries after a period of at least 5 years of Left or Center-Left rule and in (2) ethnically homogeneous countries after at least 10 years of sustained economic growth. These hypothetical results show a key feature of QCA that separates it from standard statistical analysis: It identifies multiple combinations of causal conditions that may contain causal factors in both their present and absent states. In one causal conjuncture, ethnic homogeneity is a factor in the emergence of universal pensions; in the other, its absence (i.e., ethnic diversity) is a factor.

When only a few causal conditions are examined, QCA can be implemented without the aid of a computer. However, when the number of causal conditions is more than about 5, the number of logically possible combinations of conditions increases greatly. For example, an analysis with 10 dichotomous conditions results in a truth table with 2^{10} (1,024) rows. Drass and Ragin (1989) offer a microcomputer package suitable for such analyses.

THE PROMISE OF THE BOOLEAN APPROACH

Systematic analysis of cases as configurations of causes and outcomes is the essence of case-oriented comparative work. When the number of cases and configurations is great, it is a cognitively demanding task, especially in the absence of algorithms to aid the researcher. The formalization of qualitative comparative methods sketched here (and explained in detail in Ragin 1987) allows the preservation of essential features of case-oriented work in the analysis of many cases and provides an important methodological bridge between case-oriented and variable-oriented work.

Most studies of macrosocial phenomena are dominated by either discourse on variables or discourse on cases. This bifurcation derives in part from the perception that researchers must choose between doing in-depth case studies of a small number of cases, on the one hand, or conducting quantitative cross-national analyses of many cases, on the other. This perception is unfortunate. It is as though travelers committed to reaching a particular destination – general statements valid across many cases – abandon one vehicle, case-oriented analysis, early on and then adopt a completely different mode of transportation, variable-oriented analysis, for the remainder of the trip. A lot is missed along the way, so much so that in the end it may seem like a different journey altogether. Strong generalizations should be based on strong empirical foundations.

ANNOTATED BIBLIOGRAPHY

QCA is a new technique. While the first published application appeared in a 1984 article (Ragin, Mayer, and Drass 1984), the technique was not presented in detail until 1987 (Ragin 1987). Since that time, applications have appeared with increasing frequency. The works listed below include (1) discussions of the technique, (2) applications of the technique (partial listing), and (3) information about the computer program.

General discussions of Boolean methods

Abell, Peter. 1989. "Foundations for a Qualitative Comparative Method." *International Review of Social History* 34(1):103–9.

This long and complimentary essay on *The Comparative Method* (Ragin 1987) offers a good introduction to the use of Boolean algebra in comparative analysis and suggests some directions for extending the approach.

Markoff, John. 1990. "A Comparative Method: Reflections on Charles Ragin's Innovations in Comparative Analysis." *Historical Methods* 23(4):177–81.

A second long essay on *The Comparative Method* (Ragin 1987), this discussion addresses the advances afforded by the Boolean approach and sketches its limitations. The primary limitation that Markoff addresses is the fact that the Boolean approach is a method of data analysis that requires a good prior grasp of relevant substantive and historical knowledge.

Ragin, Charles C. 1987. *The Comparative Method: Moving Beyond Qualitative and Quantitative Strategies*. Berkeley, Calif.: University of California Press.

The sharp contrast between case-oriented and variable-oriented research strategies provides a backdrop for a systematic, in-depth presentation of Boolean methods of data analysis. A cornerstone of the discussion is the problem of multiple conjunctural causation and the difficulty of assessing this type of causation with linear, statistical models. This book is essential background reading for those who want to understand Boolean methods, in general, and QCA, in particular.

1989. "New Directions in Comparative Research." In Melvin Kohn, (ed.), *Cross-National Research in Sociology*, pp. 57–76. Newbury Park, Calif.: Sage.

This discussion of trends in comparative research presents QCA as an important link between qualitative historical work and quantitative work in macrosociology and political science. The linking of these different kinds of work is integral to the future of comparative work.

Ragin, Charles C. 1989. "The Logic of the Comparative Method and the Algebra of Logic." *Journal of Quantitative Anthropology* 1(2):373–98.

This presentation of QCA uses data on 53 social movement organizations to illustrate various aspects of the Boolean approach, including the use of Boolean algebra to assess the fit between empirical results and theoretical expectations. The medium-sized data set illustrates problems that arise when there are too many cases for intensive qualitative analysis, but too few cases for sophisticated statistical analysis.

Ragin, Charles C. 1991. "Introduction: The Problem of Balancing Discourse on Cases and Variables in Comparative Social Science." In Charles C. Ragin, (ed.), *Issues and Alternatives in Comparative Social Research*, pp. 1–8. Leiden: E. J. Brill.

This introduction to a collection of essays on comparative methodology (which includes two applications of QCA) argues that the key to good comparative social science is a balance between discourse on cases and discourse on variables – a task that is simplified with QCA.

Applications of QCA

Amenta, Edwin, Bruce G. Carruthers, and Yvonne Zylan. 1992. "A Hero for the Aged? The Townsend Movement, the Political Mediation Model, and U.S. Old-Age Policy, 1934–1950." *American Journal of Sociology* 98(2):308–39.

This examination of U.S. social policy uses state-level data to test basic arguments about the Townsend movement. The qualitative comparative analysis reinforces conclusions drawn from historical and statistical analyses and shows the different paths to four movement outcomes at the state level: polity membership, concessions, co-optation, and collapse.

Berg-Schlosser, Dirk, and Gisèle De Meur. 1991. "Conditions of Democracy in Inter-War Europe: A Boolean Test of Major Hypotheses." Paper presented at the 15th World Congress of the International Political Science Association, Buenos Aires, Argentina, July 21–5, 1991.

This sophisticated examination of a variety of theoretical arguments presents a wide array of Boolean analyses using qualitative data on conditions conducive to democracy. The authors construct and then simplify truth tables for each major theoretical perspective.

Drass, Kriss A., and J. William Spencer. 1987. "Accounting for Pre-Sentencing Recommendations: Typologies and Probation Officers' Theory of Office. *Social Problems* 34:277–93.

This application of QCA took its cue from Aaron Cicourel's work on juvenile justice. While most applications of QCA use some form of macrolevel data, Drass and Spencer focus on microlevel records.

Griffin, Larry J., Christopher Botsko, Ana-Maria Wahl, and Larry W. Isaac. 1991. "Theoretical Generality, Case Particularity: Qualitative Comparative Analysis of Trade Union Growth and Decline." In Charles C. Ragin (ed.), *Issues and Alternatives in Comparative Social Research*, pp. 110–36. Leiden: E. J. Brill.

Griffin et al. present a novel adaptation of QCA to time-series data and examine causes of the diverging rates of unionization among advanced industrial democracies. Because QCA was developed for the examination of configurations of qualitative characteristics, events, and structures, it was necessary for Griffin et al. to characterize longitudinal trends in qualitative ways. They develop criteria for defining periods of time qualitatively and for comparing countries' trajectories to each other.

Kangas, Ollie. 1991. *The Politics of Social Rights: Studies on the Dimensions of Sickness Insurance in 18 OECD Countries*. Stockholm: Swedish Institute for Social Research.
This collection of studies by Kangas offers a chapter featuring Boolean analysis of sickness insurance. Kangas finds the Boolean approach useful but bases most of his conclusions in the collection on statistical results.

Lieberson, Stanley, and Eleanor O. Bell. 1992. "Children's First Names: An Empirical Study of Social Taste." *American Journal of Sociology* 98(3):511–54.
This article features a truth table approach to the interpretation of complex data patterns without taking advantage of the formal methods of simplification (i.e., deriving prime implicants and using the prime implicant chart) outlined in this chapter. Nevertheless, it illustrates a concern for configurations and the use of truth tables to represent and analyze complexity.

Musheno, Michael C., Peter R. Gregware, and Kriss A. Drass. 1991. "Court Management of AIDS Disputes: A Sociolegal Analysis." *Law and Social Inquiry* 16(4):737–76.
This novel application of QCA examines 36 AIDS-related court rulings. The goal of the analysis is to assess the impact of different combinations of contestants' characteristics and legal claims (restrictive vs. expansive) on case outcomes for dominant and subordinate parties.

Ragin, Charles C., Susan E. Mayer, and Kriss A. Drass. 1984. "Assessing Discrimination: A Boolean Approach." *American Sociological Review* 49:221–34.
This first application of QCA emphasized the lack of correspondence between legal arguments about appropriate comparisons (e.g., the idea that only similarly situated individuals should be compared) and statistical methods used to assess discrimination, which are almost universally additive and linear in orientation. QCA is offered as an alternative.

Ragin, Charles C., and York W. Bradshaw. 1991. "Statistical Analysis of Employment Discrimination: A Review and Critique." *Research in Social Stratification and Mobility* 10:199–228.
This study builds on Ragin, Mayer, and Drass (1984). It offers a more thorough examination of the legal reasoning behind debates about discrimination and a superior technique for using QCA to

assess inequality. Alternative definitions of discrimination are implemented in the analysis, using QCA. Different ways of defining discrimination produce different patterns of findings.

Wickham-Crowley, Timothy. 1991. *Guerrillas and Revolution in Latin America: A Comparative Study of Insurgents and Regimes Since 1956*. Princeton, N.J.: Princeton University Press.
This book offers a thorough Boolean analysis of the support for guerrillas and the outcomes of guerrilla movements in Latin America. It is a wide-ranging study that integrates qualitative historical analysis, ecological analysis, and Boolean analysis. Altogether, 28 cases are studied (some countries experienced guerrilla movements in both of the major waves that swept Latin America). The Boolean analysis of outcomes focuses on the different routes to failed revolutions. Part of this analysis was also published in *Issues and Alternatives in Comparative Social Research* (Ragin 1991).

Williams, Linda Meyer, and Ronald A. Farrell. 1990. "Legal Response to Child Sexual Abuse in Daycare." *Criminal Justice and Behavior* 17:284–302.

Computer programs

Drass, Kriss A., and Charles C. Ragin. 1989. *QCA: Qualitative Comparative Analysis*. Evanston, Ill.: Center for Urban Affairs and Policy Research, Northwestern University.
Currently, we are circulating QCA version 3.0 along with printed documentation for a fee of $25.00. Purchasers are welcome to make copies of the program and documentation to share with other users. The program runs on all MS-DOS computers with at least 640K of memory and is distributed on a 3.5 inch diskette. Users may create truth tables in QCA or retrieve truth tables that are saved in DOS text format (ASCII) by other programs (e.g., word processors or statistical packages). To obtain QCA, write to Audrey Chambers, Center for Urban Affairs and Policy Research, Northwestern University, 2040 Sheridan Road, Evanston, Ill. 60208.

REFERENCES

Bendix, Reinhard. 1978. *Kings or People: Power and the Mandate to Rule*. Berkeley: University of California Press.

Bonnell, Victoria. 1980. "The Uses of Theory, Concepts and Comparison in Historical Sociology." *Comparative Studies in Society and History* 22:156–73.

Drass, Kriss, and Charles C. Ragin. 1989. *QCA: Qualitative Comparative Analysis*. Evanston, Ill.: Center for Urban Affairs and Policy Research, Northwestern University.

Janoski, Thomas. 1991. "Synthetic Strategies in Comparative Sociological Research: Methods and Problems of Internal and External Analysis." In Charles C. Ragin (ed.), *Issues and Alternatives in Comparative Social Research*, pp. 59–81. Leiden: E. J. Brill.

Kohn, Mervin. 1989. "Cross-National Research as an Analytic Strategy." In Melvin Kohn (ed.), *Cross-National Research in Sociology*, pp. 77–102. Newbury Park, Calif.: Sage.

Lipset, Seymour Martin. 1963. *The First New Nation: The United States in Comparative and Historical Perspective*. New York: Basic.

Mendelson, Elliot. 1970. *Boolean Algebra and Switching Circuits*. New York: McGraw-Hill.

Mill, John Stuart. 1843/1967. *A System of Logic: Ratiocinative and Inductive*. Toronto: University of Toronto Press.

Moore, Barrington, Jr. 1966. *Social Origins of Dictatorship and Democracy: Lord and Peasant in the Making of the Modern World*. Boston: Beacon.

Przeworski, Adam, and Henry Teune. 1970. *The Logic of Comparative Social Inquiry*. New York: Wiley-Interscience.

Ragin, Charles C. 1983. "Theory and Method in the Study of Dependency and International Inequality." *International Journal of Comparative Sociology* 24:121–36.

1987. *The Comparative Method: Moving Beyond Qualitative and Quantitative Strategies*. Berkeley: University of California Press.

1989. "New Directions in Comparative Research." In Melvin Kohn (ed.), *Cross-National Research in Sociology*, pp. 57–76. Newbury Park, Calif.: Sage.

1991. "Introduction: The Problem of Balancing Discourse on Cases and Variables in Comparative Social Science." In Charles C. Ragin (ed.), *Issues and Alternatives in Comparative Social Research*, pp. 1–8. Leiden: E. J. Brill.

Ragin, Charles C., and York W. Bradshaw. 1991. "Statistical Analysis of Employment Discrimination: A Review and Critique." *Research in Social Stratification and Mobility* 10:199–228.

Ragin, Charles C., Susan E. Mayer, and Kriss A. Drass. 1984. "Assessing Discrimination: A Boolean Approach." *American Sociological Review* 49:221–34.

Ragin, Charles C. and David R. Zaret. 1983. "Theory and Method in Comparative Research: Two Strategies." *Social Forces* 61:731–54.

Roth, Charles. 1975. *Fundamentals of Logic Design*. St. Paul, Minn.: West.

Rueschemeyer, Dietrich. 1991. "Different Methods – Contradictory Results? Research on Development and Democracy." In Charles C. Ragin (ed.), *Issues and Alternatives in Comparative Social Research*, pp. 9–38 Leiden: E. J. Brill.

Skocpol, Theda. 1979. *States and Social Revolutions: A Comparative Analysis of France, Russia, and China*. Cambridge University Press.

Skocpol, Theda, and Margaret Sommers. 1980. "The Uses of Comparative History in Macrosocial Inquiry." *Comparative Studies in Society and History* 22:174–97.

Smelser, Neil J. 1959. *Social Change in the Industrial Revolution: An Application of Theory to the British Cotton Industry*. University of Chicago Press.

Tilly, Charles. 1984. *Big Structures, Large Processes, Huge Comparisons*. New York: Russell Sage Foundation.

Walton, John. 1984. *Reluctant Rebels: Comparative Studies of Revolution and Underdevelopment*. New York: Columbia University Press.

Weber, Max. 1978. *Economy and Society*. Guenther Roth and Claus Wittich (eds.), Berkeley: University of California Press.

13

A qualitative comparative analysis of pension systems

CHARLES C. RAGIN

There is nearly universal agreement in advanced capitalist democracies today that it is the responsibility of national governments to provide or at least sanction old-age support programs. Public expenditures on these programs have grown dramatically over the post–World War II period, and today expenditures on programs for the elderly outweigh expenditures on other welfare programs in most advanced countries (Quadagno 1987). Despite these commonalities, there is striking diversity among the advanced countries in how systems of old-age support are organized. Systems vary in the relative importance of public and private programs, the degree to which benefits are tied to contributions associated with paid labor, the degree to which programs have special provisions for different occupational groups or for civil servants, their relative administrative costs, and in many other ways.

Scholars have proposed a variety of explanations for these broad national differences. Three general explanations are discernible in the social scientific literature on the welfare state. According to the "logic of industrialism" explanation, both the growth of the welfare state and cross-national differences in "welfare state effort" – including pension expenditures – are by-products of economic development and its demographic and social organizational consequences (Wilensky 1975, Pampel and Williamson 1985). The "political class struggle" argument contends that the level of working-class mobilization and the strength of Left parties are the primary determinants of both the size of welfare state programs and their redistributive impact (Stephens 1979; Korpi 1983; Myles 1984; and Esping-Andersen 1990). Finally, according to "state-centered" explanations, the structure of the state and the policy-

I thank Bruce Carruthers, Mary Driscoll, Alexander Hicks, Thomas Janoski, and John Stephens for their many useful comments on various versions of this chapter.

making activities of bureaucrats (who are seen as relatively autonomous from the pressures of social forces) are the primary sources of international differences in welfare state programs and are responsible as well for the expansion of these programs through time (Heclo 1974; Weir, Orloff, and Skocpol 1988). Despite the fact that all three explanations have existed for at least a decade and have stimulated considerable empirical research, there is still a surprising level of inconsistency among the findings of studies addressing national differences in old-age support systems and in other features of the welfare state (Palme 1990, p. 14).

This chapter examines both the diversity of pension systems among the advanced capitalist democracies and the sources of this diversity. These two substantive objectives are coupled with two methodological objectives: to demonstrate qualitative comparative analysis (QCA; described in detail in Chapter 12; Ragin 1987; and Drass and Ragin 1989) and to show how to use interval-scale variables with QCA. One apparent drawback of QCA, as presented in Chapter 12, is its reliance on categorical-scale variables, a limitation also noted in Ragin (1987). There are several ways to overcome this constraint. The technique outlined in this chapter is a *preliminary* formulation of the use of cluster analysis to build a bridge between interval-scale variables and the construction of the truth table. Before presenting this extension of QCA to interval-scale variables, I examine the diversity of pensions systems and briefly survey possible causes of this diversity.

This chapter uses data from Esping-Andersen (1990) and other sources and tries to test some of the core ideas presented in his work. The results, while preliminary, challenge Esping-Andersen's (1990) threefold classification of welfare states as liberal, corporativistic, and social democratic and offer new findings on the origins of differences among welfare states.

THE DIVERSITY OF PENSIONS SYSTEMS

The recent publication of Gosta Esping-Andersen's *The Three Worlds of Welfare Capitalism* (1990) has called into question well-established ways of thinking about differences among welfare states in advanced capitalist democracies. Most previous thinking was anchored in a strongly unidimensional conception of welfare states, with weak or "liberal" welfare states such as the United States at one extreme and developed or "social democratic" welfare states such as Sweden at the other (Stephens 1979). According to this conception, countries at or near the U.S. end of this continuum tend to spend less, do more means testing, rely on the private sector when possible, and implement – to the extent feasible – a close connection between paid labor and benefits. Countries at or near the Swedish end of the continuum, by contrast, tend to spend more, do less means testing, avoid using the private sector, and conceive of benefits as rights. To these two worlds Esping-Andersen added a third, using various labels to describe it: continental, corporativistic, and Catholic-authoritarian. While this third world of welfare capitalism is in many ways intermediate between the social democratic and the liberal welfare states, it possesses specific features that differentiate it from the other two. For example, while countries with corporativistic pension systems tend to rank in the middle on most measures of pension expenditures and pension quality, they stand out in a number of occupationally based public pension programs and in expenditures on public employee pension programs.

One important issue is the degree to which these three worlds of welfare capitalism do in fact constitute distinct types, especially with respect to pension programs. Esping-Andersen proposes indicators for each of the three types, and many of these indicators are specific to differences among pension systems. The chief indicator of a *liberal* pension system is the existence of a developed private pension system parallel to the public system. Private pension systems flourish where public systems fail to meet the demands of the more affluent members of society. A *corporativistic* pension system is segmentally organized and is characterized by a large number of occupationally specific pension programs and a high level of expenditure on civil servants. The primary indicator of a *social democratic* pension system is the "decommodification" of public pensions. Pensions are decommodified when benefits are less tied to contributions associated with paid labor. A universal pension available to all citizens regardless of work history is relatively decommodified according to this reasoning. Esping-Andersen's composite measure of pension decommodification results in a ranking of countries that parallels rankings produced by Day's (1978) and Myles's (1984) composite measures of pension quality.[1]

Table 13.1 shows the relative positions of 18 advanced countries on these indicators. To simplify the presentation, countries are divided into three ordinal categories (high, medium, and low) on each of three measures. For each measure, the countries with the five highest scores are labeled "high"; the countries ranked sixth through tenth are labeled "medium"; and the remaining eight countries are labeled "low." These three categories correspond to the following breakdown of standardized scores on the three measures: High indicates scores above .5 standard deviations above the mean; medium indicates scores below .5 standard deviations above the mean but not lower than .5 standard deviations

Table 13.1. *Characteristics of pension systems*

Country	Private pensions[a]	Civil servants/ no. of programs[b]	Pension decommod.[c]	Type[d]
New Zealand	Low	Low	Low	?
Australia	High	Low	Low	Liberal
Canada	High	Low	Low	Liberal
Switzerland	High	Low	Low	Liberal
United States	High	Low	Low	Liberal
Japan	High	Medium	Medium	?
Ireland	Medium	Medium	Low	?
United	Medium	Medium	Low	?
Kingdom	Medium	Medium	Medium	?
Netherlands	Medium	High	Low	?
Germany	Low	High	Medium	Corp.
Austria	Low	High	Medium	Corp.
France	Low	High	Medium	Corp.
Italy	Low	High	High	?
Belgium	Low	Medium	High	?
Finland	Medium	Low	High	?
Denmark	Low	Low	High	Soc. dem.
Norway	Low	Low	High	Soc. dem.
Sweden				

[a] Expenditures on private pensions as a percentage of total pension expenditures.
[b] Index of corporativism combining number of occupationally specific pension programs and expenditures on public employee pension programs as a percentage of GDP.
[c] Esping-Andersen's index of pension decommodification.
[d] Preliminary assignment of cases to types, based on criteria presented in Esping-Andersen (1990); "Corp." = corporativistic, and "Soc. dem." = social democratic. Question marks indicate that no straightforward assignment is possible.

below the mean; and low indicates scores lower than .5 standard deviations below the mean.

The first measure in Table 13.1 is the private sector's share of total pension expenditures (from Esping-Andersen 1990, p. 84); high scores indicate a liberal pension system. The second is an index of pension corporativism that combines two strongly correlated measures: expenditure on pensions for public employees as a percentage of GDP (p. 84) and the number of occupationally specific pension programs (p. 70). These two measures were converted to Z-scores and then averaged to produce an index of pension corporativism. The third measure of the decommodification of pensions indicates social democratic pension systems (p. 50).

The patterns in Table 13.1 are clear (see also Janoski Chapter 3, this volume). There is a definite liberal configuration (reading across rows: high, low, low) that is shared by four countries (Australia, Canada, Switzerland, and the United States) and a clear social democratic configuration (low, low, high) shared by two countries (Sweden and Norway). There are no instances of "pure" corporativism (low, high, low); instead, three countries (Austria, France, and Italy) show a corporativistic pattern that includes moderate social democratic elements (low, high, medium). This pattern is consistent with Esping-Andersen's (1990, p. 52) characterization of the corporativistic world as intermediate between the liberal and social democratic worlds on some dimensions.

Altogether, only half (9 out of 18) countries, as presented in Table 13.1, correspond closely to the three types described in Esping-Andersen (1990; see also Castles and Mitchell 1990). New Zealand is low on all three measures, suggesting that its pension system is outside the scope of Esping-Andersen's general framework (despite this country's high level of pension spending; Castles and Mitchell 1990 offer an account of this anomaly). The other 8 countries show various mixes of the three types. These mixed results are not a simple artifact of the cutoff values chosen for the three categories. Adjusting the cutoff between medium and high produces a higher proportion of mixed types: of the countries that score in the medium range on private pensions, Denmark has the highest score. Denmark is usually treated as an example of a social democratic welfare state (Esping-Andersen 1990, p. 74). Of the countries that score in the medium range on the index of corporativism, Finland has the highest score. Finland is also treated most often as an example of a social democratic welfare state (p. 74). And of the countries that score in the medium range on pension decommodification, France has the highest score; Esping-Andersen (p. 86) treats France as an example of a corporativistic pension system.[2]

Table 13.1 challenges the view that there are three distinct worlds of old-age support among modern welfare states. There is even greater diversity among pension systems than allowed in Esping-Andersen's extension of the bipolar model (liberal vs. social democratic pension systems) to a tripartite model (the addition of the corporativistic world). As the analysis presented in this chapter demonstrates, the correspondence between constructed types and empirical cases is not strong enough to warrant simple assignment of cases to types, especially for the corporativistic type. The application of advanced clustering techniques to these data reinforces this conclusion.

CAUSES OF DIVERSITY: A BRIEF INVENTORY

Many different explanations of the diversity of pensions systems have been proposed. Skocpol and Amenta (1986) and Quadagno (1987) offer comprehensive surveys of the relevant literature; their reviews will not be reproduced here because of space limitations and because the primary objectives of this chapter are methodological. As already noted, the different explanations can be grouped under three main headings: the logic of industrialism, political class struggle, and state-centered arguments. The following analysis includes causal variables drawn from each of these perspectives. Additional variables relevant to the contextualization of the main causal variables are included as well.

According to the logic of industrialism explanation, economic development brings with it both the need and the capacity for the welfare state. The capacity for a welfare state derives simply from the greater surplus that comes with increased productivity and government's ability to tax the surplus (Lenski 1966). The need for a welfare state comes from a variety of structural sources including, among others, increased longevity associated with greater affluence, decline of the economic importance of the extended family, commodification of social relations in general, a greater dependence on labor markets, and a greater vulnerability to their fluctuations. To gauge differences among countries in conditions relevant to this perspective, I use GDP per capita, an indicator of both economic development and national wealth.

According to the political class struggle explanation, strong welfare states are built by Left political parties in alliance with organized labor. In short, "the earlier and more fully the workers become organized into centralized unions and a social democratic party, and the more consistently over time the social democratic party controls the state, the earlier and more 'completely' a modern welfare state develops" (Skocpol and Amenta 1986, p. 140). To measure the influence of Left parties on the welfare state, most researchers use some indicator of the accumulated strength of Left parties in government – for example, the number of years (over the post–World War II period) in which Left parties have formed governments on their own or in coalition with other parties (Left cabinet strength). This study follows the lead of previous research in using this measure.

Some researchers argue additionally that Catholic political parties (Wilensky 1981) or religious parties more generally (Huber, Ragin, and Stephens 1991; Palme 1990, pp. 119–29) also promote welfare state expansion, either in competition or coalition with Left parties. This study includes a measure of the strength of religious parties (accumulated cabinet strength of religious parties) to assess their impact. Van Kersbergen (1991) offers a comparative/historical study of the influence of these parties.

State-centered arguments do not deny the impact of industrialism or of class politics but locate the primary vehicle for change in the size and character of welfare state programs in (1) the structure and capacity of states, (2) the interests of government bureaucrats and the administrators of welfare programs, and (3) historical legacies that shape how key actors view policy options. The state-centered approach mandates case-oriented, historically sensitive research on specific policy enactments and changes across a range of cases and historical periods. However, as two proponents note, the approach is in an "early stage" of development (Skocpol and Amenta 1986, p. 147), and the measurement of cross-national variation in causal forces relevant to this perspective remains in its infancy. Nevertheless, this study includes one measure pertinent to the state-centered approach, the date that legislation founding the public pension system was first enacted. This measure of the age of public pension programs is relevant to state-centered arguments because the older a program, the greater (1) its entrenchment in the state, (2) its opportunity for autonomous control, and (3) its possibilities for quantitative expansion and qualitative improvement. Of course, further research on the historical development of specific programs is necessary to determine if, in fact, these enhanced capacities follow from program age.

In addition to the four causal conditions just described, the analysis also includes examination of the effects of country size (natural log of population; OECD 1986), percent Catholic (Taylor and Hudson 1972), and ethnic diversity (a fractionalization index using data from Barrett 1982). Country size is relevant because social democratic welfare states have emerged primarily in relatively small countries. Generally, smaller countries are more open to the international economy and thus more vulnerable to its exigencies. These factors encourage high levels of union centralization, centralized wage bargaining, and strong Left parties (see Wallerstein 1989, 1991; Stephens 1991). Examination of country size is central to the study of the social democratic welfare state. The percentage of Catholics is included because Catholicism is a major factor cited by Esping-Andersen to explain the corporativistic welfare state and because it is an important contextual variable for examining the influence of religious parties. Finally, ethnic diversity is included because cultural, racial, and linguistic heterogeneity pose obstacles to labor organization, to working-class political mobilization, and consequently, to Left party strength. Further, this factor is complexly confounded with both country size and wealth. Small countries tend to be relatively

Table 13.2. *Summary of causal variables*

Label	Description	Sources
LEFCAB	Left-party cabinet strength: an index measuring the accumulated participation of Left parties in government cabinets over the 1945-80 period	Mackie and Rose (1982), Castles and Mair (1984)
RELCAB	Religious party cabinet strength: measures the accumulated participation of religious parties in government cabinets over the 1945-80 period	Mackie and Rose (1982), Castles and Mair (1984)
SIZE	Size of country: population in 1980; logged to remove the influence of skew and extreme values	OECD (1986)
GDPCAP	Gross domestic product per capita: measured in 1980; national currency units converted to U.S.$ using prevailing exchange rates	OECD (1986)
ETHDIV	Ethnic diversity: measured as a fractionalization index, ca. 1980; low scores indicate relative homogeneity	Barret (1982)
PDATE	Program date: year that social security program was first established; high score indicates young program	U.S. Dept. of H.H.S. (1990)
CATH%	Catholics as a percentage of total population, ca. 1980	Taylor and Hudson (1972)

homogeneous (e.g., Scandinavian countries), but there are important exceptions (e.g., Belgium and Switzerland are small and heterogeneous, while Germany and Japan are large and relatively homogeneous). Richer countries tend to be ethnically diverse (e.g., the United States, Canada, and Switzerland), but again there are major exceptions (e.g., Scandinavian countries). Different configurations of size, wealth, ethnic diversity, and strength of Left parties could have an important impact on pension systems. QCA was specifically designed to address such complex configurations of conditions. The seven causal variables used in this study are summarized in Table 13.2.

This list of causal conditions may seem modest, especially when compared to an exhaustive inventory of the different causal conditions that researchers in this area have examined (see Skocpol and Amenta 1986). It is important to remember the following, however: First, a multiple regression analysis of these seven causal variables would be awkward with only 18 cases. A regression equation with seven predictors and 18 cases is generally considered untrustworthy, even if it can be estimated. Second, QCA addresses configurations of conditions. Once transformed into a truth table, these seven causal conditions establish a foundation for the examination of 128 (i.e., 2^7) different combinations of conditions. It is impossible to address this degree of complexity in a regression analysis of 18 cases.

ADAPTING INTERVAL-LEVEL MEASURES TO QCA

QCA was developed originally for categorical variables, and most applications using interval-level causal variables have simply transformed these variables to ordinal categories, using substantive criteria to establish cutoffs (see, e.g., Ragin, Mayer, and Drass 1984; Ragin and Bradshaw 1991). There are other ways to adapt interval-level variables to QCA. The new technique outlined here uses principles from cluster analysis to build a bridge between interval-level causal conditions and the assignment of cases to rows of the truth table (i.e., to different causal configurations; see Chapter 12). I first provide an overview of this new technique and then describe the details of its application to pension systems.

Overview of the technique

For the sake of simplicity, consider an analysis that involves only three causal variables and a single dichotomous outcome variable. A truth table for three *dichotomous* causal variables has eight rows: 000, 001, 010, 011, 100, 101, 110, and 111 (see Chapter 12). Essentially, these eight rows define eight different qualitative states, much like an eight-category independent variable, and each combination of values should be understood as a distinct configuration. These eight combinations of values, however, also can be viewed as the eight corners of a cube defined by three interval-scale variables (*X, Y*, and *Z*), each of which, in turn, ranges from −1 to +1. The first row of the truth tables (000) corresponds to values of −1 on dimension *X*, −1 on dimension *Y*, and −1 on dimension *Z*; the second row (001) translates to −1 on *X*, −1 on *Y*, and +1 on *Z*; and so on. The center of the cube is defined by values of 0 on all three interval-scale variables.

Once the three-variable truth table (eight rows) is reconceived as a cube (eight corners), it is possible to treat the problem of interval-scale causal variables as essentially a *measurement* problem. The scores for each case on the three interval-scale variables (*X*, *Y*, and *Z*) define a specific location inside the three-dimensional cube. By measuring the distance from the points defined by each case to each of the eight corners of the cube and to the center of the cube, it is possible to determine the best assignment of cases to truth table rows. For example, a case with a value of −.8 on *X*, −.6 on *Y*, and +.7 on *Z* is closest to the −1, −1, +1 corner of the cube and thus should be assigned to the 001 row of the truth table. A case with a value of −.1 on *X*, −.2 on *Y*, and +.3 on *Z* is very close to the center of the cube (0, 0, 0) and thus *cannot* be assigned safely to any row of the truth table. It is important to measure the distance between each case and the center of the cube as well as the distance between each case and the corners because cases that are closer to the center than to any corner should be excluded from the Boolean analysis. It would be hazardous to assign such cases to any of the rows of the truth table.

Cluster analysis aids this task because it is based on distance calculations. However, *classic* clustering techniques, per se, are not used because classic cluster analysis proceeds *inductively*. Cases that are close to each other are joined to form a cluster, and "cluster centers" are inductively defined by averaging the values of the cases in a cluster (e.g., computing their average scores on variables *X*, *Y*, and *Z*). Clustering procedures are used *deductively* here. Cluster centers are defined at the outset (by translating truth table values to numeric values), and they remain fixed through the course of the cluster analysis. For example, in the three-variable problem just described, eight cluster centers, based on translations of truth table values, would be input into the clustering program as fixed, though hypothetical, cluster centers. For example, truth table row 000 becomes cluster center −1, −1, −1; truth table row 001 becomes cluster center −1, −1, +1; and so on. A ninth cluster center giving the location of the center of the cube (0, 0, 0) is included as well to capture cases close to the center and therefore unassignable to any of the corners. Essentially, the clustering algorithm is used simply to streamline the calculation of distances and to automate the process of selecting the shortest distance between each case and the fixed cluster centers. Clustering cases in this deductive manner produces mathematically precise assignments of cases to truth table rows and exact calculations of the fit of a case to the row it is assigned (i.e., its distance from the fixed cluster center). In short, the cluster analysis determines the best possible assignment of cases to causal configurations defined by the truth table.

As I will show, this deductive adaptation of cluster analysis also can be used to assign cases to different outcome conditions when interval-scale variables are used to characterize outcomes. In this use of clustering procedures (which builds on ideas presented in Ragin 1983), the problem is to assess the conformity of each case's pension system (as defined by the three interval-scale variables used to construct Table 13.1) to ideal-typical configurations defined by the three constructed types described in Esping-Andersen (1990): liberal, corporativistic, and social democratic.

Cluster analysis of causal variables

This cluster analysis examines the distance between each of the 18 cases, on the one hand, and 128 cluster centers defined by truth table rows (the 2^7 combinations of seven dichotomous variables), on the other. An additional cluster center, defined by the mean values of the seven causal variables (i.e., the center of the seven-dimensional space), is also included to capture cases that do not conform well to any of the cluster centers defined by the 128 truth table rows.

Before performing the cluster analysis, however, it is necessary to transform the causal variables. First, the variables must be converted to standardized (Z) scores. Cluster analysis of cases relies primarily on the computation of distance scores. Measures with different metrics contribute differently to distance scores unless some sort of standardization is imposed. In effect, by transforming the different causal variables to a common metric, the variables are weighted equally in the computation of distance measures.

After the causal variables are standardized, they are "winsorized" to moderate the influence of extreme scores. Winsorizing a measure recodes its most extreme values (very high and very low) to values that are less extreme. For example, to winsorize a variable at the 20 percent level, all values above the 80th percentile are recoded to the value of the case at the 80th percentile; all values below the 20th percentile are recoded to the value of the case at the 20th percentile. Winsorizing was developed by scholars in the field of exploratory data analysis (Tukey 1977; Hoaglin, Mosteller, and Tukey 1983, 1985). The goal of exploratory data analysis is to develop measures and techniques that yield more robust and "resistant" estimates and findings – results that are based on the main body of the data. Most often, winsorizing a variable is a prelude to the computation of a measure of central tendency (Weisberg 1992, p. 40). In the following analysis, it is used to moderate the range of the variables used in the analysis.

The effect of a 20 percent winsorizing of standardized *LEFCAB* (accumulated cabinet strength of Left parties) is presented in Table 13.3.

Table 13.3. *Example of winsorized-standardized values: a 20 percent trim of LEFCAB*

Country	*LEFCAB*	Standardized *LEFCAB*	Winsorized-standardized *LEFCAB*
Australia	6.94	-0.43	-0.43
Austria	20.45	0.97	0.97
Belgium	13.53	0.25	0.25
Canada	0.00	-1.15	-0.95
Denmark	25.13	1.45	1.07
Finland	13.98	0.30	0.30
France	3.10	-0.83	-0.83
Germany	10.86	-0.03	-0.03
Ireland	2.79	-0.87	-0.87
Italy	2.52	-0.89	-0.89
Japan	0.00	-1.15	-0.95
Netherlands	8.20	-0.30	-0.30
New Zealand	9.92	-0.12	-0.12
Norway	28.42	1.80	1.07
Sweden	29.62	1.92	1.07
Switzerland	8.62	-.26	-0.26
United Kingdom	16.16	0.52	0.52
United States	0.00	-1.15	-0.95

As the table shows, only the values at the two ends of the distribution are changed. Winsorizing variables usually does not produce serious distortions; the Pearson correlation between untransformed *LEFCAB* and winsorized-standardized *LEFCAB* is .98. Extreme values must be moderated because they have a strong impact on the computation of distance measures in cluster analysis. All seven interval-scale causal variables used in the analysis were winsorized in this manner. Varying the value for winsorizing (using 15, 20, and 25 percent) does not alter the results reported in this chapter.[3]

After standardizing and then winsorizing the causal variables, it is necessary to identify the cluster centers to be used in the cluster analysis. The endpoints (minimum and maximum values) of the winsorized-standardized measures are used to define cluster centers. As noted, the goal of the cluster analysis is to assign cases to rows of the truth table. With seven causal variables, there are 128 rows to the truth table, which, in turn, define 128 cluster centers. The first row of the truth table contains the Boolean value of 0 for all seven variables. This corresponds to a cluster center defined by the lowest values of the seven winsorized-standardized variables. The second row of the truth table has Boolean values of 0 for the first six variables and Boolean value of 1 for the seventh. This corresponds to a cluster center defined by the lowest values of the first six winsorized-standardized variables and the highest value of the seventh. Panel A of Table 13.4 shows several representative truth table rows (with Boolean values) translated to cluster centers. As noted already, a 129th cluster center, which uses the means of the seven variables to define a cluster center, is included as well.

To assign cases to specific, user-defined cluster centers, it is necessary to use a clustering program that permits prior specification of fixed cluster centers. In SPSS/PC+, the relevant procedure is called QUICK CLUSTER, which uses the principle of nearest centroid sorting (Anderberg 1973). The assignment of cases to rows of the truth table follows from the assignment of cases to clusters in the clustering algorithm. In SPSS/PC+ this is accomplished by specifying 129 initial clusters, the 128 defined by the truth table and the 129th defined by the mean values of the seven causal variables. Panel B of Table 13.4 shows 10 of the 129 cluster centers entered into the SPSS/PC+ QUICK CLUSTER program.

The results of the cluster analysis are presented in Table 13.5, which lists the cluster numbers (corresponding to row numbers from the truth table presented in abbreviated form in Table 13.4) for the 18 countries in the analysis. With 129 cluster centers, it is not surprising to find that few countries are assigned to the same cluster and thus to the same truth table row. Denmark and Sweden are in the same cluster, and Australia and New Zealand are in the same cluster. The Netherlands is assigned to the indeterminate cluster defined by the mean values of the seven causal variables. Each of the remaining 13 countries is assigned to a different cluster center. In effect, this procedure allows each case to be unique but also specifies its uniqueness as a distinct configuration of common causal elements. Remember, however, that the use of the clustering algorithm serves simply to aid the construction of the truth table. Boolean algorithms are used to assess similarities and differences among cases and to identify patterns of convergence and divergence. In short, the results reported in Table 13.5 merely define the major truth table rows to be used in the analysis of causes of pension diversity.

Cluster analysis of outcome variables

A similar clustering procedure can be applied to the three interval-scale variables used by Esping-Andersen (1990) to elucidate the diversity of pension systems: (1) private pension expenditures as a percentage

Table 13.4. *The translation of the truth table to cluster centers*

Panel A. Partial truth table for seven causal variables: Boolean variables[a]

Row no.	*LEFCAB*	*SIZE*	*RELCAB*	*ETHDIV*	*GDPCAP*	*PDATE*	*CATH%*
1	0	0	0	0	0	0	0
21	0	0	1	0	1	0	0
33	0	1	0	0	0	0	0
40	0	1	0	0	1	1	1
55	0	1	1	0	1	1	0
69	1	0	0	0	1	0	0
75	1	0	0	1	0	1	0
80	1	0	0	1	1	1	1
97	1	1	0	0	0	0	0
108	1	1	0	1	0	1	1
114	1	1	1	0	0	0	1
128	1	1	1	1	1	1	1

Panel B. Cluster centers corresponding to truth table rows[b]

Row no.	*LEFCAB*	*SIZE*	*RELCAB*	*ETHDIV*	*GDPCAP*	*PDATE*	*CATH%*
1	-.95	-1.01	-.68	-.91	-.87	-.75	-1.13
21	-.95	-1.01	1.02	-.91	.83	-.75	-1.13
33	-.95	1.03	-.68	-.91	-.87	-.75	-1.13
40	-.95	1.03	-.68	-.91	.83	1.12	1.37
55	-.95	1.03	1.02	-.91	.83	1.12	-1.13
69	1.07	-1.01	-.68	-.91	.83	-.75	-1.13
75	1.07	-1.01	-.68	1.18	-.87	1.12	-1.13
80	1.07	-1.01	-.68	1.18	.83	1.12	1.37
97	1.07	1.03	-.68	-.91	-.87	-.75	-1.13
108	1.07	1.03	-.68	1.18	-.87	1.12	1.37
114	1.07	1.03	1.02	-.91	-.87	-.75	1.37
128	1.07	1.03	1.02	1.18	.83	1.12	1.37

[a]The outcome variable is not shown; only a subset of the 128 truth table rows are shown. The row numbers correspond to 128 rows of the truth table, in Boolean order, from row 1 (Boolean value 0000000) to row 128 (Boolean value 1111111).
[b]The numerical values are the minimum and the maximum values of the winsorized-standardized variables; see Table 13.3.

Table 13.5. ***Results of the cluster analysis of causal conditions***

Cluster no.	Causal configuration[a] 1	2	3	4	5	6	7	Country
2	0	0	0	0	0	0	1	Ireland
9	0	0	0	1	0	0	0	Australia, New Zealand
32	0	0	1	1	1	1	1	Switzerland
35	0	1	0	0	0	1	0	Japan
38	0	1	0	0	1	0	1	France
44	0	1	0	1	0	1	1	Canada
47	0	1	0	1	1	1	0	United States
50	0	1	1	0	0	0	1	Italy
54	0	1	1	0	1	0	1	Germany
67	1	0	0	0	0	1	0	Finland
69	1	0	0	0	1	0	0	Denmark, Sweden
71	1	0	0	0	1	1	0	Norway
82	1	0	1	0	0	0	1	Austria
96	1	0	1	1	1	1	1	Belgium
105	1	1	0	1	0	0	0	United Kingdom
129	x	x	x	x	x	x	x	Netherlands

[a] 1 = *LEFCAB*, 2 = *SIZE*, 3 = *RELCAB*, 4 = *ETHDIV*, 5 = *GDPCAP*, 6 = *PDATE*, 7 = *CATH%*.

of total pensions expenditures, (2) the index of corporativistic pension systems (which combines two measures – number of occupationally specific public pension programs and public employee pension expenditures divided by GDP), and (3) the index of pension decommodification. In this cluster analysis, the problem is *not* to fit the data to a truth table, but to determine which, if any, of three pension worlds each country fits best, using predetermined values for cluster centers that correspond to Esping-Andersen's constructed types.

Three hypothetical cluster centers are defined by the three worlds (see Table 13.6). The liberal cluster center is defined by a high value on private pensions and low values on both the index of corporativism and pension decommodification (the high-low-low corner of the three-dimensional cube defined by the three measures). The corporativistic cluster center is defined by a low value on private pensions, a high value on corporativism, and a medium value on pension decommodification (consistent with Esping-Andersen's portrayal of this world as intermediate between the liberal and social democratic worlds on decommodification). Finally, the social democratic cluster center is defined by low values on

Table 13.6. *Cluster analysis of characteristics of pension systems*

A. Cluster centers[a]

	Private pensions	Civil servants/ No. of programs	Pension decommod.
1. Liberal	0.83	-0.74	-0.92
2. Corporativistic	-0.94	0.94	0
3. Social democratic	-0.94	-0.74	1.25
4. Spare	0	0	0

B. Assignments of cases to clusters

1. Liberal	2. Social democratic
Australia	Denmark
Canada	Norway
Switzerland	Sweden
United States	
3. Corporativistic	**4. Spare**
Austria	Germany
Belgium	Ireland
Finland	Japan
France	Netherlands
Italy	New Zealand
	United Kingdom

[a]The values displayed are winsorized-standardized values of the variables used by Esping-Andersen (1990) to characterize the differences among pension systems, consistent with his tripartite scheme.

both private pensions and corporativism, as well as a high value on pension decommodification. A *fourth* cluster center is defined by the mean values of the three measures. The purpose of the fourth is to capture those cases that do not conform well to any of the three types specified by Esping-Andersen.

Table 13.6 shows the four cluster centers specified for the SPSS/PC+ QUICK CLUSTER program (using winsorized-standardized measures) and the resulting assignment of countries to cluster centers. The nine preliminary assignments of countries to pension worlds presented in Table 13.1 are confirmed, and additional assignments are made as well:

Denmark is added to the social democratic world, and Belgium and Finland are added to the corporativistic (these assignments confirm Esping-Andersen's conjectures). While Finland's cluster assignment contradicts Esping-Andersen's general treatment of the Finnish case as social democratic, it is consistent with his discussion of Finland's pension system as possibly corporativistic. However, he does not resolve this contradiction. Further problems surface: Germany, Ireland, Japan, the Netherlands, New Zealand, and the United Kingdom are captured by the fourth, "spare" cluster that was included to accommodate cases not conforming to any of Esping-Andersen's three worlds. With six countries, this last cluster is the largest of the four. Overall, these results indicate that the diversity of pension systems is a topic that requires further attention from students of the welfare state (see also Castles and Mitchell 1990). The three-world scheme does not capture existing diversity adequately, even when measures reported in Esping-Andersen (1990) are used, and some cluster assignments contradict the ad hoc assignments made by Esping-Andersen.

QUALITATIVE COMPARATIVE ANALYSIS OF THE CAUSES OF DIVERSITY

The results of the cluster analysis of causal configurations reported in Table 13.5 can be combined with the results of the cluster analysis of the characteristics of pension systems reported in Table 13.6 to produce three truth tables appropriate for QCA, which are presented in combined form in Table 13.7. The three main outcome clusters are represented as in Table 13.6; assignment to the fourth, spare cluster is represented with dashes. In QCA, rows with dashes are initially assigned to the "don't cares" category, which means that the algorithm can treat these as positive or negative outcomes (1s or 0s), depending on which designation in each instance produces a logically simpler solution (Mendelson 1970; Roth 1975). The Netherlands is shown along with the other 17 countries even though it is excluded from the Boolean analysis. This country's assignment to the indeterminate causal cluster mandates excluding it from the examination of causes.

Of the 128 causal configurations, instances of 15 were found among the 18 cases. For the other 113 causal combinations – those lacking empirical instances – the Boolean analysis can treat these as *negative* cases (giving them 0s on all outcome variables), as *positive* cases (giving them 1s on all outcome variables), or as "*don't cares*" (giving them dashes on all outcome variables). Generally, assigning hypothetical causal combinations to the don't care category results in more parsimonious solutions. In the interest of brevity, I use this strategy in the Boolean analysis.[4]

Table 13.7. ***Truth table for causes of diversity among pension systems***

Causal configuration[a]							Outcome cluster[b]			
1	2	3	4	5	6	7	Y_1	Y_2	Y_3	Country
0	0	0	1	0	0	0	1	0	0	Australia
1	0	1	0	0	0	1	0	1	0	Austria
1	0	1	1	1	1	1	0	1	0	Belgium
0	1	0	1	0	1	1	1	0	0	Canada
1	0	0	0	1	0	0	0	0	1	Denmark
1	0	0	0	0	1	0	0	1	0	Finland
0	1	0	0	1	0	1	0	1	0	France
0	1	1	0	1	0	1	—	—	—	Germany
0	0	0	0	0	0	1	—	—	—	Ireland
0	1	1	0	0	0	1	0	1	0	Italy
0	1	0	0	0	1	0	—	—	—	Japan
x	x	x	x	x	x	x	—	—	—	Netherlands
0	0	0	1	0	0	0	—	—	—	New Zealand
1	0	0	0	1	1	0	0	0	1	Norway
1	0	0	0	1	0	0	0	0	1	Sweden
0	0	1	1	1	1	1	1	0	0	Switzerland
1	1	0	1	0	0	0	—	—	—	United Kingdom
0	1	0	1	1	1	0	1	0	0	United States

[a] 1 = *LEFCAB*, 2 = *SIZE*, 3 = *RELCAB*, 4 = *ETHDIV*, 5 = *GDPCAP*, 6 = *PDATE*, 7 = *CATH%*, see Table 13.2.
[b] Y_1 = liberal pension system, Y_2 = corporativistic pensions system, Y_3 = social democratic pension sytem, and "-" = don't care (assignment to spare cluster).

Liberal pension systems

Boolean minimization of the truth table for liberal pension systems (Y_1 in Table 13.7) results in a very simple solution:

$$\text{Liberal} = lefcab \times ETHDIV$$

(A variable name in uppercase letters indicates presence; lowercase letters indicate absence; multiplication indicates a combination of causes – causal conjunctures; addition indicates alternate causes or alternate causal combinations – multiple conjunctural causation.) Liberal pension systems are found in countries with little or no rule by Left parties and high ethnic diversity. This causal combination conforms to the general bipolar characterization of welfare states central to the political class struggle explanation, which cites the historically decisive role of an organized working class in alliance with Left political parties to explain the emergence of social democratic welfare states. The results indicate that when a weak Left is combined with ethnic diversity, not only does a social democratic pension system fail to coalesce, but a private system emerges to cater to the needs of the more affluent members of society. More than likely, those served by the private pension system are less diverse ethnically and more ethnically advantaged than those excluded from this system.

Of the six countries assigned to the spare cluster in the analysis of characteristics of pension systems, only New Zealand conforms to the Boolean equation for liberal pension systems (the combination of weak Left parties and ethnic diversity). An intensive analysis of New Zealand's pension system might show how it conforms to the liberal model despite the weakness of its private pension system. Alternatively, this analysis might challenge the combined causes specified in the equation for liberal pension systems.

Corporativistic pension systems

Simplification of the truth table for corporativistic pension systems results in a complex solution showing multiple conjunctural causation:

$$\text{Corporativistic} = (\mathit{ethdiv} \times \mathit{gdpcap}) + (\mathit{ethdiv} \times \mathit{CATH\%}) + (\mathit{LEFCAB} \times \mathit{gdpcap}) + (\mathit{LEFCAB} \times \mathit{CATH\%}).$$

This relatively complex equation can be factored to produce a simpler equation:

$$\text{Corporativistic} = (\mathit{ethdiv} + \mathit{LEFCAB}) \times (\mathit{gdpcap} + \mathit{CATH\%}).$$

In this product-of-sums equation, addition indicates logical "or." Thus, the terms within parentheses function as causal equivalents.

The four combinations of conditions for corporativistic pension systems listed in the equation cover different and overlapping cases. The combinations *ethdiv* × *gdpcap* and *LEFCAB* × *gdpcap* cover Austria and Finland. The combination *ethdiv* × *CATH%* covers Austria, France, and Italy, while the combination *LEFCAB* × *CATH%* covers Austria and Belgium. All four causal combinations cover Austria, suggesting it is the modal or ideal typic corporativistic case.

In sharp contrast to the solution for liberal pension systems, the solution for corporativistic systems emphasizes the presence of ethnic homogeneity or Left-party strength. The presence of either of these conditions bars the liberal outcome, but one or the other must be present for the emergence of a corporativistic system. Additionally, one of these two conditions must be combined with either lower wealth or a large percentage of Catholics. In many parts of Europe, Catholicism has been associated with a collectivist orientation compatible with the segmented nature of corporativistic pensions systems. Also, lower relative wealth tends to favor the segmented growth of pension systems, with groups of occupations added to the system in stages.

Of the six countries assigned to the spare cluster in the analysis of characteristics of pension systems, four conform to the Boolean equation for corporativistic systems: Ireland, Japan, Germany, and the United Kingdom. As noted in the discussion of Table 13.1, the corporativistic world is the murkiest of the three. The cluster analysis of characteristics of pension systems presented in Table 13.6 follows Esping-Andersen's treatment of this world as intermediate between the liberal and the social democratic worlds on the decommodification index (i.e., pension quality). However, these four countries from the spare cluster combine medium or high scores on the index of corporativism with medium or high scores on private pensions – the indicator of liberal pension systems – and three of the four have *low* scores on the index of pension decommodification. The fourth, Japan, has a medium score on pension decommodification but a high score on private pensions. In short, these four countries are characterized by a combination of liberal elements and corporativistic elements in their pension systems. The results of the Boolean analysis of corporativism thus indicate that there may be two subtypes of corporativistic countries – those that lean toward the social democratic world (i.e., Austria, Finland, Italy, France, and Belgium) and those that lean toward the liberal world (i.e., Ireland, Japan, Germany, and the United Kingdom).[6]

Social democratic pension systems

Boolean minimization of the truth table for social democratic pension systems produces the most perplexing results. In contrast to the solution for liberal systems (where a single causal combination covers all cases) and the solution for corporativistic systems (where different casual combinations cover different cases), the solution for social democratic pension systems results in many different casual combinations, but each combination covers *all* cases. In short, the results for the social democratic countries are overdetermined.

Altogether, the equation for the social democratic countries includes seven different causal conjunctures:

$$\begin{aligned}\text{Social democratic} = {} & (size \times GDPCAP \times cath\%) \\ & + (size \times ethdiv \times GDPCAP) + (size \times relcab \times GDPCAP) \\ & + (LEFCAB \times GDPCAP \times cath\%) \\ & + (LEFCAB \times ethdiv \times GDPCAP) \\ & + (LEFCAB \times relcab \times GDPCAP) \\ & + (ethdiv \times GDPCAP \times cath\%).\end{aligned}$$

While perplexing, there are consistencies across the causal conjunctures. The first six terms can be factored to produce a simpler expression:

$$\begin{aligned}\text{Social democratic} = {} & GDPCAP \times (LEFCAB + size) \\ & \times (ethdiv + cath\% + relcab).\end{aligned}$$

Essentially, this equation states that greater wealth must be combined with either a strong Left or small country size, which in turn must be combined with either relative ethnic homogeneity, a small percentage of Catholics, or weak religious parties. There are many equivalent solutions to the truth table for social democratic pension systems because the social democratic countries share many causally relevant characteristics: a strong Left, small size, weak religious parties, ethnic homogeneity, greater wealth, and a small percentage of Catholics.

Because all seven causal combinations cover all cases, it is reasonable to use substantive and theoretical criteria to choose from among them. While foreign to the world of quantitative analysis, this practice is common in the qualitative analysis of small *N*s, where the number of possible explanations routinely exceeds the number of cases. (For an extended discussion of this issue and related topics, see Ragin and Hein in press.) One possible solution to the problem of overdetermination is to select terms with the maximum overlap with the solutions for the other two types (liberal and corporativistic). Of the seven equivalent causal combinations, the two terms that include greater wealth and strong Left parties ($LEFCAB \times ethdiv \times GDPCAP$ and $LEFCAB \times GDPCAP \times cath\%$) overlap the most with causal variables appearing in the equations for liberal and corporativistic systems. The combination $LEFCAB \times ethdiv \times GDPCAP$ includes two causal variables that are the opposite of those that combine to produce the liberal outcome (ethnic diversity and a weak Left: $lefcab \times ETHDIV$). The presence of *GDPCAP* in this term also distinguishes it from two terms in the equation for corporativistic systems – those that include lower relative wealth ($ethdiv \times gdpcap$ and $LEFCAB \times gdpcap$). The combination $LEFCAB \times GDPCAP \times cath\%$ from the equation for social democratic systems distinguishes these systems from the other two causal combinations in the equation for corporativistic systems – the two that include a high percentage of Catholics ($LEFCAB \times CATH\%$ and $ethdiv \times CATH\%$).

To maximize relevance to the other equations, therefore, the social democratic equation can be represented as follows:

$$\text{Social democratic} = LEFCAB \times GDPCAP \times (ethdiv + cath\%).$$

Of course, all social democratic countries combine ethnic homogeneity and a low percentage of Catholics. So the equation could be written as a single combination of the four causal factors – a strong Left, greater relative wealth, ethnic homogeneity, and a low percentage of Catholics.

This last equation is consistent with the political class struggle explanation of the social democratic welfare state. It further stipulates, however, that greater wealth and either ethnic homogeneity or a low percentage of Catholics must be combined with Left-party strength. Two of these additional conditions – greater wealth and a low percentage of Catholics – are the very factors that distinguish countries with social democratic systems from those with corporativistic systems.

DISCUSSION

Full treatment of the substantive issues raised in this chapter must await further refinement of the relevant concepts and measures. Nevertheless, it is clear, first of all, that the diversity of pensions systems (and, by implication, welfare states) is greater than that allowed in Esping-Andersen's tripartite scheme. The results presented in Tables 13.1 and 13.6 and the results of the Boolean analyses cast serious doubt on the idea of three types of welfare capitalism. They indicate especially that the corporativistic category is a mixed bag. Some corporativistic systems tend toward the social democratic pattern and others tend toward the liberal. This division into two subgroups is worthy of further research. The findings presented here add fuel to the fire started by Castles and Mitchell (1990), who focus on problems in Esping-Andersen's conceptualization of the liberal category. A second major substantive conclusion is that the main outline of the political class struggle explanation of the diversity of pension systems is supported, as in Palme's (1990) study of pension rights. The weakness of the Left appears to be a key factor in explaining the emergence of liberal systems, while the strength of the Left appears to be important to the emergence of all social democratic systems and some corporativistic systems. The third main substantive conclusion is that ethnic factors matter. Ethnic diversity appears to be important in explaining the emergence of liberal systems, while relative ethnic homogeneity seems to be important in explaining both social democratic and corporativistic outcomes. The degree to which this effect is mediated by class, by labor organization, or by political and other forces is a topic for future research.

With respect to methodological objectives, first, this chapter demonstrates the application of QCA to a modest-sized data set with 18 cases, seven causal conditions, and three outcome categories. Second, it demonstrates how to use cluster analysis to translate interval-scale variables to the qualitative states defined by a truth table. Third, it demonstrates further how to accomplish this translation for (1) interval-scale causal variables that must be matched to configurations of causal conditions defined by a truth table and (2) interval-scale outcome variables that must be matched to configurations of outcomes understood as theoretically constructed types (i.e., Esping-Andersen's three worlds). Fourth, it shows some of the interpretive art involved in using QCA, a feature it shares with other qualitative methods. The solution for social democratic systems is overdetermined. Using substantive interests as a guide, this solution can be winnowed to one that maximizes contrasts with the other two solutions.

The QCA of national-level data on pensions programs presented in this chapter demonstrates that some of the basic features of small-*N*, intensive investigation sketched in Chapter 12 can be maintained in studies with more than a handful of cases. This study shows that it is possible to understand cases as configurations of causes and outcomes, to examine multiple conjunctural causation, to find general patterns without resorting to error vectors and probabilistic statements, and to examine qualitative outcomes. While the dialogue between ideas and evidence has been limited by the priority of methodological objectives, it is clear from the results that many opportunities exist for more intensive case-oriented analysis of the countries in this study, using the results as a guide. QCA thus can be used to bridge case-oriented and variables-oriented research (Ragin 1991) by providing a platform for the qualitative analysis of configurations of quantitative variables.

NOTES

1. Curiously, Esping-Andersen (1990, pp. 85–7) does not use his own measure pension decommodification when he attempts to categorize pensions systems, despite the fact that it is the single best indicator of "population-wide social rights" characteristic of "universalistic, state-dominated" systems (see also Hicks 1991, pp. 399–401). My goal in using this indicator is to remain true to the major themes of his work in my assessment of the diversity of pension systems.
2. Esping-Andersen (1990, pp. 85–7) classifies New Zealand with the social democratic cases because of its dominance of public pensions; however, New Zealand's use of means testing prevents it from receiving a high pension decommodification score. In this same passage Esping-Andersen classifies Denmark as possibly social democratic ("universalistic, state-dominated") and Finland as possibly corporativistic.

3. It should be noted, however, that using raw values (i.e., unwinsorized data) produces results that are compatible with but not identical to the results using winsorized values.
4. Before presenting the results of the Boolean analysis, it must be emphasized that the clustering technique used here to bring interval-scale variables to QCA is a preliminary formulation. Further refinements might alter the results presented here. Also, the selection of causal and outcome variables for analysis is preliminary. A critical assessment of this literature would more than likely lead to the selection of causal and outcome variables different from the ones used here to demonstrate QCA.
5. Germany's inclusion in this list may seem curious. However, Esping-Andersen's data show that Germany has a moderate level of private pensions and a low pension decommodification score (see Table 13.1).

REFERENCES

Anderberg, M. R. 1973. *Cluster Analysis for Applications*. New York: Academic Press.

Barrett, David B. 1982. *World Christian Encyclopedia*. New York: Oxford University Press.

Castles, Francis, and Peter Mair. 1984. "Left–Right Political Scales: Some 'Expert' Judgements." *European Journal of Political Research* 12:73–88.

Castles, Francis, and Deborah Mitchell. 1990. "Three Worlds of Welfare Capitalism or Four?" Public Policy Program Discussion Paper 21. Canberra: Australia National University.

Day, Lincoln A. 1978. "Government Pensions for the Aged in 19 Industrial Countries: Demonstrations of a Method for Cross-National Evaluation." *Comparative Studies in Sociology* 1:217–33.

Drass, Kriss, and Charles C. Ragin. 1989. *QCA: Qualitative Comparative Analysis*. Evanston, Ill.: Center for Urban Affairs and Policy Research, Northwestern University.

Esping-Andersen, Gøsta. 1990. *The Three Worlds of Welfare Capitalism*. Princeton, N.U.: Princeton University Press.

Heclo, Hugh. 1974. *Modern Social Politics in Britain and Sweden*. New Haven, Conn.: Yale University Press.

Hicks, Alexander. 1991. Review of *The Three Worlds of Welfare Capitalism*. *Contemporary Sociology* 20(3):399–401.

Hoaglin, D. C., F. Mosteller, and J. W. Tukey. 1983. *Understanding Robust and Exploratory Data Analysis*. New York: Wiley.

1985. *Exploring Data Tables, Trends, and Shapes*. New York: Wiley.

Huber, Evelyne, Charles C. Ragin, and John D. Stephens. 1991. "Quantitative Studies of Variation Among Welfare States: Towards a Resolution of the Controversy." Evanston, Ill.: Center for Urban Affairs and Policy Research, Northwestern University.

Korpi, Walter 1983. *The Democratic Class Struggle*. London: Routledge & Kegan Paul.

Lenski, Gerhard. 1966. *Power and Privilege: A Theory of Social Stratification*. New York: McGraw-Hill.

Mackie, Thomas, and Richard Rose. 1991. *International Almanac of Electoral History*. Washington, D.C.: Congressional Quarterly.

Mendelson, Elliot. 1970. *Boolean Algebra and Switching Circuits*. New York: McGraw-Hill.

Myles, John. 1984. *Old Age in the Welfare State: The Political Economy of Public Pensions*. Boston: Little, Brown.

Organization for Economic Cooperation and Development. 1986. *Historical Statistics, 1960–1984*. Paris: OECD.

Palme, Joakim. 1990. *Pension Rights in Welfare Capitalism*. Stockholm: Swedish Institute for Social Research.

Pampel, Fred C., and John B. Williamson. 1985. "Age Structure, Politics, and Cross-National Patterns of Public Pension Expenditures." *American Sociological Review* 50:1424–56.

Quadagno, Jill. 1987. "Theories of the Welfare State." *Annual Review of Sociology* 13:109–28.

Ragin, Charles C. 1983. "Theory and Method in the Study of Dependency and International Inequality." *International Journal of Comparative Sociology* 24:121–36.

1987. *The Comparative Method: Moving Beyond Qualitative and Quantitative Strategies*. Berkeley: University of California Press.

1991. "Introduction: The Problem of Balancing Discourse on Cases and Variables in Comparative Social Science." In Charles C. Ragin (ed.), *Issues and Alternatives in Comparative Social Research*, pp. 1–8. Leiden: E. J. Brill.

Ragin, Charles C., and York W. Bradshaw. 1991. "Statistical Analysis of Employment Discrimination: A Review and Critique." *Research in Social Stratification and Mobility* 10:199–228.

Ragin, Charles C., and Jeremy Hein. In press. "Methodological and Conceptual Issues in the Comparative Study of Ethnicity." In John Stanfield II and Rutledge Dennis (eds.), *Race and Ethnicity: Methodological Innovations*. Newbury Park, Calif.: Sage.

Ragin, Charles C., Susan E. Mayer, and Kriss A. Drass. 1984. "Assessing Discrimination: A Boolean Approach." *American Sociological Review* 49:221–34.

Roth, Charles. 1975. *Fundamentals of Logic Design*. St. Paul, Minn.: West.

Skocpol, Theda, and Edwin Amenta. 1986. "States and Social Policies." *Annual Review of Sociology* 12:131–57.

Stephens, John D. 1979. *The Transition from Capitalism to Socialism*. London: Macmillan Press.

1991. "Industrial Concentration, Country Size, and Trade Union Membership." *American Political Science Review* 85(3):941–9.

Taylor, Charles L., and Michael Hudson. 1972. *World Handbook of Political and Social Indicators*. New Haven, Conn.: Yale University Press.

Tukey, J. W. 1977. *Exploratory Data Analysis*. Reading, Mass.: Addison-Wesley.

U.S. Department of Health and Human Services. 1990. *Social Security Around the World*. Washington, D.C.: U.S. Government Printing Office.

van Kersbergen, Kees. 1991. *Social Capitalism: A Study of Christian Democracy and the Post-War Settlement of the Welfare State*. Ph.D. diss., European University Institute.

Wallerstein, Michael. 1989. "Union Organization in Advanced Industrial Democracies." *American Political Science Review* 83(2):481–501

1991. "Union Concentration, Country Size, and Trade Union Membership." *American Political Science Review* 85(3):949–53.

Weir, Margaret, Ann Shola Orloff, and Theda Skocpol. 1988. "Introduction:

Understanding American Social Politics." In Margaret Weir, Ann Shola Orloff, and Theda Skocpol (eds.), *The Politics of Social Policy in the United States*, pp. 1–37. Princeton, N.J.: Princeton University Press.

Weisberg, Herbert F. 1992. *Central Tendency and Variability*. Sage University Paper Series on Quantitative Applications in the Social Sciences, 07–083. Newbury Park, Calif.: Sage.

Wilensky, Harold. 1975. *The Welfare State and Equality*: Berkeley: University of California Press.

1981. "Leftism, Catholicism, and Democratic Corporatism: The Role of Political Parties in Recent Welfare State Development." In P. Flora and A. Heidenheimer (eds.), *The Development of Welfare States in Europe and America*, pp. 345–82. New Brunswick, N.J.: Transaction Books.

14

The politics of social security: on regressions, qualitative comparisons, and cluster analysis

OLLI KANGAS

Recent debates in macrosociological and comparative methodology have revolved around the respective merits of the "variable-oriented" and "case studies" approaches. In its extreme form, the methodological debate has presented these two approaches as mutually antagonistic strategies and even as epistemologically distinct ways to interpret social reality. They have been contrasted by exemplifying them as nomothetic versus idiosyncratic brands of social sciences, or "inquiry from the outside" versus "inquiry from the inside" (see Bryman 1988).

Indeed, there are essential differences that seem to legitimate the sharp distinction. The variable-oriented approach attempts to apply standard quantitative methods in comparative analysis on a wider sample of countries, while the case approach is more focused on qualitative and historical analysis of individual cases. As a rule, the variable-oriented approach is theory-centered (see Ragin 1987, p. 55; Kiser and Hechter 1991). Hypotheses are derived from theories in order to test the relevance of the theory by submitting it to empirical examination that is usually conducted with the help of multivariate techniques. Thus, the approach is hypothetical-deductive in character and is employed in order to obtain results that can legitimately be generalized to the broadest possible sample.

By contrast, case studies are not aimed at testing theories per se; instead, the formulation and evaluation of theories proceeds simultaneously with historical narration. Since such inquiry tends to reveal that causes necessary and sufficient to bring about various social outcomes may differ between places and periods, practitioners of this method have been inclined to develop explanations that are limited to certain

I would like to thank Göran Ahrne, Eero Carroll, Walter Korpi, Joakim Palme, and Irene Wennemo for valuable comments.

spatiotemporal units (Skocpol and Somers 1980, p. 181; Kiser and Hechter 1991).

Each of these two orientations have their strengths as well as weaknesses. The strong point of the case studies design is that it gives a detailed description of the state of affairs and the processes through which actual historical developments took shape. It is sensitive to time, place, agency, and process (Ragin 1987, p. 11; Allardt 1990). In addition, the investigator is able to evaluate more effectively the complexity and variability of causal conditions by concentrating on one or a few cases. However, an increase in the number of cases will complicate the handling of causal conditions. A further problem is that it is hard to make generalizations on the basis of detailed historical story telling: the relative importance of singularities is difficult to determine from setting to setting (Tilly 1984, pp. 87–96).

By contrast, the variable-oriented approach is focused on establishing similar patterns over the sample analyzed. Thus, the merit of the approach lies in figuring out a general standard against which individual cases can be evaluated. But the approach has been accused of being linear and monocausal, that is, of assuming that the causal links between explanandum and explanans work in a similar fashion from case to case regardless of the variation in other attributes in a wider social and historical framework (e.g., Ragin 1987, p. 59; Allardt 1990, pp. 184–5).

The crucial question when balancing the case orientation against the variable approach thus appears to be how to obtain the generality produced by the latter without sacrificing the complexity achieved by the former. Recently, some suggestions on alternative middle-of-the-road strategies have been presented. Ragin (1987) suggests a comparative strategy that tries to combine the strengths of the case-oriented approach with the advantages of the variable-oriented studies. In this synthetic strategy of qualitative comparative analysis (QCA), whole cases are compared as configurations of parts, which allows us to preserve the complexity of case studies and generality of the variable research design (see Ragin 1987; Chapters 12 and 13, this volume).

In a parallel way, in his analysis of welfare capitalism, Esping-Andersen (1990) emphasizes that the development of national welfare states must be understood in terms of social categories instead of linearly distributed variable values. Therefore, an approach based on the maxim "the more x, the better y" is simply not sufficient. The Esping-Andersenian typology of welfare capitalism yields three distinct ideal regime types: the social democratic, the liberal, and the corporatist clusters, each of them emerging from a different political configuration.

Since the study of welfare state development has been an expanding area of sociology, these methodological debates are of particular relevance for this field. Therefore, the empirical data used in this chapter refer to cross-national differences in social protection in 18 advanced OECD countries.

The purpose of this chapter is to evaluate the possible extent to which multivariate techniques suggest the same conclusions as alternative middle-of-the-road methodological approaches in explaining welfare state expansion. We begin with traditional regression models, results from which are compared with findings from QCA and cluster analysis. The latter method may be a fruitful tool to evaluate the existence of homogeneous welfare state clusters. Although cluster analysis is not a causal method, the clusters – providing that they are found – can be interpreted causally, as Esping-Andersen (1990) does when explaining the emergence of the three types of welfare capitalism.

For the sake of simplicity, our explanatory variables are limited to three sets of political factors most often offered as the explanation to the cross-country differences in the level of welfare state development. Hence, we shall consider the relative importance of working-class mobilization, the strength of Christian democratic parties, and the weakness of the political Right.

This chapter is organized as follows. First, the three political explanations evaluated in subsequent analyses are discussed and specified. Second, data and variable operationalizations are explicated. The evaluation of the methods begins with application of the ordinary least squares (OLS) regressions techniques, followed by separate sections of the QCA and cluster analysis. Finally, results from different methods are compared, and the merits and limits of various methodological choices are discussed.

THREE POLITICAL EXPLANATIONS TO THE WELFARE STATE

In contrast to various structural explanations of welfare state expansion, many studies emphasize the crucial role played by various societal actors. (For a fuller discussion see, e.g., Alber 1982; Uusitalo 1984; Quadagno 1988; and Korpi 1989.) In the power resource approach, changes in the distribution of power resources are assigned a key role for the development of social policy in Western countries. In this approach, the emergence of mass democracy in the wake of industrialism – especially the rise of leftist political parties and labor unions, reflecting the new class structure of Western societies – are seen as a major cause of changes in the distribution of power resources between societal actors (Korpi 1985). These changes often motivated strategic action by previously established interest groups and conservative or liberal parties, aimed at forestalling working-class mobilization. However, in many countries, left-wing parties eventually managed to attain positions in government. In this context, working-class organizations can be regarded as indirectly or directly important for the formation of the welfare state, and political power is seen as purposefully being used to modify the outcomes of the play of market forces and to shelter individuals against different kinds of social risks (Korpi 1980, 1989; and Esping-Andersen and Korpi 1984; Esping-Andersen 1985, 1990). To sum up the hypothesis: the higher the degree of working-class mobilization, the higher the quality of social protection.[1]

In some theories that emphasize the importance of social agency, the composition of bourgeois parties has been given special attention. According to Castles (1978, 1982), the existence of internal splits among the bourgeoisie is a crucial factor when explaining post–World War II developments in social policy. Where such splits are absent, nonsocialist parties have been able to resist labor demands to expand welfare measures. Thus, on the basis of this hypothesis we can expect disunity on the political Right to be associated with high social security.

In other theories, nonsocialist parties play a more active role than that of a failing brakeman. Bourgeois parties have even been given credit for actively accelerating the growth of the welfare state. Thus, for example, Baldwin (1990) questions the prevailing assumption of the close relationship between socialist rule and universalist social policy in Scandinavia. The impact of the rural population and, later, demands from the middle classes enlarged the extension of coverage in social insurance far beyond the traditional working class (cf., Marklund 1982; Kuhnle 1983; Therborn 1984; and Esping-Andersen and Korpi 1984, 45–6). In many studies, the crucial role of denominational parties has been pointed out. Wilensky (1981) and Stephens (1979), for example, emphasize that the more intense the political competition between denominational parties and labor, the more the parties in power will spend on social security. Thus, this hypothesis leads us to expect that the higher the degree of mobilization of denominational parties, the higher the quality of social protection.

DATA AND VARIABLES

Until recently, analyses of the expansion of the welfare state have predominantly concentrated on social spending. However, in recent years, attempts have been made to compile sets of comparable data that can be used as alternatives to expenditure data. Such data on "social rights" have also been applied in this study (cf. Korpi 1989). This chapter focuses on one of the main aspects of social protection, that is, the quality of health insurance. In order to test if the relationships between variables have changed during the post–World War II period, we perform identical analyses for 1950 and for 1985.

When performing regression and QCA analyses, our dependent variable is operationalized as an additive index of the quality of health provisions. The index consists of the income loss replacement ratio (net benefit as a percentage of net wage), the coverage rates, the number of waiting days, and the length of the contribution period required for the access to benefits.[2] In the search for welfare state clusters, these variables are introduced separately into cluster analysis.

The explanatory political variables employed in the analyses are operationalized as follows: *Working-class mobilization* is a mean of three different mobilization measures: union density (the number of unionized workers/total labor force), the percent share of parliamentary seats held by members of left-wing parties, and the proportion of cabinet portfolios held by leftist ministers. *Christian democratic power* is measured as a mean of the share of parliamentary seats and the share of cabinet positions held by members of denominational parties. Concerning *splits on the right*, as proposed by Castles (1978, 1982), we can expect that where the nonsocialist bloc has been split into many competing fractions, the representatives of the working class have been able to push through their sociopolitical reforms better than in countries with a unified Right. In this study, the weakness of the Right is operationalized as the average number of nonsocialist parties that receive more than 5 percent of parliamentary seats – the 5 percent limit was applied in order to eliminate the possible bias caused by tiny parties.

In the analysis for 1950, the political variables were computed as averages for the period 1947–50, while in the analysis for 1985 we used averages for the whole 35-year period between 1950 and 1985. Data on social rights, as well as on all background variables, have been gathered as part of a larger ongoing research project (see Korpi 1989; Palme 1990; and Kangas 1991).

REGRESSION MODELS

The impacts of our three explanatory variables are at first evaluated by utilizing OLS regressions, a method most frequently employed in this kind of comparative study. However, the regression approach has been blamed for its tendency to make too strong presuppositions on relationships between the dependent and independent variables. Critics have warned against assuming that similar scores for explanatory variables

Table 14.1. *OLS regression of the level of social rights in health insurance in 1950 and 1985 (standardized coefficients, T-statistics within parenthesis)*

Independent variable	1950 (1)	1950 (2)	1985 (1)	1985 (3)
Working-class mobilization	0.228	0.341*	0.499*	0.535*
	(1.390)	(3.206)	(2.749)	(2.820)
Christian democratic power	0.754***	0.820***	0.368	0.191
	(4.509)	(7.387)	(2.058)	(1.010)
Weak Right	0.120	0.230	0.348	0.501*
	(.725)	(2.090)	(1.916)	(2.662)
df	14	12	14	11
Adjusted R^2	0.550	0.834	0.460	0.551
Stan. error of est.	72.405	42.155	79.847	58.804

Note: (1) Includes all 18 countries, (2) excludes Finland and Japan, and (3) excludes Australia, Germany, and the United States.
$*p \leq 0.005$; $**p \leq 0.01$; $***p \leq 0.001$.

result in similar outcomes from case to case (Ragin 1987; Esping-Andersen 1990). Therefore, in order to find out which cases the model fits particularly badly we apply a number of control techniques to analyze if the residuals reveal some systematic bias, outliers, or influential cases strongly affecting the parameter estimates. If such cases are identified, they are omitted from the sample and reanalyses are performed to see how sensitive the results are to these particular observations.

Results from the regression analyses are presented in Table 14.1. First of all, the table tells us that the relative importance of the independent variables greatly depends on the time point under study.

In 1950, the only agency-related variable resulting in significant impacts on the level of health benefits is the strength of denominational parties. In fact, Christian democratic power is clearly the most important variable in the model. The coefficient for working-class mobilization goes in the expected direction but is not significant. The coefficient for the weak Right variable is also positive but far from significant.

Residual analysis of the 1950 data reveal two principal deviations from the regression line: the level of health benefits in Japan is higher than what would be predicted by the model, while the level of Finnish benefits is much lower than predicted. The omission of these peculiar cases (Equation 2) considerably improves the general fit of our model (R^2 increases from .550 to .834). Betas for each of the explanatory variables increase, and the coefficient for working-class mobilization turns out to be statistically significant. Also the weak Right predictor performs better in the smaller sample.

In the 1985 data, the relative importance of the independent variables has changed markedly. The working-class mobilization variable turns out to be more important than the other two political measures, coefficients of which are positive as hypothesized but not quite significant.

The residual analysis reveals three problematic cases: Germany, with a higher level of benefits than predicted, and Australia and the United States, displaying benefits lower than predicted. The omission of these cases (Equation 3) modestly improves the fit of the model (R^2 increases from .460 to .551). In the reduced sample, the weak Right also becomes statistically significant, whereas the role of denominational parties is greatly circumscribed.

To sum up, our analyses show that the relative importance of the weak Right, working-class mobilization, and the strength of the Christian Democratic parties depends on the point of time under study. In the 1950 data, the hypotheses about the importance of denominational parties are strongly supported, while the 1985 data lend more support to the working-class mobilization hypothesis. The thesis on the importance of cleavages among nonsocialist parties is also better supported by the later data. This would appear to indicate that the causal patterns behind improvements of social security may have changed during the postwar period.

The analysis of residuals reveals that the model fits considerably better to some cases than to others. This gives us cause for criticism of overly mechanical generalizations of causal relationships from one context to another. However, it must be emphasized that by applying a well-defined formal model, we can determine not only the degree of overall fit between the model and the data, but also some standard against which deviant cases can be contrasted. These deviant cases can then be submitted to detailed analyses of why they display specific causal patterns. Thus, the variable approach can be nuanced by introducing historical interpretations of individual cases. In the regression models presented, outliers were simply excluded from further analyses. However, explanations for the problematic cases noted fall beyond the scope of the present chapter. Such accounts have been presented elsewhere.[3]

THE QUALITATIVE COMPARATIVE METHOD

As stated, the regression approach has been criticized for the dilution of important contextual configurations through the disaggregation of cases into variable values that are separated from their meaningful contexts. Since contextual factors may vary from case to case, the impacts of explanatory variables, despite identical scores of the variables in question, may take different forms. By contrast, case-oriented methods entail considering cases as wholes, and it is precisely the understanding of historical context that gives substance and meaning to individual variables (see Bryman 1988, p. 65). Due to this contextual holism, the case approach is assumed to enable the researcher to take better account of the complexity of causal combinations.

The problem here is that the increase in the number of cases will lead to overwhelming problems with handling multiple causal conjunctures. Ragin's (1987) QCA offers a possibility to bridge the gap between variable-oriented and case-oriented methods.

The first step in Ragin's method is basically the same as in the traditional variable-oriented research design: to identify the fundamental causal mechanisms and relevant variables measuring the working of those mechanisms. In the following exercise, we will employ the same variables already used and analyze the same causal connections.

Since all variables employed in QCA must be dichotomous nominal-scale measures, the second task is to express them in binary form. Here, the original interval scales are therefore dichotomized. If the actual value of a variable exceeds the mean value of that variable for all 18 countries, it is assigned a value of 1; if its value does not exceed the mean it is assigned a value of 0.

The raw data matrix is presented in the form of truth tables (Tables 14.2 and 14.3), which summarize the various combinations of independent variables and their links with the outcomes. As can be seen, a specific outcome may be a result of several different combination of conditions. In the 1950 data (Table 14.2), seven different combinations of political factors are achieved, two of them resulting in a high level and three in a low level of social protection. Two combinations of causes are contradictory, that is, the same combinations result in both high and low benefit levels. In Denmark, Finland, and Sweden, high working-class mobilization combined with a splintered bourgeois bloc and the absence of denominational parties produce low social protection, while in Norway the same combination produces a high benefit level. Also the Netherlands and Switzerland display contradictory results. The problems caused by contradictions are discussed later.

Table 14.2. *Truth table for causes of quality of health insurance provisions in 1950*

Combination			Outcome	
W	*C*	*F*	*S*	Cases
1	0	0	0	Australia, New Zealand, the United Kingdom
1	1	0	1	Austria, Belgium
0	0	0	0	Canada, United States
1	0	1	0	Denmark, Finland, Sweden
1	0	1	1	Norway
0	1	0	1	France, Germany, Italy
0	0	1	0	Ireland, Japan
0	1	1	1	Netherlands
0	1	1	0	Switzerland

Note: *W* = high working-class mobilization; *C* = strong Christian democratic power; *F* = fragmented bourgeois bloc; *S* = high level of social provisions in health insurance

Table 14.3. *Truth table for causes of quality of health insurance provisions in 1985*

Combination			Outcome	
W	*C*	*F*	*S*	Cases
1	0	0	0	Australia, New Zealand, the United Kingdom
1	1	0	1	Austria
0	0	0	0	Canada, Ireland, Japan, United States
1	0	1	0	Denmark, Finland, Norway, Sweden
0	1	0	1	Germany, Italy
0	1	1	0	Belgium
0	1	1	1	Netherlands, Switzerland
0	0	1	0	France

The next step is to eliminate "unneeded" terms from variable combinations and to reduce the number of logically necessary equations. (For a fuller description of the principles of the elimination, see Ragin, Chapters 12 and 13, this volume). The application of the minimization algorithms[4] produces the equation $S = Cf$, where uppercase letters represent high levels (presence) and lowercase letters represent low levels (absence) of variables. The equation thus demonstrates that in 1950 there was only one combination of political variables necessary to explain the high social protection (*S*): a unified nonsocialist bloc with religious affiliations (*Cf*). This pattern is exemplified by France, Germany, and Italy. Working-class mobilization and the weakness of the Right seem to be of less importance in this context. Although benefits are high in Austria and Belgium, where the scores for working-class mobilization are high, the reduced equation suggests that Christian democracy deserves more credit for the outcome than does working-class mobilization. In addition, in the Scandinavian countries, with the exception of Norway, working-class mobilization did not produce a high level of benefits. Thus, according to QCA, both working-class mobilization and the weakness of the Right are of negligible importance when explaining cross-national differences in the quality of social security provisions in 1950.

To round out this picture, combinations of conditions linked to relatively low health provisions are also analyzed. The minimization confirms the preceding results. The equation achieved ($s = F + c$) reveals that two logical combinations cover all the instances presented in Table 14.2. A low level of benefits is related to the absence of a significant denominational party or the weakness of the Right.

In 1985, seven different causal combinations can be discerned. Three of these combinations are related to a high benefit level and three to a low benefit level, with the one remaining combination leading to contradictory results (Belgium vs. the Netherlands and Switzerland in Table 14.3). The minimization process leads into the following two logical functions: $S = WF + Cf$. The first causal combination indicates that the benefit level is high in countries with strong labor mobilization, combined with fragmentation among right-wing parties (*WF*). This pattern is typical in the Scandinavian countries, as indicated by the truth table. The second combination indicates that a unified bourgeois bloc, providing that its political ideology is Christian Democratic (*Cf*), also guarantees a high level of social rights. This route is typical to the Central European countries. As indicated in the discussion of the 1950 data, this causal combination seems to have longer historical roots than the "social democratic" one.

Complementary analyses were performed here as well to see which political configurations are associated with a low level of benefits. The equation obtained ($s = wc + cf$) reveals that a low benefit level is found in countries with low working-class mobilization in combination with the absence of influential religious parties (*wc*) and in cases of a homogeneous and secular bourgeois block (*cf*).

To sum up, QCA analyses of cross-national differences in health insurance provisions in 1950 give strong support to the hypothesis of the importance of denominational parties, whereas the differences cannot be explained by the weakness of the Right or by working-class mobilization. The 1985 data support all three hypotheses, but only to a qualified extent. For example, results indicate that working-class mobilization as such is not a sufficient cause for high social provisions, as exemplified by Australia, New Zealand, and the United Kingdom. Each of these countries has had a relatively high degree of working-class mobilization but nevertheless scores low benefit levels. In line with Castles's thesis on the importance of the weakness of the Right, the results from QCA demonstrate that only where working-class mobilization is accompanied by a split bourgeois bloc will the outcome be a high level of social security. However, the QCA results also indicate deficiencies in the weakness of the Right thesis: a relatively strong bourgeois bloc, providing that it has religious affiliations, tends to introduce social benefits of high quality, whereas a strong and unified bourgeois group without denominational associations tends to produce social protection of lower quality.

As indicated in Tables 14.2 and 14.3, we have some contradictory logical conjunctures: a similar combination of explanatory variables resulted in high and low benefit levels. In the Dutch case, low working-class mobilization combined with high denominational party strength and a fragmented bourgeois bloc resulted in a high level of social protection, while the opposite was true for the Swiss case. Outcomes in the Scandinavian group were also contradictory: strong working class mobilization combined with a fragmented bourgeois bloc produced high benefits in Norway, whereas provisions were low grade in the other three countries.

A more detailed study of problematic cases and an introduction of additional variables are suggested as a general remedy for tackling this problem of contradictions (Ragin 1987, pp. 113–18). However, there are some alternative procedures as well: the researcher could code all ambiguous cases to nonexistent combinations or rely on the frequency criteria. The latter solution would in our case suggest that the Norwegian case should, as in the cases of the three other Scandinavian countries, be recoded as a country low in social protection. However, the results would be the same as those already presented. The results also remain the same if contradictory terms are recoded to nonexistent scores. Of these methods to handle problematic cases, a more detailed examination of troublesome combinations is the most "orthodox" way of seizing contradictions. In a way, this is a parallel method to residual analysis applied in conjunction with traditional regression techniques, as exemplified in the section entitled "Regression Models." This accentuates a problem that the qualitative comparative approach has in common with the traditional variable-oriented studies: how to select the relevant variables, as well as how to code and present the empirical world satisfactorily in the form of variable values, either in dichotomous or continuous form.

CLUSTER ANALYSIS

Interestingly enough, the results from the QCA analyses seem to provide indirect support to Esping-Andersen's (1990) notion of three welfare state regimes, each of which has its own internal political dynamics. In Central Europe, high-quality benefits result from the strength of the denominational parties, in Scandinavia from high working-class mobilization accompanied by weakness of the Right. In the English-speaking countries, neither the Central European nor the Scandinavian prerequisites are fulfilled, and consequently, the level of social protection guaranteed to citizens is lower.

Cluster analysis seems to be a sufficient method to evaluate the adequacy of Esping-Andersen's typology. (For a description of cluster analysis, see, e.g., Loether and McTavish 1988, pp. 378–84). The variables used are the same as those used for the construction of the index of the quality of health insurance provisions, but now they are introduced separately into the analysis.

In cluster analysis, different scales of measurement may greatly affect the results. Variables with numerically large values are likely to be more decisive than variables with smaller numbers. To circumvent this problem caused by different scales, the variables are here standardized by dividing them by the observed maximum value of the sample for the entire period under study.

The dendrogram plots shown in Figure 14.1 not only indicate which clusters are combined, but also display the relative distances at which the grouping of nations took place.[5] In the 1950 data, Canada, Finland, and the United States are distinctive because of the complete lack of legislated health insurance programs. Denmark and Sweden are merged together, later to be joined with a cluster including Ireland and the United Kingdom. Australia and New Zealand, due to their means-tested schemes, at first form their own group that is later joined to the cluster that consists of the Central European nations as well as Norway and Japan. Thus, inspection of the dendrogram for 1950 lends qualified support to the idea of welfare state clusters. We can distinguish embryos

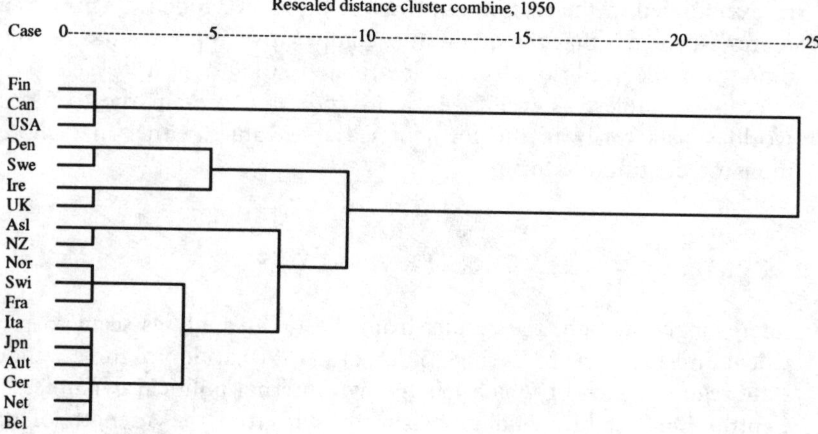

Figure 14.1. Dendrogram plots on characteristics of health insurance schemes in OECD countries in 1950 .

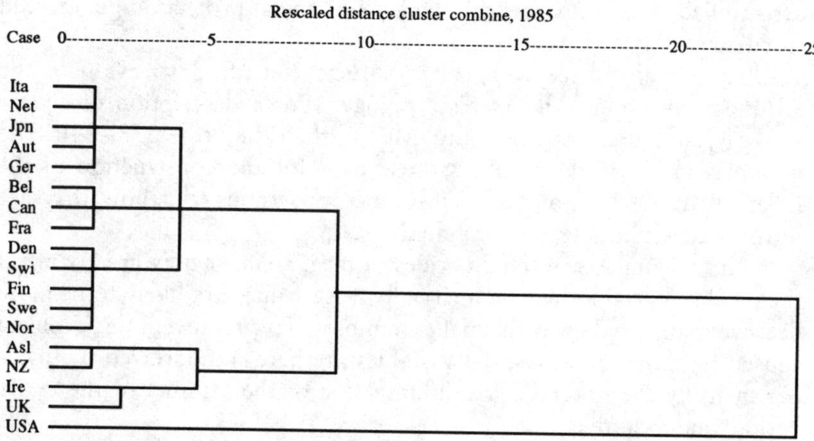

Figure 14.2. Dendrogram plots on characteristics of health insurance schemes in OECD countries in 1985.

of the Scandinavian cluster (Denmark and Sweden) and the continental European cluster. But the problem is that a homogeneous liberal cluster is harder to find.

In the data for 1985, shown in Figure 14.2, the formation of different clusters is somewhat more pronounced. At first Italy, the Netherlands, Japan, Austria, and Germany are grouped together in a cluster of corporatist regimes. This cluster can be characterized by medium-to-high income-loss compensations, with coverage limited to employees. The core of the social democratic regime can also be distinguished from the very beginning: Denmark, Finland, Sweden, and Norway are combined into one single group at the first clustering stage. Switzerland can also be added to this group. Emblematic of this group of countries is high replacement rates and high coverage among the population age 15–64. Again, however, it is hard to distinguish any clear liberal regime cluster. Undeniably, the two subclusters of Antipodean countries and Ireland and the United Kingdom are merged together, but the United States and Canada are problematic cases.

Recently, Castles and Mitchell (1990) have suggested certain modifications to the three-regime model. Instead of postulating a single Liberal regime, they distinguish two subclusters within the group of nations usually assigned to it. In the first subcluster, which includes the two Antipodean nations, politics have been based on coalitions between the liberals and the labor party. This configuration of political forces has led to means-tested and tax-financed welfare arrangements. The other subcluster consists of Canada and the United States, where conservative liberals achieved political hegemony. This group of nations is characterized by a heavier reliance on private-sector solutions and a lower level of redistributive effort (see Fritzell 1991, pp. 146–8).

Our analyses seem to lend some support to the idea of different welfare state regimes. The results from previous regression analyses and qualitative comparative analyses, in particular, seem to provide a political explanation for the development of welfare state regimes. However, it must be noted that distances found between the regimes are rather negligible. In control runs including more variables measuring the characteristics of legislated health insurance schemes, the clustering distances were larger, a finding that further supports the idea of distinct social policy regimes. In addition, it must be emphasized that our analysis was based on cross-sectional data that may affect the composition of welfare state clusters. The development within a cluster may be similar but not necessarily simultaneous.[6]

DISCUSSION

Recently, some alternative, middle-of-the-road strategies have been presented in order to bridge the gap between the case studies approach and variable orientation. In this chapter, efforts were made to ascertain the extent to which results from these middle-of-the-road strategies are compatible with the traditional regression techniques. The alternative methods employed were cluster analysis and qualitative comparative analysis. The analysis focused on the quality of social protection for the sick in 18 advanced OECD countries. Three political hypotheses most commonly offered as explanations of welfare state expansion were examined: working-class mobilization, the strength of religious parties, and the weakness of the Right.

Results from the regression analyses indicated that the relative importance of the political factors greatly depends on the point of time under study. In the data for 1950, the hypothesis on the importance of denominational parties was strongly supported, while analyses based on the data for 1985 provided stronger support to the hypotheses of working-class mobilization and the weakness of the right.

Practitioners of the regression approach have been blamed for their proclivity for generalizing their findings beyond the scope of actual historical contexts. However, it can be argued in defense of regression techniques that by applying a formal model we can determine not only the degree of overall fit between the model and the data, but also a standard against which individual cases can be evaluated. Problematic nations can then be "explained" away by submitting them to a more detailed historical scrutiny. Thus, the variable approach can be nuanced by introducing historical accounts of crucial cases.

The overall results from regression analyses were more or less confirmed by findings from QCA: on the basis of 1950 data the impact of denominationalism could clearly be viewed as the most important cause of high levels of social protection, while analyses of 1985 data indicated that high levels of social protection have been obtained both in countries with strong and unified Christian democratic parties and in countries with strong working-class mobilization and a weak right-wing bloc. Thus, all three of our hypotheses were supported. However, there were some important reservations conditioning the impacts of variables, and these reservations somewhat nuanced the impression given by the regression models. For example, the results derived from QCA indicated that the impacts of high working-class mobilization are different depending on the composition of the bourgeois bloc: where working-class mobilization is accompanied by a split bourgeois bloc, the outcome will be high social security, whereas the level of social provision tends to be rather low in countries with a unified bourgeoisie even where labor is highly mobilized – something that seems to support the weakness of the Right thesis. However, QCA also helps us to outline some qualifications of the thesis of the weak Right: a relatively strong bourgeois bloc, providing that it has religious affiliations, tends to introduce social benefits of high quality.

The great merit of QCA compared with traditional case studies is that it is easier to handle a larger number of cases. Compared with the conventional regression approach, the qualitative method can more effectively reveal multiple causal interactions in research designs where the limited number of cases does not otherwise allow for effective utilization of interaction terms in regression equations. Thus, the causal mechanisms suggested are more nuanced than those underlying regression analyses.

However, there are also limitations and deficiencies in this approach. First, a change in the value of a single variable may cause essential shifts in causal conjunctures. This sensitivity to changes in variable values may be a more severe problem for analysts using QCA than for those using multivariate methods. In addition, the presentation of the quality of social security systems – as well as many other social phenomena – in the dichotomous present–absent form is in many cases an oversimplification. In the real world of social protection, cross-country differences and longitudinal development within single countries are more adequately described as continuous measures than as purely dichotomous variables.

Second, in comparison to the regression approach, the QCA seems to be a method with which it is more difficult to estimate the relative significance of causal factors (cf., Lieberson 1991). In the regression analysis, the relative importance of different explanatory variables is specified from the beginning, which signals the researcher to exclude superfluous variables. In QCA, no variable originally introduced into the causal combinations is omitted unless it is logically unnecessary. Thus, explanatory factors that are relatively unimportant for producing the outcome in question are treated equally with factors that actually have vital impacts on the dependent variable. However, the problem can be minimized by paying careful theoretical attention to the selection of explanatory factors. The parallel use of regression techniques can also help to circumvent the problem caused by the low degree of selectivity in the QCA approach.

The other middle-of-the road method applied in this study was cluster analysis. The goal here was to test the three-fold typology of welfare state regimes. Our analyses lent some support to the distinction between social democratic, corporatist, and liberal ideal types of legislated social protection. In particular, results from regression models and QCA seem to provide elements of a multidimensional political explanation for the emergence of these welfare state types.

All in all, although the different approaches can be regarded as appropriate tools when seeking answers to different kinds of research problems, this study has shown that the results from analyses using divergent methods seem to be fairly compatible with each other, at least in the area of welfare state studies. Therefore, treating these approaches as mutually exclusive – not to speak of epistemologically contradictory –

would be an exaggeration. Rather than mutually exclusive, they are alternative or parallel research options for expanding our understanding of social reality.

NOTES

1. It must be emphasized that the political explanations are here presented in strongly simplified form. Very seldom, if ever, have the proponents of political approaches presented their theories as one-factor explanations. For example, the working-class mobilization thesis captures much more than purely left-wing power. In fact, it pertains to a broader political context in which strategic behavior and coalition making by different actors are conditioned by a relatively strong representation of working-class interests (Korpi 1989).
2. Net replacement ratios have been calculated separately for two family types: for a single person and for a married couple (with two children), each of them working with an average industrial wage. Separate replacement rates are also calculated for short-term absences of 1 week and for long-term absences lasting 26 weeks. Coverage rates are expressed as the percentage of insured persons in the population ages 16–64. Since it is hard to define the actual coverage rates in the means-tested Australian and New Zealand programs, coverage is not included in the index calculation for these two countries. The number of waiting days and the number of contribution weeks are finally subtracted from the sum of the four separate replacement ratios and the coverage figure. Since replacement levels and coverage ratios are measured as percentages, while qualifying conditions are given in absolute numbers, it is not possible directly to subtract the number of waiting days. Here the actual number of waiting days and the number of contribution weeks are divided by the observed maximum (14 days and 52 weeks) and multiplied by 100. Thus, our index weights the replacement by four, whereas the other measures are unweighted.
3. For more detailed narratives and case studies of these peculiar cases, see, e.g., Bodenheimer (1990) and Fein (1989) for the United States; Castles (1989) for Australia; Immergut (1986) for Germany; and Kangas (1991) for Finland.
4. Here, the minimization of combinations leading to high sickness allowances has been done by utilizing the QCA PC-software program (Drass 1988). In reducing the minimum number of causal combinations, all causal combinations were taken into consideration, that is, those combinations that are logically possible but that are not necessarily presented in the truth table. The exclusion of those combinations that do not appear in the truth table caused no changes in the results from analyzing 1950 data, whereas the minimized logical expression of high social protection in 1985 would be as follows: $S = WcF + Cf$.
5. The clustering method used here is the complete linkage method, where the distance between two clusters is calculated as the distance between their two furthest points. In order to evaluate the possible bias caused by the applied method, test runs on the 1985 data were also performed by using other procedures available in the SPSS-PC+ soft-ware package. The results were more or less the same, although the clustering distances varied slightly.

6. The replacement level of health insurance was raised and made taxable in 1974 in Sweden, 1978 in Norway, and 1982 in Finland, just to give an example of similar but not simultaneous development.

REFERENCES

Alber, Jens. 1982. *Vom Armenhaus zum Wohlfahrtsstaat. Analysen zur Entwicklung der Sozialversicherung in Westeuropa.* Frankfurt: Campus.

Allardt, Erik. 1990. "Challenges for Comparative Social Research." *Acta Sociologica*, 33(3):183–93.

Baldwin, Peter. 1990. *The Politics of Social Solidarity*. Cambridge University Press.

Bodenheimer, Thomas. 1990. "Should We Abolish the Private Health Insurance Industry?" *International Journal of Health Services* 20(2):199–220.

Bryman, Alan. 1988. *Quantity and Quality in Social Research*. London: Unwin Hyman.

Castles, Francis. 1978. *The Social Democratic Image of Society*. London: Routledge.

1982. "The Impact of Parties on Public Expenditure." In Francis Castles (ed.), *The Impact of Parties*, pp. 21–96. Newbury Park, Calif.: Sage.

1989. "Social Protection by Other Means: Australia's Strategy of Coping with External Vulnerability." In Francis Castles (ed.), *The Comparative History of Public Policy*, pp. 16–55. Cambridge: Polity.

Castles, Francis, and Deborah Mitchell. 1990. Three Worlds of Welfare Capitalism or Four? Australian National University, Public Policy Program, Discussion Paper, no. 21, Oct. 1990. Canberra.

Drass, Kriss. 1988. "QCA 1.03, Qualitative Comparative Analysis." Dallas: Department of Sociology, Southern Methodist University. Stencil.

Esping-Andersen, Gøsta. 1985. *Politics Against Markets*. Princeton, N.J.: Princeton University Press.

1990. *The Three Worlds of Welfare Capitalism*. Cambridge: Polity Press.

Esping-Andersen, Gøsta, and Walter Korpi. 1984. "Social Policy as Class Politics in Post-War Capitalism: Scandinavia, Austria, and Germany." In John Goldthorpe (ed.), *Order and Conflict in Contemporary Capitalism*, pp. 179–208. Oxford University Press.

Fein, Rashi. 1989. *Medical Care Medical Costs. The Search for a Health Insurance Policy*. Cambridge, Mass.: Harvard University Press.

Fritzell, Johan. 1991. *Icke av Marknaden allena: Inkomstfördelningen i Sverige*. Stockholm: Almqvist & Wicksell.

Immergut, Ellen. 1986. "Between State and Market: Sickness Benefits and Social Control." In Martin Rein and Lee Rainwater (eds.), *Public/Private Interplay in Social Protection*, pp. 57–98. Armonk, N.Y.: Sharpe.

Kangas, Olli. 1991. *The Politics of Social Rights: Studies on the Dimensions of Sickness Insurance in 18 OECD Countries*. Stockholm: Swedish Institute for Social Research.

Kiser, Edgar, and Michael Hechter. 1991. "The Role of General Theory in Comparative-Historical Sociology." *American Journal of Sociology* 1:1–39.

Korpi, Walter. 1980. "Social Policy and Distributional Conflict in the Capitalist Democracies." *West European Politics* 3(3):296–316.

1985. "Power Resources Approach vs. Action and Conflict: On Causal and Intentional Explanations in the Study of Power." *Sociological Theory* 3(2):31–45.

1989. "Power, Politics, and State Autonomy in the Development of Social Citizenship: Social Rights During Sickness in Eighteen OECD Countries Since 1930." *American Sociological Review*, 54(3):309–28.

Kuhnle, Stein. 1983. *Velferdsstatens utvickling – Norge i komparativt perspektiv*. Bergen: Universitetsforlaget.

Lieberson, Stanley. 1991. "Small *N*'s and Big Conclusions: An Examination of the Reasoning in Comparative Studies Based on a Small Number of Cases." *Social Forces* 70(2):307–20.

Loether, Herman, and Donald McTavish. 1988. *Descriptive and Inferential Statistics*. Boston: Allyn & Bacon.

Marklund, Staffan. 1982. *Klass, stat och socialpolitik*. Lund: Arkiv.

Palme, Joakim. 1990. *Pension Rights in Welfare Capitalism. The Development of Old-Age Pensions in 18 OECD Countries 1930 to 1985*. Stockholm: Swedish Institute for Social Research.

Quadagno, Jill. 1988. *The Transformation of Old Age Security: Class and Politics in the American Welfare State*. Chicago: University of Chicago Press.

Ragin, Charles. 1987. *The Comparative Method: Moving Beyond Qualitative and Quantitative Strategies*. Berkeley: University of California Press.

Skocpol, Theda, and Margaret Somers. 1980. "The Uses of Comparative History in Macrosocial Inquiry." *Comparative Studies in Society and History* 22:174–97.

Stephens, John. 1979. *The Transition from Capitalism to Socialism*. London: Macmillan Press.

Therborn, Göran. 1984. "Classes and States: Welfare State Developments, 1881–1981." *Studies in Political Economy* 13:7–41.

Tilly, Charles. 1984. *Big Structures, Large Processes, Huge Comparisons*. New York: Russel Sage Foundation.

Uusitalo, Hannu. 1984. "Comparative Research on the Determinants of the Welfare State: the State of the Art." *European Journal of Political Research* 22:403–22.

Wilensky, Harold. 1981. "Leftism, Catholicism, and Democratic Corporatism: The Role of Political Parties in Recent Welfare State Development." In Peter Flora and Arnold J. Heidenheimer (eds.), *The Development of the Welfare States in Europe and America*, pp. 345–82. New Brunswick N.J.: Transaction Books.

15

Conclusion: quo vadis *political economy? Theory and methodology in the comparative analysis of the welfare state*

THOMAS JANOSKI AND ALEXANDER M. HICKS

Before answering where the political economy of the welfare state may be going in the near future, we should first explain what we mean by that powerful but elusive term – "political economy." Political economy can encompass a maddeningly wide range of studies. In a book aptly titled *What Is Political Economy?* Martin Staniland asks what it means to title a work "The political economy of . . ." (1985, p. 1). He concludes that "there is no such thing as 'the theory of political economy,' and there never will be, in the sense of a single universally accepted complex of assumptions and methodology" (p. 198). He goes on to say that the use of the term "refers to a continuing intellectual enterprise, a particular agenda, a specific object of theoretical ambition" (p. 198). These diverse ways of viewing political economy range from classical and neoclassical economics through Marxist analysis, sociological studies of economic processes in institutional context, and political science analyses of "politico-economic interactions" (Frey 1979; Caporaso and Levine 1992). We will briefly review each approach and place this volume within the overall context of political economy.

The editorial board of the Library of Political Economy at Oxford University Press lists a somewhat earlier definition from economics:

> POLITICAL ECONOMY is the old name for economics. In the hands of the great classical economists, particularly Smith, Ricardo and Marx, economics was the study of the working and development of the economic system in which men and women lived. Its practitioners were driven by a desire to describe, to explain and to evaluate what they saw around them. No sharp distinction was drawn between economic analysis and economic policy nor between economic behavior and its interaction with the technical, social and political framework. (Shalev 1992, frontispiece)

This economically oriented definition can loosely encompass much of what is meant by political economy today, so long as wide latitude is allowed for economic "interaction" with the "technical, social and political." However, more narrowly economic definitions of political economy have been more recently and frequently offered. For example, Eyestone (1972, p. 2) has stated that "political economy can be thought of as a body of suggested practices for solving the basic economic problems of a society," thereby conflating political economy with orthodox, marginalist economics (see, e.g., Samuelson 1992). Meltzer, Cukierman, and Richard focus on a similarly narrow field of "individual choice by voters who maximize subject to constraints" (1991, p. vii). Chichilnisky calls for a political economy that focuses on "the general competitive model rather than dealing with *ad hoc* market imperfections" (1990, p. 38). Although some economists of various unorthodox persuasions may object to such narrow stipulations (Knight 1944, Stigler 1959, 1988; Hagen 1960; Heilbroner 1970; Kaldor 1972; Klein 1980; and Robbins 1981), the heart of the mainstream economic approach lies in the primacy of economic variables, the problem of efficient allocation, and the theory of rational decision making. Most of the authors in this volume do not take such a narrowly economic or economically deterministic view of political economy.

Marxist analysis lays a strong claim for the term "political economy." The strength of this claim lies in the theory of Marxism ignoring disciplinary borders and ranging over the academic landscape to include economics, politics, and even culture in its analyses. The determining force, while not free choice or markets, still lies in the "economic camp," that is, in the mode of production (Chattopadhyay 1974). Neo-Marxists have taken great pains to emphasize the partial autonomy of the state and the play of class interests, and hence, to give a strongly political slant to their view of political economy. However, the approaches used in this book, while incorporating many neo-Marxist concerns, do not typically begin with the mode of production.[1]

The approaches taken by most authors in this book are not as narrow as an economic approach to political economy, and they mainly come from sociology and political science. These approaches are quite well encompassed by the following statement by Dietrich Rueschemeyer, Evelyne Huber Stephens, and John D. Stephens:

> We employ, like most of the comparative historical work from Max Weber to Guillermo O'Donnell, a "political economy" perspective that focuses on actors – individual as well as collective actors – whose power is grounded in control of economic and organizational resources and/or of coercive force and who vie with each other for scarce resources in the pursuit of conflicting goals. (1992, p. 5)

Collective actors with their power grounded in economic and in organizational resources exert the persuasive and coercive influences that lead to particular social policy outcomes. The emphasis on interest group power – especially labor and capital – resembles the power resources theory (Shalev and Korpi 1980; Korpi 1989), while the grounding of power resources in state institutions would fit state-centered theory or political-institutional theory (Skocpol 1985).

And leading back to the lair of the economists, many public choice economists, rational choice political scientists, and a small group of sociologists have pushed their paradigm of rational politics to the point where it addresses the choices of group actors pursuing diverse goals under socio-political constraint within both political and economic arenas (Olson 1982; Przeworski and Wallerstein 1988; Tsebelis 1990; and Kiser and Hechter 1991). In their introduction to the Cambridge series in the Political Economy of Institutions and Decisions, James Alt and Douglas North see political economy as being comparative and historical. They define "political economy" as a term

> built around attempts to answer two central questions: How do institutions evolve in response to individual incentives, strategies, and choices; and how do institutions affect the performance of political and economic systems? (in Lewin 1988, p. ix)

The chapters in this volume reveal authors in a complex love–hate relationship with much of economics. On the one hand, economics' penchant for a narrow focus seems confining and unnecessarily individualistic to these authors. On the other hand, econometric techniques are admired and find their way into nearly all the methodological introductions, except, perhaps the Boolean comparisons. In the end, this volume mostly reflects the Rueschemeyer, Stephens, and Stephens concern with the power of individual and collective actors over economic, organizational, and coercive resources.[2]

WHERE IS POLITICAL ECONOMY GOING METHODOLOGICALLY?

Given continued dissemination of the tools discussed in this volume – time-series, pooled, event history, and Boolean analyses – how will the comparative political economy of the welfare state develop? In the introduction we presented four possible scenarios. In this conclusion, we will give our best guess about where the methods outlined in this book may take us in the future on the theoretical and substantive playing fields of political economy. Our hypothetical predictions of future tendencies involve tensions between generalizing and particularizing, inductive and deductive, and scientific and interpretive polarities already very evident in the political economy literature.

1. *Quantitative analyses will increasingly use pooled data not merely to solve the "small-n" problem, but to extend the reach of generalizing formulations across culture, society, and time and to integrate systematically considerations of context, either as contextual forces or mediations, into theoretical articulation and testing.* The use of pooled methods and event history will provide increasing evidence for generalizations that were not previously validated in quantitative analysis. Pooling will almost certainly lead to the greater testing of theories that come from cross-sectional and time-series results. Systematic institutional and historical contextualization of general propositions will be advanced as in Hicks's subordination of governmental impacts on economic performance to the cohesiveness of national unions (see Chapter 7) and in O'Connell's specification of the causes of worker compensation to contexts as particular as that of post-OPEC neocorporatism (see Chapter 8). However, strains toward the nuanced treatment of context – for the contextualization of the general, as well as the exhaustive explanation of the particular – will continue to call out for more specificity. In open systems, additional contingencies and fresh nuances of structural and conjunctural embeddedness can always be addressed, especially where exhaustive understanding of the particular is sought. One must welcome strains toward more idiographic analyses and qualitative descriptions than pooling alone can provide.

2. *New modes of analyses that are explicitly designed to induce new patterns from the evidence will address conjunctural or configurational explanations, alter native pathways and other revelations of the specific for the general, and will extend the boundaries of nomothetic social science along the methodological frontier with cultural, institutional, and historical particularity.* The vector autoregression approach allows for inductive specification of complex explanatory systems beyond the limits of extant theoretical developments. It may also advance the articulation of highly general and complex theory as the Freeman and Alt essay does (see Chapter 5). Event history models will focus more on legislative enactments and unique implementations in order to illuminate statutory bases of policy that expenditure models leave largely unexamined (see Chapters 10 and 11). Boolean analyses will empower our pursuit of small-*n* (as well as large-*n*) comparisons. However, more distinctively, they will refine our treatment of conjunctural causation and inform the dialogue between generalizing and narrative (variable- and case-oriented) accounts as in the Ragin and Kangas contributions

(see Chapters 13 and 14). Both the Marxist penchant for "conjuncturally mediated" explanations and the historians' devotion to relentless contextual, idiographic, and disaggregative refinement will be well served by these new techniques. This is true despite the addition, even as we write, of new, even more contextually sensitive techniques than those presented here to the social scientific tool kit. We refer in particular to the "emerging" applications of event-structure analysis to compare the details of events such as lynchings and the organization of epochal strikes in different countries (Griffin 1991, 1992).[3]

3. *Quantitative analysis will tend increasingly toward nation- and period-specific time-series and historical analyses of epochs that constrain the boundaries of nomothetic social science.* Under the pressures of increasing concern for internal analysis and postmodernity, more and more attention will be given to subnational analyses, narrative, and theoretical assumptions. Statistical methods will take a role somewhat subordinate to clearly identifying periods and grasping them holistically. This will accentuate a trend toward qualitative analysis, idiographic explanation, and discourse analyses and interpretation. It may also lead to the introduction of postmodern theories into comparative political economy. The search for "the big *n*" will be replaced by defining the appropriate "coherent period" when particular institutional and discursive frames hold sway, while in the next or previous period other values transform relationships between variables and redefine repertoires of relevant variables. Moving covariance models will help analysts reflect and articulate the nuanced subtleties and epochal divides of temporal process as Isaac, Carlson, and Mathis demonstrate (see Chapter 4). Postmodernity, however, will not lead to a year-to-year relativism that may even dissolve distinctions among periods and challenge claims for "best" models or "causality," because distinct periods will still exist.[4] Parts of sociology and political science will gravitate toward these positions, while most of economics and rational choice will remain committed to nomothetic conceptions of knowledge.

However, as the frontiers of time are constrained, new expectations and tensions will emerge as many social scientists push the limits of time. In Hage, Hanneman, and Gargan's (1989) analyses of a small set of European countries, the period considered is extended to include the 1870s to the 1960s, with probable movement to the 1990s.[5] This will clearly create strains with the time-varying parameter approach, if distinctive subperiods are not created. Further, a changing regime approach can be included in time-series regression equations that implement "switching regressions" (Kennedy 1985, pp. 74–6). Further expanding the frontiers of time will introduce autoregressive moving average (ARIMA) models, which often have had limited application in comparative research because time periods have been relatively short (McCleary and Hay 1980; SAS 1986). This will bring a more detailed focus on white noise, make cointegration and unit roots much more important (Fomby and Rhodes 1990; Cuthbertson, Hall, and Taylor 1992, chap. 5, this volume), and proliferate the use of vector autoregression (VAR) with its elaborate attention to noise (Freeman and Alt, Chapter 5). But oddly enough, white noise and chaos theory may take away from postmodernity's furious particularity and lead back again to nomothetic approaches. Researchers should expect heated methodological debates and perhaps major breakthroughs as these trends develop.

4. *The political economy of the welfare state will gravitate toward the type of deduction from first principles embodied in rational choice models.* Amidst inductive, idiographic, and interpretive pressures, the social scientific strain toward nomothetic generalization and abstraction will be increasingly advanced by means of formal models within the rational choice tradition. This may now be broadly construed to include the old orthodoxies of individual rational egotism and market clearing and such "new heresies" as Przeworski and Wallerstein's (1982, 1988) dualistic and tripartite "oligopolies" of national political economic power. Models rooted in rational choice are particularly propitious carriers of the tradition of deductive theory because they harmonize usually discrepant rationalist, psychological, interpretive, and macrosociological insights. Rational choice reconciles powerful mathematical techniques of deductive reasoning with a degree of behavioral and psychological reality by elaborating a particular rationalist interpretation of individual subjectivity and behavior (Kiser and Hechter 1991). Such models reconcile this stylized, formally powerful interpretation of human decision and action to social structure by means of the theory of constrained optimization and the elaboration of society as constraint and opportunity structure (Alt and Chrystal 1983; Lewin 1988; Elster 1989; and Moene and Wallerstein 1991). With their links to (rational) historical interpretation on the one hand and their highly formal theoretical generalization (and econometric testing) on the other, rational choice theories and methods seem likely to consolidate a prominent position on the generalizing flank of the social scientific battlefield.

The rampant differentiation of social scientific approaches is unlikely to come to a halt soon. We believe that as *comparative political economies* undergo strains and tensions in many directions – generalizing versus particularizing, induction versus deduction, science versus interpretation, and periodization versus extending time – they will progress in all four directions at once.

Conclusion: quo vadis *political economy?*

WHERE IS POLITICAL ECONOMY GOING SUBSTANTIVELY?

In as much as Staniland is correct in stating that "the theory of political economy" does not exist (1985, p. 198), that the range of substantive areas that comparative political economy of welfare states will focus on will remain quite open. In this section, we will focus on four areas: expenditures and programs; organizational structures and the state; economic growth, unemployment, inflation, and investment; and the popularity of political leaders and voting (see Table 15.1 for the variables in these four approaches). Finally, we will speculate on some areas of the comparative welfare state that will emerge from very recent and massive social changes, which we believe will produce a comparison of continental units with subunit variations (e.g., NAFTA and the EEC).

First, the political economy of the welfare state will continue to go in the direction of analyzing state and program expenditures. This may seem surprising given Esping-Andersen's claim that analysts should focus on program characteristics and results rather than expenditures:

> Expenditures are epiphenomenal to the theoretical substance of welfare states. Moreover, the linear scoring approach (more or less power, democracy, or spending) contradicts the sociological notion that power, democracy, or welfare are relational and structured phenomena. (1990, p. 19)

However, we see welfare expenditures as one of three equally important aspects of complex and interrelated welfare state phenomenon. Just as the analysis of strikes moved from frequency alone to strike volume composed of frequency (number of strikes per year), participants (number of persons affected), and duration (the length of strikes), studies of the welfare state need to do the same with budgeted expenditures, program participants, and the nature of benefit programs. Budgets will continue to be important as macroeconomic *manipulanda* and records of allocative struggles, as well as facets and shorthand indicators of program benefits. To quote Schumpeter in "The Crisis of the Tax State":[6]

> "The budget is the skeleton of the state stripped of all misleading ideologies" – a collection of hard, naked facts which yet remain to be drawn into the realm of sociology. The fiscal history of a people is above all an essential part of its general history. (Swedberg 1991, p. 100)

Consequently, the short history of "fiscal sociology" will not end but will be interwoven in new ways with program characteristics and participation.

Nonetheless, the institutional or organizational approach to welfare states will still be a second increasingly prominent focus of attention in

Table 15.1. *The substance of political economy studies*

Type of study	Dependent variables	Independent variables
1. Welfare state expenditures and programs	Welfare state spending, program characteristics, and legislation.	Interest group and class goals and resources; demographic structure;and and economic performance.
2. Neoinstitutional and state-centric theories	Institutional, bureaucratic, and organizational variables; detailed program characterisitics and processes.	State structures: centralization, constitutional characteristics, policy regimes, elite orientations, and traditionalism.
3. The political economy of economics and growth	Economic variables: unemployment, inflation, economic growth, and investment.	Associational scope, cohesion, and cooperativeness; partisan government; assets and effectiveness.
4. The political economics of politics and economic policy	Popularity of political leaders and voting (political business cycle).	Economic performance; government's goals and expectations; mass stratification.

comparative political economy (Myles 1989; Esping-Andersen 1990; Schmid, Reissert, and Bruche 1992). While case study and qualitative approaches have tended to predominate in the sociological state-centric approach, economic public choice approaches have made a frontal assault on bureaucratic growth and spending. From political science, the neo-institutional approach will forge a synthesis with state-centric approaches and perhaps come up with a durable research stable. Here the battle lines are set with increasing attention to nonrational, organizational theories (are we near a garbage can theory of the state?) and the rational choice approaches of segments of political science and most, if not nearly all, of economics. Time-varying parameter models and event structure analysis may play an emerging role in this debate because of their accentuation of events and conjunctures. (See also Lewin's 1988 approach to crises that synthesizes rational choice and historical conjuncture.)

Third, while economics has invaded organizational and institutional areas, sociology and political science are similarly invading traditional areas of economics such as growth, unemployment, inflation, and investment (Freeman and Alt, Chapter 5; Hicks, Chapter 6; and O'Connell, Chapter 8, this volume). The direction of this research is for increasing application of social and political variables to the growth or decline of economies. The major debate over the net benefits or burdens of social organization (e.g., trade union and solidarity effects) will continue between the "social sclerosis" approach (Olson 1982, Mueller 1983) and the Left-corporatist commutarian view (Lange and Garrett 1985, 1986; Hicks and Patterson 1987). Resolution in this area will not come soon for the recent focus on "special interest" organizations on the one hand and on "encompassing" ones on the other hand is being complicated by the new communitarian literature on the associational fabric of social responsibility (Boswell 1990; Campbell, Hollingsworth, and Lindberg 1991).

In a fourth vein, some see "political economics" as being distinct from "political economy" (Alt and Chrystal 1983; Kuhnle 1987, pp. 452–3). In this arena, there are two strands. One strand looks at how the state of the economy influences the popularity functions and electoral fortunes of elected officials. The other area focuses on the effects that politicians making economic policies have on economic outcomes. The political business cycle literature is central to this realm and it most often focuses on time-series analyses (Tufte 1978; Robertson 1982; Monroe 1984; Kellman and Izraeli 1985; Hibbs 1987; and Radcliff 1992). The other strand includes historical and comparative studies of how economic policy is formulated and implemented, as well as what effects it may ultimately have (Katzenstein 1984; Hall 1986; Hayward

1986; and Calder 1988). The direction of this field of research will be of increasing statistical sophistication as rational choice applications and econometric extensions evolve complicated but new institutional insights. For its qualitative arm, shifting political circumstances and polity-community tastes in macroeconomic instruments will continue to drive substantive changes within a durable case study tradition (see Becker and Ragin 1992; Feagin, Orum, and Sjoberg 1992).[7]

Finally, in view of recent worldwide watersheds, the political economy of welfare states will expand in geographic focus and complexity. In Eastern Europe, the massive changes in the former communist countries will bring state programs and processes to light for the first time. Boolean analyses of the breakdown are already possible, and in 10 years' time, interrupted time-series analysis of changes will begin. The eventual analysis of Eastern Europe will also be highly dependent on pooled analysis since long time series of postfall welfare states for 30 years obviously will take at least 30 years. Nonetheless, the access of these countries' political-economic processes to more informed social scientific scrutiny will increase the range of countries generally considered. Also, many Third World countries will be developing modern democratic welfare states, with those in South America and Asia, as well as some on the Mediterranean rim, being the most probable.

The unification of Western Europe through the EEC and the attempts at free trade agreements in North America, despite occasional doses of Danish gloom and opposition to low-wage Mexican labor, will force a reorganization of cross-Atlantic research. The result will probably focus on Europe and North America as whole units, with internal analyses of states, departments, provinces, *Landern*, etc. Much of this may lead to comparative cross-sectional examinations, pooled analyses, event history methods, Boolean comparisons, and the application of many other methods too. While this will not be a full world system analysis, it will focus on continental systems and trading blocs that interact with each other.

These changes will present new substantive concerns and massive data collection requirements. Comparative historical research on welfare states and social policy concerns would benefit immensely from an "Inter-university (or indeed national) Consortium for Comparative Political and Economic Research" (ICCPER) that would store data from different projects, facilitating secondary data analysis. In essence, this field needs what the ICPSR supplies for survey research projects. The Luxembourg project has gone far to consolidate data sets on stratification (mostly based on individual-level data),[8] and Peter Flora has performed an impressive task for the political economic community by publishing data on a large number of countries over a long period of time; however, these massive and increasing data collection tasks should rest with the international research community as a whole and not with particular subsets of the field and/or individual scholars.

CONCLUSION

The macroanalysis of welfare states in advanced industrialized countries is a complex and growing field (Smith 1993, p. 351). Strains and tensions between the various approaches to political economy embedded within and between academic disciplines will continue. However, these conflicts should lead to real progress in methods, theories, and substantive knowledge, at least within the limits of theoretical "pluralism" (Levine 1985). The political economy of the welfare state will continue to produce exciting work. Intellectual tension begets progress, or as the Ross family motto says about the rose – *Quo spinosior fragrantior*, or "the more thorny, the greater the fragrance" (Mawson 1976). We have given our best estimate what directions the field of political economy may take. The measure of knowledge that might emerge from the decades' plurality of research approaches lies some distance beyond our current viewpoint and the moment's proliferating postmodern thicket.

NOTES

1. Although Marxist discussions of political economy are legion (Chattopadhyay 1947), one important synthetic approach is by Oskar Lange. He states that "political economy is . . . the study of the social laws governing the production and distribution of the material means of satisfying human needs" (Lange 1963, p. 1). In a similar definition, James Russell defines "political economy" as a "discipline that studies economic production and exchange" (1980, p. 88).
2. Two broad "multidisciplinary" approaches to research and theory dominate the social sciences – cultural analysis and political economy. In an even more basic way, we can reduce these approaches to ideas – symbols, values, ideologies, and Weltanschauungen – and material interests in goods and services. The cultural approach gives primacy to ideas and values, and this is expressly what this book is not about. For instance, Mereleman isolates cultural factors in television, advertisements, civics books, and corporate reports to show how ideas toward participation motivate society (1991). Ideology and values can be integrated into a political economy approach (Burstein 1985; Janoski 1990), but they cannot not be given exogenous force. Studies that do give ideas exogenous or primary force cannot be considered to be political economy (e.g., see Wuthnow et al. 1984; Thompson, Ellis, and Wildavsky 1990). Wuthnow's *Communities of Discourse* (1989) is an attempt to navigate a compromise position between political economy and a strong cultural approach.
3. As Griffin (1992, p. 405) states in his introduction to papers by Abbott, Aminzade, and Quadagno and Knapp: "They idenfity the real issue to be not

the age of the data or events but rather the nature of the data – the representation of the events – and what is actually done with those data."

4. Ironically, this periodization will reduce the size of samples and accelerate the push for pooled analysis!
5. Hage et al. (1989) do periodize in their analysis; however, they also consider the full length of the entire period that they examine (i.e., 1870 to 1968).
6. Schumpeter is quoting R. Goldscheid's *Staatssozialismus order Staatskapitalismus*, which was published in 1917.
7. A number of additional areas provide promise for political economy, but they are still emerging in a comparative context. The attention given to citizenship will grow (Janoski 1990; Brubaker 1992). Research in the area of diffusion, networks, and policy domains should significantly impact on comparative welfare state studies (Lauman and Knoke 1987; Burstein 1991; and Knoke and Pappi 1991).
8. The Luxembourg Income Study (LIS) provides over 30 large microdata sets on income and economic well-being in 15 welfare states. It is located at CEPS/INSTEAD in Walferdange, Luxembourg.

BIBLIOGRAPHY

Alt, James, and K. Alec Chrystal. 1983. *Political Economics*. Berkeley: University of California Press.

Apple, Nixon. 1980. "The Rise and Fall of Full Employment Capitalism." *Studies in Political Economy* 4:5–39.

Anonymous. 1925–6. "Political Economy" Palgrave's *Dictionary of Political Economy*. Vol. 3.

Becker, Howard, and Charles Ragin. 1992. *What Is a Case?* Cambridge University Press.

Block, Fred. 1986. "Political Choice and the Multiple 'Logics' of Capital." *Theory and Society* 15(1–2):175–92.

Bollen, Kenneth. 1979. "Political Democracy and the Timing of Development." *American Sociological Review* 44:572–88

Bollen, Kenneth, and Robert Jackman. 1985. "Political Democracy and the Size Distribution of Income." *American Sociological Review* 50:438–57.

Boswell, Jonathan. 1990. *Community and Economy*. London: Routledge.

Brubaker, Rogers. 1992. *Citizenship and Nationhood in France and Germany*. Cambridge, Mass.: Harvard University Press.

Burstein, Paul. 1981. "The Sociology of Democratic Politics and Government." *Annual Review of Sociology* 7:291–319.

1985. *Discrimination, Jobs, and Politics*. Chicago: University of Chicago Press.

1991. "Policy Domains: Organization, Culture, and Policy Outcomes." *Annual Review of Sociology* 17:327–50.

Calder, Kent. 1988. *Crisis and Compensation: Public Policy and Political Stability in Japan, 1949–1986*. Princeton, N.J.: Princeton University Press.

Campbell, John L., J. Rogers Hollingsworth, and Leon N. Lindberg. 1991. *The Governance of the American Economy*. Cambridge University Press.

Caporaso, James, and David Levine. 1992. *Theories of Political Economy*. Cambridge University Press.

Chattopadhyay, Paresh. 1974. "Political Economy: What's in a Name." *Monthly Review* (Apr.): 23–33.

Chichilnisky, Graciela. 1990. "On the Mathematical Foundations of Political Economy." *Contributions to Political Economy* 9:25–41.

Choucri, Nazli. 1980. "International Political Economy: A Theoretical Perspective." In Ole Holsti, Randolph Siverson, and Alexander George (eds.), *Change in the International System*, pp. 103–29 Boulder, Colo.: Westview.

Clark, Barry. 1991. *Political Economy: A Comparative Approach*. New York: Praeger.

Clark, John G. 1990. *The Political Economy of World Energy: A Twentieth-Century Perspective*. New York: Harvester-Wheatsheaf.

Cuthbertson, Keith, Stephen Hall, and Mark Taylor. 1992. *Applied Econometric Techniques*. Ann Arbor: University of Michigan Press.

Elster, Jon. 1989. *The Cement of Society: A Study of Social Order*. Cambridge University Press.

Esping-Andersen, Gøsta. 1990. *Three Worlds of Welfare Capitalism*. Princeton, N.J.: Princeton University Press.

Eyestone, Robert. 1972. *Political Economy: Politics and Policy Analysis*. Chicago: Markham.

Feagin, Joe, Anthony Orum, and Gideon Sjoberg. 1992. *A Case for the Case Study*. Chapel Hill: University of North Carolina Press.

Flora, Peter (ed.). 1987. *Growth to Limits: The Western European Welfare States Since World War II: Volume 4: Appendix*. Berlin: De Gruyter.

Fomby, Thomas, and George Rhodes (eds.). 1990. *Advances in Econometrics: Co-Integration, Spurious Regressions, and Unit Roots*. Vol. 8. Greenwich, Conn.: JAI.

Frey, Bruno S. 1979. *Modern Political Economy* Oxford: Martin Robertson.

Fulcher, James. 1991. *Labour Movements, Employers and the State: Conflict and Co-operation in Britain and Sweden*. Oxford University Press.

Grant, Wyn. 1985. *The Political Economy of Corporatism*. New York: St. Martin's.

Griffin, Larry J. 1991. "Event Structure Analysis and Comparative-Historical Research." Paper presented at the New Compass of the Comparativist conference, Duke University, April 26–7.

1992. "Temporality, Events, and Explanation in Historical Sociology" *Sociological Methods and Research* 20(4):403–27.

Gurley. John. 1971. "The State of Political Economics." *American Economic Review* 61(2):53–62.

Gustafsson, B. A., and N. A. Klevmarken (eds.). 1989. *The Political Economy of Social Security*. Amsterdam: North Holland.

Hage, Jerald, Robert Hanneman, and Edward Gargan. 1989. *State Responsiveness and State Activism*. London: Unwin Hyman.

Hagen, Everett. 1960. "Turning Parameters into Variables in the Theory of Economic Growth." *American Economic Review* 50(2):623–25.

Hall, Peter. 1986. *Governing the Economy: The Politics of State Intervention in Britain and France*. Oxford University Press.

Hayward, Jack. 1986. *The State and the Market Economy: Industrial Patriotism and Economic Intervention in France*. Brighton: Wheatsheaf.

Heilbroner, Robert. 1970. "On the Possibility of a Political Economics." *Journal of Economic Issues* 4(4):1–22.

Hibbs, Douglas A., Jr. 1987. *The American Political Economy: Macroeconomics and Electoral Politics*. Cambridge, Mass.: Harvard University Press.

Hibbs, Douglas A., and Heino Fassbender (eds.). 1981. *Contemporary Political Economy: Studies on the Interdependence of Politics and Economics*. Amsterdam: North Holland.

Jackman, Robert. 1984. "Cross-national Research and the Study of Comparative Politics." *American Journal of Political Science* 28:161–82.

Jackson, P. M. 1982. *The Political Economy of Bureaucracy*. Oxford: Philip Allan.

Janoski, Thomas. 1990. *The Political Economy of Unemployment: Active Labor Market Policy in West Germany and the United States*. Berkeley: University of California Press.

Kaldor, Nicholas 1972. "The Irrelevance of Equilibrium Economics." *Economic Journal* 328:1237–55.

Kalecki, Michael. 1943. "Political Aspects of Full Employment." *Political Quarterly* 14:322–1.

Katzenstein, Peter. 1984. *Corporatism and Change: Austria, Switzerland, and the Politics of Industry*. Ithaca, N.Y.: Cornell University Press.

Kellman, Mitchell, and Oded Izraeli. 1985. "Rhythms in Politics and Economics." In P. Johnson and W. Thompson, *The Political Business Cycle. An International Perspective*, pp. 71–83. New York: Praeger.

Kennedy, Peter. 1985. *A Guide to Econometrics*, 2d ed. Oxford: Blackwell Publisher.

Kiser, Edgar, and Michael Hechter. 1991. "The Role of General Theory in Comparative-Historical Sociology." *American Journal of Sociology* 97(1):1–30.

Klein, Philip. 1980. "Confronting Power in Economics: A Pragmatic Evaluation." *Journal of Economic Issues* 14(4):871–96.

Knight, Frank. 1944. "Economics, Political Science, and Education." *American Economic Associations: Papers and Proceedings* 34(1):68–76.

Knoke, David, and Franz Pappi. 1991. "Organizational Action Sets in the U.S. and German Labor Policy Domains." *American Sociological Review* 56(4):509–23.

Korpi, Walter. 1989. "Power, Politics and State Autnomy in the Development of Social Citizenship." *American Sociological Review* 54:309–28.

Kuhnle, Stein. 1987. "Political Economics." In Vernon Bogdanor (ed.), *The Blackwell Encyclopaedia of Political Institutions*, pp. 452–4. London: Blackwell Reference.

Lane, Jan-Erik, and Svante Ersson. 1990. *Comparative Political Economy*. London: Pinter.

Lange, Peter, and Geoffrey Garrett. 1985. "The Politics of Growth." *Journal of Politics* 47:792–827.

1986. "The Politics of Growth Reconsidered." *Journal of Politics* 48:257–74.

Lange, Oskar. 1963. *Political Economy*. New York: Macmillan.

Lauman, Edward, and David Knoke. 1987. *The Organizational State*. Madison: University of Wisconsin Press.

Levine, Donald. 1985. "Simmel as a Resource for Sociological Metatheory." *Sociological Theory* 7:161–74.

Lewin, Leif. 1988. *Ideology and Structure: A Century of Swedish Politics*. Cambridge University Press.

MacRae, Duncan. 1973. "Normative Assumptions in the Study of Public Choice." *Public Choice* 16:27–41.

March, James, and Johan Olsen. 1989. *Rediscovering Institutions*. New York: Free Press.

Mawson, C. O. S. 1976. *Dictionary of Foreign Terms*. New York: Crowell.

McCleary, Richard, and Richard Hay. 1980. *Applied Time Series Analysis for the Social Sciences*. Newbury Park, Calif.: Sage.

Meltzer, Allan, Alex Cukierman, and Scott F. Richard. 1991. *Political Economy*. New York: Oxford University Press.

Merelman, Richard. 1991. *Partial Visions: Culture and Politics in Britain, Canada, and the United States*. Madison: University of Wisconsin Press.

Mitchell, William. 1967. "The Shape of Political Theory to Come: From Political Sociology to Political Economy." *American Behavioral Scientist* 11(2):8–20.

1968. "The New Political Economy." *Social Research* 35(1):76–110.

Moene, Karl Ove, and Michael Wallerstein. 1991. "Solidaristic Bargaining." Paper presented at the New Compass of the Comparativist conference, Duke University, April 26–7.

Monroe, Kirsten. 1984. *Presidential Popularity and the Economy*. New York: Praeger.

Mueller, Dennis (ed.). 1983. *The Political Economy of Growth*. New Haven, Conn.: Yale University Press.

Myles, John. 1989. *Old Age and the Welfare State: The Political Economy of Public Pension*. Rev. ed. Lawrence: University of Kansas Press.

Oliver, Henry. 1973. "Study of the Relationships Between Economic and Political Systems." *Journal of Economic Issues* 7(4):543–51.

Olson, Mancur. 1982. *The Rise and Decline of Nations*. New Haven, Conn.: Yale University Press.

Oppenheimer, Joe. 1980. "Small Steps Forward for Political Economy." *World Politics* 33(1):121–51.

Peretz, Paul. 1983. *The Political Economy of Inflation in the United States*. Chicago: University of Chicago Press.

Przeworski, Adam. 1991. *Democracy and the Market*. Cambridge University Press.

Przeworski, Adam, and Michael Wallerstein. 1982. "The Structure of Class Conflict in Democratic Capitalist Societies." *American Political Science Review* 76:215–29.

1988. "Structural Dependence of the State on Capital." *American Political Science Review* 82:11–21.

Radcliff, Benjamin. 1992. "The Welfare State, Turnout, and the Economy: A Comparative Analysis." *American Political Science Review* 86(2):444–54.

Ratner, R. S., and Paul Burstein. 1980. "Ideology, Specificity, and the Coding of Legal Documents." *American Sociological Review* 45:522–5.

Robbins, Lionel. 1981. "Economics and Political Economy." *American Economic Review: Papers and Proceedings* 71(2):1–10.

Robertson, John D. 1982. "Economic Policy and Election Cycles: Constraints in Nine OECD Countries." *Comparative Social Research* 5:129–45.

Rueschemeyer, Dietrich, Evelyne Huber Stephens, and John D. Stephens. 1992. *Capitalist Development and Democracy*. Chicago: University of Chicago Press.

Russell, James. 1980. "Political Economy." In R. James (ed.), *Marx–Engels Dictionary*, p. 88. Westport, Conn.: Greenwood.

Samuelson, Paul. A. 1992. *Economics. 14th ed.* New York: McGraw-Hill.

SAS. 1986. *SAS System for Forecasting Time Series*. Cary, N.C.: SAS.
Schmid, Günter, Bernd Reissert, and Gert Bruche. (1992). *Unemployment Insurance and Active Labor Market Policy: An International Comparison of Financing Systems*. Detroit: Wayne State University Press.
Shalev, Michael. 1992. *Labour and the Political Economy in Israel*. Oxford University Press.
Shalev, Michael, and Walter Korpi. 1980. "Working Class Mobilization and American Exceptionalism." *Economic and Industrial Democracy* 1:31–61.
Sklar, Richard. 1975. "On the Concept of Power in Political Economy." In D. Nelson and R. Sklar (eds.), *Toward a Humanistic Science of Politics*, pp. 179–206. Lanham, Md: University Press of America.
Skocpol, Theda. 1985. "Bringing the State Back In." In Peter Evans, Dietrich Rueschemeyer, and Theda Skocpol (eds.), *Bringing the State Back In*, pp. 3–37. Cambridge University Press.
Smith, W. Rand. 1993. "International Economy and State Strategies." *Comparative Politics* 25(3):351–72.
Staniland, Martin. 1985. *What Is Political Economy? A Study of Social Theory and Underdevelopment*. New Haven, Conn.: Yale University Press.
Stigler, George. 1959. "The Politics of Political Economists." *Quarterly Journal of Economics* 73(4):522–32.
Stigler, George (ed.). 1988. *Chicago Studies in Political Economy*. Chicago: University of Chicago Press.
Swank, Duane. 1992. "Politics and the Structural Dependence of the State in Democratic Capitalist Nations." *American Political Science Review* 86(1):38–54.
Swedberg, Richard (ed.). 1991. *Joseph A. Schumpeter: The Economics and Sociology of Capitalism*. Princeton, N.J.: Princeton University Press.
Thompson, Michael, Richard Ellis, and Aaron Wildavsky, 1990. *Cultural Theory*. Boulder, Colo.: Westview.
Tsebelis, George. 1990. *Nested Games*. Berkeley: University of California Press.
Tufte, Edward. 1978. *Political Control of the Economy*. Princeton, N.J.: Princeton University Press.
Wellisz, Stanislaw. 1968. "Oskar Lange." In *International Encyclopedia of the Social Sciences*, pp. 591–4. David Sills (ed.), New York: Macmillan and Free Press.
Whiteley, Paul. 1983. "The Political Economy of Economic Growth." *European Journal of Political Research* 11:197–213.
1986. *Political Control of the Macroeconomy: The Political Economy of Public Policy-Making*. London: Sage.
Winch, D. M. 1977. "Political Economy and the Economic Polity." *Canadian Journal of Economics* 10(4):547–64.
Wuthnow, Robert. 1989. *Communities of Discourse*. Cambridge, Mass.: Harvard University Press.
Wuthnow, Robert, James Hunter, Albert Bergesen, and Edith Kurzweil. 1984. *Cultural Analysis: The Work of Peter L Berger, Mary Douglas, Michel Foucault and Jürgen Habermas*. London: Routledge.
Young, Oran. 1980. "International Regimes: Problems of Concept Formation." *World Politics* 32:331–56.

Author index

Author index

Subject index

Subject index

Subject index

Subject index

Subject index